# Cosmic Christology in the Gospel of Matthew

**Biblical Hermeneutics Rediscovered**

The Series as the name suggests will focus on Biblical Hermeneutics, i.e., literary works concerned with methods of interpreting the Old and New Testaments of Bible via different stream of topics like Literature & Poetry, Indigenous Philosophizing, Ethical response towards Ecology, Health & Healing, Science & Technology, Feminist Theology, Sociological approach towards Human Rights, Law & Politics, Arts, History of Ideas, Ancient Civilizations, Cultural Contiguity, Religious Cosmologies & Mysticism, Appraisal of various Theologians, World Peace & Harmony, Global Capitalism, Network Marketing, Cybertheology, Population & Demographics, Epigraphic Studies, Contextualized Education, and many others. We welcome a Mss. on any topic/s mentioned, whether they are original works, scholarly monographs, collections of conference papers, revised dissertations, or translations of historical documents. Through the Series we, the Publishers, are striving to put forward published works that may help Institutions, Academic Bodies, Researchers, Scholars and the World at large in furthering their respective knowledge and understanding on the concerned subject. We welcome your comments on our efforts and further suggestions on how we can enshrine new ray of analysing & explaining the written Texts through our upcoming books.

*Biblical Hermeneutics Rediscovered - 45*

# Cosmic Christology in the Gospel of Matthew

## Matthew's utilization of Nature Miracles and Jewish Cosmology

**Lalramchhana RC**

Christian World Imprints

First Published in 2021 by

**Christian World Imprints**
*Christian Publishing & Books from India*
C-3, Wazirpur Industrial Area
**Delhi-110052**
cwidelhi2017@gmail.com
www.ChristianWorldImprints.com
Phone: +91 11 41526079

ISBN: 978-93-5148-556-8 (HB)
ISBN: 978-93-5148-557-5 (PB)



Printed in India.

**HMINGTHANSANGI (NU-I)**
**KUM - 75**
**23.6.1944 - 17.4.2019**

# Foreword

I am pleased to write a foreword to this book written by Rev. Dr. Lalramchhana, who completed his doctoral studies with me. It was a thrilling and pleasant journey as the author could connect brilliantly nature miracles performed by Jesus with the identity of Jesus. He claims: "The study mainly focuses on the understanding of nature miracles in Matthew's Gospel where there could be found significance connection to cosmic Christology. The lack of the study of miracle stories for the formulation of Matthew's Christology is established. Though Christological titles and typologies in Matthew's Gospel are the main sources for Matthew's Christology, miracle stories in general and nature miracles in particular have been neglected. This study of nature miracle stories elucidates Matthew's interest in Jesus's cosmic significance. Reviewing of relevant literature set out the basic methodology that emphasizes that the contact between Christology and cosmology in Synoptic Gospels, and especially nature miracles is largely untouched. The study also finds out that cosmic Christology is neglected in the study of Matthew's Christology." (Abstract, p.1)

It is significant today to promote contextual and creative exegetical works of the Bible specifically in the field of Christology. It is mainly because of the contemporary challenges we encounter in terms of the practice and propagation of our faith. Rev. Dr. Lalramchhana is a very pleasant person and demonstrate his perspectives very clearly and firmly. This book is a classic example of his innovation and exploration.

I wish and pray that may God continue to use him as a theological educator and biblical scholar.

**Rev. Dr. C. I. David Joy**
Principal, KUT Seminary
Board Member SBL-ICI

# Preface

This book is an attempt to study nature miracles by utilizing various exegetical tools in order to develop and highlight the presence of cosmic Christology in Matthew's Gospel. As miracle stories are neglected during the formulation of various Christologies of Matthew, the book offers new trajectory for further research. Though titles and typologies are the main ingredients in developing Matthew's Christologies, this attempt finds that stories of nature miracles are embedded with rich sources to enhance the overall picture of Jesus in the Gospel of Matthew. The work also focuses on the contact between Christology and cosmology in Synoptic Gospels which is largely untouched by any other research. The basic methodology is projected from the study of relevant literature especially the cosmological worldview found in Jewish literatures. It also finds out that cosmic Christology is neglected in the study of Matthew's Christology.

The original title of the thesis is "Nature Miracles in the Gospel of Matthew as the basis for developing Cosmic Christology." Changes and improvements have been made by inculcating examiners' comments. My heartfelt thanks to my supervisor Rev. Prof. C. I. David Joy, and examiners Rev. Dr. V. J. John and Rev. Dr. P. C. Gine.

**Lalramchhana RC**
Dawrpui
Aizawl, Mizoram

# List of Abbreviations

| | |
|---|---|
| AAR | The American Academy of Religion |
| ABS | Archaeology of Biblical Studies |
| ADLR | The Ages Digital Library References |
| AFER | African Ecclesial Review |
| AM | Asia Minor |
| ANE | Ancient Near East |
| APQ | American Philosophical Quarterly |
| ATRSup | Anglican Theological Review Supplement Series |
| AW | Ancient World (alternative for Ancient Near East) |
| BASOR | Bulletin of the American Schools of Oriental Research |
| BCE | Before Common Era |
| BibW | Biblical World |
| BJRL | Bulletin of the John Rylands Library |
| BLS | The Bible and Liberation Series |
| BSac | Bibliotheca sacra |
| BTF | Bangalore Theological Forum |
| ca. | *Circa*/About |
| CBQ | Catholic Biblical Quarterly |
| CBR | Catholic Biblical Quarterly |
| CE | Common Era |
| cf. | confer, compare |
| ch(s) | chapter(s) |
| CJT | Canadian Journal of Theology |
| CogL | Cognitive Linguistics |
| CurTM | Currents in Theology and Mission |
| DBI | A Dictionary of Biblical Interpretation |
| DNT | Dictionary of New Testament |

| | |
|---|---|
| DTIB | Dictionary of Theological Interpretation |
| e.g. | example |
| ed(s). | editor(s), edited by, edition |
| EDNT | Exegetical Dictionary of the New Testament |
| esp. | especially |
| et al. | *et alii*, and others |
| etc. | *et cetera*, and so forth, and the rest |
| EvQ | Evangelical Quarterly |
| ExAud | Ex Auditu |
| ExpTim | Expository Times |
| FCS | Faith and Cultures Series |
| FrS | Franciscan Studies |
| GDNT | Greek Dictionary of the New Testament |
| GTIS | Guides to Theological Inquiry Series |
| GTJ | Grace Journal |
| HTR | Harvard Theological Review |
| HTS | Harvard Theological Studies |
| HUCA | Hebrew Union College Annual |
| IB | Interpreter's Bible |
| ICC | The International Critical Commentary |
| IEJ | Israel Exploration Journal |
| Int | Interpretation: A Journal of Bible and Theology |
| IR | International Review |
| IRM | International Review of Mission |
| IRT | Issues in Religious and Theology |
| JBL | Journal of Biblical Literature |
| JETS | Journal of the Evangelical Theological Society |
| JHI | Journal of the History of Ideas |
| JRH | Journal of Religious History |
| JSJud | Journal for the Study of Judaism |
| JSNT | Journal for the Study of the New Testament |
| JTTS | Journal of Tribal Studies |
| MisT | Mission Today |
| MITJT | MIT Journal of Theology |
| n.d. | no date |
| n.p. | no place, no publisher, no page |
| NAC | The New American Commentary |
| NEI | North East India |

| | |
|---|---|
| NEISBS | North East India Society of Biblical Studies |
| NICNT | The New International Commentary on the New Testament |
| NIGCT | The New International Greek Testament Commentary |
| NovT | Novum Testamentum |
| NT | New Testament |
| NTS | New Testament Studies |
| OT | Old Testament |
| PQ | Philosophical Quarterly |
| RelS | Religious Studies |
| repr. | Reprinted |
| rev. | revised (by) |
| SBJT | Southern Baptist Journal of Theology |
| SBL | Society of Biblical Literature |
| SBLDS | Society of Biblical Literature Dissertation Series |
| ScrH | Scripta Hierosolymitana |
| SCSS | Septuagint and Cognate Studies Series |
| SNTSMS | Society for New Testament Studies Monograph Series |
| SPCK | Society for Promoting Christian Knowledge |
| *sic* | *Sicra* |
| SPCK | Society for Promoting Christian Knowledge |
| SR | Studies in Religion |
| Supp | Supplementary |
| TDCC | Tribal Development and Communication Centre |
| TDNT | Theological Dictionary of the New Testament |
| TDOT | Theological Dictionary of the Old Testament |
| TEx | The Expositors |
| ThB | Theologische Beiträge |
| ThTo | Theology Today |
| TLNT | Theological Lexicon of the New Testament |
| TLOT | Theological Lexicon of the Old Testament |
| TPI | Theological Publications in India |
| trans. | translator, translated by |
| TS | Theological Studies |
| TSIS | Tribal Studies of India Series |
| TSS | Tribal Study Series |
| TTJ | Torch Trinity Journal |
| TynBul | Tyndale Bulletin |
| v. | Verse |

| | |
|---|---|
| VJTR | Vidyajyoti Journal of Theological Reflection |
| VTSup | Vestus Testamentum Supplementary Series |
| vv. | Verses |
| WBC | Word Biblical Commentary |
| WCom | Written Communication |
| WUNT | Wissenschaftliche Unterschungen zum Neuen Testament |

## Old Testament Books

| | |
|---|---|
| Gen | Genesis |
| Exod | Exodus |
| Lev | Leviticus |
| Num | Numbers |
| Deut | Deuteronomy |
| Josh | Joshua |
| Judg | Judges |
| 1-2 Sam | 1-2 Samuel |
| 1-2 Kgs | 1-2 Kings |
| 1-2 Chr | 1-2 Chronicles |
| Ezra | Ezra |
| Job | Job |
| Ps/Pss | Psalm/Psalms |
| Prov | Proverbs |
| Isa | Isaiah |
| Jer | Jeremiah |
| Ezek | Ezekiel |
| Dan | Daniel |
| Zech | Zechariah |

## New Testament Books

| | |
|---|---|
| Matthew | Matt |
| Mark | Mark |
| Luke | Luke |
| John | John |
| Acts | Acts |
| Romans | Rom |
| 1-2 Corinthians | 1-2 Cor |
| Galatians | Gal |
| Ephesians | Eph |

| | |
|---|---|
| Philippians | Phil |
| Colossians | Col |
| 1-2 Thessalonians | 1-2 Thess |
| 1-2 Timothy | 1-2 Tim |
| Titus | Titus |
| Philemon | Philm |
| Hebrews | Heb |
| James | Jas |
| 1-2 Peter | 1-2 Pet |
| 1-2-3 John | 1-2-3 John |
| Jude | Jude |
| Revelation | Rev |

## Ancient Sources

| | |
|---|---|
| LXX | Septuagint |
| 2 Bar. | 2 Baruch |
| 1 En. | 1 Enoch (Ethiopic Apocalypse) |
| 2 En. | 2 Enoch (Slavonic Apocalypse) |
| 3 En. | 3 Enoch (Hebrew Apocalypse) |
| 4 Ezra | 4 Ezra |
| Pss. Sol. | Psalms of Solomon |
| Sir | Sirach/Ecclesiasticus |
| Tob | Tobith |
| Wis | Wisdom of Solomon |

## Rabbinic

| | |
|---|---|
| B. Bat. | Baba Batra |
| Num. Rab. | Numbers Rabbah |
| Sanh. | Sanhedrin |

## Josephus

| | |
|---|---|
| *Ag. Ap.* | Against Apion |
| *Ant.* | Antiquities of the Jews |
| *J.W.* | Jewish War |

## Philo

| | |
|---|---|
| *Alleg. Interp.* | Allegorical Interpretation |
| *Ep.* | Seneca, Epistles |
| *Hist. eccl.* | Eusebius Ecclesiastical History |

Chapter 1

# Introduction

## 1.1. The Problem

Christological titles and typologies in Matthew's Gospel are the main sources for the formulation of Matthew's Christology, but miracles in general and nature miracles in particular have not been adequately studied for this purpose. The study of these miracle stories (the stilling of the storm – 8:23-27; the walking on the water – 14:22-33; and the feeding of the multitudes – 14:13-21; 15:32-39) may show Matthew's keenness to depict Jesus' authority over nature and his creative powers.

## 1.2. Elaboration of the Problem

The miracles of Jesus in Matthew's Gospel and other Synoptic Gospels are termed as mighty acts (δυνάμεις). Clubbing together both the mighty works and the preaching, they are described as the works of Christ in Matthew's Gospel (τὰἔργατοῦ Χριστοῦ, 11:2, 5). For the Gospel writers, the modern notion of the laws of nature is irrelevant.[1] What is more relevant for them in their perspective is the effect toward the witnesses. For the first-century Palestinian point of view, the miracles were understood as extraordinary actions that evoked astonishment and awe.[2]

1 Mark R. Saucy, "Miracles and Jesus' Proclamation of the Kingdom of God," *BSac* 153 (1996): 281-307. For footnote, bibliography, quotation and abbreviations, this research has followed *Society for Biblical Literature Handbook of Style*, 2nd ed. (Atlanta, GA: SBL, 2014).

2 Saucy, "Miracles and Jesus' Proclamation," 282, citing G. H. Boobyer, "The Gospel Miracles: Views Past and Present," in *The Miracles and the Resurrection* (London: SPCK, 1964), 32; Anton Vögtle, "The Miracles of Jesus against Their Contemporary

Peter's preaching in Acts 10 makes it clear that the early church did not think of Jesus' miracles as additional function to his ministry. The close relationship between Jesus' words and deeds is apparent in the mind of the early Christians. The summary statements in Matthew 4:23 and 9:35 denote clearly that Matthew understood Jesus as possessing authority over everything.[3] Furthermore, with this passing comments Matthew makes it apparent that he understood Jesus as possessing authority over creation. And by looking at the nature miracles in Matthew's Gospel, it is evident that the disciples are beyond doubt that Jesus is not only the Christ but also God incarnated among human beings.[4] The nature miracles, therefore, is a graphic manifestation of a God-like image of Jesus as Lord over the cosmological reality.[5]

### *1.2.1. Cosmic Christology*

Several New Testament texts, such as John's Prologue, 1 John 1:1-3, Colossians 1:15-20, and Ephesians 1:3-14, provide crucial evidence that inform the reader that the earliest followers of Jesus recognised the significance of Jesus' life as surpassing his time on earth.[6] These texts indicate a development of faith among the members of the earliest Jesus' movement. The understanding of faith among the earliest followers of Jesus "shifted from an encounter of the historical Jesus to a belief that in and through Jesus the divine purpose is revealed and achieved."[7] Faith develops when consequences change, and also when new climate of understanding emerges.

The thought that Jesus is authorized by God to have authority over the cosmological powers could be attained from different parts of Matthew's Gospel. The infancy narrative (1:18-2:23), the passion narrative (26:1-27:66) and especially the resurrection scene (28:1-20) present Christ as possessing power over cosmology.

The expression cosmic Christology has been used in various contexts and intellectual movements. To define the phrase broadly, it has to be

---

Background," in *Jesus in His Time*, ed. Hans Jurgen Schultz, trans. Brian Watchorn (London: SPCK, 1971), 96-105 (96-97).

3 Saucy, "Miracles and Jesus' Proclamation," 283.

4 James R. Harrison, "Modern Scholarship and the 'Nature' Miracles: A Defence of their Historicity and Affirmation of Jesus' Deity," *Church History* 3 (2006): 493-510.

5 Graham H. Twelftree, *Jesus the Miracle Worker: A Historical and Theological Study* (Downers Grove, IL: IVP, 1999-2011), 235.

6 Peter Callaghan, "Cosmic Christology and the Reclamation of Christ's Relevance in the 21st Century," *Graduate Annual* 3 (2015): 3, http://digitalcommons.lasalle.edu/cgi/viewcont-ent.cgi?article=1034&context=graduateannual.

7 Callaghan, "Cosmic Christology," 3, citing Zachary Hayes, "Christ, Word of God and Exemplar of Humanity: The Roots of Franciscan Christocentrism and its Implications for Today," *Cord* 46.1 (1996): 7-8.

understood that cosmic Christology includes an attempt to connect the created beings - cosmos, human beings, and spiritual entities; the bonding of creation, redemption, and consummation with the different activities of Christ - the creator, redeemer, and sustainer through the phases of his life in history - incarnation, death, and resurrection.[8] It seriously considers the relevant verses (Col 1:16 and John 1:1-8) where the incarnated Christ is stated as the point of origin for all things. The creation is now different after the incarnation took place. And the universe without losing its quality of metaphysical reality becomes an entity assumed by its creator. This Christological dimension also presents the question of the destiny of the universe. This world is apprehended as a chaotic process moved by blind chemical, physical, and genetic forces.[9] It is an apparent disorganisation, but there would be a point of attraction, an orientating principle of the whole reality, which is to be explained by the idea of cosmic Christology.[10]

Cosmic Christology concerns with the preexistence of Jesus, the one who has full fledge control over the cosmos, and the one who became incarnate in history. It points Jesus as divine person, who took the human flesh through the mystery of incarnation.[11] Like Paul who explicitly regards Christ as, "The image of the unseen God and the first-born of all creation, for in Him were created all things in heaven and on earth: everything visible and everything invisible, thrones, ruling forces, sovereignties, powers - all things were created through Him and for Him (Col 1:15-16)," Matthew also indicates the idea of cosmic Christology throughout his narrative. As already stated, the infancy narrative, the passion narrative and the resurrection all pointed toward Jesus as possessing authority over cosmic reality. Even the healing miracles depicted the same content, and the nature miracles are special indication of the idea of cosmic Christology in Matthew.

Matthew's nature miracles project cosmic Christology in a way that emphasizes Jesus' authority over nature and creation. Jesus' words could make sense for the storm and materialistic elements. The stilling of the storm in Matthew 8 affirms Jesus' authority over nature. The feeding of the five thousand is unique because all Gospel writers mention it (Matt 14:13-21; Mark 6:30-44; Luke 9:10-17; John 6:1-14). The miracle illustrates the authority of Jesus over nature and the divine intervention on behalf of others. The walking on the

---

8 Lucio Florio, "Cosmic Christology and Pneumatology: Updating a Traditional Theological Topic to Approach a Dynamic Universe," (paper presented at the program of the Metanexus Institute, Philadelphia, USA, 3-7 June 2006, n.p., https://www.academia.edu/567401/Cosmic_Christolo-gy_and_Pneumatology.

9 Florio, "Cosmic Christology," n.p.

10 Florio, "Cosmic Christology," n.p.

11 Ferdinand Nwaigbo, "Cosmic Christology and Eco-theology in Africa," *AFER* 53/2 (2011): 437-461.

water in Matthew 14 is another example for Jesus' authority over nature. This is not a biological design, but the evangelist seems to have presented what he had heard or read from Jesus' tradition. When Jesus came toward the disciples, it revealed his authority over nature. Thus cosmic Christology refers Jesus as Christ, and the aspect of God which pervades all of creation, the Christ who "fills the universe in all its parts" (Eph 1:23).

### *1.2.2. Matthean Community*

Matthew clearly exhibits its rootedness within the community.[12] The gospel is also not the product of an isolated author, but reflects the life and concerns of a particular Christian community. Matthew's Gospel has long been known as the most ecclesiastical Gospel, the only gospel to use the word *church* to describe the community of believers (16:18; 18:17). Matthew's church has obviously been involved in an intense relationship with the surrounding dominant Jewish community and the Roman imperial presence.[13] This community could be best referred to as the "real readers" of Matthew. The initial clue as to the place in history of the Matthean community comes from Matthew himself, as implied author. In such passages as 24:15 (let the reader understand), 27:8 (until this day), and 28:15 (until this day), Matthew bursts the bounds of the story he is telling of the life and ministry of Jesus in order to address his readers directly. Temporally, these passages locate the real readers at a point after the resurrection but short of the Parousia. Matthew himself describes this point as the time of the messianic woes, which will issue in the final judgment (24:8). The time of the messianic woes, therefore, is also the time in which the real readers of Matthew's Gospel were living.[14] However, the ongoing problem is that the time of the messianic woes cannot be tied down to any particular date.

Many of the commentators tentatively place the Matthean Community in Syria and most probably in Antioch, which is home to a large Jewish-Christian congregation from at least the time of Acts 11:19-30 (no later than 46 CE) and lasting well into the second century.[15] J. Zumstein has revived the thesis that

---

12 Graham N. Stanton, *A Gospel for a New People: Studies in Matthew* (Louisville: T&T Clark, 1993), 45-47.

13 M. Eugene Boring, *The Gospel of Matthew: Introduction, Commentary, and Reflections*, NIB 8, eds. Leander E. Keck, *et.al.* (Nashville: Abingdon Press, 1995), 97; Warren Carter, *Matthew and the Margins: A Sociopolitical and Religious Reading* (Sheffield, England: SAP, 2000), 36-40.

14 Kingsbury, *Matthew as Story*, 120.

15 Robert R. Hahn, "Judaism and Jewish Christianity in Antioch: Charisma and Conflict in the First Century," *JRH* 14 (1987): 341-360, cited by Craig L. Blomberg, *Matthew*, NAC 22 (Nashville: Broadman, 1992), 37.

Matthew's Gospel originated in Antioch,[16] to explain the existence of Jewish and Gentile Christian tendencies side by side in the Gospel.[17] Warren Carter later defends Antioch as the place for Matthew by stating that "The earliest citations of this gospel are found in writings that have connections with Syria, and Antioch in particular."[18] He also cites the works of Ignatius (bishop of Antioch) who was wrote about it in first decade of the second century, where he utilizes material unique to Matthew. Carter also uses *Didache* to give weight to his argument by citing the presence of the Lord's Prayer in Matthean version.[19] Therefore, Antioch as the place for Matthew makes a stronger case than any other suggested places.

Apart from the struggle faced within the Jewish context, Matthew's audience, like any other community under imperial rule encounters an added context in Antioch. Matthew's Gospel presents a story in which Jesus offers an alternative. Jesus' "inclusive social vision and conflicts with the religious leaders, members of the ruling elite, allies of Rome, and defenders of a hierarchical structure sanctioned by Rome"[20] could be deduced from Matthew. The need to picture Jesus as the supreme authority could also be the result of the oppressing powers of the emperor. Matthew emphasizes Jesus' kingly rule and divine authority. Looking at Jesus' last words in Matthew, he speaks of his supreme authority, "All authority in heaven and on earth has been given to me. Go therefore and make disciples of all nations... teaching them to observe all that I have commanded you; and lo, I am with you always..." (Matt 28:18-19). God is alone "Lord of heaven and earth" (Matt 11:25), and Jesus shares this total authority. Matthew also shows Jesus' authority over nature by his miracles, his authority over sins by forgiving them, and his authority over death by his resurrection.

It is a common knowledge that New Testament was born and developed in the milieu where miracle stories are more common than today's scientific context. In Graeco-Roman antiquity miracle stories were wide spread, and

---

16 J. Zumstein, "Antioche sur l'Oronte et l'évangileselon Matthieu," cited by Gerd Theissen, *The Gospels in Contexts: Social and Political History in the Synoptic Tradition*, trans. by Linda M. Maloney (Edinburg: T&T Clark, 1992), 17; The classic defence of Antioch as the place appears in B. H. Streeter, *The Four Gospels: A Study of Origins, Treating of the Manuscript Tradition, Sources, Authorship, & Dates* (London: Macmillan, 1924), 500-523.

17 Theissen, *The Gospels in Contexts*, 17; for a detail discussion on this thought, see also Donald Senior, "Between Two Worlds: Gentiles and Jewish Christians in Matthew's Gospel," *CBQ* 61 (1999): 14-18.

18 Carter, *Matthew and the Margins*, 15.

19 Carter, *Matthew and the Margins*, 15.

20 A. J. Saldarini, "Pharisees," *ABD* 5:289-303, quoted by Carter, *Matthew and the Margins*, 36.

there are claims that a god or a hero controls nature.[21] Miracle workers mostly related their abilities with the gods (Apollonius started out in the temple of Asclepsis). There are also cases where they were believed to be divine.[22] There are stories of stilling the storm[23] walking on water (Poseidon), and changing water into wine (Dionysus). These nature miracles were attributed to deities and heroes. Roman emperors Julius Caesar's devotees claim for him a destiny that will not allow any sea storm to claim his life; and Augustus Caesar, whose great *Pax* is said to have stilled the storms of the world.[24] At this juncture a crucial strategy "to reframe the audience's thinking and their way of viewing the present and future" is an interpretational motive of Matthew. Thus, Matthew could have proceeded from cosmic Christological framework in presenting Jesus as the Lord of heaven and earth.

### *1.2.3. Son of God in Matthew's Gospel*

Generally, studies of New Testament Christology tend to focus on the titles conferred on Jesus in the Gospels and other New Testament writings. Titles such as Son of God, Son of man, Christ, Lord, and others are understood in a sense as code words that convey the early Christians' confession of Jesus' identity.[25] Christology is one area in which students of Matthew's Gospel have not as yet achieved anything like a consensus of opinion.[26] And major studies include and revolve around certain christological titles designated to Jesus and typology in Matthew.

Jack D. Kingsbury has consistently affirmed that the key title for Matthew's Christology is that of the Son of God.[27] According to his understanding this is not the most frequent title for Jesus in Matthew, but its use and content mark it as the most significant title to which all other titles

---

21 Wendy Cotter, *Miracles in Greco-Roman Antiquity: A Sourcebook for the Study of New Testament Miracles Stories* (London: Routledge, 1999), 131-174.

22 Davids, *DLNTD*, 437.

23 With respect to the control of sea storms, the gods of the Greco-Roman pantheon most commonly mentioned are Poseidon/Neptune, who reigns over the sea, and also Aphrodite/Venus, probably by virtue of the fact that she was supposed to have been born from the sea foam. Outside the Olympian pantheon, five other deities or groups of deities were prayed to for the cessation of storms: (1) the Dioscuri, brothers who once sailed with the Argonauts and later became divine; (2) the Samothrace deities, sea rescue gods who had their own mystery cult; (3) Isis, that major deity from Egypt whose devotion around the Mediterranean also included mystery initiations, (4) Serapis, a deity from Hellenized Egypt, a god of the underworld but merciful in saving his devotees from death at sea.

24 Cotter, *Miracles in Greco-Roman Antiquity*, 134.

25 Donald Senior, *The Gospel of Matthew*, IBT (Nashville: Abingdon Press, 1997), 54.

26 Jack D. Kingsbury, *Matthew: Structure, Christology, Kingdom* (Philadelphia, PA: Fortress, 1975), 41.

27 Kingsbury, *Matthew*, 44.

for Jesus are subordinated. Kingsbury argues by analysing the structure of the gospel, and notes that reference to the title Son of God occurs in all the principal sections of Matthew.

Donald Senior also notes that 'Son of God' is the most significant title Matthew gives to Jesus in his writing and D. R. Bauer goes further to say that Jesus as the Son of God is the overarching theme of Matthew's writing.[28] Matthew has retained all of the references to 'Son of God' contained in the Gospel of Mark and added some of his own and some from the Q source.[29] Matthew uses this title to denote several characteristics of the relationship that Jesus has with God.[30] Jesus' origin is in and through God as he has been conceived through the Holy Spirit (Matt 1:20-21). Jesus as Son of God has an intense and intimate relationship with his Father; "All things have been handed over to me by my Father; and no one knows the Son except the Father, and no one knows the Father except the Son and anyone who the Son chooses to reveal him" (Matt 11:27). The phrase *Πάντα* denotes the cosmic totality in which Jesus is the authoritative divine agent.

Jesus is described by God, Peter, centurions and demons as the Son of God and describes himself in this way also.[31] In the passage that narrates the baptism of Jesus, the Spirit of God descends upon him and the voice of God is heard saying "this is my Son, the beloved, with whom I am well pleased" (Matt 3:17). According to Bauer, Matthew often uses the title of Son of God at particularly significant places within the text, especially at the climaxes of the main divisions of his Gospel.[32] An example of the use of this device is Peter's confession of Jesus as "the Messiah, the Son of the Living God" (Matt 16:16) which ends the second division of Matthew's Gospel concerned with the work and mission of Jesus and the people's response to it.

The healing miracles are no doubt important for Matthean Christology, but Matthew's presentation of nature miracles contains explicit Christological emphasis; as in the walking on the water where the story concludes with the disciples' worshiping Jesus as truly the Son of God ('Ἀληθῶς θεοῦ υἱὸς εἶ - 14:33).[33] The appearance of the title in Matthew 3:17 when the voice from

28 Senior, *The Gospel of Matthew*, 54; D. R. Bauer, *The Structure of Matthew's Gospel: A study in Literary Design*, JSNTSup (Wiltshire: SAP, 1989), 143.

29 D. A. Carson, "Christological Ambiguities in the Gospel of Matthew," in *Christ the Lord: Studies in Christology Presented to Donald Guthrie*, ed. Harold H. Rowdon (Leicester: IVP, 1982), 97-114 (111).

30 Bauer, "The structure of Matthew's Gospel," 145.

31 Terence L. Donaldson, "The Vindicated Son: A Narrative Approach to Matthean Christology," in *Contours of Christology in the New Testament*, ed. Richard N. Longenecker (Michigan: Eerdmans, 2005), 100-121 (109).

32 Bauer, "The Structure of Matthew's Gospel," 144.

33 Senior, *The Gospel of Matthew*, 59.

heaven (God) declares Jesus as "my Son, the Beloved" (οὗτός ἐστιν ὁ υἱός μου ὁ ἀγαπητός). However, even before this dramatic declaration, Matthew already introduces Jesus as God's Son in the infancy narrative, the virginal conception of Jesus, the naming of Jesus as Emmanuel (μεθ'ἡμῶν ὁ θεός – God-with-us - 1:23), the repeated references to Jesus as the child (1:20; 2:2, 8, 9, 11, 13, 14, 20, 21), and the quotation of Hosea 11:1 "Out of Egypt I have called my son" (ἐξ Αἰγύπτου ἐκάλεσα τὸν υἱόν μου- Matt 2:15). In line with his thesis, Kingsbury maintains that the entire miracle section of chapters 8-9 presents Jesus primarily as the powerful Son of God.

The confession of Jesus as Son of God begun in the introductory chapters of Matthew's story and continues throughout the Gospel. In 11:25-27, Jesus identifies himself as God's unique Son. The disciples confess Jesus as Son of God after the miracle of his walking on the water (14:33), and Peter solemnly confesses Jesus as Son of God at Caesarea Philippi (16:16). Similar to the scene of Baptism, a voice from heaven (a euphemism for God) once again on the mountain of transfiguration declares Jesus as God's beloved Son (17:5). In the parable of the vineyard and its wicked tenants, the designation of Jesus as Son again plays a significant role (21:33-46), as it does in the following parable of the king who gave a wedding banquet for his son" (22:1-10). The charge against Jesus in the trial before the Sanhedrin is his claim to be the Son of God (26:63). The passersby mock Jesus for this (27:40, 43), while the climactic declaration of the centurion and his companion is: "Truly this man was God's Son!" (27:54); and these are the evidences that can be drawn out from Matthew's narratives.

Even though the title is not used in the final scene of Matthew's Gospel (28:16-20), Kingsbury still argues that it underlies the majestic appearance of Jesus on the mountain and his declaration that all authority in heaven and on earth has been given to him.[34] In effect, the challenge to Jesus' identity as Son of God in the passion is vindicated through Jesus' resurrection.

Matthew's infancy narrative details the Jewishness of Jesus. The genealogy notes Jesus as a descendant of both David and Abraham. Matthew situates Jesus firmly within a culture waiting and expecting for a promised Messiah.[35] The story parallels the exodus and return of the Israelites as Jesus and his family flee to Egypt (Matt 2:13-15 and Exod 4:19-20),[36] which serves to strengthen the role of Jesus as the promised Messiah. Jesus' identity as Son of God is affirmed by more than just explicit use of the title in the infancy narrative. Matthew underlines Jesus as King and Messiah with the visit of the

34 Kingsbury, *Matthew*, 76-77.

35 Earl Richard, *Jesus: One and Many. The Christological Concept of New Testament Authors* (Wilmington: Michael Glazier, 1988), 146.

36 Dale C. Allison, *The new Moses: A Matthean Typology* (Minneapolis: Fortress, 1993), 141-142.

Magi to his place of birth, bringing gifts worthy of a true King.[37] The infancy narrative of Matthew introduces the reader to the fundamental beliefs about Jesus as Christ; that he is the divine Son of God, truly the King of the Jews and Emmanuel, the very presence of God with us.[38]

### *1.2.4. Other Christological Titles in Matthew's Gospel*

Most scholars will not deny the importance of the title Son of God in Matthew's Christology, but there are others who do not accept Kingsbury's contention of other Christological titles as subordinate to the title Son of God. Graham Stanton and others have highlighted the significance of the title Son of David in Matthew.[39] The observation is that, this title appeared nine times in Matthew's Gospel (compared with only three times in Mark). The title is particularly employed in healing stories (9:27; 12:23; 15:22; 20:30, 31) and also in some of the conflicts with Jesus' opponents (e.g., 12:42). For Stanton, this title enables Matthew to assert the distinctive features of Jesus' messianic identity.

David Hill opines that other titles given to Jesus in Matthew are not necessarily subordinate to the Son of God title.[40] He contends that Matthew's intention in his use of other titles may indicate his effort to add particular nuance to the Son of God designation. Hill's suggestion, for an example is the Servant designation; which Matthew applies to Jesus and his mission in the long citation from Isaiah 42:1-4 (see Matt 12:17-21). The humble and compassionate qualities of the Servant of God typify the nature of Jesus' messianic authority as the Son of God.

John Meier also contests Kingsbury's view about the function of the Son of Man title in Matthew's Gospel.[41] He argues that the title is strongly influenced by its use in the apocalyptic theology of Daniel (7:17). Matthew applies this title to various parts of Jesus' ministry. Although, Matthew does not use the title in his final scene, Meier argues that Matthew has in mind the identity of Jesus as Son of Man. Matthew's portrayal of the risen Christ, who holds all authority in heaven and on earth and who returns triumphantly to his community of disciples is, in a sense, a foreshadowing of the end time when the Son of Man will come in glory.[42] Matthew's portrayal of the triumphant

---

37 Bernard P. Robinson, "Matthew's Nativity Stories: Historical and Theological Quesions for Today's Readers," in *New Perspectives on the Nativity*, ed. Jeremy Corley (London: Continuum, 2009), 110-131 (125).

38 Robinson, "Matthew's Nativity Stories," 131.

39 Stanton, *A Gospel for a New People*, 180-185.

40 David Hill, "The Figure of Jesus in Matthew's Gospel: A Response to Professor Kingsbury's Literary-Critical Probe," *JSNT* 21 (1984): 37-52.

41 John P. Meier, *The Vision of Matthew* (New York: Paulist, 1978), 210-219.

42 "A Proleptic Parousia" as Meier calls it – the assigning of the event of parousia to a period earlier than the actual occurrence or the representation of something in the future as if

Jesus in this scene recalls the glorified Son of Man in the book of Daniel. Thus the Son of Man designation is not subordinate to the Son of God title but used alongside it. Matthew may even have in mind the qualities of this title as well as the Son of God title in those passages when God addresses Jesus simply as "My Son" (see 3:17; 17:5).

It is crucial to note that one title cannot be understood as more significant to other titles, and to argue that other titles are subordinate to a particular title is irrelevant for the purpose of this research. It is comprehensible that all these three titles (Son of God, Son of David, and Son of Man) connote christological significance and thus to consider them for Matthew's Christology is inevitable. Senior argues that to pin down the meaning and role of various titles of Jesus in Matthew is a difficult task.[43] The titles or especially a particular title could not sufficiently render the meaning and significance of Matthew's Christology. For Senior, other features of Matthew's story also have contribution to offer for the understanding of Matthew's Christology. Therefore, it is reasonable to understand these studies as depicting Matthew's Christ as closely related to God, and the power and authority of Christ overarches cosmic totality.

### *1.2.5. Cosmic Christology in Matthew's Gospel*

The Synoptic Gospels record a wide variety of healing miracles and testify that Jesus of Nazareth possessed an extraordinary power. Though healing miracles are impressive manifestations they particularly identify Jesus as healer. In other miracles called nature miracles in the Gospels, Jesus does something contrary to the known laws of nature. The stilling of the storm, the walking on the water, the conversion of water into wine, the multiplying of food, the cursing of the fig tree and the taking out of coin from the fish mouth, are all miraculous acts that defy the known nature of law. They are dealing with the realm of creation and providence.[44] These miracles, even if they could be explained scientifically or not, provide the bedrock for the idea of cosmic Christology.

Matthew employs cosmic signs to reinforce Jesus' significance; the star at his birth, and earthquakes at his death and resurrection. Divine interventions through angels and dreams signal the importance of events, and Jesus' relation with cosmic elements. Matthew's ways of dealing with his source is foreign to modern thinking. His technique of playing with numbers; introducing earthquakes and cosmic signs, finding proofs from prophecies which originally meant something else are noteworthy. Matthew's

---

already existed or had occurred.

43 Senior, *The Gospel of Matthew,* 58.

44 Larry R. Helyer, *The Witness of Jesus, Paul and John: An Exploration in Biblical Theology* (Downers Grove, IL: IVP, 2008), 284.

presentation of Jesus as possessing power over the created order of the known world is impressive. It is not difficult to interpret cosmic Christology in different parts of Matthew's narratives. Furthermore, nature miracles may particularly provide more information and path for the formulation of cosmic Christology in Matthew.

John Riches remarks that Matthew uses both titles and motives from tradition to develop his view about Jesus' person and relationship with God. He moves on to assert that to understand Matthew's Christology it is inevitable to consider the narrative setting of the titles and their interaction with motives.[45] How does this relate to nature miracles? This fuller "narrative – sensitive"[46] reading of Matthew's Christology enables us to see the contributions from nature miracles of the First Gospel. When examining these nature miracles, Matthew understands Jesus' identity as clearly aligned with the divine side. Jesus' identity is very much defined by the powers he had possessed over nature.

Jonathan T. Pennington in his 2007 book *Heaven and Earth in the Gospel of Matthew*, argues that Matthew's presentation of Jesus is divine by repeatedly identifying him with the realm of heaven (3:6; 4:17; 11:27) in contrast to the earth which is repeatedly identified with the human (6:19-21; 18:18-20; 21:25-26; 23:9).[47] Furthermore, Jesus' divinity and his authority are clearly seen in nature miracles. After Jesus' stilling of the storm, the question arises "What sort of man is this, that even the winds and the sea obey him?" (8:27). After Jesus' walking on the water the disciples exclaimed "Truly you are the Son of God." (14:33). The feeding stories do not immediately contain this kind of direct assertion from the audience but when looking at the feeding of the four thousand, the next pericope started with the testing to show a sign from heaven. All these narratives confirm that there is a working framework to develop cosmic Christology in Matthew's Gospel. The idea of cosmic Christology in Matthew's Gospel may further develop a framework to look into the challenges to contribute to the development of contextual eco-theology.

### *1.2.6. Eco-Theology for the Mizos*

One concern for the Mizos at this present reality is to understand the concept of cosmic Christology and to provide a framework to develop and to move further the importance of eco-theology among the churches of Mizoram. In the North-East India's context, eco-theology "aims to liberate both an

45 John Riches, *Matthew* (Sheffield: SAP, 2001), 123.

46 Jonathan T. Pennington, *Heaven and Earth in the Gospel of Matthew*, NovTSup 126 (Leiden: Brill, 2007), 83.

47 Pennington, *Heaven and Earth*, 83.

oppressed people and creation to establish a more sustainable society."[48] It also has concerned with preserving and caring for nature.[49] The Mizo concept of a three-way relationship: God, nature and human, may be best described as communitarian model which affirms the common origin and interconnectedness of all creation.[50] God is seen as the originator and ground of community. This means that the universe (including the earth with all its creatures) lives and moves and has its being in God. The dependency on God and nature for livelihood and survival is significantly embedded in the understanding of the interrelated connections between God, nature and human. God is conceived by the Mizos as being organically related to the whole creation. God ceases to be God and is inactive when there is no land and creation.[51]

Human beings are the stewards of the land which belong to the creator, God. The ownership of land by the community or individual is thus "to be understood within the greater recognition that the land belongs to the Supreme Being."[52] The land equally belongs to all with equal rights and freedom to live in it and is to be shared among the members of the community, and thus the produce of the land is eagerly shared in traditional Mizo society. Mathew George observes that an eagerness to share is the most beautiful tribal virtue.[53] In traditional tribal society, the season right after the harvest is when generosity arises. The feasts and celebrations of this season indicate the eagerness of the individual to share with the wider community.

However, this traditional virtue has been lost through generations. The understanding of the interrelated connection between God, nature and human being began to cease in the present reality. Though the awareness of environmental issues and concerns had been given importance by the church, it is crucial to formulate convincing arguments for the Mizos to reignite the significance of the traditional understanding of nature. Thus, to connect cosmic Christology with eco-theology is important in order to promote responsibility of the churches in preservation and caring for nature and creation.

---

48 Yiepetso Wezah and Tereso C. Casiño, "Towards a Relevant Theology of Nature: North-East India Tribal Perspective," *TTJ* 14 (2011): 99-115.

49 K. C. Abraham, "Christian Ethics: Methodological Issues," in *Doing Christian Ethics: Context and Perspectives*, ed. Hunter P. Mabry (Bangalore: BTESSC, 1996), 78.

50 Lawmsanga, "A Critical Study on Christian Mission with Special Reference to Presbyterian Church of Mizoram," (Ph.D. diss., University of Birmingham, 2010), 259.

51 Lawmsanga, "A Critical Study on Christian Mission," 266.

52 Lawmsanga, "A Critical Study on Christian Mission," 267.

53 Mathew George, "Sources of Tribal Theology," *Mission Today* 4 (2000): 290-300.

The following questions form focus of discussion and pave way for further investigation:

- Is it appropriate to interpret nature miracles in Matthew's Gospel as having cosmic christological significance?
- Are these miracle stories in Matthew's Gospel to be taken as the projection of Jesus as Lord over nature and the cosmic totality?
- What did Matthew intend to communicate by these miracle stories?

## 1.3. Previous Research

Study of Matthew's Christology usually moves along several strands of interest. During the fruitful age of redaction criticism and the dominance of two-source hypothesis, Matthew, Mark and Q were carefully compared.[54] Later, scholars have their focus on the meaning and function of particular christological titles.[55] At the same time, there is another direction of study that concentrates on particular passages that contain christological language and symbolism.[56] This last direction will not be taken up at this point; when it comes to the idea of Christology, commentaries and arguments found in the studies of miracles are generally passing comments without much of an in depth treatment. Thus, it is appropriate to take up few struggles and attempts in developing Matthew's Christology from the study of titles and typologies. However, it is evident from the outset that the studies on titles and typologies did not bring us to a point where one can make legitimate conclusion on the subject of Matthew's Christology.

---

54 For example, G. M. Styler, "Stages in Christology in the Synoptic Gospels," *NTS* 10 (1963-64): 398-409; Robert H. Gundry, *Matthew: A Commentary on His Literary and Theological Art* (Grand Rapids: Eerdmans: 1981).

55 On "Lord" see G. Bornkamm, G. Barth and H. J. Held, *Tradition and Interpretation in Matthew* (London: SCM, 1963), 52-57; On "Son of God" see especially Kingsbury, *Matthew*, and critique by David Hill, "Son and Servant: An essay on Matthean Christology," *JSNT* 6 (1980): 2-16; On "Son of David," cf. Dennis C. Duling, "The Therapeutic Son of David: An Element in Matthew's Christological Apologetic," *NTS* 24 (1978): 392-410; and for background study, Christoph Burger, *Jesus als Davids sohn: Eine traditions geschichtliche Untersuchung* (Göttingen: Vandenhoeck & Ruprecht, 1970).

56 Carson thinks that O. Michel's "Der Abschluss des Matthaus evangeliums," and of the many works that have sprung up from this work on Matthew 28:16-20, and more recent work of Brian M. Nolan's book on Matthew, *The Royal Son of God*, which develops a Christology shaped by the Davidic covenant are all basing their broad conclusions on their findings. Carson, "Christological Ambiguities," 97, citing O. Michel, "Der Abschluss des Matthaus evangeliums," *EvT* 10 (1950-51): 16-26; Brian M. Nolan, *The Royal Son of God: The Christology of Matthew 1-2 in the Setting of the Gospel* (Vandenhoeck & Ruprecht, 1979).

Kingsbury calls attention to the three-fold division of Matthew's structure, the formula at 4:17 and 16:21 marks the division, "From that time on Jesus began...", and divides Matthew's Gospel into-the Person of Jesus Messiah (1:1-4:16); the Proclamation of Jesus Messiah (4:17-16:20); the Suffering, Death and Resurrection of Jesus Messiah (16:21-28:20). The detailed examination of the structure of Matthew's Gospel is to support the main argument of the book, which is the real purpose and its view on the person of Christ. He disputes the claim that Matthew's real concern is ecclesiological, and rightly draws attention to his view of the Person of Christ, which he finds particularly expounded by means of the title Son of God, supported by the titles Lord (κύριος) and Son of Man.[57] Kingsbury's interest in the relationship between the structure of the book and its Christology is interesting, but miracle stories are out of his scope.

Carson's article, "Christological Ambiguities in the Gospel of Matthew" takes up some recent studies on Matthew's Christology and questions the presupposition of Matthew's Gospel as containing christological anachronisms. He presents a brief analysis of five christological titles: Christ, Son of David, Lord, Son of God and Son of Man. According to Carson, these christological titles are evidence that Matthew made an attempt to "distinguish his own christological understanding at the time he wrote, and that of Jesus' contemporaries, including his disciples, during the days of his ministry."[58] Carson also understands Matthew's Gospel as setting forth his own christological commitments; and these titles gained significance after the post-passion period. However, the article fails to move beyond titles, and this is where other works will come in.

As is already mentioned, Senior's contribution on the study of Matthew's Christology cannot be neglected here; especially his 1997 book *The Gospel of Matthew* that contains two sub topics in the fifth chapter, the study on titles and beyond titles.[59] He acknowledges that the study of christological titles in Matthew's Gospel drawn from the Old Testament or Judaism, and some borrowed from Greek culture or at least that are given new layers of meaning in Hellenistic context, can yield significant contribution to Matthew's Christology.[60] After reviewing different stance taken by Matthean scholars like Kingsbury, Graham Stanton, David Hill and John Meier, he concludes that it is not an easy task to put together the titles ascribed to Jesus by Matthew. He further states that, it is more difficult to define the interrelationship of different

57 Kingsbury, *Matthew*, 27.

58 Carson, "Christological Ambiguities," 114.

59 Senior, *The Gospel of Matthew*, 52-62.

60 Senior, *The Gospel of Matthew*, 54.

titles employed in the Gospel of Matthew.[61] Therefore he moves on beyond titles and deals with typology in Matthew's Gospel. As the Jewish and Biblical world is interested in typology, it played an important role in giving meaning to a person or an event.[62] However, the link between miracles, especially nature miracles and Christology in Matthew's Gospel is lacking in the work.

Scholars who see the limits of articulating Matthew's Christology from the study of titles alone thus move toward beyond titles and started digging in the significance of typology for Matthew. Dale C. Allison presents how Matthew portrays Jesus as New Moses. Drawing from the Exodus stories that portrayed Moses as lawgiver, leader, liberator, and saviour of his people, worker of miracles, revealer, prophet, and the one who suffered on behalf of his people; a strong connection is made between Jesus and the Pentateuch. The presentation of Jesus as lawgiver (Chaps. 5-7), his intimate knowledge of God (11:25-30), the transfiguration on the mountain (where Moses is explicitly named, 17:1-9), and the commissioning of his disciples in the last scene of Matthew's Gospel are in Allison's view some of the most obvious places where Jesus is portrayed by Matthew as a new Moses.[63]

Larry R. Helyer in his 2008 book *The Witness of Jesus, Paul and John*, talks about the significance of miracles, and especially the nature miracles provide a key building block for cosmic Christology.[64] According to him, the healing miracles fall short of cosmic Christology, but simply testify Jesus as possessing an extraordinary power. As nature miracles deal with the realm of creation and providence, Jesus is asserted as being the cosmic Christ. According to Helyer, by adding transfiguration and resurrection of Jesus, we have "the grand demonstration and vindication of the Son of God."[65] However, this study is not concentrated on the Synoptic Gospels, but rather it is an effortless argument without much elaboration, in order to find out the possible sources for Paul's cosmic Christology.

From the brief survey, it is clear that it is now imperative to move further or beyond the study of titles. Focus must be given upon an attempt to define Jesus by the stories and traditions, which is called Narrative Christology. Reading and interpreting miracles, especially the nature miracles of Jesus to make significant contribution in the study of Matthew's Christology is rare.

---

61 Senior, *The Gospel of Matthew*, 58.

62 Senior, *The Gospel of Matthew*, 59.

63 Allison finds a number of passages where Matthew has clothed the figure of Jesus in the mantle of Moses. According to this perspective Moses typology is surely present in the opening chapters of the gospel where a wicked king slaughters the children of Israel in an attempt to destroy the infant messiah (Matt 1-2; cf. Exod 1:1-2:10) and when Jesus faces a test in a desert (Matt 4:1-11; cf. Exod 16:1-17:7).

64 Helyer, *The Witness of Jesus,* 283-284.

65 Helyer, *The Witness of Jesus,* 284.

Thus, this research will pursue to examine nature miracles in Matthew's Gospel with wider perspective.

## 1.4. Method of Study

The research will employ various methodological approaches, and to locate the socio-cultural-political milieu of miracle stories, historical-critical methods need to be employed. The insights from sociological criticism will provide the main foundation for the research. For contemporary biblical studies, varieties of methodologies are not mutually exclusive. To adopt a particular methodology does not mean that other approaches are to be ignored. It is also true with Cultural Intertextuality that combines new methodologies with older approaches.[66]

### *1.4.1. Cultural Intertextuality*

Julia Kristeva explains Cultural Intertextuality as locating a text "within (the text of) society and history."[67]Abstract ideas such as society and history are viewed figuratively as texts and must be considered in the interpretation. Thus, the readers of Matthew's Gospel have the task to place the text within the general culture of which they are a part of it and which is in turn a part of them.[68]

Carter's formulation of six-fold approach is required to locate the Gospel texts within the text of their society and history. Historical studies, classical and archaeological studies, social-science models, insights from cultural anthropology, post-colonial approaches, and forms of literary criticism (audience-oriented and narrative studies) are all accommodated in this approach.[69] Moreover, this multi-disciplinary approach has more relevance for a person who experiences the reality of growing up in a colony of the former British Empire.

Cultural intertextuality can be understood as a text's interaction or relation with cultural knowledge that is known only to a particular people. This may

---

66 Cultural Intertextuality is best described as multi-layered or inter-disciplinary approach that enables access to various dimensions of the interaction between Gospel texts and the imperial world. Warren Carter, "Matthew and Empire," in *Empire in the New Testament*, NTS, ed. Stanley E. Porter & Cynthia Long Westfall (Oregon: Pickwick, 2011), 90-119. For surveys of intertextuality and its counterparts, see G. Miller, "Intertextuality in Old Testament Research," *CBR 9* (2011): 238-309.

67 Julia Kristeva, "Word, Dialogue and Novel," in *Desire in Language: A Semiotic Approach to Language and Art*, ed. Leon S. Roudiez; trans. T. Gora, et al. (New York: CUP, 1980), 64-91, cited by Carter, "Matthew and Empire," 92.

68 Carter, "Matthew and Empire," 92, cited by Joel Willitts, "Matthew," in *Jesus is Lord, Caesar is Not: Evaluating Empire in New Testament Studies*, ed. Scot Mc. Knight and Joseph B. Modica (Downers Grove: IVP, 2013), 82-100 (86).

69 Carter, "Matthew and Empire," 92.

appear in word and concept patterns, values, codes, systems, and myths. Thus, within a text, cultural intertextuality could be seen as references and, allusions, and echoes.[70] As texts materialize cultural systems of communication and discourse, intertextuality includes the interaction of cultural texts of all sorts, including performances, concepts, images, and metaphors, as well as literary texts.[71] The research will mainly utilize three specific approaches namely, sociological, rhetorical and postcolonial approaches.

### *1.4.2. Sociological Criticism*

As the interpreters have the task to expose ancient text and its culture by modern methods and theories of sociology, C. I. David Joy, in his 2012 book *Hermeneutics: Foundations and New Trends: A Postcolonial Reading of John 4*, rightly talks about the risk faced by the interpreters in interpreting the world of the text.[72] The attempt to expose ancient text and its culture by modern methods and theories of sociology is truly a daunting task. But by applying these principles, it is evident that the exegesis could provide location for the social and cultural condition of the text as accurately as possible.[73] Stephen J. Pattenson's study of Thomas' Christianity justifies the usefulness of using such tool to arrive at a proper location for identifying the cultures behind the texts.[74] Thus, it is evident that the continuous search for the historical context of the texts and their historical development is still looming large at this present theological exercise.

The analysis of likely daily conditions experienced by the earliest followers of Jesus within the empire could serve as a starting point. As already noted in the previous section, the provenance of Matthew's Gospel is not clear but the careful suggestion made by Carter is the Antioch-on-the-Orontes, the provincial capital of the Roman province of Syria.[75] Certainty for the provenance of Matthew's Gospel is not possible, but what is clear is that Matthew's audience lives in a world in which negotiating Roman imperial

---

70 Duane F. Watson, ""Keep Yourselves from Idols": A Socio-Rhetorical Analysis of the Exordium and Peroratio of 1 John," in *Fabrics of Discourse: Essays in Honor of Vernon K. Robbins*, ed. David B. Gowler, L. Gregory Bloomquist and Duane F. Watson (Harrisburg: Trinity Press International, 2003), 281-302 (296).

71 Richard Valantasis, "The Nuptial Chamber Revisited: The Acts of Thomas and Cultural Intertextuality," *Semeia* 80 (1997): 261-276.

72 C. I. David Joy, *Hermeneutics: Foundations and New Trends. A Postcolonial Reading of John 4* (Delhi: ISPCK, 2012), 29.

73 Joy, *Hermeneutics*, 30-31, citing John H. Elliot, *A Home for the Homeless: A Sociological Exegesis of 1 Peter: Its Situation and Strategy* (Philadelphia: Fortress, 1981), 3.

74 Joy, *Hermeneutics*, 30-31, citing Stephen J. Patterson, *The Gospel of Thomas and Jesus* (Sonomo: Polebridge, 1993).

75 Carter, *Matthew and the Margins*, 14-17.

power is a daily task. If the Gospel addresse a community in Antioch in Syria, it is not possible for a community to exist in that city without negotiating the Empire. The encounter with numerous expressions of Roman imperial power: coins, buildings, troops, administrative officials, taxes, festivals - is inescapable for Matthew's audience.[76]

The impact made by sociological approach on New Testament study is significant and overwhelming. It ushers the researcher into the realm and environment of the early Christianity. Especially for a reader with a contemporary Western mindset, this method is necessary to explore the Bible in its original context and setting.[77] John H. Elliot mentions that "Social scientific presuppositions, like theological presuppositions, pertain to three aspects of the interpretive enterprise: the interpreters, the objects to be interpreted, and the method of interpretation."[78] Philip F. Esler also states, "New Testament documents speak to us from particular social worlds and need to be investigated using disciplines developed specifically to comprehend the social dimensions of the human experience. Without this, our understanding of the texts will be unnecessarily impaired."[79] There is a potential in this method to bring the reader to the awareness of the realities of the communities behind the texts.

### *1.4.3. Rhetorical Approach*

Rhetorical approach recognizes the themes and arguments that are embedded in miracle stories. Significantly it takes form, source, tradition, redaction, history, and theology not as individual elements but accommodates them as interactive elements in miracle stories.[80] The traditional criticisms that see miracle stories as primarily acts as vehicle to reveal manifestations of divine power is now broadened with rhetorical approach. Miracle stories are no longer understood as having a single purpose of revealing divine authority, but now it is recognized that they have multiple function within the narrative in which it is embedded. This also moves further in saying that they also played significant roles within the social and cultural contexts in which the narrative itself is employed.

As Vernon K. Robbins, in his essay "Argumentative Textures in Socio-Rhetorical Interpretation," the New Testament discourses are to be understood as an interwoven system that made use of the Old Testament discourse as one

76 Willitts, "Matthew," 86.

77 Gerald Bray, *Biblical Interpretation: Past and Present* (Downers Grove: IVP, 1996), 512.

78 John H. Elliott, *What is Social-Scientific Criticism,* 36.

79 Philip F. Esler, *The First Christians in their Social Worlds* (New York: Routledge, 1994), 2.

80 Duane J. Watson, "Introduction," in *Miracle Discourse in the New Testament*, ed. Duane J. Watson (Atlanta: SBL, 2012), 1-16.

major resource within Mediterranean discourse.[81] This "highly process of rhetorical invention during the first century," according to Robbins, enable the early Christians "to create their new form of discourse."[82] Thus, the basic literary forms such as biographical history, epistle, and apocalypse are carved out from wisdom, prophetic, apocalyptic, precreation, priestly, and miracle discourses of Old Testament and Mediterranean sources. Sociorhetorical approach sees each mode of discourse as a rhetorolect, which is simply a contraction of the phrase "rhetorical dialect."[83] The presupposition is that "each early Christian rhetorolect emerged in relation to multiple social and cultural spaces, functioned in dynamic ways in multiple public setting, and responded in appealing ways, both then and now, to multiple kinds of evil in the world. Early Christians blended the six rhetorolects in multiple ways."[84] In this sense, the potential for each rhetorolect to function in multiple ways will surely enable the early Christians with a wide range of speech and argumentation to articulate their Christology.

The blending of these different modes of discourse is called rhetorolects, which Robbins defines it as "a form of language variety or discourse identifiable on the basis of a distinctive configuration of themes, topics, reasonings, and argumentations."[85] According to Robbins, the miracle rhetorolect in the New Testament, "presupposes that God responds to humans in context of danger or disease and that Jesus is the mediator of these benefits to humans," and commonly situated in the context of fear, cowardice, and the response of belief.[86] Miracle stories are thus composition of a blend of miracle rhetorolect and one or more of the other rhetorolect.[87] A major portion of miracle discourse

---

81 Vernon K. Robbins, "Argumentative Textures in Socio-Rhetorical Interpretation," in *Rhetorical Argumentation in Biblical Texts: Essays from the Lund 2000 Conference*, ed. Anders Eriksson, Thomas H. Olbricht and Walter Übelacker (Harrisburg: Trinity Press International, 2002), 27-65; Vernon K. Robbins, "The Dialectical Nature of Early Christian Discourse," *Scriptura* 59 (1996): 353-362.

82 Robbins, "Argumentative Textures," 28.

83 Robbins, "The Dialectical Nature of Early Christian Discourse," 356.

84 For conceptual blending, see Gilles Fauconnier and Mark Turner, *The Way We Think: Conceptual Blending and the Mind's Hidden Complexities* (New York: Basic, 2003); Todd V. Oakley, "Conceptual Blending, Narrative Discourse, and Rhetoric," *Cognitive Linguistics* 9.4 (1988): 321-360; Todd V. Oakley, "The Human Rhetorical Potential," *Written Communication* 16.1 (1999): 93-128; Vernon K. Robbins, "Conceptual Blending and Early Christian Imagination," in *Explaining Christian Origins and Early Judaism: Contribution from Cognitive and Social Science*, BIS 89, ed. Petri Luomanen, Ilkka Pyysiäinen, and Risto Uro (Leiden: Brill, 2007), 161-195; Robert von Thaden, *Sex, Christ, and Embodied Cognition: Paul's Wisdom for Corinth*, ESEC 16 (U.K.: Deo, 2012).

85 Robbins, "The Dialectical Nature of Early Christian Discourse," 356.

86 Robbins, "The Dialectical Nature, 358; Watson, "Introduction," 3.

87 Watson, "Introduction," 3.

in Matthew's Gospel is inductive narrative, thus without rationales introducing deductive reasoning and argumentation simply moves from cases to results. Robbins sees the importance of rhetorical investigation to analyse and interpret how inductive narrative of miracle stories is nurtured into argumentative discourse within the New Testament.[88]

These rhetorolects do not exist in a pure form in normal discourse, but "by their nature, rhetorolects interpenetrate one another and interact with one another like dialects do when people from different dialectical areas converse with one another."[89] The task is thus not simply to identify unique rhetorolects, but to identify how separate and unique rhetorolects interwoven to create discourse.[90]

Wilhelm Wuellner opines that there are two ways in which rhetorical discourse elaborates topoi, which is based on the insights of ancient rhetorical treatises. The two ways are (1) amplificatory-descriptive and (2) argumentative-enthymematic.[91] Robbins thus argues from a rhetorical perspective and states that discourse contains both rhetography (narration that creates pictures) and rhetology (assertions that create reasoning).[92] Nature miracles in Matthew's Gospel also present pictorial narration (rhetography) of the topos of Jesus' cosmic authority. The miracle stories that are to be dealt with in the later section will clearly show how important it is to read the stories from rhetorical perspective. The narration of miracle stories is usually straightforward and epideictic in Matthew's Gospel, and implies a positive view or praise of Jesus and his actions.[93]

---

88 Vernon K. Robbins, "Sociorhetorical Interpretation of Miracle Discourse in the Synoptic Gospels," in *Miracle Discourse in the New Testament*, ed. Duane J. Watson (Atlanta: SBL, 2012), 17-84.

89 Robbins, The Dialectical Nature, 356; cf. L. Gregory Bloomquist, "The Role of Argumentation in the Miracle Stories of Luke-Acts: Toward a Fuller Identification of Miracle Discourse for use in Sociorhetorical Interpretation," in *Miracle Discourse in the New Testament*, ed. Duane J. Watson (Atlanta: SBL, 2012), 85-124 (88).

90 Bloomquist, "The Role of Argumentation in the Miracle Stories of Luke-Acts," 88.

91 Robbins, "Sociorhetorical Interpretation of Miracle Discourse," 21, citing Wilhelm H. Wuellner, "Toposforschung und Torah interpretation bei Paulus und Jesus," *NTS* 24 (1977/1978): 467.

92 Vernon K. Robbins, "Rhetography: A New Way of Seeing the Familiar Text," in *Words Well Spoken: George Kennedy's Rhetoric of the New Testament*, SRR 8, ed. C. Clifton Black and Duane F. Watson, (Waco: Baylor University Press, 2008), 81-106, cited by Robbins, "Sociorhetorical Interpretation of Miracle Discourse," 21-22.

93 Robbins, "Sociorhetorical Interpretation of Miracle Discourse," 22.

### *1.4.4. Postcolonial Biblical Criticism*

Postcolonial Biblical Criticism basically assumes that the dominating culture wrote the Bible, and even decided the process of canonization. Even the language used in this literature became propagating and subjugating tools to oppress the colonized.[94] The task is mainly to critique the Western assumptions of what literature has been canonized and an attempt to reinterpret the texts with an awareness of their imperialist assumptions.[95] The second task is an attempt to attach due attention to the literature of the colonized, and the third task is to discuss postcolonial diaspora, pan-nationalism, and nationalism.[96] The third task "includes discourses on the production of culture and the complexity of identity-the inherent hybridity of both the colonist and the subjugated people."[97]

Sugirtharajah in his 2012 book *Exploring Postcolonial Biblical Criticism: History, Methods, Practice*, also states "The debates about postcolonialism center roughly around three things: the fact of colonial and postcolonial reality; the resultant political, historical, and cultural changes; and the scholarly study of the work that emerged out of the colonial encounter."[98] Thus, postcolonialism confirms the culturally influenced and determined nature of interpretation, and that all interpretation is culturally conditioned. Therefore, the term postcolonialism can generally be understood as the multiple political, economic, cultural and philosophical responses to colonialism from its inauguration to the present day, and is somewhat broad and extensive in scope.[99]

New Testament scholarship gains fresh insights through the process of postcolonial reading. The reading crystallized the presence of imperial process defined by Roman Empire in the New Testament texts. Thus, the possibility of applying this approach to the New Testament is further pursued. Simon Samuel, in his analysis of Mark's portrait of Jesus in *A Postcolonial Reading of Mark's Story of Jesus*, concludes that "Mark can be seen as a postcolonial discursive strategy that creates a strategic space for the transcultural community in-between the relatively dominant native Jewish and the Roman colonial

94 Donald E. Hall, *Literary and Cultural Theory: From Basic Principles to Advanced Applications* (Boston: Houghton Mifflin, 2001), 268-269.

95 W. Randolph Tate, *Biblical Interpretation: An Integrated Approach* (Grand Rapids: Baker, 1991), 312-313.

96 Aparajita Sagar, "Postcolonial Studies," *DCCT*: 562-567.

97 Tate, *Biblical Interpretation*, 313.

98 R. S. Sugirtharajah, *Exploring Postcolonial Biblical Criticism: History, Methods, Practice* (Chichester: Wiley-Blackwell, 2012), 176.

99 Jane Hiddleston, *Understanding Postcolonialism* (Stocksfield: Acumen, 2009), 1.

discourses."[100] This analysis situates the postcolonial community between native Jewish traditions and the colonizing Rome. Joy in his 2008 book *Mark and its Subaltern*, also argues that Herodians, Scribes and the priestly class who collaboratively promoted colonial values in Palestine and the Roman imperialism through its various means are responsible for creating oppression and exploitation to ordinary people.[101]

In her postcolonial essay on John, Dube notes that "The Gospel of John engages in a long and extended subordination of all other Jewish figures and the cultural spaces of power associated with them."[102] Dube further argues that John redraws the spatial maps in a quest for power on the same terms as its imperial oppressors and their collaborators. She further argues that the Gospel's strategy of elevating Jesus above any other cultural figure among the Jews and in the world is a colonizing ideology.[103] In this regard, Adele Reinhartz, in her essay "The Colonizer as Colonized" argues that Johannine community forges an identity from its spiritual superiority over other subordinate groups and even the dominant group, and takes on the role of the colonizer, at least in theology, language and narrative.[104]

These works are an example of how postcolonial reading revolutionized New Testament interpretation, and this approach thus convincingly present itself as a major shift in biblical hermeneutics. The Mizos traditional cosmological worldview resembles closely to New Testament's or Jewish cosmological worldview, but got degraded through colonial influence. Therefore, it is important to acknowledge the significance of traditional religious worldview of the Mizos to come up with a stronger theology of nature.

## 1.5. Purpose of Research

Matthew presents Jesus as having authority over all creation. The majority of christological studies of Matthew's Gospel focus on the titles of Jesus. As these studies lack adequate explanation and meaning of a complex Christology in Matthew's Gospel, other aspects need to be examined. The study on typology

100 Dean B. Deppe, review of *A Postcolonial Reading of Mark's Story of Jesus*, by Simon Samuel, *CTJ* 44 (2009): 413-414.

101 C. I. David Joy, *Mark and its Subaltern: A Hermeneutical Paradigm for a Postcolonial Context* (London: Equinox, 2008), 123.

102 Musa W. Dube, "Savior of the World but not of this World: A Post-Colonial Reading of Spatial Construction in John," in *The Postcolonial Bible*, ed. R. S. Sugirtharajah (Sheffield: SAP, 1998), 118-135.

103 Dube, "Savior of the World," 128-129.

104 Adele Reinhartz, "The Colonizer as Colonized: Intertextual Dialogue between the Gospel of John and Canadian Identity," in *John and Postcolonialism: Travel, Space and Power*, eds. Musa W. Dube and Jeffrey L. Staley (London: SAP, 2002), 170-192.

and other features of Matthew's stories are also taken up to provide better understanding of Matthew's Christology. However, miracle stories, especially nature miracles are neglected, and the purpose is to analyse these miracles to provide more contributions to the overall Matthew's Christology. Another purpose is to situate the religious cosmological worldview of traditional Mizos in order to formulate a more intimate eco-theology.

## 1.6. Scope and Limitation

The studies of titles, typology and narratives could help the research to uncover the general idea of cosmic Christology that is present in Matthew's Gospel. The study will focus mainly on three of the nature miracles in Matthew: the stilling of the storm (8:23-27), the walking on the water (14:22-33), and the feeding of the multitudes (14:13-21; 15:32-39). Matthew's two stories of feeding of the multitudes will be taken as one miracle because they both contain the same elements needed for the research. Another point of interest is the Mizo traditional concept of Khuanu, which will be taken up as a test case or an example of how cosmic Christology and traditional concepts could be related or connected. Thus, an exhaustive dealing of traditional Mizo concepts of deities is not to be expected in this thesis.

## 1.7. Tentative Outline

The first chapter will present the rationale and definition of the methodology. The second chapter will study Matthew's community and will try to situate the community to a particular context. The third chapter will make an attempt to highlight how nature miracles are understood in ancient tradition, and how God, nature and miracle are intertwined under the cosmological worldview of the Old Testament, Graeco-Roman, and Second Temple Judaism.

Nature miracles within the cosmological worldview of the New Testament will also be considered. The fourth chapter will briefly deal with other New Testament writings where cosmic Christology to be found. The fifth chapter is an attempt to formulate Cosmo-Christological framework in Matthew's Gospel that is to be utilized for the exegesis. The exegetical chapters will deal with nature miracles of Matthew's Gospel in the light of Matthew's christological framework, and Matthew's cosmological worldview cannot be neglected. Thus, the study will proceed to develop cosmic Christology in Matthew's Gospel from these nature miracles, and shall be related to traditional Mizo's religious traditional worldview. However, the thesis will concentrate mainly on the concept of *Khuanu*, and other deities could not be taken up because the main argument of this thesis deals with Matthew's nature miracle stories and their significance for the formulation of cosmic Christology in the Gospel.

The understanding of Khuanu as creator and the one who sustained the village and its inhabitants, including human beings and all other created things shall be taken up as an enhancement of eco-theology for the Mizos. For the Mizos, God as creator and sustainer of all created things is not a foreign concept, especially before the colonial rule. By looking at folktales and myths of the Mizos, it is understandable that the Mizos never identified God as being isolated from creation.

Chapter 2

# Socio-Historical Context of Matthew's Gospel

## 2.1. Introduction

To understand the teachings of nature miracles of Matthew's Gospel,[1] and in order to uncover the historical context, there is a need to examine the cultural milieu and the historical settings of that time. Historical analysis of the text would need an exploration of the religious, cultural and sociological milieu of the origin of Matthew.[2] There is also a need to explore the purpose of Matthew's Gospel.[3] During the time of the writing of this Gospel, several oral traditions and perhaps written sources may seem to flourish. Why did Matthew not simply make a copy of these traditions? Why did he decide to write another Gospel and what did he wish to accomplish?[4] Thus, it is always an exciting endeavour to look at Matthew's Gospel to find out the purpose of his Gospel, and the fact that there is no explicit declaration of his intention becomes intriguing.

This chapter will make an attempt to situate Matthew's Gospel as earliest as possible. As the Gospel was accepted as having apostolic credential according to the earliest tradition, without dragging Mark's Gospel to an

1 This thesis uses "Matthew" to refer to the evangelist without in any way suggesting that the evangelist is to be identified as the apostle Matthew.

2 Bernard Lategan, "Mapping the Hermeneutical Process," in *Focusing on the Message: New Testament Hermeneutics, Exegesis and Methods*, ed. Du Toit A. (Pretoria: Protea, 2009), 65-105 (65).

3 Lategan "Mapping the Hermeneutical process," 65; Kevin Gary Smith, *Academic Writing and Theological Research: A Guide for Students* (Johannesburg: SATSP, 2008), 172.

4 Cf. John Yieh, *Conversation with Scripture: The Gospel of Matthew*, AABSSS (Harrisburg: Morehouse Publishing, 2012), 4.

earlier date Matthew's Gospel could be dated around 60 CE - 100 CE. Though Matthean Community is dealt with briefly in the first chapter, here in this chapter Matthean community will be dealt with in relation to Formative Judaism, and the term "crowds" in Matthew's Gospel will be analysed. The socio-economic status, social and religious climate, the idea of discipleship and mission among the members of the community are another interest. The geographical details and topographical significance in the literary design of Matthew's Gospel also need to be highlighted. There is another significant term "place" in Matthew's Gospel, and Gerd Theissen's understanding of Christianity as a movement of wandering charismatics also need attention and will be dealt with in this chapter.

## 2.2. Author

Ancient tradition unanimously credited the Apostle Matthew as the author of this Gospel. The earliest evidence is found in the statement of Papias, Bishop of Hierapolis (usually dated about 130-140 CE) which was asserted by Eusebius (*Ch. Hist. iii.39.16*). This is repeated in important ancient writers, some of them are Irenaeus (*Against Heresis*, iii. I.1), Pantaenus (quoted by Eusebius, *Ch. Hist.* v. 10.3), Tertullian (*Against Marcion*, iv. 2), Origen (quoted by Eusebius, *Ch. Hist.* vi. 25.4), and Eusebius (*Ch. Hist.* vi. 25.3).[5] Apart from this ancient traditional assertion, the patristic tradition is also explicit and unanimous in saying that the apostle Matthew wrote this Gospel in Hebrew. However, this traditional view that Matthew's Gospel was written by the Apostle Matthew himself is open to serious question after the emergence of Source Criticism.

As reflected in the Canon of the New Testament, Matthew was the first written Gospel having apostolic credential according to the early church. Problems have been found with this view over the years, and Mark's Gospel was widely accepted as the first and foremost written Gospel, and Matthew's utilization of it became prominent in New Testament Studies. As Matthew provided a more sophisticated Greek in terms of grammar and style, it is widely accepted that "Matthew gave Mark some extra literary polish rather than the other way around."[6] Matthew may have also utilized the Q source as distinctive themes were displayed throughout the Gospel such as Wisdom Christology, apocalyptic prophecy, and imminent judgment.[7] It is accepted that Matthew and Luke had common additional material, but the exact nature

5 Cf. Floyd V. Filson, *The Gospel According to St. Matthew*, BNTC (London: Adam & Charles Black, 1960), 16; R. T. France, *Matthew*, TNTC (Leicester: IVP, 1985), 29-30; W. D. Davies and D. C. Allison, *Introduction and Commentary on Matthew I-VII*, vol. 1 of *A Critical and Exegetical Commentary of the Gospel According to Saint Matthew* (London: T&T Clark, 1988), 7-8.

6 Yieh, *Conversation with Scripture*, 5.

7 Yieh, *Conversation with Scripture*, 5.

of this Q source is not clear. Scholars also opined that there may be another source apart from Mark's Gospel and Q, which is assumed as a special source for Matthew called M. In short, Matthew probably utilized Mark's Gospel, Q source and in addition his special M source.

Warren Carter's argument is quite strong, as he states that the disciple Matthew "has no other prominence in the Gospel, no privileged meetings with Jesus."[8] He further demonstrates that the author is not a special witness of Jesus' private events, such as the baptism or the transfiguration.[9] The statement by Papias that made its way to Eusebius, has been interpreted in various ways, and could be confusing. D. A. Carson and Douglas J. Moo advise examiners how these words are "notoriously difficult to translate."[10] The arguments from linguistic scholars also claim that the early Greek version (late second or early third century) does not carry any evidence that the Gospel is a work of translation. One question needs to be answered; did the quotation of Papias by Eusebius means "in the Hebrew language" or "in a Hebrew rhetorical style"?

D. J. Harrington argues that the Greek language in Matthew's Gospel is "as good in a simplistic straight forward style."[11] He also believes that it is an improvement on Mark's Greek, and the language is also in line with Septuagint which he calls "Semitic Greek with Hebrew idioms."[12] Harrington further explains that there are writings in the Gospel that show lack of awareness of Jewish practices. He points out that the parable of the unforgiving debtor (18:23-24) uses torture to extract a debt and this according to him was not certainly a Jewish practice.[13] The conclusion for him is thus the words attributed to Papias were ambiguous and argues that early copies of the Gospel did not claim an apostolic authorship.

Though the consensus weighs heavily toward a non-apostolic authorship, J. J. Greisbach (1745-1812) was the first to reject the idea that Mark's Gospel was earlier than Matthew's Gospel. According to his hypothesis, Mark and Luke edited Matthew's Gospel using Q as well, and Luke did it more than Mark. This view has become known as Griesbach Hypothesis and is largely

---

8 Warren Carter, *Matthew and Margins: A Socio-Political and Religious Reading* (Sheffield: SAP, 2000), 14.

9 Carter, *Matthew and Margins*, 14.

10 Eusebius (ca. 340) in his *Ecclesiastical History* 3.39.14-15 cites the second-century bishop Papias, who claimed that he had learned from an elder that "Matthew collected the oracles (of Jesus) in the Hebrew language." D. A. Carson, Douglas J. Moo and Leon Morris, *An Introduction to the New Testament*, 2nd ed. (Grand Rapids, MI: Zondervan, 1992), 143.

11 Daniel J. Harrington, *The Gospel of Matthew*, vol. 1, SPS (Collegeville, MN: The Liturgical Press, 1991), 3.

12 Harrington, *The Gospel of Matthew*, 3.

13 Harrington, *The Gospel of Matthew*, 3.

rejected by modern scholars. The reasons being that; modern scholars assume a dating too late to be written by Mathew and is also assumed that the Gospel could not be a product of the follower of Jesus from Galilee.[14] However, R. T. France inclined towards the apostolic authority.[15] In contrast to this view M. Davies believes that the apostle did not write the Gospel, but was attributed to him only late in the second century, this is mainly for the purpose of apostolic authority.[16] He further states that no external evidence could be found for the apostle to have been the actual writer of the Gospel.[17]

Coming back to the external evidence, however is heavily inclined towards apostolic authorship, but the interpretation of these evidences may differ. It is always clear that the early church is unanimous in accepting Matthew, the apostle as the writer of the Gospel. Papias writes "Matthew put together the oracle in the Hebrew language, and each one interpreted them as best he could."[18] It may be an impossible task to precisely attribute the Gospel to a particular name, and thus a current argument over whether the Gospel has a single author or a group of author as a school is not to be ignored.[19] Craig S. Keener's argument carries weight "Even if Matthew wrote at one stage of the tradition, we have no guarantee that the finished product is largely from Matthew's hand."[20] Though Papias' evidence may not provide solid foundation for the early church belief in apostolic authorship, the findings and hypothesis that are forged out by the application of source criticism are in their true nature, postulation.

France's argument is important when he talks about three lines of approach[21] to this unsolved problem of authorship, is convincing when he

14 R. T. France, *Matthew – Evangelist and Teacher* (Exeter: The Paternoster Press, 1989), 77.

15 France, *Matthew – Evangelist and Teacher*, 78-79. France believes that it is reasonable to accept Matthew as the author as there are reasons to suggest that the work of the "tax-collector apostle." While it cannot be proved, there is also no reason to believe that the early church merely guessed that Matthew was the author or that is was a pseudonym. Thus, he concludes that it can be reasonably assumed that the apostle Matthew is the author of the gospel.

16 M. Davies, *Matthew* (Sheffield, England: JSOT Press, 1993), 1.

17 Davies, *Matthew*, 1.

18 Alexander Roberts, James Donaldson and A. Cleveland Coxe, eds., "Fragments of Papias," in *The Apostolic Fathers: Justin Martyr – Irenaeus*, vol. 1 of *The Ante-Nicene Fathers* (New York: Charles Scribner's Sons, 1903), 151-155.

19 Charles H. Talbert, *Matthew*, PCNT (Grand Rapids, MI: Baker Academics, 2010), 4.

20 Craig S. Keener, *A Commentary on the Gospel of Matthew* (Grand Rapids, MI: Eerdmans, 1999), 39.

21 Three lines of approach: 1. To take *logia* in its normal sense, and to conclude that, whatever Eusebius thought, Papias was not talking about the Gospel, but about a collection of Jesus' sayings in Aramaic (possibly something like the hypothetical Q). In that case this quotation

argues that Papias' and Eusebius' evidences do not help to concretize apostolic authorship.[22] What is significant is the recognition that Matthew's Gospel is written by a Jewish Christian author, who possess "extensive knowledge of and a strong interest in the Old Testament, familiar with scribal traditions and the methods of Rabbinic debate, and capable of writing in good Greek, even though his own cultural background was clearly Semetic."[23]

It must also be recognised that the author was well informed regarding the literatures of Second Temple Judaism, such as Rabbinic Literature, Wisdom Literature, Enochic writings and the Book of Jubilees.[24] In this line of thought there may be numbers of candidate who might have fit the description among the followers of Jesus. Thus, Matthew also fits the description, but needs more reasons to affirm his position as a more likely candidate than other followers.[25]

There are two facts in regard to Matthew's distinction from other disciples; that Matthew was a tax-collector, and his other name is Levi (Matt 9:9; Mark 14; Luke 5:27). Scholars utilize both these facts to support apostolic authorship for Matthew's Gospel. France argues that a tax-collector due to his office must be fluent in Greek, which further assures that he is literate and used to keeping important records.[26] M. Eugene Boring also notes that Matthew's Gospel shows a better linguistic skill than the relatively unpolished Greek of Mark.[27] Robert H. Gundry also notes that Matthew's ability to use short-hand writing would have helped him to record Jesus' teaching with ease.[28]

France points out that the name Levi was taken as a tribal name by some scholars, and an indication that Matthew was a Levite.[29] In this same line, the argument developed by W. F. Albright and C. S. Mann move toward a

---

has no direct bearing on the authorship of the Gospel; 2. To accept Eusebius' view that Papias was talking about the Gospel, and to conclude that he was simply mistaken about its being written in a Semetic language (perhaps being led to this guess by noticing the 'Jewish' character of the Gospel); 3. To opt for the meaning 'in a Semetic style,' and to conclude that Papias is correctly recording the origin of the Greek Gospel of Matthew. France, *Matthew*, 31-32.

22 France, *Matthew*, 31-32.

23 France, *Matthew*, 32; cf. Sean McDowell, *The Fate of the Apostles: Examining the Martyrdom Accounts of the Closest Followers of Jesus* (London: Routledge, 2016), 223.

24 This argument is strongly supported by the findings of Chapter Three, which is the next chapter.

25 France, *Matthew*, 32.

26 France, *Matthew*, 33.

27 M. Eugene Boring, *An Introduction to the New Testament: History, Literature, Theology* (Louisville: WJK, 2012), 534.

28 Robert H. Gundry, *The Use of the Old Testament in St. Matthew's Gospel*, SNT 18 (Leiden: E. J. Brill, 1967), 182-185; see also France, *Matthew*, 33.

29 France, *Matthew*, 33.

suggestion that; as Matthew was a Levite turned tax-collector, ridicule from his more orthodox fellow-Levites is to be expected.[30] They further argue that this is the reason why Matthew was liable to record Jesus' conflicts with orthodoxy with vigorous emphasis. Matthew's purpose thus serves as his own self-defence and a guideline for other potential new comers to the church.[31]

With all these facts and arguments, though it cannot be taken as proof of authorship, Matthew fits the description of the author of this Gospel. Though there were other people among the early disciples, the unanimous tradition of the early church offers a candidate who fits best for being an author of this Gospel. However, this does not rule out the possibility of the stages of composition. According to France, "The later the Gospel is dated, the more likely it becomes that Matthew's contribution was at an earlier stage than the final 'edition.'"[32] No one stands in a position to name the actual writer of the Gospel, but what could be found from these evidences serve as a pointer toward the possibility of Matthew's participation in the composition of Matthew's Gospel.

## 2.3. Date

The absence of manuscript for evidence to locate the exact date as to when Matthew's Gospel was written is acknowledged by scholars.[33] There are scholars who suggest a date for the writing of the Gospel is somewhere around 80-90 CE.[34] As it is generally accepted that Matthew used Mark's Gospel as a source, and Mark's Gospel is thought to be written around 60 CE thus, most of the argument of the date for Matthew depends on relative dating.[35]

Carter's opinion hangs on the understanding that Matthew referred to the destruction of the Temple in the Gospel. This understanding acts as a proof that Matthew cannot be written before 70 CE. It is largely the acceptance of Matthew's account as giving a theological interpretation of why the events happened, the events being the fall of Jerusalem.[36] John Drane also states that it is wide spread belief that Matthew was written after Luke. This is based on the duel assumption that the fall of Jerusalem in 70 CE is being referred to in

30 W. F. Albright and C. S. Mann, introduction, translation and notes to *The Anchor Bible Dictionary*, vol. 26: *Matthew* (New York: Doubleday, 1971), CLXXVII-CLXXXIV.

31 Cf. France, *Matthew*, 33.

32 Cf. France, *Matthew*, 34.

33 Carter, *Matthew and Margins*, 16.

34 Carter, *Matthew and Margins*, 16.

35 Carter, *Matthew and Margins*, 16; David A. DeSilva, *An Introduction to the New Testament: Contexts, Methods and Ministry Formation* (Downers Grove, IL: InterVarsity Press, 2004), 238.

36 Carter, *Matthew and Margins*, 16.

Matthew 22:7 and 24:3-28, also this was not a prophetic statement before the event.[37]

As noted earlier the 80-90 CE dating is quite common, but does not necessarily stand up to reason according to David A. DeSilva.[38] The basis of this is that the presence of tensions between the Jewish and the early Christian communities could be seen right after the ascension of Christ. The idea that this Gospel was written after 70 CE during the rise of the Pharisaic tradition does not provide sufficient foundation. The relationship with Judaism that is reflected in Matthew's Gospel is difficult to define with exact clarity. France rightly put it by saying that it is a matter of "subjective impression, not of demonstration."[39] The tension between two distinct communities that is evident in the Gospel can also be seen as the period when church and synagogue were in dialogue, which is not necessarily a hostile one.

The reading of passages like Matthew 16:17-19 and 18:15-20 as evidence for late dating could also be taken as a presupposition of the pattern of development in the earlier church. Again, this pattern of development is not easy to demonstrate or fit properly into a chronological scheme.[40] To identify clearly when an aspect of theological thought or language occurred is another critical issue. Therefore, the suggestion of a date after 80 CE is far from conclusive.[41]

France further argues that Matthew's reference to the destruction of Jerusalem could well be attributed to prophecy.[42] If the prophecy was already fulfilled there would be references to the fulfilment of these prophecies according to France.[43] If the destruction of a city in Matthew 22:7 can be understood as referring to the Jewish war and the destruction of Jerusalem in particular, one question that is needed to be answered is, why did Matthew mention it only once and in such an indirect way?[44] However, if Antioch or another location which is situated further away from Jerusalem is accepted for the place of writing, then the lack of focus on the destruction of the city could be explained.

Another reason to disagree with the 80 CE or later dating is that the date for Mark's Gospel cannot be tied down to an exact date. The belief of the early

37 John Drane, *Introduction to the New Testament*, rev. ed. (Oxford: Lion Publishing, 1999), 208.

38 DeSilva, *An Introduction to the New Testament*, 238.

39 France, *Matthew*, 29.

40 France, *Matthew*, 29.

41 France, *Matthew*, 29.

42 R. T. France, *The Gospel of Matthew*, NICNT (Grand Rapids, MI: Eerdmans, 2007), 825.

43 France, *Matthew – Evangelist and Teacher*, 85.

44 Robert H. Mounce, *Matthew*, UBCS 16 (Grand Rapids, MI: Baker, 2011), 3.

church that Matthew's Gospel was written earlier than Mark's Gospel would give a date as early as 60 CE. Irenaeus dated Matthew's Gospel in the early 60's, and France argues that evidence is unavailable to contradict Irenaeus.[45] Douglas A. Hagner argues that even if Matthew draws upon Mark it does not necessarily mean that there is a long gap of time between the two writings.[46]

Apart from the patristic tradition, which dates Matthew's Gospel before Mark's Gospel, the Gospel itself contains evidences of an early date. References to practices in connection to the temple (5:23-24; 23:16-22) would have been excluded by the author, especially after the temple ceased to exist in 70 CE. Even the discussion of the temple tax (17:24-27) would have been unnecessary because the tax was already diverted to the temple of Jupiter in Rome after 70 CE. Matt 23:2-3 contains respectful attitude towards the position of the scribes and also the Pharisees, and to heed their teachings.[47] Jesus however teaches them not to do as they do. This kind of teaching found in the Gospel better fits the period before the total opposition between the church and the synagogue.[48] In this same line, the content of the Gospel itself makes it clear that the Gospel was written during a period of uneasy tension. The time frame that allows the author of the Gospel to experience an uncomfortable tension during the middle and latter parts of the first century in relation to the synagogue cannot be put aside easily.[49]

These two sides of the arguments are interesting but the real problem is that there are no explicit chronological data in the Gospel itself, and makes it impossible to pinpoint the exact date of writing for the Gospel. France's argument is still valid, that all such conclusions made depend on how other various writings and events are dated.[50] To come to terms with earlier dating and latter dating, conclusion could be made in this manner. Firstly, the recognition of Matthew's Gospel and Matthean tradition by both Didache and Ignatius helps us to determine that the Gospel cannot be written after 100 CE. Secondly, accepting Matthew's dependence on Mark does not help much, because the dating of Mark is more difficult than Matthew. As there is less evidence to be found, and thus according to Craig L. Blomberg, "the evidence

45 France, *Matthew – Evangelist and Teacher*, 88.

46 Donald A. Hagner, *Matthew 1-13*, WBC 33a (Dallas: Word Books, 1993), lxxiv; Grant Macaskill, *Revealed Wisdom and Inaugurated Eschatology in Ancient Judaism and Early Christianity* (Boston: Brill, 2007), 117.

47 Robert H. Gundry, *Matthew: A Commentary on His Literary and Theological Art* (Grand Rapids: Eerdmans, 1981), 599-609.

48 Cf. France, *Matthew*, 30.

49 France, *The Gospel of Matthew*, 17; see also J. Andrew Overman, *Church and Community in Crisis: The Gospel According to Matthew*, NTC (Pennsylvania: Trinity Press International, 1996), 19-26.

50 France, *Matthew*, 30.

is highly inferential."[51] Thirdly, Mark's Gospel is dated mostly under the Neronian persecution in about 60 CE. Thus without even dragging Mark to an earlier date, it seems safe to posit 60 CE - 100 CE for the writing of Matthew's Gospel.

## 2.4. Place of Writing

The actual location in which the Gospel was written remains and continues to be a matter of debate. The earliest tradition points to Judea as the provenance of not the present Gospel but the assumed Aramaic Gospel.[52] To point to an exact location for Matthean community, scholarly arguments pointed toward several places: Palestine (Galilee, Caesarea, Jerusalem), Syria (Tyre, Sidon, Antioch), Trans-Jordan (Pella).[53]

The Alexandrian provenance of Gospel of Matthew was also argued especially by S. Brandon in his 1951 book *The Fall of Jerusalem and the Christian Church.*[54] After a special consideration is given to B. H. Streeter's favour for Syrian city, Brandon argues for another city. Streeter's did not explain clearly why he suggests that a party of Jerusalem Christian fled for refuge to Antioch after the death of James. Brandon argues that it is improbable that the flight toward North had taken place at any time during the course of the war in 66 CE - 70 CE because of the Roman campaigns (Cestius Gallus and Vespasian) against the insurgents entered Palestine from the North.[55] Instead of taking flight towards North to the city of Antioch, it is natural direction for the Jews are southwards or to the east across the Jordan.[56]

Recent discussion maintains the origination of Matthew in Antioch, especially after Streeter. If the origin of the Gospel is to be sought in an important church outside Palestine, for Streeter, Antioch is the only one. He observes the primacy of Peter in Matthew's Gospel and the role and prominence of Peter in Antioch. He thus argues that the church in Antioch with its enormous population of Jews would have provided fitting climate for Matthew's Gospel to prosper.[57] W. G. Kümmel states "Most scholars assume, relying on Streeter,

---

51 Craig L. Blomberg, *Matthew*, NAC 22 (Nashville: Broadman, 1992), 41, citing Gundry, *Mattthew*, 601, who notes that there is less evidence for dating Mark than for dating Matthew, so the former can scarcely be allowed to control the latter.

52 Benedict T. Viviano, *Matthew and his World: The Gospel of the Open Jewish Christians Studies in Biblical Theology* (Göttingen: Vandenheock & Ruprecht, 2007), 23.

53 Boring, *An Introduction to the New Testament*, 536.

54 S. G. F. Brandon, *The Fall of Jerusalem and the Christian Church: A Study of the Effects of the Jewish Overthrow of A.D. 70 on Christianity* (London: SPCK, 1951), 217-222.

55 Brandon, *The Fall of Jerusalem and the Christian Church*, 218.

56 Brandon, *The Fall of Jerusalem and the Christian Church*, 218.

57 B. H. Streeter, *The Four Gospels: A Study of Origins, Treating of the Manuscript Tradition, Sources, Authorship, & Dates* (London: Macmillan, 1924), 504.

that Matthew was written in Antioch, or, more generally, in Syria."[58] Without much discussion Raymond E. Brown in his work on the infancy narrative also follow Streeter in locating the place of writing for Matthew.[59] Streeter also did consider Caesarea but his main argument against it is that, it was "the port of entry of Samaria" but Matthew's Gospel contains "...enter no town of the Samaritans" (10:5).[60] This is inconceivable for Streeter to accept Caesarea for the place of writing Matthew's Gospel.[61]

G. D. Kilpatrick in his 1962 book *The Origins of the Gospel According to St. Matthew*, also concludes that "Matthew was written in a Greek-speaking community with little or no contact with the Semitic tongue, probably in a Syrian port."[62] Kilpatrick disagrees with Streeter, and he is in favour of Phoenician, suggesting a place like Tyre and Sidon as the actual place of writing the Gospel. He argues that Ignatius of Antioch, almost contemporaneous with the writing of the Gospel, "shows no trace of the Jewish influence which is so strong in the Gospel."[63] Other scholars such as Carson and Donald Guthrie prefer a provenance from the rural community of the Syrian axis near Galilee or Decapolis.[64] However, most scholars accept the Syrian provenance for Matthew.[65]

## 2.5. Matthean Community

For David C. Sim, the Matthean community is that group for which the Gospel was written for.[66] The inconceivable question is that, is the Matthean community's participation to be understood as from which or by which the Gospel was written?[67] To take the community's view as identical with the

58 W. G. Kümmel, *Introduction to the New Testament* (Nashville: Abingdon, 1957), 119.

59 Raymond E. Brown, *The Birth of the Messiah: A Commentary on the Infancy Narratives in the Gospels of Matthew and Luke* (New York: Doubleday, 1993), 45-47.

60 Streeter, *The Four Gospels*, 502.

61 Contrary to this there is a suggestion that Caesarea was likely a place for authorship. Viviano, *Matthew and his World*, 16-20.

62 G. D. Kilpatrick, *The Origins of the Gospel According to St. Matthew* (Philadelphia: Fortress, 1962), 195.

63 Kilpatrick, *The Origins of the Gospel According to St. Matthew*, 132.

64 Carson, Moo and Morris, *An Introduction to the New Testament*, 75; Donald G. Guthrie, *New Testament Introduction: The Gospels and Acts* (Chicago: IVP, 1965), 38.

65 Mounce, *Matthew*, xiv; Davies and Allison, *Introduction and Commentary on Matthew I-VII*, 138-147; Blomberg, *Matthew*, 37.

66 David C. Sim, *The Gospel of Mathew and Christian Judaism: The History and Social Setting of the Matthean Community*, SNTW (Edinburgh, T&T Clark, 1998), 27, 36, 115, 141, 257, 285.

67 Mark Goodacre, review of *The Gospel of Mathew and Christian Judaism*, by David C. Sim, *Heythrop Journal* 41 (2000): 334-336.

author's view could be simply an assumption without demonstration, but still, when there is no evidential material to be found to locate the exact date and the author, it is understandable.

The attempt to identify the original reader of Matthew's Gospel is another difficult task. There is no evidence to suggest who they are, and even a search outside the New Testament literature does not help.[68] The Gospel has long been known as the most ecclesiastical Gospel, the only one to use the word church to describe the community of believers (16:18; 18:17). Matthew's church has obviously been involved in an intense relationship with the surrounding dominant Jewish community.[69] In such passages as 24:15 (let the reader understand), 27:8 (until this day), and 28:15 (until this day), Matthew bursts the bounds of the story he is telling of the life and ministry of Jesus in order to address his readers directly. Temporally, these passages locate the real readers at a point after the resurrection but short of the parousia. Matthew himself describes this point as the time of the messianic woes, which will issue in the final judgment (24:8). The time of the messianic woes, therefore, is also the time in which the real readers of Matthew's Gospel were living.[70] However, the ongoing problem is that the time of the messianic woes cannot be tied down to any particular date.

According to Keener and others the primary reader would be Jewish Christians.[71] Due to the amount of Jewish specifics and Old Testament references found in the Gospel, scholars widely held this view. Adopting Jewish Christians as primary readers as Keener suggested does not mean that Gentile Christians are excluded but rather the Gentiles would have realised that they were adopting Jewish faith.[72] According to Michael J. Wilkins there is evidence to be found in the text of Gentile Christians being addressed.[73] Therefore, a move from a Jewish-centric mission to a Gentile-centric mission needs further investigation.

Benedict T. Viviano has little doubt that the early members of Matthean community were Jewish, highlighted by the mention of the covenant with Abraham, Moses and David.[74] This seems like a most probable argument, but the inclusion of the Gentiles in Matthean community could not be easily ruled

68 T. C. Long, *Matthew* (Louisville: WJK, 1997), 1.

69 M. Eugene Boring, *The Gospel of Matthew: Introduction, Commentary, and Reflections*, NIBC 8, eds. Leander E. Keck, *et.al.* (Nashville: Abingdon, 1995), 97.

70 Jack D. Kingsbury, *Matthew as Story* (Philadelphia: Fortress, 1986), 120.

71 Craig S. Keener, *The IVP Bible Background Commentary: New Testament* (Downers Grove, IL: IVP, 1993), 49; Long, *Matthew*, 2.

72 Keener, *The IVP Bible Background Commentary*, 49.

73 Michael J. Wilkins, *Matthew*, ZIBBC 1 (Grand Rapids, MI: Zondervan, 2001), 39.

74 Benedict T. Viviano, *The Gospel According to Matthew*, NJBC (London: Chapman, 1990), 630-674.

out. Cedric E. W. Vine notes that Matthew portrays variety of responses to Jesus from various characters in the Gospel. The positive characterisation of the magi (2:1) and the guards at the crucifixion (27:54) is to be recognised while locating the community.[75]

According to Vine, the cure of the centurion's servant (8:5-13) and the story of the Canaanite woman (15:21-211) represent further positive examples of Gentile faith, which is against pejorative references to the Gentiles (5:47; 6:7, 32; 18:17). The importance of the great commission (28:19) could enlighten the identity of Matthean community. When one allows for a development in plot in which Matthew enlarges the mission to the house of Israel (10:5-6) to the mission to all nations (28:19), the author's relationship with Judaism needs more scrutiny.[76]

The ethnicity of the author of Matthew's Gospel is debated for a long time, and the discussion does not become less intense. The significant proportion of Matthean scholars lean towards the Gospel as Jewish rather than Gentile.[77] In contrast to the Jewishness of the Gospel, scholars like Nepper Christensen and S. van Tilborg support the notion and view that the Gospel has a fundamentally Gentile and anti-Jewish perspective.[78] However, David E. Orton is convincing when he says that "the Gospel reads perfectly coherently on the understanding that the whole work has a Jewish-Christian setting."[79] Orton opines that the Matthean community was predominantly a Jewish church, and there is evidence that the community is in the process of accommodating the increasing numbers of Gentile members.[80] This kind of context might provide a solution to the ongoing tension between the church and the synagogue which is identified in Matthew's Gospel. It can be further argued that the predominating Jewish-Christian are "still very much aware and protective" of their heritage, and thus creates tension between and may be even among the members of Matthean community and synagogue at large.[81]

As the Jewish Christians undoubtedly hold the majority among Matthean community, the members of the community seem to have been non-participants or hesitant participants of the synagogues. The reason is that the Gospel refers

75 Cedric E. W. *Vine, The Audience of Matthew: An Appraisal of the Local Audience Thesis*, LNTS (London: Bloomsbury, 2014), 67.

76 Vine, *The Audience of Matthew*, 68.

77 David E. Orton, *The Understanding Scribe: Matthew and the Apocalyptic Ideal* (London: T&T Clark, 2004), 22.

78 Nepper Christensen, *Das Matthäus Evangelium – Ein Juden Christliches Evangelium?* (Aarhus: Universitetsforlaget, 1958); S. van Tilborg, *The Jewish Leaders in Matthew* (Leiden: Brill, 1972).

79 Orton, *The Understanding Scribe*, 22.

80 Orton, *The Understanding Scribe*, 22.

81 Orton, *The Understanding Scribe*, 22.

the synagogues with third person plural pronoun "their synagogues" and the negative vibe added in the Gospel toward the Jewish religious authorities.[82] This further suggests and makes it clear that part of the members of the Matthean community had already being discouraged by the synagogues or voluntarily walked out from the participation in the synagogues. Thus, the Matthean community has to cope with the reality to work out their own life, hesitantly or unwillingly, away from their Jewish heritage and to sort out how to adapt into the new situation of the Christian faith with their fellow Gentile church members.

### *2.5.1. The Matthean Community in Relation to Formative Judaism*

During the time after the Jewish war the pre-70 Pharisaic party were in competition with other surviving Jewish groups and established itself as a definitive group. Boring states that the Matthean community was a movement related to formative Judaism.[83] Matthean community sees itself as the eschatological people of God, a messianic community, and regarded itself as the authentic people of God. It also identifies itself as a minority experiencing persecution at the hands of the dominant Pharisaic leadership (e.g. Matt 5:13-16; 10:23, 32-33, 40-42; 25:31-46).[84]

The work of J. Andrew Overman in 1990 explicitly relates the Matthean community to formative Judaism.[85] He argues that Matthean community was profoundly influenced by the "competition and conflict"[86] it had with formative Judaism.[87] Formative Judaism and the community of Matthew both involved in a process of social construction and definition. Formative Judaism was like any other movements during the time, struggling to gain more control and influence. Matthean community and formative Judaism were both in the process of becoming.[88] Both were emerging movements in search of self-definition at that time.

If Judaism was to survive, a new religio-cultural synthesis was needed to be established. This synthesis and the process of the emergence and development of a movement after the Jewish war is what scholars referred to

82 Long, *Matthew*, 2.

83 The term "Formative Judaism" was coined by J. Neusner, *Formative Judaism: Religious, Historical and Literary Studies* (Chico: Scholars Press, 1982); Boring, *The Gospel of Matthew*, 539.

84 Boring, *The Gospel of Matthew*, 539.

85 J. Andrew Overman, *Matthew's Gospel and Formative Judaism: The Social World of the Matthean Community* (Minneapolis: Fortress, 1990).

86 E. J. Vledder and A. G. van Aarde, "The Social Location of the Matthean Community," *HTS* 51 (1995): 388-408.

87 Overman, *Matthew's Gospel and Formative Judaism*, 2.

88 Overman, *Matthew's Gospel and Formative Judaism*, 2.

as formative Judaism.[89] There is a long process for rabbinic Judaism to become more and more normative, probably several hundred years.[90] In all probability, this process was set in motion by the council of Jamnia. This period of time is when the Matthean community had to oppose the dominant role, which is being played by the Pharisees.

### *2.5.2. The Crowds*

Carter states that "Even though "the crowds" (ὄχλοι) appear fifty times in the Gospel of Matthew, their role in this story has perplexed interpreters."[91] By applying audience-oriented criticism and seeing Matthean community as being already separated from the synagogue, he analyses the appearances of the term "crowds" in the Gospel. He concludes that the crowds' function is not a peculiar one, but as a part of a larger matrix, functions in similar ways for the audience in the same line with that of the Jewish leaders (Matt 12:14), birth narrative (Matt 2), discourses such as beatitudes (Matt 5:10-12) and parables (Matt 13), and also the eschatological discourse (Matt 24-25) in the Gospel.[92] Though he sees the crowds as just a part of the matrix of characters, plot, setting, points of view and symbols, the crowds still play an important part to interpret the reality of Matthean community and legitimates its experience, and also provides valuable encouragement for the coming future.[93]

For Paul S. Minear, the crowds are not amorphous and neutral group, but are playing a positive role and represent a major objective of Jesus' ministry.[94] From the beginning of Jesus' ministry, the crowds accepted Jesus and follow him. They bring their sick to Jesus to be healed, and recognize Jesus as a prophet and glorify God. Minear also argues that the crowds are sharply distinguished from the disciples, as the latter are the select group appointed to care for the former.[95] He further notes that though Matthew prefers the plural ὄχλοι but argues that the difference in meaning between singular and plural is

89 Vledder and Aarde, "The Social Location of the Matthean Community," 396.

90 Overman, *Matthew's Gospel and Formative Judaism*, 37; R. A. Wild, "The encounter between Pharisaic and Christian Judaism: Some Early Gospel Evidence," *NovT* 27 (1985): 105-124; Howard C. Kee, "The Transformation of the Synagogue after 70 CE: Its Import for Early Christianity," *NTS* 36 (1990): 1-24.

91 In Matthew, the singular ὄχλος appears nineteen times, while the plural ὄχλοι appears thirty-one times. As the plural is used more often than the singular form, it is commonly used in academic discussions. Warren Carter, "The Crowds in Matthew's Gospel," *CBQ* 55 (1993): 54-67.

92 Carter, "The Crowds in Matthew's Gospel," 67.

93 Carter, "The Crowds in Matthew's Gospel," 67.

94 Paul S. Minear, "The Disciples and the Crowds in the Gospel of Matthew," *ATR* Supplement Series 3 (1974): 28-44.

95 Minear, "The Disciples and the Crowds," 30.

not to be found in Matthew's Gospel. To support the argument, he cites the two uses in Matt 13:2, first a plural, then a singular, but both pointing to the same group. In the arrest and trial scenes, the same group is referred three times in the singular (Matt 26:47; 27:15, 24), and two times in the plural (Matt 26:55; 27:20).[96] In contrast, while dealing with the significance of discourses for the structure in Matthew's Gospel, Terence J. Keegan argues that there is a difference between the singular and the plural uses of the term ὄχλος in the Gospel.[97] For him the use of the plural signifies the crowds in the technical sense as the object of Jesus' ministry, and every use of the singular is either found in traditional material and lacks special significance in the Gospel or used in a non-technical sense.

Two of the singular uses in the arrest and trial scenes (Matt 27:15, 24) is with reference to the crowd in relation to Pilate, and is a general usage. The third singular in the arrest and trial scenes (Matt 26:47) is a traditional material and is also found in Mark and Luke. Keegan asserts that the two plurals in the arrest and trial scenes are "significant portrayals of the crowds as the object of Jesus' ministry, a body which Jesus seeks to enlist as followers (26:55) but which is susceptible as well to persuasion by the Jewish authorities (27:20)."[98] Thus, the crowds are mainly the objects of Jesus' ministry according to Keegan.

According to Jack D. Kingsbury, the crowds form the "applauding backdrop" for the actions of Jesus, the Israel of the unique "time of Jesus."[99] He argues that Matthew chapter 13 signals the great "turning point" within the structural framework of Matthew's Gospel, and then Jesus turns away from the Jews, including the crowds to the disciples.[100] Both the crowds and the Jewish leaders comprise the Jews. After chapter 13 Jesus' attitude toward the crowds becomes changed according to Kingsbury. For him, though Matthew did not treat the crowds and their leaders as separate identities, but distinction is to be found, especially in the passion narrative. He further argues that "Matthew is fundamentally well-disposed towards them," because Matthew depicts the crowds as being sharing directly in Jesus' ministry.[101]

---

96 Minear, "The Disciples and the Crowds," 29.

97 Terence J. Keegan, "Introductory Formulae for Matthean Discourses," *CBQ* 44 (1982): 415-430.

98 Keegan, "Introductory Formulae," 426. Other uses of the singular in Matthew's Gospel are either clearly non-technical (Matt 9:23, 25; 14:5; 21:26) or appear in passages with Synoptic parallels (Matt 13:12b; 14:14; 15:10, 32, 33, 35; 17:14a; 20:29, 31; 21:8).

99 Jack D. Kingsbury, *The Parables of Jesus in Matthew 13: A Study in Redaction-Criticism* (Richmond: John Knox, 1969), 24-28.

100 Kingsbury, *The Parables of Jesus in Matthew 13*, 130.

101 Kingsbury, *The Parables of Jesus in Matthew 13*, 26-27; cf. J. R. C. Cousland, *The Crowds in the Gospel of Matthew*, NovTSup 102 (Leiden: Brill, 2002), 10.

As the crowds do not belong to the church, for Kingsbury, they are to be associated with the Jewish leaders. He also proposes another concept, that the crowds have a "flat" character, because they lack both the faith of the disciples and the hostility of the Jewish leaders.[102] Tilborg also identifies the distinction between the disciples and the crowds, and finds that the crowds, unlike the Jewish leaders "react very positively in the appearance of Jesus."[103] It is thus understandable that Ulrich Luz also regards them as "potential disciples."[104] Tilborg further argues that the disciples enjoy special position, and are the ones who function as mediators of Jesus to the crowds, and thus "bring the ὄχλοι into contact with Jesus."[105]

The problem of coming to a consensus is partly due to the fact that the crowds in Matthew's Gospel have been introduced in various presentations throughout the Gospel. After surveying past views regarding the identity of the crowds and concluding that none is entirely accurate, J. R. C. Cousland in his 2002 book *The Crowds in the Gospel of Matthew*, argues that since the crowds are Matthew's literary construct and are not necessarily historical crowds, "it is probably fruitless to ascertain the makeup of the crowds."[106] The central problem that he tackles is the dimension of Matthew's crowds. Matthew, in various places describes the crowds, like the disciples as following Jesus. The crowds regularly show favourable reactions to Jesus' words and deeds. However, Matthew explicitly contrasted the crowds with the disciples. The crowds and the disciples are on different points of "spiritual understanding spectrum"[107] during the teaching of parables of the mystery of the kingdom. What is striking here is that Jesus' evaluation comes soon after the explicit contrast exhibited between the crowds and the Pharisees (12:23).

---

102 Kingsbury, *Matthew as Story*, 23-24. The contrast between the crowds and the Jewish leaders has also been observed by D. E. Garland, *The Intention of Matthew 23*, NovTSup 52 (Leiden: Brill, 1979), 36; W. D. Davies and Dale C. Allison, *The Gospel According to Matthew*, ICC, 2 vols. (Edinburgh: T&T Clark, 1988).

103 S. van Tilborg, *The Jewish Leaders in Matthew* (Leiden: Brill, 1972), 158.

104 Ulrich Luz, *Matthew 1-7* (Minneapolis: Augsburg, 1989), 456; see also W. D. Davies and Dale C. Allison, *A Critical and Exegetical Commentary on the Gospel According to Saint Matthew*, ICC, 3 vols. (Edinburgh: T&T Clark, 1988), 1:419-420. Davies and Allison also state that the crowd is a neutral group, out of which come those who will become disciples or those who will decide against Jesus.

105 Tilborg, *The Jewish Leaders in Matthew*, 163, 171; cf. Cousland, *The Crowds in the Gospel of Matthew*, 12; see also Francis W. Beare, *The Gospel according to Matthew* (San Francisco: Harper & Row, 1981), 122; Gundry, *Matthew*. For Beare and Gundry, they are the laity of Matthew's church who are ministered to by the community leaders (the disciples).

106 Cousland, *The Crowds in the Gospel of Matthew*, 49.

107 Michael J. Wilkins, *Discipleship in the Ancient World and Matthew's Gospel*, 2nd ed. (Eugene: Wipf&Stock, 2015), 230.

The crowds, unlike the Pharisees are ready to acknowledge Jesus' messianic status. However, further in the Gospel, the crowds approve Jesus as both Son of David and prophet in the Triumphal Entry, but unexpectedly they participate actively in his arrest and crucifixion. Therefore the following represents the ambivalent roles played by the crowds in Matthew's Gospel: The crowds followed Jesus (4:25), expected healing from him (15:30); applauded him and his teaching (7:28; 21:9-10); but at other setting laughed at him (9:23-25); came to arrest him (26:47); influenced by the chief priests and the elders to choose Barabbas over him (27:20); and finally, as the "people," they are responsible for the blood of Jesus (27:24). Though the assumption "that the crowds' betrayal of Jesus is dictated by tradition," and they do not really change is for Cousland a logical assumption,[108] but C. Clifton Black argues that the crowds do change in Matthew's Gospel, and unlike Kingsbury's "flat" character, he understood the crowds as a "round" character.[109] Black also notes that in literary works the major characters are usually the one who change, and the minor ones who remain constant.[110]

Cousland's analysis further suggests that Matthew's interest in the crowds is less "historical or mimetic" than "literary and theological."[111] Matthew distinguishes the crowds from the Jewish leaders, and represents them as one constituent of Israel. The distinction is significant for "Matthew's theologizing of the crowds" and may have been identified from the description found in Mark 6:34 – "sheep without a shepherd."[112] Such imagery to depict Israel's suffering under the corrupt leadership such as in Ezekiel 34 was probably also influential. This imagery "becomes programmatic for Matthew's portrayal of the crowds," who "are no longer simply the fortunate bystanders to Jesus' public ministry," as in Mark's Gospel.

In Matthew's Gospel, they have become "the present exemplars of the covenant people of God, who... have suffered from bad leadership and await divine intervention."[113] Therefore, the crowds represent a particular group that participate actively in Jesus' ministry. It is also clear that Matthew presents the disciples as being "with Jesus," the Jewish leaders as being "against Jesus,"

---

108 Cousland, *The Crowds in the Gospel of Matthew*, 48.

109 C. Clifton Black, "Depth of Characterization and Degrees of Faith in Matthew," *SBL 1989 Seminar Papers* (Atlanta: Scholars Press, 1989): 604-623 (619).

110 Cousland says that Black bases his judgments of literary character on Mary Doyle Springer, *A Rhetoric of Literary Character* (Chicago: UCP, 1978), 11-44.

111 Cousland, *The Crowds in the Gospel of Matthew*, 49-52.

112 Cousland, *The Crowds in the Gospel of Matthew*, 93.

113 Cousland, *The Crowds in the Gospel of Matthew*, 98.

and the crowds as being in the juncture to make decision to be either "with him or against him."[114]

### 2.5.3. Socio-Economic Status

Kingsbury opines that there are indications in the Gospel that the real readers were a well-to-do community.[115] In comparison with Mark, Matthew's Gospel seems to be more urbanized.[116] The words "city"(πόλιvς) and "village" (κώμη) is used eight times and seven times respectively in Mark's Gospel, but the word "village" is used only four times in Matthew's Gospel. Matthew's alteration of the setting of Jesus' ministry is clearly seen in his preference of the word "city" which is seen no fewer than twenty-six times. The city is thus the setting for a significant part of Jesus' life and ministry and for the ministry of the disciples as well. It has been argued on various grounds that Matthean community was a generally prosperous one.

Socio-historical data as well as textual evidence point to the Matthean community as more urbanized, and according to Avi-Yonah, Graeco-Roman culture in Syria and Palestine "was marked by a steep rise in material standards of living."[117]As Matthew's Gospel was most likely to have been written for an urban community, the members probably consist of the well to do and also the poor. Graham N. Stanton suggests that Matthew writes for a loose network of communities over a wide geographical area, and thus may not have first hand information about the life situation of all the communities.[118] Therefore, it is very difficult to reconstruct the exact setting of Matthew's Gospel.

By holding to the idea of an urban setting Smith further says that the community included landholders, merchants, businessmen, and entrepreneurs.[119] Matthew's words on debtors and courts in Matthew 5:25-26 may be a good communication tool for people at higher rank. Matthew's

114 Cf. Matt 12:30; Mark 9:40; Luke 9:50 – the saying in Matthew is the more restrictive. Matthew and Luke record the statement, "The one who is not with me, is against me, and the one who does not gather with me scatters" (Matt 12:30/ Luke 11:23). Mark and Luke have the reverse statement, "The one who is not against us, is for us" (cf. Mark 9:40; Luke 9:50), a saying not found in Matthew. Wilkins, *Discipleship in the Ancient World and Matthew's Gospel*, 231.

115 Kingsbury, *Matthew as Story*, 125.

116 Michael H. Crosby, *House of Disciples: Church, Economics, & Justice in Matthew* (New York: Orbis Books, 1988), 30-40.

117 Crosby, *House of Disciples*, 40, quoting Aharon Kempinski and Michael Avi-Yonah, *Syria-Palestine II: From the Bronze Age to the End of the Classical World [2200 B.C. – 324 A.D.]* (Geneva: Nagel, 1979), 129.

118 Graham N. Stanton, "Revisiting Matthew's Communities," *HTS* 52 (1996): 376-394 (378).

119 Robert H. Smith, "Were the Early Christians Middle-Class? A Sociological Analysis of the New Testament," *CurTM* 7 (1980): 260-276 (266).

Gospel is a literary piece according to James Hope Moulton, who makes it clear that the use of Greek in the Gospel is sophisticated in construction and theological argument than that of Mark's Gospel.[120] C. F. D. Moule also argues that Matthew was "an educated person commanding sound Greek with considerable vocabulary."[121] The well-to-do in the community may also be startled by the suggestions regarding generosity in Matthew 5:39-42 and the casual attitude toward sound financial planning in Matthew 6:19, as they sound illogical.

The comparison between the kingdom of heaven and the merchant in search of pearls (Matt 13:45-46) could perhaps communicate better to businessmen. The equal wages given by the landowner to the laborers in Matthew 20:1-16 could also serve as a warning to those who are not willing to share their wealth in the community.[122] Therefore, it seems plausible that the people with higher status in the community are encouraged by Matthew not to accumulate wealth but to share. It also seems fair to postulate that the rich are not willing to participate in sharing their wealth among the community.

While Jesus in Luke's Gospel pronounces a blessing on the poor (Luke 6:20) Jesus in Matthew's Gospel pronounces on the poor in spirit (Matt 5:3). While in Mark's Gospel, Jesus commands the disciples to take with them "no copper coin" – that is, small change in their missionary journey (Mark 6:8), but in Matthew's Gospel, Jesus commands them to take neither "gold, nor silver, nor copper coin" (Matt 10:9). Matthean community seems to be well accustomed with a wide range of money, as Matthew's Gospel contains "a more extensive vocabulary of coinage and wealth" than the other synoptic Gospels.[123] Jesus tells a parable about "minas" in Luke's Gospel (Luke 19:11-27), but in Matthew's Gospel the parable is about "talents" (Matt 25:14-30), and talents worth approximately fifty times to minas. These are the indications and also a pointer that the members of the Matthean community were well-to-do.[124]

In Mark's Gospel and Luke's Gospel (Mark 15:43; Luke 23:50-51), Joseph of Arimathea is a member of the council who is looking for the Kingdom of God, but in Matthew's Gospel he is "a rich man… who also was a disciple

---

120 James Hope Moulton, *A Grammar of New Testament Greek* (Edinburgh: T&T Clark, 1919), 29, 169; cf. Smith, "Were the Early Christians Middle-Class," 267.

121 C. F. D. Moule, *The Birth of the New Testament* (New York: Harper and Row, 1962), 219; see also F. Blass and A. Debrunner, *A Greek Grammar of the New Testament*, trans. and rev. by R. W. Funk (Chicago: UCP, 1961), 485, 492; cf. Smith, "Were the Early Christians Middle-Class," 267.

122 Smith, "Were the Early Christians Middle-Class," 266.

123 Smith, "Were the Early Christians Middle-Class," 267.

124 Cf. Kingsbury, *Matthew as Story*, 125.

of Jesus" (Matt 27:57).[125] It is clear that not all of Jesus' followers were poor and destitute, but there are also well-to-do people in their midst. Therefore, as Kingsbury concludes it seems safe to say that the real readers of Matthew's Gospel were "prosperous and in no sense materially disadvantaged."[126]

Banking was another popular business of the time. Both the Jewish and Roman business worlds had organized banking systems. Under the early Greeks (and even much later), temples played the part of safe deposits, but in the early Roman Empire we also find regular banking establishments, sometimes owned by a number of partners. The function of such was first to arrange for the business of foreign exchange, and second to enable people to make deposits and to draw upon them whenever necessary. Lending money, having huge amounts of debt was not an uncommon thing during this time.[127] Therefore, for the Matthean community this kind of accumulating wealth and having debts could be understood without much difficulty.

This alteration of the setting of Jesus' ministry could perhaps be the outcome of the economic realm of Matthean community. It is also understandable that Matthew's redactional work seen in the parables and other texts are the outcome of socio-economic reality of the community. The importance of the sharing of wealth is seen in Mathew 25:31-46 (The judgment of nations). Matthew may perhaps encourage the well-to-do in the community to participate in sharing. In this line of thought the parable of the judgment of nations could best be interpreted as "the warning about the fate of those who have world's goods but fail to share their resources with 'the least of these my brethren."[128]

### *2.5.4. Social and Religious Climate*

The social and religious climate in which the Matthean community found itself appears to be one of intense conflict. If we can use the text to reflect the actual situation of the community, they were seemingly being hauled into court by gentile authorities, judicially harassed (handed over to tribulation), hated "by all," and even put to death (10:18, 22; 13:21; 24:9).[129]

125 Kingsbury, *Matthew as Story*, 125.

126 Smith, "Were the Early Christians Middle-Class," 266.

127 Alan Coates Bouquet, *Everyday Life in New Testament Times* (Great Britain: A Carousel Book, 1974), 133.

128 Smith, "Were the Early Christians Middle-Class," 266.

129 Emmanuel M. Jacob, "Discipleship and Mission: A Perspective on the Gospel of Matthew," *IRM* 91 (2002): 102-110 (104); Kingsbury, *Matthew as Story*, 126, citing Douglas R. A. Hare, *The Theme of Jewish Persecution of Christians in the Gospel According to St. Matthew* (Cambridge: CUP, 2005), 106-108, 124; see also Kenton L. Sparks, "Gospel as Conquest: Mosaic Typology in Matthew 28:16-20," *CBQ* 68 (2006): 651-663.

On the other hand, it likewise seems that they were living in close proximity to a vigorous Jewish community. The evidence for this is multiple. For instance, the parable of the tares (13:24-30) may refer to this directly, for it is possibly with a view to the church's relationship to Israel that Matthew reports Jesus as saying, "Let both grow together until the harvest" (13:30).[130] In a similar vein, if the story of the payment of the temple tax (17:24-27) can be interpreted to mean that the Jewish Christians in Matthean community were being encouraged, despite their freedom, not to offend Jews by refusing to participate in the collection of contributions in support of the Patriarchy at Jamnia, then this unit, too, may speak for close contact between the Jews and the real readers of Matthew's Gospel.[131]

### 2.5.5. Instruction for Discipleship in the Community

The instruction found in the great commission (28:16-20) at the end of the Gospel makes it clear that Matthew intended to signify discipleship to the community. The command to teach disciples also relates back to the five discourses of which the Sermon on the Mount is one of them. As Matthew is the only evangelist to use the word ἐκκλησία (16:18), Drane opines that Matthew is concerned with the church community and discipleship. Collection of Jesus' teachings to provide instruction for the community is also believed by Drane as to provide easy to use lessons to assist new members of the community.[132] This does not necessarily mean that the writing is only meant for the new addition to the Matthean community.

Seán Freyne states that it is an unnecessary task to look for apparent distinction between the community members and their apostolic leaders, except perhaps on the introduction of the mission discourse (9:36-10:4) and also in 16:16-20 (Peter's confession) and 28:16-20 (great commission).[133] The apostles are the foremost disciples and the instructions they receive are to be transferred to those in the community who would follow their footsteps in

130 Jack D. Kingsbury, *The Parables of Jesus in Matthew 13: A Study in Redaction-Criticism* (Richmond: John Knox, 1969), 63-76.

131 Kingsbury, *Matthew as Story*, 126. One important observation to note here is that of Michael Crosby, who argues that the author wrote to show Jesus as the model who broke the rules (8:7) and was able to rise above the social alienation which was tearing the Matthean Community apart. Michael H. Crosby, *Spirituality of Beatitudes: Matthew's Challenges for 1st World Christians* (New York: Orbis Books, 1982), 10; see also Gene R. Smillie, "'Even the dogs': Gentiles in the Gospel of Matthew," *JETS* 45 (2002): 73-97.

132 Drane, *Introduction to the New Testament*, 206.

133 Seán Freyne, *The Twelve: Disciples and Apostles: A Study in the Theology of the First Three Gospels* (London: Sheed & Ward, 1968), 185, cited by Joel Willits, "The Twelve Disciples in Matthew," in *Jesus, Matthew's Gospel and Early Christianity: Studies in Memory of Graham N. Stanton*, eds. Daniel M. Gurtner et al. (London: T&T Clark, 2011), 166-179 (174).

discipleship. Guthrie comments how Jesus taught humans to live their lives individually responsible before God, but also with concern for the society in which they belong.[134] This is very true when we picture a community of believers seeking to follow Jesus in the backdrop, and is the nature of discipleship found in Matthew's Gospel.

Another distinctive feature of Matthew's instruction of discipleship is that it has relevance for his community and even for the contemporary audience at large. The great commission makes it clear that Matthew's instruction of discipleship is not confined to the disciples alone, but discipleship is required of all nations that follow Jesus. Matthean community is also linked to the Twelve and the other disciples of Jesus' time because the later generations of disciples relate to a resurrected and present Jesus.

### *2.5.6. Mission in Matthean Community*

Matthew's Gospel contains two mission mandates and their relationship has been an exegetical crux for a long time. To find a "satisfactory theological explanation" between Jesus' restriction of the mission to "the lost sheep of the house of Israel" (Matt 10:6) and the extension of the mission to "all nations" (Matt 28:19) is difficult.[135] The problem here is if Matthew's Gospel was written after 70 CE, could the Gentile mission still pose a problem for the community? The question arises; did the church bid farewell to Judaism at one single point?[136] It is more plausible to argue that the turning to Gentile mission took place in several stages.[137] The complicated scenario is evident in these scenes, because there was no occasion in Jesus' ministry where he either "send[s] them to preach to gentiles or prohibit them from doing so."[138]

Douglas R. A. Hare in his 1967 book *The Theme of Jewish Persecution of Christians in the Gospel according to St. Matthew*, places the Gospel in a Jewish-Christian setting, and argues that "the invitation which Israel has refused so rudely is now to be offered exclusively to the Gentiles."[139] Consequently this argument "assumes the abandonment of the mission to Israel."[140] Graham N. Stanton, in his 1977 article "5 Ezra and Matthean Christianity in the Second Century," provides a parallel view and also places Matthew's Gospel

134 Donald G. Guthrie, *New Testament Theology* (England: IVP, 1985), 153-154.

135 Schuyler Brown, "The Matthean Community and the Gentile Mission," *NovT* 22 (1980): 1193-221 (193).

136 Brown, "The Matthean Community and the Gentile Mission," 194.

137 Krister Stendahl, *The School of St. Matthew, and its use of the Old Testament* (Philadelphia: Fortress, 1968), xiii-xiv; cf. Brown, "The Matthean Community and the Gentile Mission," 194.

138 Brown, "The Matthean Community and the Gentile Mission," 194.

139 Hare, *The Theme of Jewish Persecution of Christians*, 147.

140 Hare, *The Theme of Jewish Persecution of Christians*, 148.

in a Jewish-Christian milieu.[141] Stanton also states that Matthean community are considering themselves as a new people over against both the Jews and the Gentiles.[142] Therefore, what is plausible is that Matthew's Gospel is written before 70 CE and the community is struggling and is in the process of transformation to accommodate the gentile believers.

There are synoptic tradition that recorded the miracle stories for the benefit of the Gentiles (Matt 8:5-13; Luke 7:1-10; Mark 7:24-30). Matthew's insertion of the saying "I tell you, many will come from east and west and will eat with Abraham and Isaac and Jacob in the kingdom of heaven, while the heirs of the kingdom will be thrown into the outer darkness, where there will be weeping and gnashing of teeth." (Matt 8:11-12) into the healing of the centurion's servant reflects his concern for the Gentile Mission.[143]

However, there is no clear cut concern at this point in the Gospel, but only an allusion is to be found. The significance is fully revealed only in the great commission at the end of the Gospel (Matt 28:19). In the parable of the great banquet (Luke 14:15-24), the substitute guests are the publicans and sinners. However, in the parable of the wedding banquet in Matthew 22:1-14, the substitute guests are now gentiles.[144] There is an interest towards the gentiles, and perhaps it means that Matthew had altered the common source he possessed with Luke.

David L. Barr sees the healing narrative of the daughter of the Canaanite woman (Matt 15:21-28) as "a brilliant scene that allows Matthew to show that Jesus himself made the shift to gentile inclusion."[145] Right after this healing story Matthew has Jesus venturing into Gentile territory, and the people "glorified the God of Israel" because of Jesus (15:31). The scheme does not put aside Israel from the centre, but stabilizes it. In this way, though Gentiles were now admitted into Israel, the centre remains unchanged.

## 2.6. Geography in Matthew's Gospel

What sets apart the canonical gospels from that of Gnostic gospels such as the Gospel of Thomas is in providing details of geography and time. The canonical

---

141 Graham N. Stanton, "5 Ezra and Matthean Christianity in the Second Century," *JTS* 28 (1977): 67-83.

142 Graham N. Stanton, *A Gospel for a New People: Studies in Matthew* (Louisville: T&T Clark, 1993), 11-12. Cf. 113-131, he however sees Matthew's Gospel as being written "in the wake of a recent painful parting from Judaism," but he still claims that though Matthew and his community are "*extra muros*" they are still responding to local synagogues in various ways. This argument does not negate the early date for Matthew's Gospel.

143 Brown, "The Matthean Community and the Gentile Mission," 195.

144 Brown, "The Matthean Community and the Gentile Mission," 195.

145 David L. Barr, *New Testament Story: An Introduction*, 4th ed. (Australia: Wadsworth Cengage Learning, 2009), 324.

gospels do not just narrate the words and deeds of Jesus, but tells the reader the location and time of activities. One of the distinctive features of them is thus the contents of geographical and temporal details they contain.

In his 1998 article "The Purpose and Plan of the Gospel of Matthew, Part 1," Ernest De Witt Burton argues that as the writer of Matthew's Gospel is a Palestinian Jew, he shows himself familiar with the geography of Palestine.[146] Burton is careful in his assumption and points out that these geographical details could well be derived from a documentary source, and is possible even for a non Palestinian to have them in writing. According to Burton, Bethlehem of Judea was distinguished from Bethlehem in the tribe of Zebulun (2:1). The phrase "a city called Nazareth" (2:23) does not suggests that the writer was unfamiliar with the place, but an intended phraseology to call attention to the name and its relation with references in the Old Testament.[147]

Other examples given by Burton are as follows: The wilderness of Judea (3:1); the circuit of the Jordan (3:5; cf. Gen. 13:10); Galilee and the Jordan (3:13); Nazareth and Capernaum (4:12, 13), and the relation of these to the ancient tribal boundaries; Galilee and the lands adjacent (4:23-25); the country of the Gadarenes placed on the opposite side of the Sea of Galilee from Capernaum (8:5,23, 28); Gennesaret on the Sea of Galilee (14:34); Tyre and Sidon (15:21); Magadan, (cannot be certainly identified today) (15:39); Caesarea Philippi, and the high mountain in that vicinity (16:13; 17:1); Judea beyond Jordan (19:1); Jericho (20:29); Bethphage (not certainly identified) (21:1); and the Mount of Olives near Jerusalem (24:3); Bethany (21:17; 26:6).[148]

In contrast with Burton, C. C. McCown in his 1941 article, strongly states that Matthew's geography is more unreal and less clear than that of Mark's Gospel.[149] He argues that in the material drawn from Mark's Gospel, Matthew sometimes makes addition to his geographical details to make it more precise, and sometimes attempts to correct and omits Mark's data.[150] He further gives an examination of why Matthew lacks geographical interest and geographical feeling, and also the contradictions and inconsistencies found.

McCown analysis finds out that Matthew improved Mark's geography only in three places: the centurion of Capernaum (8:5), the wilderness locale of John's preaching (11:7), and the fact of Jesus preaching in Chorazin and

---

146 Ernest De Witt Burton, "The Purpose and Plan of the Gospel of Matthew, Part 1" *BibW* 11 (1898): 37-44.

147 Burton, "The Purpose and Plan of the Gospel of Matthew," 38.

148 Burton, "The Purpose and Plan of the Gospel of Matthew," 38-39.

149 C. C. McCown, "Gospel Geography: Fiction, Fact, and Truth," *JBL* 60 (1941): 1-25.

150 McCown, "Gospel Geography," 9.

Bethsaida (11:21).[151] Matthew could not add a definite locale for the healing of the leper (8:1), the Sermon on the Mount, or any of the incidents left without a home or country.[152] After a series of Jesus' healing miracles, which are not given specific location, Jesus' action and movements in different timeframe also lack mentioning of the place.[153]

Matthew and Mark both provided names of places from where people came to Jesus. Unlike Mark's arrangement - Galilee, Judea, Jerusalem, Idumea, beyond Jordan, and the vicinity of Tyre and Sidon (Mark 3:7), Matthew's order differ - Galilee, the Decapolis, Jerusalem, Judea, and beyond Jordan, (4:25). McCown, in various ways talks about how Matthew edited his sources, and opines that Matthew lacks geographical feeling or orientation.[154] However, it has to be understood that Matthew might have reasons to alter Mark's order, and it is not fair to boldly charge Matthew as lacking geographical orientation just by comparing his order of places with that of Mark.

Donald J. Verseput, in his article "Jesus' Pilgrimage to Jerusalem and Encounter in the Temple: A Geographical Motif in Matthew's Gospel" deals with how Matthew presents "the final journey of Jesus and his sojourn in Jerusalem in a unique way."[155] He argues that Matthew intensifies Jesus' decisive encounter with the inhabitants of Jerusalem who oppose the messianic ministry by using pilgrimage motif with the announcement of the journey to Jerusalem in Matthew 16:21.[156] Matthew's use of geography helps the interpreter to gain insight into the narrative strategy of the Gospel. After Peter makes a confession that Jesus is the Messiah, Matthew starts to narrate "From that time on Jesus began (Ἀπὸ τότε ἤρξατο ὁ Ἰησοῦς) to explain to his disciples that he must go to Jerusalem and suffer many things at the hands of the elders, the chief priests and the teachers of the law, and that he must be killed and on

151 McCown, "Gospel Geography," 10; Boring argues that Mark's confusing geography of the location for the feeding of the five thousand is clarified in Matthew 14:22-24 (Jesus' walking on the water). The feeding miracle took place on the east bank of the Sea of Galilee, and the disciples go by boat to the west bank, where they land. Boring, *The Gospel of Matthew*, 327.

152 McCown, "Gospel Geography," 10.

153 Jesus' ministry tour in 9:35, sending out the Twelve in 10:5, another Jesus' ministry tour in 11:1, Jesus' passing through the fields on the Sabbath in 12:1 (cf. Mark 2: 23), and entering of the synagogue in 12:9 (cf. Mark 3:1) are all without location. McCown, "Gospel Geography," 10.

154 McCown, "Gospel Geography," 10.

155 Donald J. Verseput, "Jesus' Pilgrimage to Jerusalem and Encounter in the Temple: A Geographical Motif in Matthew's Gospel," *NovT* 36 (1994): 105-121 (105). For the broad geographical framework of the Gospel narrative, see especially 118-120.

156 Verseput, "Jesus' Pilgrimage to Jerusalem," 105.

the third day be raised to life" (Matt 16:21).[157] Consequently, Matthew assigns the city of Jerusalem a dominant role in 16:21-25:46, which is another pointer to geographical motive in the Gospel. While approaching the city gates, Jesus is exalted with the royal "Son of David" acclamation.[158] Verseput understands the plot of 16:21-25:46 as a description of "the returned of the exiled king to confront the city of his forefather's throne."[159] Matthew's geography thus enhances his messianic motif in such a way that Jesus is presented as the one who endures all oppositions and to come back triumphantly to claim his rightful place in Jerusalem.

Though Matthew could be seen as being very familiar with the Palestinian topography or lacking geographical interest or orientation according to Burton and McCown, it is undeniably true that geography plays a significant role in the Gospel. Matthew's second chapter is dominated largely by a geographical motif, and the geographical significance is underlined with Scripture.[160] Matthew uses geographical details throughout the Gospel, but only in the second chapter that they are all associated with Scripture texts introduced by fulfilment formulae.[161]

Jesus' travelling from place to place is often provided with a note of explanation of fulfilment prophecy from the author of the Gospel. Jesus' birth in Bethlehem comes with a reminder of how the prophetical writing is fulfilled (2:5; cf. Micah 5:2). Jesus' flight to Egypt becomes a background to fulfil Hosea's "Out of Egypt I called my son" (2:15; cf. Hos 11:1) and the prophetic saying "He will be called a Nazarene" (2:23).[162] Jesus' leaving Nazareth and

157 For Matthew, Jesus is a Judean by birth. In the beginning of the Gospel the child Jesus is introduced by Matthew as the Son of David, the messianic king from Bethlehem, engrafted at God's behest into the royal lineage of Israel but driven out of his native homeland by the jealous hostility of Herod and-at least in sentiment- "all Jerusalem with him" (Matt 2:3). As a result of this opposition, the messianic family is forced to wander, and later in the narration they come at last to rest at Nazareth in Galilee in accordance with the words of the prophets (Matt 2:23).

158 Patrick Screiner, "Matthew's Geographical Overlay: The Return of the Exiled King," *Transformed Blog*, https://www.westernseminary.edu.

159 Verseput, "Jesus' Pilgrimage to Jerusalem," 118-119.

160 Thomas R. Hatina, "From History to Myth and Back Again: The Historicizing Function of Scripture in Matthew 2," in *The Gospel of Matthew*, vol. 2 of *Biblical Interpretation in Early Christian Gospel*, ed. Thomas R. Hatina, (London: T&T Clark, 2008), 98-118 (98).

161 Hatina, "From History to Myth and Back Again," 98.

162 "He will be called a Nazarene," do not match any exact text in the Old Testament. However there is a suggestion that it could be wordplay on Judges 13:5: "because you will conceive and give birth to a son. No razor may be used on his head, because the boy is to be a Nazirite, set apart to God from birth, and he will begin the deliverance of Israel from the hands of the Philistines." (NIV). Wordplay here could explain Matthew's creativity in focusing the past history of Israel onto the person of Jesus.

settlement in Capernaum, in the region of Zebulun and Naphtali (4:13) is associated with the fulfilment of Isaiah 9:1.[163] Matthew's sense of geographical reality seems to be mostly controlled by his fulfilment motive.

### *2.6.1. Significance of Topography in Literary Design of Matthew's Gospel*

Matthew covers the period between the birth of Jesus and the resurrection. These are both expanded backward and forward by means of references to the past (retrospections) and to the future (anticipation): the creation of the world (Matt 19:4, 8) and the coming of the Son of Man (Matt 24:3, 27, 29, 39) or the end of the ages (Matt 13:39-40, 49).[164] The indication of time in Matthew's Gospel, except in the passion narrative is vague and plays a role as temporal organisation of the story.[165] However, most of the topographical details found in the Gospel are related to Jesus.

The whole series of Jesus' topographical refrain and progression in Matthew's Gospel is significant. The wise men and Joseph are the subject of ἀναχωρέω (to withdraw - Matt 2:12-14, 22), and after John had been imprisoned Jesus continues to be the subject of ἀναχωρέω (Matt 4:12). Jesus' life was threatened first by Herod the Great (Matt 2:12-14) and his sons Archelaus (Matt 2:22) and Antipas (Matt 4:12; 14:13). Further in the Gospel, the circle of enemies for Jesus expanded with the Pharisees (Matt 12:14; 15:21), and even the region of Galilee became unsafe for Jesus. Thus, Jesus begins to avoid populated areas and stay in solitary places (Matt 14:13), and further travelling in the direction of the district of Tyre and Sidon (Matt 15:21). He left behind the Pharisees and the Sadducees (Matt 16:4) and continues his ministry in the region of Caesarea Philippi (Matt 16:13-28).

---

163 According to France, *The Gospel of Matthew*, 141, Matthew gives an abbreviated quotation of Isaiah 8:23-9:1 in a form closer to the Hebrew than to the LXX, but not fully corresponding to the sense of either. George M. Soares-Prabhu, *The Formula Quotations in the Infancy Narrative of Matthew*, Analecta Biblica 63 (Rome: Biblical Institute Press, 1976), 86-104, after examining the textual character of the quotation in relation to the Hebrew, LXX and targum texts, he concludes "an *ad hoc* christologically oriented translation, made directly from the original (proto-Masoretic) Hebrew, but influenced in its language by that of the LXX." The actualization of earlier texts in new situations, by various exegetical strategies (Midrash, Pesher, Targum, etc.) makes it evident that all early Christian literature is profoundly intertextual. See Seán Freyne, *Galilee and Gospel: Collected Essays*, WUNT 125 (Tübingen: Mohr, 2000), 289; Seán Freyne, "Reading the Gospels in the Light of the Window of the Evangelists at Chartres Cathedral," in *Radical Pluralism and Truth, David Tracy and the Hermeneutics of Religion*, ed. W. Jeanrond and J. Rike (New York: Crossroad, 1991), 107-120.

164 Wim J. C. Weren, *Studies in Matthew's Gospel: Literary Design, Intertextuality, and Social Setting* (Boston: Brill, 2014), 24.

165 Cf. McCown, "Gospel Geography," 11.

These moves remarkably increase Jesus' radius of action, and the continuing presence of large crowds even in uninhabited areas signify Matthew's topography. According to Weren, Matthew's insertion of fulfilment quotations in connection to this refrain also makes it clear that Matthew understands Jesus' wandering as not a restless traveling out of fear, but in obedience to God.[166] This understanding makes Weren to conclude that Jesus distances himself from Jerusalem and Judea, but he sees these moves as anticipating the events related in Matthew 26:17-28:15.[167]

Weren's work is a literary-synchronic perspective to find out how Matthew's Gospel is structured, but the significance of topography in Matthew's literary work is somehow highlighted. It must also be understood that according to the perspective chosen, the outcome will vary widely. In consideration of the structure of Matthew's Gospel, Benjamin W. Bacon the Gospel is divided by Matthew in such a way to signify the books of Moses, which are five blocs.[168] He sees it as being independent of each other that he considers them as five books.[169]

After this consideration, question arises. Why is Matthew's Gospel being preserved in this present form? The question concerns the reason why these individual incidents were arranged in a certain way in relation to one another

166 Weren, *Studies in Matthew's Gospel*, 26.

167 Weren, *Studies in Matthew's Gospel*, 25-27.

168 Benjamin W. Bacon, "The Five Books of Matthew Against the Jews," *The Expositor* 8 (1918): 56-66; cf. Raymond E. Brown, *An Introduction to the New Testament* (New York: Doubleday, 1997), 172. For Charles H. Lohr, Matthew's Gospel consists of six narrative sections and five discourses because he sees Matthew 23-25 as a single discourse. "Oral Techniques in the Gospel of Matthew," *CBQ* 23 (1961): 403-435 (427).

169 Jesus' discourse is concluded five times with a stereotypical formula (καὶ ἐγένετο ὅτε ἐτέλεσεν– Matt 7:28; 11:1; 13:53; 19:1; 26:1). The five books are framed by a preamble (Matt 1-2) and an epilogue (Matt 26-28). Book one – Matt 3:1-7:29 (Narrative: 3:1-4:25, Discourse: 5:1-7:27, Formula: 7:28-29); Book Two – Matt 8:1-11:1 (Narrative: 8:1-9:35, Discourse: 9:36-10:42, Formula: 11:1); Book Three – 11:2-13:53 (Narrative: 11:2-12:50, Discourse: 13:1-52, Formula: 13:53); Book Four – 13:54-19:1a (Narrative: 13:54-17:20, Discourse: 17:22-18:35, Formula: 19:1a); Book Five – 19:1b-26:1 (Narrative: 19:1b-22:46, Discourse: 23:1-25:46, Formula: 26:1). Cf. Weren, *Studies in Matthew's Gospel*, 14. This view is supported by Christopher R. Smith in his literary analysis of the structure of Matthew's Gospel. Christopher R. Smith, "Literary Evidence of a Fivefold Structure in the Gospel of Matthew," *NTS* 43 (1997): 540-551. However, following Edgar Krentz, Kingsbury argues that Matthew's Gospel actually consists three parts. Edgar Krentz, "The Extent of Matthew's Prologue: Toward the Structure of the First Gospel," *JBL* 83 (1964): 409-414; Jack D. Kingsbury, "The Structure of Matthew's Gospel and His Concept of Salvation History," *CBQ* 35 (1973): 451-474; see also Jack D. Kingsbury, *Matthew: Structure, Christology, Kingdom* (Philadelphia, PA: Fortress, 1975), 1-39; David R. Bauer, *The Structure of Matthew's Gospel: A Study in Literary Design*, JSNTSup 31 (Sheffield: SAP, 1988), 73-108.

by their mutual temporal and causal relations.[170] Frank J. Matera argues that a long and complex story such as Matthew's Gospel is not simply a collection of individual incidents.[171] Each individual incident cannot be given equal weight in consideration of the plot of the Gospel. There are events that can be understood as a turning point in the narrative and further influences the continuation of the narrative. Matera calls such significant incidents "kernels."[172]

These kernels are the essential parts of the narrative, and without them the development of the plot became unsteady. Thus, Matera sums up six passages in which there is a decisive turning point: the birth of Jesus (2:1a); the beginning of Jesus' ministry (4:12-17); John's question (11:2-6); the conversation in the district of Caesarea Philippi (16:13-28); the cleansing of the temple (21:1-17); the sending out of the disciples (28:16-20). In all these kernels, what is significantly evident is that Matthew embedded explicit topographical references.

### *2.6.2. The Term "Place" in Matthew's Gospel*

Matthew's understanding of the term "place" is not only confined to geographical place names because the setting for particular events in the Gospel also carries symbolic significance.[173] Ian Boxall states that "The Gospel's references to 'the sea' (only occasionally identified explicitly as the Sea of Galilee: 4.18; 15.29) evokes the Bible's association of the sea with danger and chaos (e.g. Gen. 1.2, 9; Job 38.8-11; Ps. 74.13-15; 104.6-9; 107.23-30)."[174] Matthew located two of Jesus' nature miracles at the sea (8:23-27; 14:22-33). The sea is also the place where the demon possessed pigs are sent to death (8:32). The shore of the sea is a place of receptivity where Jesus teaches in parables to the large crowds who gathered around him.

Matthew's phrases like "their synagogues" or "your synagogues"; and "Jesus teaches in their synagogues" (4:23; 9:35; 13:54) and occasionally heals in "their synagogue" (12:9-14), are marks of bitterness. These visits result in people taking offence (13:57) or even conspiring to destroy him (12:14), and Jesus' teaching to the disciples to expect flogging in "their synagogues" (10:17; cf. 23:34) is not an unexpected response. Thus, the synagogues,

170 Weren, *Studies in Matthew's Gospel*, 28.

171 Frank J. Matera, "The Plot of Matthew's Gospel," *CBQ* 49 (1987): 233-253.

172 Matera, "The Plot of Matthew's Gospel," 237.

173 Ian Boxall, *Discovering Matthew: Content, Interpretation, Reception* (Grand Rapids, MI: Eerdmans, 2014), 59.

174 Boxall, *Discovering Matthew*, 59.

presumably the ones dominated by the opponents of Jesus are presented as places of hostility and separation in Matthew's Gospel.[175]

Another prominent topographical role in Matthew's Gospel is played by mountains. Apart from the borrowing from Mark's Gospel, Matthew has several more to offer. The mountain on which Jesus prays before walking on the water (14:23); the high mountain of the Transfiguration[176] (17:1); the Mount of Olives to the east of Jerusalem (21:1; 24:3; 26:30), are all from Mark's source.

The account of the temptation of Jesus recalls the devil showing Jesus the kingdom of the world from "a very high mountains" (4:8; cf. Luke 4:5 – the devil simply "led him up"). In Matthew's Gospel Jesus delivers his first and last sermons from a mountain in Galilee and Mount of Olives respectively (5:1; 8:1), paralleling his last sermon, delivered on the Mount of Olives (24:3). Jesus heals many while seated on "the mountain" overlooking the Sea of Galilee, perhaps the mountain of the earlier sermon (15:29; cf. Mark 7:31-32). At the culmination of the Gospel's narrative Jesus meets his disciples on a mountain in Galilee after his resurrection (28:16). Matthew's insertion of the phrase "all authority in heaven and on earth" contrasts deliberately with the temptation by the devil on the very high mountain.[177]

Terence L. Donaldson in his 1985 book *Jesus on the Mountain: A Study in Matthean Theology*, presents an analysis of the six narratives in Matthew's Gospel where Jesus ascends to a mountain.[178] Donaldson notes that the place "mountain" also appears in sayings material five times (5:14; 17:20; 18:12; 21:21; 24:16), but opines that they have no direct bearing on Matthew's redaction or theology.[179] The two components of his analysis are the function of mountains in the milieu of Matthew's Gospel and the theological use of the mountain motif.[180]

Extensive redactional studies led Donaldson to draw conclusions concerning the relation of the mountain motif in Matthew's Gospel. In sum, the Temptation and Transfiguration stories relate to Jesus' true sonship and the path of obedience. The ecclesiology of the eschatological community is the focus of the Sermon on the Mount, the Feeding of the five thousand and the Commissioning narratives. "Salvation history" is the focus of the Olivet

175 Boxall, *Discovering Matthew*, 59.

176 This mountain is traditionally identified as Mount Tabor in Galilee. Boxall, *Discovering Matthew*, 59.

177 Boxall, *Discovering Matthew*, 60.

178 Terence L. *Donaldson, Jesus on the Mountain: A Study in Matthean Theology,* JSNTSS 8 (*Sheffield: JSOT Press, 1985*).

179 *Donaldson, Jesus on the Mountain*, 12.

180 *Donaldson, Jesus on the Mountain*, 13; see also K. C. Hanson, "Transformed on the Mountain: Ritual Analysis and the Gospel Matthew," *Semeia* 67 (1994), 147-70.

Discourse.[181] He further states that mountain symbolism in Matthew's Gospel is primarily dependent upon the Judean Zion traditions.

## 2.7. The Wandering Charismatics: In Relation with Miracles

Theissen, in his 1978 book *The First Followers of Jesus: A Sociological Analysis of Earliest Christianity*, understands early Christianity as a movement of wandering charismatics.[182] The movement is identified as being called by Jesus as Son of Man and the bearer of revelation. Though Theissen's theory has found much acceptance and became so widespread that it is almost a consensus today but there are other scholars who charge him of having limited empirical foundation and ambiguous sociological model.[183] J. A. Draper states that the only real evidence asserted by Theissen is the account of the sending of the disciples (10:1-11:1; Mark 6:6-56; Luke 9:1-11, 10:1-12), but he further argues that these accounts "provide evidence of a purposeful strategy of Jesus, a mission of sending and returning, rather than of radical itinerancy."[184] However, Theissen's theory of wandering charismatics remains as trendsetter and widespread as ever. The evidence makes it clear that wandering charismatics, like the first disciples of Jesus were supported by small communities of sympathizers, and continued to be a common phenomenon of early Christianity.

Theissen understands the radical sayings of Jesus as "belonging to the lived experience of those charismatic wanderers who adapted for themselves both the words and the lifestyle of Jesus."[185] He insists that "turning the other cheek" (5:38-48) must have had an existential relevance in the lives of the wandering charismatics. The interpretation of this virtue among the settled

---

181 *Donaldson, Jesus on the Mountain*, 196.

182 Gerd Theissen, *The First Followers of Jesus: A Sociological Analysis of Earliest Christianity*, trans. John Bowden (London: SCM, 1978).

183 Wolfgang Stegemann, "Vagabond Radicalism in Early Christianity? A Historical and Theological Discussion of a Thesis Proposed by Gerd Theissen," in *God of the Lowly: Socio-Historical Interpretations of the Bible*, ed. W. Schottrof and Wolfgang Stegemann (Maryknoll: Orbis, 1984), 148-168; J.G. Gager, "Social Description and Sociological Explanation in the Study of Early Christianity: A Review Essay," in *The Bible and Liberation*, ed. N. K. Gottwald (Maryknoll: Orbis, 1983), 428-440; Bruce Malina, "The Social Sciences and Biblical Interpretation," in *Bible and Liberation: Political and Social Hermeneutics*, ed. N. Gottwald (Maryknoll: Orbis, 1983), 11-25; J. H. Elliot, "Social Scientific Criticism of the New Testament and its Social World," *Semeia* 35 (1986): 1-33; Richard A. Horsley, *Sociology and the Jesus Movement* (New York: Crossroads, 1989).

184 J. A. Draper, "Wandering Radicalism or Purposeful Activity? Jesus and the Sending of Messengers in Mark 6:6-56," *Neotestamentica* 29.2 (1995): 187-207.

185 Gerd Theissen, *The Gospels in Context: Social and Political History in the Synoptic Tradition*, trans. Linda M. Maloney (Edinburg: T&T Clark, 1992), 144.

householders even in the early communities will have taken over distinct elements.

Three out of four characteristics of wandering charismatics given by Theissen, could be found in Matthew's Gospel.[186] Firstly, homelessness: Jesus reminds a prospective follower that the Son of Man does not have home, but foxes and birds do have their own (8:20). Jesus' instruction to the followers track upon this same route of homelessness (10:5-13). Secondly, lack of family ties: This second characteristic is not explicitly mentioned by Matthew, but Luke and Mark did mention it in the sense of hating father, mother, wife and children (Luke 14:26; cf. Mark 10:29). Thirdly, lack of possessions make them depend upon the hospitality of the surrounding people: "Take no gold, nor silver, nor copper in your belts, no bag for your journey… for the laborer deserves his food. And whatever town or village you enter, find out who is worthy in it, and stay with him until you depart (10:9-11). Lastly, lack of security and protection: "...But if any one strikes you on the right cheek, turn to him the other also (5:38-42); "…And if the house is worthy, let your peace come upon it; but if it is not worthy, let your peace return to you (10:12-13). Theissen sees that this last characteristic could hardly be a norm of Christian householders because the requirement to give in to abusive behavior could be much more in line with the livelihood of wandering charismatics. He was persuaded that only the "transient charismatic" could "turn the other cheek."[187]

Georg Strecker believes that Jesus has a home in Nazareth.[188] Jesus moves from Nazareth to Capernaum in order to make it his second hometown (4:16), and has a house there (9:10; 17:24-27). Interestingly, Matthew's story

186 Gerd Theissen, *Sociology of Early Palestinian Christianity*, trans. John Bowden (Phildelphia: Fortress, 1978), 12; see also Bernard J. Lee, *The Galilean Jewishness of Jesus: Retrieving the Jewish Origins of Christianity*, vol. 1 of *Conversation on the Road not Taken* (New York: Paulist Press, 1988), 130-131; Carroll D. Osburn, *Essay on Women in Earliest Christianity*, 2 vols. (Eugene: Wipf & Stock, 1993), 187.

187 Aaron Milavec, *Didache: Faith, Hope, and Life of the Earliest Christian Communities, 50-70 C.E.* (New York: The Norman Press, 1989), 744, citing Theissen, *The Gospels in Context*, 149. Especially in pages 741-746, Milavec summarizes Theissen's reading of the text of Matthew's Gospel and makes comparison with wandering charismatics of Didache. Theissen adds that Jesus is portrayed as wonder-worker in some popular tales, "without any specifically *Christian* traits." Gerd Theissen, "Historical Scepticism and the Criteria of Jesus Research: My Attempt to Leap Over Lessing's Ugly Wide Ditch," in *How to Study the Historical Jesus*, ed. Tom Holmén and Stanley E. Porter, vol. 1 of *Handbook for the Study of the Historical Jesus* (Leiden: Brill, 2011), 549-588 (560).

188 Georg Strecker, *Der Weg der Gerechtigkeit: Untersuchung zur Theologie de Matthäus*, FRLANT 82 (Göttingen: Vandenhoeck, 1962), 94-96, cited by Gerd Theissen, "Jesus as an Itinerant Teacher: Reflections from Social History of Jesus' Roles," in *Jesus Research: International Perspective*, ed. J. H. Charlesworth and P. Pokorny (Grand Rapids: Eerdmans, 2009), 98-122. Strecker believes that in Matthew 8:14; 9:10, 28; 13:1, 36; 17:25 the reference in each case is to the same house in Capernaum, his "own town."

of Jesus had him entering into Peter's home instead of his own, on Jesus' first appearance in Capernaum (8:14). Of all the places that Jesus has been, Matthew places Jesus' saying on the homelessness of the Son of Man, in his hometown (8:20). Graham H. Twelftree in his 1993 book *Jesus the Exorcist*, also argues that Jesus seems to have worked from a home he had in Capernaum (4:13) and some of the Galilean towns mentioned in the Gospels are within the walking radius of Capernaum.[189] But according to Theissen's recent article, "Jesus as an Itinerant Teacher: Reflections from Social History of Jesus' Roles," in *Jesus Research: International Perspective*, the treatment of Capernaum as a hometown for Jesus is "intended to improve his image as a homeless itinerant preacher to some extent," but other parts of Matthew's Gospel also present the overall picture of a wandering life.[190]

## 2.8. Summary

The early Christians' testimony unanimously identifies the apostle Matthew as the author of the First Gospel, but the nineteenth-century scholarship differs in this aspect. The possibility of the stages of composition or naming the apostle Matthew as an earlier contributor is worth noting. It is also to be pointed out that tradition and critical scholarship need not to be put in opposition. Matthew, the Jewish disciple of Jesus, a tax collector in Galilee would have been exposed to both Greek and Semitic languages of Palestine. The apostle Matthew fits rather well the profile of what modern scholars suggest as the author of Matthew's Gospel. Though it cannot be ignored that to ascertain the real author at this point, little is known of the apostle Matthew but among other figures he is still a suitable candidate. Consequently, placing Matthew's Gospel as early as 60 CE may yield the best sense of the text for the original readers.[191] The Syrian provenance for Matthew's Gospel is perhaps the most satisfactory answer to the question of the setting of the Gospel. Matthean community spreads over a wide geographical area. Though they were living in close proximity to a vigorous Jewish community, they are in the process of making a distinct community.

In regards to the identification of geographical details the canonical gospels did better than that of Gnostic gospels. Mark's and Matthew's arrangement and order of places differs, and this is the reason why it was understood that Matthew might have lack geographical orientation. Is it a lacking of orientation or is there a reason behind Matthew's order of places?

---

189 Graham H. Twelftree, *Jesus the Exorcist: A Contribution to the Study of the Historical Jesus* (Eugene: Wipf & Stock, 1993), 214.

190 Theissen, "Jesus as an Itinerant Teacher," 104-105.

191 Cf. Curtis Mitch and Edward Sri, *The Gospel of Matthew*, CCSS (Grand Rapids, MI: Baker Academics, 2010), 20-21.

Especially Matthew's second chapter provides visible geographical motif, and Matthew intensifies its significance with Scripture. The prominence of the city of Jerusalem is a pointer to geographical motive in the Gospel. Geography enhances Matthew's messianic motif. Matthew's comprehension of the term "place" is not confined only to geographical spaces also interacts with symbolic significance.

Chapter 3

# Nature Miracles in Ancient Traditions

## 3.1. Introduction

Miracle cannot be defined or contained in a definite perception free of incoherency. The issue of miracle stories becomes more significant especially in relation to the person of Jesus and the Gospel writers, and also their theological or contextual motifs. Another important note to make here is the interest on nature miracles in ancient literature. The peculiarity of traditional worldviews when compared to modern sciences must be acknowledged. This chapter is mainly to understand and locate their place within the framework of the cosmological worldview of the ancient writers.

## 3.2. Brief Re-visit to the Cause of the Rejection of Nature Miracles

The disparity between the worldviews of both the Old Testament and modern mind may need no further investigation, and thus the development of the rejection of nature miracles may be briefly mapped out here. The exclusion of spiritual causes from the natural world was one of the factors that paved a way for the birth of modern science in the sixteenth century. Francis Bacon (1561-1626) attempted to separate metaphysics, the investigation of the ultimate nature of reality, sharply from physics that concerned only with efficient and material causes. According to him, empirical sciences must have nothing to do with the alleged purposes of finite objects, such as angels, demons or gods, because they are not parts of science proper.[1]

1 Keith Ward, *The Big Questions in Science and Religion* (Pennsylvania: Templeton Foundation Press, 2008), 85-86.

René Descartes, contemporary to Bacon also characterized rational method in thought as that of seeking evidence for beliefs.[2] He divided each problem encountered into its constituent parts, beginning from the simplest to the most complex one, and finally offers exhaustive details of the topic under review. This method was in fact a development of the previous work of Robert Grosseteste (1186-1253), who perceived mathematics as the "hidden language of nature."[3]

Isaac Newton later championed the understanding of the laws of nature. Thus, he "constructed a few simple laws of mechanics that seemed to apply to all phenomena when they were considered in relative abstraction from the very complex real-world situations in which they were perceived by common sense."[4] His mathematical abstraction and postulation of a set of universal principles that govern the behaviour of the simplest parts of physical objects is published in his great work *Principia Mathematica* in 1687.[5]

The revolution in physics that began with the criticism of Aristotelian principles by Copernicus and Galileo was completed and halted. Thus, the universe was comprehended as a mechanical system, the understanding of the world as continually intervened by supernatural spirits now became obsolete. This causes a huge revolution in human thinking, but to be noted here is that it was not prompted then in any sense by opposition or rejection to religion and its beliefs. These prominent thinkers saw mathematics as the language of God, and also think that human beings, as an image of God could understand the language. Though Newton was not bothered by the biblical miracles and wrote many books about them, Richard Westfall writes "Newton both believed in and did not believe in miracles."[6] He continues to point out that Newton, in his unwillingness to "relinquish his belief in a providential and interposing Deity" makes himself inconsistent.[7]

David Hume's essay, "Of Miracles," which appeared in his larger work *An Inquiry Concerning Human Understanding* first published in 1748 initiates an attention to historical debate on miracles in New Testament study.

2 Ward, *The Big Questions in Science and Religion*, 86.

3 Ward, *The Big Questions in Science and Religion*, 86.

4 Ward, *The Big Questions in Science and Religion*, 86. Aristotle had thought that projectiles need a positive force or impetus to keep them moving or they will fall down to earth after a while. However, Newton demonstrated that this common sense view is mistaken, since it is factors like air resistance and gravity that cause projectiles to fall down. An abstract consideration tells that objects will continue moving in a straight line without any special impetus, unless something stops them.

5 Ward, *The Big Questions in Science and Religion*, 86.

6 Richard Westfall, *Science and Religion in Seventeenth Century England* (New Haven, 1970), 204, quoted by Peter Harrison, "Newtonian Science, Miracles, and the Law of Nature," *JHI* 56 (1995): 531-553 (531).

7 Westfall, *Science and Religion*, 5, 89, cf. Harrison, "Newtonian Science," 531.

Hume understands miracle as "a violation of the laws of nature"[8] and this definition became the focus of discussion for a long time. As the law of nature is established by "firm and unalterable experience,"[9] for him miracle cannot in anyway takes place. Hume's understanding is in part generated by his thoughts on people's love of gossiping about marvellous and surprising events and things in general, and also the lack of sufficient numbers of witnesses for any miracles in history.[10] Though the term "sufficient" is a problematic one and also the phrase "love of gossiping" is limited in nature, Hume's understanding of miracle is one of the most significant chapters in miracle study.

Friedrich Schleiermacher argues that the miracle stories narrated in the Bible were "literalizations of purely spiritual truths."[11] He understood the term miracle as simply the religious name for an event.[12] His attempt was mainly to preserve simultaneously, both the scientific understanding of nature and the idea of omnipresent divine agency.[13] Rudolf Bultmann also regarded miracles as wholly legendary.[14] He was more interested in understanding Christianity as a search for the possibility of a new understanding of human existence and inner spiritual renewal, rather than the occurrence of odd facts in antiquity.

Albert Schweitzer asserts that the study of the life of Jesus falls into two periods, "that before Strauss and that after Strauss."[15] The main interest in the former period was the question of miracle and the question of possible terms between a scientific treatment of the life of Jesus and the acceptance of supernatural events. According to Shweitzer, the deliberate rejection of all miracles and the elimination of everything supernatural which intrudes itself into the life of Jesus were first consistently carried through by Heinrich E. G. Paulus (1761-1851).[16] Paulus' aim according to Hendrik Van der Loos is "to make the thorough acquaintance of the purely historical Christ and his original

8 David Hume, *An Enquiry Concerning Human Understanding*, 2nd ed., ed. Eric Steinberg (Indianapolis: Hackett, 1993), 79.

9 Hume, *An Enquiry Concerning Human Understanding*, 114.

10 Hume, *An Enquiry Concerning Human Understanding*, 116-117; see also Richard Swinburne, *The Concept of Miracle*, NSPR (London: Macmillan, 1970), 13-22.

11 Ward, *The Big Questions in Science and Religion*, 88.

12 Friedrich Schleiermacher, *On Religion: Speeches to Its Cultured Despisers*, trans. John Oman (New York: Harper & Brothers, 1958), 88.

13 Ralph Del Colle, "Miracles in Christianity," in *The Cambridge Companion to Miracles*, CCR, ed. Graham H. Twelftree (Cambridge: CUP, 2011), 235-253.

14 Ward, *The Big Questions in Science and Religion*, 88.

15 Albert Schweitzer, *The Quest of the Historical Jesus: A Critical Study of its Progress from Reimarus to Wrede*, trans. W. Montgomery (London: A&C Black, 1910), 10.

16 Schweitzer, *The Quest of the Historical Jesus*, 28.

Christianity as handed down to us by the apostles."[17] Paulus sees the necessity to separate opinions of the story-teller or authors whose are prompted by the circumstances of their contexts from the actual facts.[18] Although, he insisted that the main point of his study was not to explain away miracles, he rejected all miracles a priori.[19] This kind of rejection and the understanding of miracles as later legendary fabrication influence and command the path of the study of miracle stories for decades.

Richard Bauckham however contends that eyewitnesses were available when the Gospels were written, and became a main source for the recorded Gospel's documents.[20] In this aspect he opposes the generally accepted view of form criticism. Form critics who opine that the Gospels are collection and records of collective communal traditions that was in circulation in the early church. The circulation took some time before putting down on writings, and that in the process of transmission and recording they were redacted to serve the theological purposes of the different communities from which they arose.[21]

Therefore, it implies that miracle stories are transmitted from eyewitnesses, and to simply reduce it as novelistic flourishes or legendary accretions is biased and unfair, but the redactional works evident in them could not be put aside. The redactional work especially the logic of how the evangelists organize their material assists New Testament study. Without arguing for the actuality of miracles, it is reasonable to note that the distinction between natural and supernatural is initiated in the Enlightenment period,[22]

---

17 Hendrik van der Loos, *The Miracles of Jesus* (Leiden: Brill, 1965). 16, quoting Heinrich Paulus, *Exegetisches Handbuch uber die drei ersten Evangelien*, 3 vols. (Heidelberg: Winter, 1830-1833), I. 2: iii.

18 Cf. Loos, *The Miracles of Jesus*, 16-17.

19 Cf. William Lane Craig, "The Problem of Miracles: A Historical and Philosophical Perspective," in *Gospel Perspectives*, ed. David Wenham and Craig Blomberg (Sheffield: JSOT Press, 1986), 4: 9-40.

20 Richard Bauckham, *Jesus and the Eyewitnesses: The Gospels as Eyewitness Testimony* (Grand Rapids: Eerdmans, 2006), 7.

21 Bauckham, *Jesus and the Eyewitnesses*, 6, 241-246; for contradicting argument from psychological perspective, see Judith C. S. Redman, "How Accurate are Eyewitnesses? Bauckham and the Eyewitnesses in the Light of Psychological Research," *JBL* 129 (2010): 177-197. Redman's conclusion makes it clear that the continued presence of eyewitnesses in the Christian communities during the recording of Gospel documents is only an evidence of the preservation of the community's agreed version, but not of the exact details of the event itself. Therefore, Bauckham's work fails to present an empirical evidence for the historicity of the Gospels. See also Samuel Byrskog, *Story as History – History as Story*, WUNT 123 (Tübingen: Mohr, 2000).

22 Evans summarizes the typical conclusion of the Enlightenment rationalism that religious belief is irrational: (1) To be rational a belief must be based on evidence that is highly objective and certain; (2) science is the paradigm of a belief system that fulfils this requirement; (3) the evidential support for religious beliefs is completely unlike the

but this was not the case during the writings and development of miracle stories in the first century or during the earlier years of modern science. The difficulty to classify miracle stories is apparent in the history of miracle study, but the classifications of nature miracles are more or less similar among the scholars.

## 3.3. Attempts for the Classifications of Biblical Miracle Stories

It is important to note the significance of the classifications of miracle stories proposed by various scholars. The tendency to group and classify miracle stories was apparent in history, but to come to a consensus seems impossible and perhaps not imperative, due to the variety of miracle stories recorded in the Gospels, and also because of the theological interests and motifs of an individual writer of the Gospels. In this section, brief history of the discussion of miracles will be highlighted to attain a better grip on the foundation of scholarly endeavours in this subject.

### *3.3.1. Arthur C. Headlam*

Arthur C. Headlam was one of the firsts to classify miracle stories in his *The Miracles of the New Testament*, published in 1914.[23] He accepts the twofold division of miracles of healings and wonders. In summarizing Mark's Gospel, he states that "twelve of the former (miracles) are recorded, and they give the impression of having been selected or remembered as typical. Three of them are described as 'possession by unclean spirits,' four as defects of sight, hearing, or speech, two paralysis, one fever, one leprosy, one issue of blood."[24] The other Miracles are classed as "Wonders." They are the calming of the wind and sea, the bringing to life of the daughter of Jairus, the feeding of the five thousand (and the four thousand), the walking on the lake, and the making of the fig-tree wither. According to him the difference between the two cannot be easily identified, because both types of miracles were narrated in the same vivid and simple way. He further argues that the difference lies in the character of the event.[25] Headlam's wonders could be understood as nature miracles, but with the inclusion of the revivification of Jairus' daughter.

---

evidential support that scientific beliefs possess. He further concludes that "all of these assumptions are eminently dubious," because according to him externalist, coherentist, and pragmatist epistemologies all agree in challenging the first. A major part of contemporary philosophy of science challenges the second, and a lot of interesting work in contemporary philosophy of religion challenges the third. C. Stephen Evans, *The Historical Christ and the Jesus of Faith: The Incarnational Narrative as History* (Oxford: Clarendon Press, 1996), 65-66.

23 Arthur C. Headlam, *The Miracles of the New Testament* (London: John Murray, 1914).

24 Headlam, *The Miracles of the New Testament*, 201.

25 Headlam, *The Miracles of the New Testament*, 201-202.

### *3.3.2. Brooke Foss Westcott*

Another exhaustive classification of miracles is seen in the work of Brooke Foss Westcott, in the Appendix of his *Introduction of the Study of the Gospels with Historical and Explanatory Notes* makes three main divisions and subdivided them into various sub categories.[26] His three main points are: Miracles on nature, miracles on human being, and miracles of the spirit-world. As there are numerous subdivisions and analyses, Jordan states the confusion and did not help in the understanding of synoptic view, and sometimes look more like a dissection.[27] Westcott's classification of nature miracles differ from Headlam's because only those miracles which are in contact with natural order are grouped together, and the revivification of Jairus' daughter is dropped from the list.

### *3.3.3. T. H. Wright*

T. H. Wright in his article, "Miracle" in *Hasting's Bible Dictionary* classifies the miracle stories into eight groups.[28] He omitted the subdivisions of Westcott: (1) Healing bodily ailments, (2) Healing nervous diseases, (3) Healing nervous and psychical disorders, (4) Manifestations of power in his own Nature, (5) Manifestations of Power in Nature and the Organic World, (6) Manifestations of power upon the organic world, (7) Manifestations of power upon the inorganic world, (8) Raising the dead. As the personality of human beings is a complicated matter that (1), (2), and (3) continually impose to each other, and are not easily separated from (8). (4), (6), and (7) are also closely interwoven.[29] Wright's observation is significant because he prefers the term spiritual rather than supernatural while defining the nature miracles.[30] He also asserts that nature miracles are as well attested in the Gospels as the works of healings, because they are found in each period of Jesus' ministry, in the Fourth Gospel, in the Synoptic tradition, and both in the double and triple traditions.[31] However, what is also noteworthy in his classification is the dissection of nature miracles in this classification.

---

26 Brooke Foss Westcott, *Introduction of the Study of the Gospels with Historical and Explanatory Notes* (New York: Macmillan, 1882), 466-469.

27 G. J. Jordan, "The Classification of Miracles," *ExpTim* 46 (1934-1935): 310-316 (311).

28 T. H. Wright, "Miracle," *DCG* 2:186-191 (190).

29 Jordan, "The Classification of Miracles," 312.

30 Wright, "Miracle," *DCG* 2:186.

31 Wright also gives chronological list of miracles, and places them under different periods of Jesus' ministry. He places three miracles under the group: *Preliminary period, from Baptism to call of leading apostles*; nineteen miracles (under *First period of Galilean ministry, to death of John the Baptist*; nine miracles under *Second period of Galilean ministry, to its close*; six miracles under *Ministry in Judea and Peraea*; four miracles under *Closing days of life*. Wright, "Miracle," *DCG* 2:189.

### *3.3.4. G. J. Jordan*

G. J. Jordan, after pointing out the lack of cohesion in classifications made by Headlam, Westcott, and Wright, he proposes a classification which focuses on the identification of human needs in miracle stories. He argues that the common and primary element in all the miracle stories is the human needs which are intended to be met.[32] According to Jordan the miracles when studied sympathetically makes it apparent that, for example in the marriage feast at Cana of Galilee, the needs of the guests are far more fundamental than the operation on the water. In the stilling of the storm, the fears of the disciples are more the concern of the master than his action upon the storm and the sea.[33] By comparing the miracles he concludes:

> Just as in the classification of the Parables we found the Evangelists had given us a common factor by their unconscious inclusion of the nature of the audience to which each Parable was addressed, so in the accounts of the Miracles we find them offering to us the central human need which each Miracle was calculated to meet.[34]

Therefore, Jordan sees the intrinsic significance of the needs of human beings as more fundamental than the action in the miracle stories. Though it might seem unconvincing to apply this in the classification of miracle stories, the emphasis upon human needs stand out as an important understanding while dealing with miracle stories, especially in the context of liberation and ecological theologies.

### *3.3.5. David Friedrich Strauss*

David Friedrich Strauss, by initiating his discussion of miracles from the tension between Gospels and Acts notes the presence of miracles in the Gospels and the lack of miracles in the epistles.[35] He also cites the negative response by Jesus to the Pharisees' asking for a sign, and finds this in accord with the absence of miracles in epistles, and thus concludes "that the miracles have no rightful place in history but are simply mythical elements in the sources."[36] After careful examination of all the categories of miracle stories found in the Gospels, he finds that some of the miracle stories are pure myths, and his example is the healing of the blind, which has no historical foundation in his view.

---

32 Jordan, "The Classification of Miracles," 312-313.

33 Jordan, "The Classification of Miracles," 312.

34 Jordan, "The Classification of Miracles," 313.

35 Charles H. Talbert, ed., *Reimarus Fragments* (London: SCM, 1971), 230-234.

36 Graham H. Twelftree, *Jesus the Miracle Worker: A Historical and Theological Study* (Downers Grove, IL: IVP, 1999), 33.

Until Strauss the general agreement of the occurrences of miracles had been the consensus, and the subject is mainly on the matter of how they were explained in the Gospels. But, Strauss changed the course by asserting that these miracle stories in the Gospels actually never happened, and the narratives are unhistorical tales which are determined by myth and legend.[37] Strauss rejects both the conspiratorial theory of Reimarus and the natural explanation theory of Paulus, and proposes an explanation of the miracle stories "in terms of myth, legend, and redaction."[38] According to William Lane Craig, Strauss dissolved the central dilemma of eighteenth century orthodoxy's argument for the miracles of Jesus. Strauss' criteria for discerning mythological motifs were rooted upon the presupposition of the impossibility of miracles. Therefore any narratives of events which cannot be accommodated under "the inviolable chain of natural causes and effects was *ipso facto* unhistorical and therefore to be mythologically accounted for."[39] This was the legacy of Strauss followed by Bultmann, the naturalistic assumption that guided historical investigations. However, it is important here to note that Strauss treated the Old Testament as the most significant backdrop to the miracle stories of the Gospels.

### *3.3.6. Rudolf Bultmann*

Unlike Strauss, Rudolf Bultmann turns to non-Christian and rabbinic stories. Whether the materials were used in the writing of the Gospels does not have so much of importance but it is implied that these miracle traditions were actually attributed to Jesus. Bultmann's form critical study of John's Gospel *Da Evangelium des Johannes* (*The Gospel of John*) is a history of religions approach to the miracle stories of John's Gospel; and for Bultmann the changing of water into wine is probably drawn from the Dionysian cult and was adapted to portray Jesus as a Revealer.[40] His "New Testament and Mythology" also left a profound effect to modern study of miracle stories, and initiated the debate on demythologization.[41] He argues that mythological thought regards God's activity as interfering with nature, and thus rejects it, and further explains his reasoning:

> A miracle-i.e. an act of God – is not visible or ascertainable like worldly events. The only way to preserve the unworldly,

37 Craig, "The Problem of Miracles," 12.

38 Craig, "The Problem of Miracles," 12-13.

39 Craig, "The Problem of Miracles," 13.

40 Rudolf Bultmann, *The Gospel of John: A Commentary*, trans. G. R. Beasley-Murray, R. W. N. Hoare and J. K. Riches (Philadelphia: Westminster Press, 1971), 120.

41 Rudolf Bultmann, "New Testament and Mythology: The Mythological Element in the Message of the New Testament and the Problem of Its Re-interpretation," in *Kerygma and Myth: A Theological Debate*, ed. Hans Werner Bartsch (London: SPCK, 1957), 1-44.

> transcendental character of the divine activity is to regard it not as an interference in worldly happenings, but something accomplished *in* such a way that the close weft of history as it presents itself to objective observation is left undisturbed.[42]

This understanding undermines the Gospel's writers as being unable to discern mythical or analogical and language that was not and also dissolves the idea of miracle in the Gospels. Bultmann however explains the reason why modern person do not acknowledge miracles. The reason is mainly due to the thinking that operates and is trapped inside the framework of modern rational order of the universe.[43] Though the determining factor in classifying nature miracles is the understanding of the stories as legendary and created by the early Christians, Bultmann's differentiation of nature miracles is nevertheless noteworthy.[44] Then this kind of viewing miracle stories become a common concern, but there are other works that give much importance to the accounts of the eyewitnesses. Consequently they provide arguments that miracle reports cannot be simply ruled out a priori because they dominated many narratives of the Gospel writings.

Bultmann's form critical study of miracles opened up a new arena for miracle discussion.[45] As signs of dissatisfaction to this approach appeared in the mid-1950s, new strategies emerged. An influential movement rejected the nineteenth-century quest for the historical Jesus and presented a critique of mythical approaches.[46] There is an argument for the concept of God's revelation in time-space history from scholars like Wolfhart Pannenberg and other theologian sometimes called the "Pannenberg circle."[47] The emphasis on the acknowledgement of the significance of God's role in both past and

---

42 Bultmann, "New Testament and Mythology," 10, quoted by Twelftree, *Jesus the Miracle Worker*, 36.

43 Rudolf Bultmann, *Jesus Christ and Mythology* (New York: Charles Scribner's Sons, 1958), 37-38.

44 Rudolf Bultmann, *The History of the Synoptic Tradition*, trans. John Marsh, rev. ed. (New York: Harper & Row, 1976), 234-239; for similar understanding see G. Bornkamm, *Jesus of Nazareth* (London: Hodder & Stoughton, 1960), 131; see also David E. Aune, "Magic in Early Christianity," in *Aufstieg und Niedergang der Römischen Welt II, ed. Hildegard Temporini and Wolfgang Haase (Berlin: de Gruyter, 1980),* 1507-1557.

45 R. Douglas Geivett and Gary R. Habermas, introduction to *In Defense of Miracles: A Comprehensive Case for God's Action in History* (Downers Grove, IL: IVP, 1997), 9-26 (13).

46 Studies includes James M. Robinson, *A New Quest of the Historical Jesus*, JBT 25 London: SCM Press, 1959; and G. Bornkamm, *Jesus of Nazareth* (London: Hodder & Stoughton, 1960).

47 For the seminal work written by a group of theologians," see Wolfhart Pannenberg, ed., *Revelation as History*, trans. David Granskou (London: Collier-Macmillan, 1968).

present history is another arena that appeared.[48] R. Douglas Geivett and Gary R. Habermas argue that "the last few decades of the Twentieth century have witnessed the efflorescence of various approaches to the study of miracles... there is no identifiable consensus among current scholars, [but] there has been a somewhat positive assessment of the need to investigate the historicity of Jesus."[49] There is also a new interest and acknowledgement of the Jewish background and context of Jesus' life and teachings.[50]

### *3.3.7. Reginald H. Fuller*

Reginald H. Fuller in his 1963 book *Interpreting the Miracles*, states that even though no New Testament writers would have thought of classifying nature miracles in a separate group, but, perhaps unconsciously, they differentiate between nature miracles, and the healings and exorcisms.[51] The primary concern in this line of thought is the witnessing of miracles, and disciples are the only one who witnessed or recognised these nature miracles. He argues that there is no suggestion that the crowd knew what exactly happened during the feeding of the multitude, but is wronged by the Johannine version that says "the people saw the sign which he had done" (John 6:14).[52] While dealing with miracle stories, he gives much emphasis to the later theology of the writers of the Gospels, and sees that it is not possible to recover what actually happened.

This is significant and is true that in all probability the Gospels contain fabricated or theologized stories of miracles, not as a made up stories but to serve the purpose of writing. However he sees the tradition of Jesus' performing of healings and exorcisms as presenting a very strong case. But he further argues that it is still impossible to authenticate any actual miracle story in the Gospels because "most of them have probably been shaped out of generalized memories."[53] What is significant in this study is the observation that the differentiation between various types of miracles is evident in the writings of the Gospels.

---

48 Jürgen Moltmann, *Theology of Hope: On the Ground and the Implications of a Christian Eschatology*, trans. James W. Leitch (New York: Harper and Row, 1967).

49 Geivett and Habermas, introduction to *In Defense of Miracles*, 13.

50 Geivett and Habermas, introduction to *In Defense of Miracles*, 13; citing some major works, Geza Vermes, *Jesus the Jew: A Historian's Reading of the Gospels* (New York: Macmillan, 1973); E. P. Sanders, *Jesus and Judaism* (Philadelphia: Fortress, 1985); James H. Charlesworth, *Jesus Within Judaism* (Garden City, N.Y.: Doubleday, 1988); John P. Meier, *A Marginal Jew: Rethinking the Historical Jesus* (Garden City, N.Y.: Doubleday, 1991); John P. Meier, *Mentor, Message, Miracle* (Garden City, N.Y.: Doubleday, 1994).

51 Reginald H. Fuller, *Interpreting the Miracles* (London: SCM, 1963), 37.

52 Fuller, *Interpreting the Miracles*, 37; see also Twelftree, *Jesus the Miracle Worker*, 350.

53 Fuller, *Interpreting the Miracles*, 39.

### 3.3.8. Jesus Seminar[54]

Coming to the 20th Century, the Jesus Seminar has been receiving much attention mainly due to "its controversial procedures and results and also its concerted marketing campaign."[55] Ben Witherington discredits the Jesus Seminar by stating that its decision-making and its results under critical examination reveals serious flaws. This is mainly due to the fact that the group applies voting system[56] on Jesus' sayings and thus "leaves little room for nuances and probabilities, and, more importantly, yields a picture of Jesus with which no one scholar fully agrees."[57] The members of the group meet twice a year in order to discuss and assess the sayings of Jesus; and one of their goals, which is to produce a red-letter edition of the Gospels. This goal to highlight what Jesus did and did not say has been realized with the publication of *The Five Gospels*, which is edited by Robert W. Funk, the Seminar's founder and Roy W. Hoover.[58] However, the conclusions presented in this work are seen as dubious and Richard B. Hays thus remarks:

> The depiction of Jesus as a Cynic philosopher with no concern about Israel's destiny, no connection with the concerns and hopes that animated his Jewish contemporaries, no interest in the interpretation of Scripture, and no message of God's coming eschatological judgment is – quite simply – an ahistorical fiction, achieved by the surgical removal of Jesus from his Jewish context.[59]

---

54 The Jesus Seminar was founded by Robert W. Funk, and consists of about 50 critical biblical scholars and 100 laymen. The group originated under the auspices of the Wester Institute, Sonoma, California, and are quite active though the 1980s and 1990s, and also in the early 21st century. It is not a group sponsored by either of the two major scholarly guilds: the Society of Biblical Literature (SBL) or the group that originated in Europe and now, like SBL, is an international organization, the Society for the Study of the New Testament (SNTS).

55 Ben Witherington, *The Jesus Quest: The Third Search for the Jew of Nazareth*, 2nd ed. (Downers Grove, IL: IVP, 1997), 42.

56 Using coloured beads to cast votes on the sayings of Jesus: A red bead to indicate "Jesus surely said this," pink for "he probably said that," gray for "he probably didn't say this," and black for "it is very unlikely that he said anything like that. Only 18 percent of the Gospel sayings attributed to Jesus were actually spoken by him according to this approach".

57 Witherington, *The Jesus Quest*, 42.

58 Robert W. Funk and Roy W. Hoover, eds., *The Five Gospels* (New York: Macmillan, 1993).

59 Richard B. Hays, "The Corrected Jesus," *First Things* 43 (1994): 43-48 (47).

The Jesus Seminar,[60] on the historicity of the miracles of Jesus are positive, especially accepting Jesus as practicing exorcism and healing, as long as the cures were related to psychosomatic maladies.[61] However they frequently rejected nature miracles outright, assuming that they "more readily indicate supernatural events.[62] However, there are scholars like Gerhard Delling and Franz Mussner who see the miracle stories in the Gospels as having been originated from the reports of the eyewitnesses of Jesus' ministry.[63] The difference between cosmological worldviews of the ancient writers and modern readers is apparent in the work of Jesus Seminar, because the Gospel writers were not in a position to offer medical diagnosis.

During this time, though there are scholars who defend miracles from philosophical perspective, there is a long list of renowned scholars who proposed philosophical objections.[64] However, the study is not interested to look into all the philosophical and theological objections of miracles, because the interest is not the possibility or the impossibility of the miracles, instead the interest lies in how Matthew utilizes the materials, especially nature miracles

---

60 For more details about the Seminar's history and purpose, see Chapter Two (Jesus the Talking Head) of Witherington, *The Jesus Quest*, 42-57; see also the preface of Craig A. Evans, *Jesus and His Contemporaries: Comparative Studies* (Boston: BAP, 2001), vii-viii.

61 Twelftree, *Jesus the Miracle Worker*, 18. For the Jesus Seminar, see W. Barnes Tatum, *John the Baptist and Jesus: A Report of the Jesus Seminar* (California: Polebridge, 1993).

62 Gary R. Habermas, "Did Jesus Perform Miracles," in *Jesus Under Fire: Modern Scholarship Reinvents the Historical Jesus*, ed. Michael J. Wilkins and J. P. Moreland (Grand Rapids, MI: Zondervan, 1995), 117-140 (133).

63 Twelftree, *Jesus the Miracle Worker*, 18, citing Gerherd Delling, "Das Verständnis des Wunderim Neuen Testament," *ZST* 24 (1955): 265-280; Gerhard Delling, "Botschaft und Wunder in Wirken Jesu," in *Der historische Jesu und der kerygmatische Christus*, ed. Helmut Ristow and Karl Matthiae, 3rd ed. (Berlin: Evangelische Verlagsanstalt, 1964), 389-402; Franz Mussner, *The Miracles of Jesus: An Introduction* (Notre Dame: University of Notre Dame Press, 1968).

64 Twelftree, *Jesus the Miracle Worker*, 39, examples of works in defence of miracles are R. F. Holland, "The Miraculous," *APQ* 2 (1965): 43-51; and Richard Swinburne, *The Concept of Miracle*, NSPR (London: Macmillan, 1970); and also R. C. Wallace, "Hume, Flew and the Miraculous," *PQ* 20 (1970): 230-243. Examples of names of scholars who object miracles are Benedict de Spinoza, "Tractatus Theologico-Politicus," in *The Chief Works of Benedict de Spinoza*, trans. R. H. M. Elwes, 2 vols. (London: George Bell & Son, 1883-1884), 1:81-97; David Hume, *An Enquiry Concerning Human Understanding*, 2nd ed., ed. Eric Steinberg (Indianapolis: Hackett, 1993); Alastair McKinnon, "'Miracle' and 'Paradox'," *APQ* 4 (1967): 308-314; Malcolm L. Diamond, "Miracles," *RelS* 9 (1973): 307-324; Patrick Nowell-Smith, "Miracles–The Philosophical Approach," in *Philosophy of Religion: Selected Readings*, ed. William L. Rowe and William J. Wainwright (New York: Harcourt Brace Jovanovich, 1973), 392-400; George Chryssides, "Miracles and Agents," *RelS* 11 (1975): 319-327.

in the Gospel. Jesus Seminar also implicitly classified nature miracles in one group by means of alienating them altogether.

### *3.3.9. Gerd Theissen*

To distinguish and classify miracle stories is evidently difficult and an ideal classification may be impossible. They have been classified in different groups, and some in speculative way. Theissen in his *Miracle Stories of the Early Christian Tradition* highlighted three different levels of classification – functional, compositional and paradigmatic.[65] It is an attempt to treat the miracle stories in the Gospels from the synchronic, diachronic and functional point of view.

#### *3.3.9.1. Classification by Function*

G. Schille proposes a classification in functional terms and according to him all miracle stories have different purposes but fundamentally belong to "missionary discourse genres."[66] "Pure exorcisms and miracle stories" are those that seek to draw attention to Jesus, and "mission legends" are those that give account of existing Christian communities. These legends are again distinguished into two groups: "community foundation legends" that deal the origin of individual communities and "area legends" that are concerned with missionary activity in districts as a whole. Therefore, the story of Bartimaeus is understood as a foundation legend of the Jericho community and the story of the Syrophoenician woman is identified as an area legend of Syria and Phoenicia. Theissen argues that this classification of the genre offers nothing, but contributes to the functional analysis of miracle stories.[67]

#### *3.3.9.2. Classification by Composition*

Martin Dibelius also made a distinction between paradigms and novellas, and according to Theissen both are part of mission.[68] They differ in that paradigms, as model sermons are integrated into a wider genre of sermon, but novellas stand on their own without integrating into other wider genre. This classification also falls under compositional level of classification of miracle stories, due to the fact that the distinction between paradigms and novellas is based basically on observations at the compositional level. The paradigms are characterized by their brevity and simplicity and novellas by their longer and

65 Gerd Theissen, *Miracle Stories of the Early Christian Tradition*, trans. Francis McDonagh, ed. John Riches (Edinburgh: T&T Clark, 1983), 81-85.

66 G. Schille, *Die urchristliche Wundertradition: Ein Beitrag zur Frage nach dem irdischen Jesus* (Stuttgart: CalwerVerlag, 1967), 24-27, cited by Theissen, *Miracle Stories of the Early Christian Tradition*, 81.

67 Theissen, *Miracle Stories of the Early Christian Tradition*, 81-82.

68 Theissen, *Miracle Stories of the Early Christian Tradition*, 82.

descriptive for their own sake.[69] However, these distinctions are not that vivid when miracle stories are given careful examination.

The healing miracles in each of Dibelius category, four of the five paradigms and four of the seven novellas are of the same average length, i.e., six verses. The paradigmatic story of the paralytic in Mark 2:1-12 is also longer than the average healing novella, and the novelistic account of the blind man of Bethsaida in Mark 8:22-26 is not long at all. The healing of the blind man near Jericho in Mark 10:46-52 is told at least as vividly as the cure of the leper in Mark 1:40-45.[70]

Bultmann, by using this same criterion comes to a very contrasting conclusion. He removes all miracle stories that contain teaching by Jesus from the genre of miracle story and places them under the umbrella of apophthegms.[71] He distinguishes nature miracles from other miracle stories and attempts to show that Mark's Gospel which is the common source for Matthew and Luke does not include such stories, and also proposes non-Jewish Hellenistic sources for nature miracles.[72] Those miracle stories, especially the healing stories that are not told in the style of miracle stories were composed as a framework for the saying, and have been "completely subordinated to the point of an apophthegm."[73] Thus, when there is a teaching of Jesus present in the miracle story, sometimes the teaching and sometimes the miracle is the "occasion" for the story.[74]

Erich Fascher does not agree with Bultmann's method and contends that the origin of the miracle stories still remains dark.[75] He also states that

69 Martin Dibelius, *From Tradition to Gospel*, trans. Bertram Lee Woolf (New York: Charles Scribner's Sons, 1967), 37-103.

70 Laurence J. McGinley, "Form-Criticism of the Synoptic Healing Narratives," *TS* 4 (1941): 451-480 (214).

71 Theissen, *Miracle Stories of the Early Christian Tradition*, 82-83; Bultmann, *The History of the Synoptic Tradition*, 11. Bultmann used the term *apophthgemata* for the pericopes in which the culmination of the stories is developed by the authoritative sayings of Jesus. See also Stephen H. Travis, "Form Criticism," in *New Testament Interpretation: Essays on Principles and Methods*, ed. I. Howard Marshall (Exeter: Paternoster, 1977), 153-164 (155-156).

72 Bultmann, *The History of the Synoptic Tradition*, 227-231. He classified miracle stories into four groups, such as Exorcisms of demons, other healings, raisings from the dead, and nature miracles.

73 Bultmann, *The History of the Synoptic Tradition*, 12, 220; Twelftree, *Jesus the Miracle Worker*, 351.

74 Bultmann, *The History of the Synoptic Tradition*, 11-39, 209-244; Theissen, *Miracle Stories of the Early Christian Tradition*, 82-83.

75 Erich Fascher, *Die formgeschichtliche Methode: eine Darstellung und Kritik*, BZNW (Giessen: Alfred Töpelmann, 1924), 130, cited by Robert M. Grant, *Miracle and Natural Law in Graeco-Roman and Early Christian Thought* (Eugene, OR: Wipf & Stock, 1952), 168.

the attitude towards the question of authenticity depends mostly on the presuppositions of the person. Vincent Taylor and others also emphasize this same point.[76] Bultmann understands nature miracles as being derived from non-Jewish sources does not enjoy much acceptance today, due to the interest and findings of embedded influences of Jewish tradition in the Gospels.

### *3.3.9.3. Classification by Subject and Object*

Miracle stories could be distinguished from other genres without much confusion, but to further classify them into sub-groups is a difficult task. The classification of miracle stories by identifying and drawing out the embedded motifs or combination of motifs in the stories is also not sufficient to enable them into sub-groups.[77] Bultmann's separate listing of the motifs of exorcism is convincing, but he makes no fundamental distinction from miracle stories of healings.[78] Theissen talks about the problem of defining themes, as some motifs intermingle with various themes, and some themes may appear in specific motifs without sharing identical focus.[79] Therefore, attempts of form critical classifications to define such themes are destabilized by the accepting of different elements of the content as the basis for classification.

Further, another classification within the genre is the observation of interaction between subject and object. T. A. Burkill distinguishes the types of miracles performed through human agency into firstly, an exorcism and a non-exorcism class and secondly, miracles in the natural world and miracles in the human world.[80] Theissen observes that both these classifications overlapped each other, because there are exorcisms in the natural world as well as in the human world.[81] Miracle stories have been also classified in regards to the presence of certain objects (loaves of bread or a lake) or their characters (the lame or the blind). Van der Loos makes a simple division between healing and nature miracles, but he also provides 19 sub-categories, and attempts to come in terms with the methodological problems in dealing with both text and tradition. Gerhard Delling, in consideration with the ancient miracle tradition, has proposed a typological classification, and distinguishes cures, prodigies,

76 Vincent Taylor, *The Formation of the Gospel Tradition* (London: Macmillan, 1953), 119-141, cited in Grant, *Miracle and Natural Law in Graeco-Roman and Early Christian Thought*, 168.

77 Theissen, *Miracle Stories of the Early Christian Tradition*, 83.

78 Bultmann, *The History of the Synoptic Tradition*, 231-232.

79 Theissen, *Miracle Stories of the Early Christian Tradition*, 83.

80 T. A. Burkill, "The Notion of Miracle with Special Reference to St. Mark's Gospel," *ZBG* 50 (1959): 33-48, esp. 43-44.

81 Theissen, *Miracle Stories of the Early Christian Tradition*, 84.

epiphanies of gods, proof miracles that demonstrate supernatural character, rescue and punishment miracles.[82]

Theissen opines that the best classification must be the one that combines the most aspects of these approaches, and provides a catalogue of miracle stories according to themes: exorcisms, healings, epiphanies, rescues, gifts and rule miracles.[83] Apart from the exorcisms, the Gospel writers generally do not make distinctions among the kinds of miracle stories that they relate (cf., e.g. Mark 1:32-34, and Luke 7:22). Therefore any categorization other than this would be an imposition on the Gospel writers.[84]

### *3.3.10. Graham H. Twelftree*

Graham H. Twelftree differs from most of the scholars that have been already mentioned, and he finds that there are no warrants in the Gospel tradition for delineating healing miracles from nature miracles.[85] In his argument against Fuller, he states that the distinction between nature miracles and other miracles cannot strictly be held. He cites both Robert W. Funk and the Jesus Seminar, and further argues that although Jesus does not explicitly make any statement that would suggest that he performed what is called nature miracles, the "deeds of power" said to be done in Chorazin and Bethsaida could have been intended to be or include nature miracles.[86] He also quoted James D.G. Dunn's statement that Jesus' saying that a person of faith could command a mountain to be cast into the sea "could indicate a conviction on Jesus' part that the spiritual powers at work in him and through him could affect and alter the course of nature."[87] The understanding that close correspondence to stories or the incorporation of significant themes of the Old Testament as setting apart the nature miracles is not convincing for him, because Old Testament themes are also apparent in many other stories of the New Testament.[88]

However, it is significant that Twelftree understands what he terms it as so-called nature miracles, if they are able to be included in the authentic material that can be traced back to the life of the historical Jesus, "they in

---

82 Gerhard Delling, "ZurBeurteilung des Wundersdurch die Antike," in *Studien zur Neuen Testament und zum hellenistischen Judentum: Gesammelte Aufsätze*, ed. Ferdinand Hahn, Traugott Holz and Nicolaus Walter (Göttingen: Vandenhoeck & Ruprecht, 1970), 53-71, cited by Theissen, *Miracle Stories of the Early Christian Tradition*, 84.

83 Theissen, *Miracle Stories of the Early Christian Tradition*, 85-112.

84 Twelftree, *Jesus the Miracle Worker*, 351-352.

85 Twelftree, *Jesus the Miracle Worker*, 350-351.

86 Robert W. Funk and the Jesus Seminar, *The Acts of Jesus: What Did Jesus Really Do?* (New York: HarperCollins, 1998), 34, cited by Twelftree, *Jesus the Miracle Worker*, 350.

87 James D. G. Dunn, *Jesus and the Spirit* (London: SCM, 1975), 72, quoted in Twelftree, *Jesus the Miracle Worker*, 350-351.

88 Twelftree, *Jesus the Miracle Worker*, 351.

particular can give clear indication that Jesus thought he was acting for God."[89] Twelftree's argument mainly relies on the ambiguity of classifying healing miracles and nature miracles separately. Consequently his main thrust is probably to remove the prejudice against nature miracles in the Gospels.

## 3.4. God, Nature and Miracle within the Cosmological Worldview of the Old Testament Writers

The Old Testament commences with a grandiose cosmological account of the creation of the universe. In Genesis 1:1–2:4a, which came down from the P tradition according to documentary hypothesis, presents that the activity of creation by God took six days. Another creation account from J tradition is Genesis 2:4b-24, which is a much more anthropocentric version. Apart from the presence of tensions between the two accounts, they introduces the reader into the cosmological worldview where God, miracle, and natural order of life were not thought of as opposing to each other or being in tension, but depict a view that they correlate to each other from the beginning.

Yair Zakovitch and Rimon Kasher (source in Hebrew) were two scholars from Israel who exhaustively dealt with the definition of miracle.[90] Zakovitch proposes "control mechanisms," as a means to discover the indication present in the extraordinary events that lead the narrator to see the event as a miracle.[91] He defined miracle as being ultimately occasioned by God, and considered magic as a human act that utilizes special techniques to force nature.[92]

Kasher is however not much interested in defining miracle but provides a catalogue of the types of miracles: (1) Miracles announced in advance and worked solely by the human agent, (i.e. the miracle worker only announces, but does not perform the miracle); (2) Miracles performed by the human miracle-worker in accordance with precise instructions by God; (3) The initiative for the miracle comes from a human agent but its implementation is ascribed to God; (4) Both the initiative and the implementation are assigned exclusively

89 Twelftree, *Jesus the Miracle Worker*, 358.

90 Yair Zakovitch, *The Concept of the Miracle in the Bible* (Tel-Aviv: MOD Books, 1991); and Rimon Kasher, "The Theological Conception of the Miracle in the Bible," (PhD diss., Bar-Ilan University, 1981), cited by Michael Avioz, "Splitting the Sea, Manna from Heaven, Defeating Amalek: What Makes Something a Miracle?" *The Torah: A Historical and Contextual Approach*, n.d., http://thetorah.com/what-makes-something-a-miracle.

91 Controlled mechanisms proposed: (1) A messenger of the Lord making announcement prior to the event; (2) The extraordinary nature of the miraculous action, with regard both to its duration and place; (3) The subsequent restoration of the previously existing state of affairs; (4) The specification of the miracle's theological objective; and (5) When a miracle encompasses only a certain well-defined group and bypasses another. See Yair Zakovitch, "Miracle (Old Testament)," *ABD* 4:845-856; see also Avioz, "Splitting the Sea?"

92 Zakovitch, *ABD* 4:850.

to the miracle-worker.[93] Integrating the outcome of these two studies may help to come to a proper understanding of the miracle narratives especially those of exodus event and the Old Testament as a whole.[94] As the task here is not to delve into ideal definitions for miracle, a general overview of various terminologies and concepts evident in the Old Testament writings will suffice to understand the cosmological worldview.

What can be called as nature miracles occur in various events of the exodus. The reported extraordinary events that relates or occurs in the natural world are: the burning bush not consumed by the fire (the initiation of exodus event – Exod 3:2), the plagues of Egypt (Exod 7:20-12:30), a pillar of cloud and fire guarding the multitude (Exod 13:21-22, 14:19), the Red sea parted (Exod 14:21-29), Egyptians chariots made swervè and the army drowned in the sea (Exod 14:25-31), bitter waters of Marah sweetened and made drinkable (Exod 15:23-25), manna sent daily except on Sabbath and quail to provide meat (Exod 16:14-35), water from the rock (Exod 17:2-6, Num 20:2-13), the wind brings the quail (Num 11:31), the ground opens and swallows Korah (Num 16:19-35), the budding of Aaron's staff (Num 17:1-11), and the crossing of the river Jordan that ceases to flow (Josh 3).[95]

In the Old Testament these miracles provide evidence that God is in action and in charge and the will of God will certainly comes to pass. They are the testaments to the authority and supremacy of God. Norman L. Geisler argues that the miracles in the Old Testament "fit the monotheistic concept of God that permeates the entire Old Testament record."[96] He further argues that, by nature a theistic God is a "miracle-working God."[97] This is exactly how God is presented in the Old Testament, God who created the cosmos, and thus involved in supernatural acts from the very beginning of the Bible. God's intervention in the cosmos is another running theme of the Old Testament.

Apart from the theological framework, cosmological worldview also plays an important role in the Old Testament understanding of miracles. When a particular worldview of a specific culture in a certain period of time is considered, it is always clear that there are differences between them. This is also true with the Old Testament and modern interpreters; it is not difficult to perceive a wide gap of difference between them. Events that appear, from the perspective of modern mind to be a part and parcel of the matrix of the

---

93 Avioz, "What Makes Something a Miracle?"

94 Avioz, "What Makes Something a Miracle?"

95 For natural explanation of these miracles from the scientific point of view, see Colin J. Humphreys, *The Miracles of Exodus: A Scientist's Discovery of the Extraordinary Natural Causes of the Biblical Stories* (New York: Harper Collins, 2004).

96 Norman L. Geisler, *Miracles and the Modern Mind: A Defence of Biblical Miracles* (Eugene, OR: Wipf & Stock, 1992), 141.

97 Geisler, *Miracles and the Modern Mind*, 141.

natural order are consistently pointing to the divine intervention in the Old Testament.[98]

The phrase *sign and wonder* with its plural form appears ten times in the Pentateuch, it is used in reference to God's performing of extraordinary events on behalf of Israel. Six of them refer to God's action in exodus event (Deut 4:34, 6:22, 7:19, 26:8, 29:3, 34:11). These signs and wonders from Yahweh in Egypt can be depicted in English as "great" (סילדג– Deut 6:22, 29:3), "disastrous" (סיערו– Deut 6:22), "great trials" תסמה) תלדגה– Deut 7:19, and 29:3), "great terrors" (סילדג סיארומבו– Deut 4:34, 26:8, and 34:12), "war" (המחלמ– Deut 4:34) and accompanied by God's "strong hand" (הקזח דיבו– Deut 4:34, 6:21-22, 7:19, 26:8, and 34:11-12) and "outstretched arm" (עורזבו היוטנ– Deut 4:34, 7:19, and 26:8), with eyewitness authentication (e.g. "before your eyes") being a noteworthy emphasis (Deut 4:34, 6:22, 7:19, 29:3, and 34:11-12). It is also employed in other parts of the Old Testament in reference to exodus events (Neh 9:10, Ps 78:43, 105:27, 135:9, and Jer 32:20-21), and also in identifying the role of prophets (Isa 8:18, and 20:3).[99] The absence of the term or phrase that can be translated as miracle makes it apparent that the cosmological worldview of the Old Testament does not comprehend modern scientific law of nature.

The use of signs and wonders mirrored the term miraculous, especially in the context of Joshua 3:5, in reference to the parting of the Jordan. Joshua declares, "Sanctify yourselves; for tomorrow the LORD will do wonders among you." Gideon in Judges 6:13 also use the same word to refer to the exodus events while he was speaking to the angel of the Lord. He asks the angel for a sign to authenticate his message (Judg 6:17).[100] The destruction of the altar at Bethel in response to the word of a prophet is also termed as a sign, but the actual Hebrew word used here is תפומ (môpēt) (1 Kgs 13:3). Miracles attributed to Elisha are also called "great things" in 2 Kings 8:4 (אלפנו - gĕdōlôth).[101]

### *3.4.1. Sign, Wonder, and Marvel*

The etymologies of the two words "sign" ('ôth) and "wonder" (môpēt) in the Old Testament are not without perplexity and complexity, but as minor as it may seem, few differentiations could be made between them. The usage of sign shows that the emphasis is burdened upon any aspect of the physical

98 Samuel A. Meier, "Signs and Wonders," *DOTP*: 755-762.

99 Meier, *DOTP*: 756.

100 Ernest C. Lucas, "Miracles," *DOTHB*: 695-701.

101 Lucas, *DOTHB*: 695.

world that is deliberately selected to inform, instruct or remind someone.[102] F. J. Helfmeyer's functional classification could be useful to clarify that a sign may have been used to impart information (cosmological sign – Gen 1:14; plagues in Egypt – Exod 7:3-5), to protect (Cain – Gen 4:15, Passover blood – Exod 12:13, altar covering – Num 17:3, and preservation of Aaron's rod – Num 17:1-11), to recall a covenant in particular (rainbow – Gen 9:12-17, circumcision – Gen 17:11, and Sabbath – Exod 31:13, 17), to confirm or corroborate (transformation for Moses – Exod 4:1-9, 30-31), or to symbolize a message (Isaiah and his children – Isa 8:18; 20:3, Ezek 4:3; 24:24).[103] It is also used of the banners that identified individual Israelite tribes in Numbers 2:2. Outside of Pentateuch, the sign often confirms or authenticates a divine or prophetic word (Judg 6:17, 1 Sam 2:34; 10:7, 9, and 2 Kgs 19:29; 20:9).

In other cases (Judg 6:17, and 1 Sam 10:7) the sign confirms a divine commissioning, also in the case of Moses in the book of Exodus (Exod 3:12). In the book of Joshua, the acts of God associated with the events from Exodus to the settlement in Canaan were described as great signs (Josh 24:17). Two different meanings of sign are clear in the Old Testament. The stones taken from the bed of the river Jordan are a sign in the sense that it functions as a memory for the Israelites to always remember something God had done for them. The other meaning is in the sense of wonder.[104]

The word wonder in Deuteronomy is always a part of the phrase sign(s) and wonder(s). In the book of Exodus, except in one place, the phrase always refer to the events that accompany the exodus (Exod 4:21, 7:9, and 11:9, 10).[105] Outside the Pentateuch the disaster that has overtaken an individual can become a môpēt (wonder) to others (Ps 71:7), just as Ezekiel becomes an omen or warning sign of calamities that will overtake Israel when he was acting in a bizarre way to illustrate Israel's condition (Ezek 12:6, 11; cf. Is 8:18; 20:3). The linking of the word with God's judgments in 1 Chronicles 16:12 and Psalm 105:5 are pointers to theological significance embedded in the use of the word. Nehemiah 9:10 can also be taken as an evidence that explicitly states the purpose of those signs and wonders as to impart knowledge about

---

102 R. Walter L. Moberly, "Miracles in the Hebrew Bible," in *The Cambridge Companion to Miracles*, CCR, ed. Graham H. Twelftree (Cambridge: CUP, 2011), 57-74.

103 Meier, *DOTP*: 758-759.

104 Lucas, *DOTHB*: 695. "Signs and wonders" in the Old Testament may not be suitably translated as miracles. However, as the interest of the study rest on the Old Testament's worldview and understanding of the relationship between the divine and natural world, comparison between terminologies does not gain interest. Comparison probably does not hinder the logical sequence of the study.

105 Meier, *DOTP*: 757; see also Moberly, "Miracles in the Hebrew Bible," 58-62. Exodus is another book in which this word appears (five times) in the Pentateuch.

God. The fundamental concern is thus to bring people to acknowledge that "the LORD is God; there is no other besides him" (Deut 4:35).[106]

There is a third term "marvel" (niplā'oth) that overlaps in meaning with "sign and wonder," but is employed only two times in the Pentateuch: used once in an anticipation of Exodus marvels (Exod 3:20) and the other time in an anticipation of the unique phenomena that will accompany the conquest of Canaan (Exod 34:10). This term is more prominent in Psalms and hymnic texts. The term could be translated in English as both marvel and wonder because it signifies the limited nature of human understanding or ability.[107] The word can also refer to a judicial decision that is too difficult for human beings to judge (Deut 17:8) or natural phenomena that are too marvellous for human beings to fathom (Prov 30:18-19). The root word is used also used in expression of the salvific acts of God in the exodus.[108] As noted before, it is significant that this word finds its correlation with extraordinary deeds in Judges 6:13 and Nehemiah 9:17. Furthermore, Joshua utilizes this same word in reference to the crossing of the Jordan (Josh 3:5). The cognate term péle (wonder, marvel) also appears in the context of the crossing of the Red Sea, and attributed the wondrous act to Yahweh (Exod 15:11).[109]

### 3.4.2. Mapping the Framework of the Old Testament's Worldview

It is also not startling that there is no Hebrew vocabulary which unequivocally corresponds to the English word "miracle." There is a danger in using the English word with reference to the Old Testament, as one may import unnecessary implications and overtones from historic debate.[110] As already noted, what the modern mind termed it as miracle could have easily been a sign of the activity of God according to an ancient Israelite.[111] Due to different philosophical and cosmological worldviews, the gap is widening when these literatures are viewed from modern lens.[112] The Old Testament connotation of a sign does not need to carry the implication of miraculous acts, but the term

106 Lucas, *DOTHB*: 695-696. Like the word sign, wonder can also refer to an event that confirms a prophetic word (1 Kgs 13:3, 5).

107 Lucas, *DOTHB*: 696; see also Meier, *DOTP*: 757.

108 Lucas, *DOTHB*: 696.

109 Meier, *DOTP*: 757.

110 Moberly, "Miracles in the Hebrew Bible," 57.

111 Meier, *DOTP*: 758; see also Herman Hendrickx, *The Miracle Stories of the Synoptic Gospels* (London: Geoffrey Chapman, 1987), 3-5.

112 A worldview is an understanding of the world that guides the way one lives in the world. It shapes one's answers – consciously or unconsciously – to the existential questions. Cosmology refers to the understanding of the whole universe as an organized, structured entity. Strictly speaking, it can be distinguished from cosmogony, which is an account of how the structured universe came into being. Cosmology and worldview are clearly related to each other, but a worldview is rather broader and vaguer than a cosmology. A

wonder may correlate closer to miracle. However, every wonder in the Old Testament could not be interpreted as miracle in modern sense.

### *3.4.2.1. Cause-and-Effect Nexus as Providence*

The appointment of Joseph over Egypt (Gen 41:41) was an uncomplicated decision made by Pharaoh in modern sense, but Joseph claimed that his deportation and even his appointment over Egypt were the will and acts of God (Gen 45:8-9). When Pharaoh hardened his heart (Exod 8:15, 32), it was also an act of God in the Old Testament and is notified many times (Exod 7:3; 9:12; 10:20, 27; 11:10). In the Pentateuch, conquering one's enemies (Gen 14:20), finding what one sought (Gen 21:19; 24:27, 48), the provision of rain and ground water (Gen 49:25), an individual's premature death (Gen 38:7, 10, and Exod 21:13), multiplication of flocks and herds (Gen 24:35; 26:12-14; 31:5-9), the mockery of one's peers (Gen 21:6), and the ability of a woman to bear children (Gen 16:2; 17:16; 20:17-18; 21:1-2; 25:21; 29:31; 30:2, 17, 22), are all in correlation with acts of God.[113]

What a person finds extraordinary depends largely on one's own worldview, which represents one's own prior knowledge, experience, and comprehension. Something which is unfathomable for an observer needs not to be inexplicable by natural laws; the understanding depends solely on a certain worldview.[114] Proverbs 30:18-19 profoundly highlights the degree of amazement for contemporary understanding of the natural world. The timing of occurrences made thing extraordinary, as seen in Saul's meetings with three different groups of people in sequence, each one as random encounter thus constitutes a series of signs (1 Sam 10:2-7).[115] There are other events that clearly relate with or deny the law of nature, such as the retreating shadow on the sundial due to the call of God by Isaiah in 2 Kings 20:11. Hezekiah, Isaiah or the writer of the book was well aware of the fact that the shadow of the sun normally did not retreat on the sundial. The thunderstorm at harvest season after Samuel's prayer to God also does not negate the knowledge of the people that thunderstorm normally did not happen during this time (1 Sam 12:16-18).

What is fundamental to this ancient worldview is the belief that the world is the creation of Yahweh (e.g. Gen 1:1-2:4a, Ps 8; 104, Isa 40:28).[116] Apart from the creation account of Genesis, Amos 5:8 also describes Yahweh as the one who created the stars and the one who continues to rule over day and night, and to cause the rains. In Isaiah 42:5 Yahweh is again described as the creator

---

worldview is however shaped to some degree by the cosmology held by a person or the community. Ernest C. Lucas, "Cosmology," *DOTP*: 130-139.

113 Meier, *DOTP*: 757-758.

114 Lucas, *DOTHB*: 696.

115 Lucas, *DOTHB*: 696.

116 See John H. Walton, "Creation," *DOTP*: 155-168.

of heaven and earth and also the one who gives *breath* and *spirit* to the people. Yahweh having created the world sends the rain (Ps 104:13) and causes the plants to grow to provide food for animals and human beings (Ps 104:14). Yahweh is also the one who takes away the breath/spirit of creatures so they die (Ps 104:29-30. Yahweh is clearly depicted as the creator and the sustainer of the world and its inhabitants.[117]

### *3.4.2.2. Nature as Autonomous*

Hugo Anthony Meynell, a philosopher argues that though the term nature is not to be found in the Old Testament, we can still employ it. The fact "that the Bible has no term corresponding to 'nature', does not enable us to answer the question whether, to make explicit what is implicit in the biblical account, we ourselves may have to use the term, or at least one more or less identical with it in meaning."[118] Therefore, the occurrences of natural elements in the Old Testament is not inappropriate to class and to envelope them under the term nature. The tension that can arise in the discussion between the definition of nature and experience of the natural world is apprehended, but the main object of the study is the question of how God and nature or natural world are generally correlated and co-existed without tension within the cosmological framework of the Old Testament.

John W. Rogerson in his paper read at the Joint British-Dutch Old Testament Conference held at Louvain in 1976 clearly asserts that, "Old Testament has no concept of nature corresponding to our idea of nature."[119] He also warns the reader of the Old Testament to make adjustment of the mind in order not to mislead oneself, and used Gerhard von Rad's argument to reinforce this warning.[120]

> We must now transfer uncritically our accustomed ways of thinking to Israel. We must, rather, face the exacting demand of thinking ourselves into ideas, into a 'view of life', which are unfamiliar to us... This can easily be shown in the case of the concept of 'nature', a concept which has become so indispensible to us but of which Israel was quite definitely unaware. Indeed, if we use the term in

117 Lucas, *DOTHB*: 697.

118 Hugo Anthony Meynell, *God and the World: The Coherence of Christian Theism* (London: SPCK, 1971), 92, quoted by John W. Rogerson, "The Old Testament View of Nature: Some Preliminary Questions," in *Instruction and Interpretation: Studies in Hebrew Language, Palestinian Archaeology and Biblical Exegesis* (Leiden: Brill, 1977), 67-84.

119 Rogerson, "The Old Testament View of Nature," 67.

120 Rogerson, "The Old Testament View of Nature," 67.

> the interpretation of Old Testament texts, then we falsify something that was quite specific to Israel's view.[121]

However, Rogerson feels that in the matter of the experience of the natural world, the differences between the Old Testament and modern experiences have been exaggerated. Thus, he argues for an alternate understanding that the experience of the natural world in the Old Testament in many respects may have been similar to modern experience, but the way of representing the experience may differ.[122]

Walther Eichrodt in his second volume of *Theology of the Old Testament* observes that "It is hardly going too far to describe this Old Testament view of the maintenance of the world as *creation continua*."[123] This understanding reflects that there is no effective distinction between God and nature, but the Old Testament depicts nature as having its own autonomy.[124] Isaiah 35:1-2 states the rejoicing of nature at the return of the exiles to Zion. Also in Isaiah 1:2 and Micah 6:1-2 state that the heavens and earth are called upon to bear witness of the case between Yahweh and people of Israel, and the case is to be presented before the mountains and the hills. The call of nature to praise God is quite common in the book of Psalms (e.g. Ps 69:34). It is unnecessary to ascribe the "animation of nature" entirely as the working of poetry, and also need not to be attributed to the psychological states of the psalmists, or their choices of literary devices.[125] This kind of perception and interpretation is thus a strong pointer to the Old Testament's consideration and worldview of autonomous character for both God and nature.

There is also probability of seeing that the Old Testament alluded to a belief in the psychic affinity between human beings and the celestial bodies. "Thus, according to Job (38:7), the stars were not mere passive spectators when God created the world, but joined in that cosmic praise which nature renders to God,

---

121 Gerhard von Rad, *Wisdom in Israel*, trans. James D. Martin (London: SCM, 1972), 71.

122 Rogerson, "The Old Testament View of Nature," 68.

123 Walther Eichrodt, *Theology of the Old Testament*, trans. J. A. Baker, 2 vols., OTL (London: SCM, 1964), 2:154.

124 Lucas, *DOTHB*: 697.

125 Daniel Grossberg, "The Literary Treatment of Nature in Psalms," in *Boundaries of the Ancient Near Eastern World: A Tribute to Cyrus H. Gordon*, ed. Meir Lubetski, Claire Gottlieb and Sharon Keller, JSOTSup 273 (Sheffield: SAP, 1998), 69-87; for further studies of nature in the Psalms, see Terence E. Fretheim, "Nature's Praise of God in the Psalms," *Ex Auditu* 3 (1987): 16-30; Benedict Janecko, "Ecology, Nature, Psalms," in *The Psalms and Other Studies on the Old Testament*, ed. Jack C. Knight and Lawrence A. Sinclair (Nashotah: Nashotah House Seminary, 1990), 96-108; R. J. Raja, "Eco-Spirituality in the Psalms," *Vidyajyoti Journal of Theological Reflection* 53 (1989): 637-650.

enjoying a position of beings provided with consciousness."[126] The psalmist in Psalm 148 not only addresses the animals and natural phenomena on the same level as human being, and also enjoins these animals and elements to celebrate the Lord as human beings do.[127] The hymn includes the whole of creation, and is notable that the western distinctions between inanimate and animate, non-human beings and human beings are absent.[128] Claus Westermann puts it "all that exists is one in creatureliness."[129] He has been also quite sensitive to what the Bible says about nature, and especially to its importance for Christian faith. Thus he "notes that Psalm 148 is seldom used in Christian worship because such worship deals almost exclusively with relationships between God and humans, and other creatures hardly ever appear."[130]

The particular interest in the Old Testament's worldview is not exhaustive, but seems to suffice the foundation for this present study. A major difference between the Old Testament's worldview and particularly to that of general modern outlook is that the ancient thought is not self-contained in terms of the physical causes of events but linger onto the one who was the author of the events.[131] Due to this difference, John P. Ross in his essay, "Some Notes on Miracle in the Old Testament" in an edited *Miracles: Cambridge Studies in Their Philosophy and History* makes a convincing conclusion for the reason of the cause of the outlook of Old Testament.[132] Thus, according to Ross, the world was not primarily a physical structure for the Old Testament, but it is a power structure.[133] It is a power structure in the sense of the understanding of God's sustenance.

Though nature is partly viewed as being autonomous, the regular and normal working of natural world is not seen too much as self mechanism but

126 Luis I. J. Stadelmann, *The Hebrew Conception of the World*, AnBib 39 (Rome: Pontifical Biblical Institute, 1970), 94, cited by Grossberg, "The Literary Treatment of Nature in Psalms," 85.

127 Grossberg, "The Literary Treatment of Nature in Psalms," 85.

128 Ann Jeffers, "The Earth is Full of Your Creatures," The Way, 24- 33 (26), http:/www.theway.org.uk/ba-ck/s087Jeffers.pdf.

129 Claus Westermann, *The Living Psalms* (Edinburg: T&T Clark, 1989), 259.

130 James Limburg, "Quoth the Raven: Psalm 147 and the Environment," in *A God So Near: Essays on Old Testament Theology in Honor of Patrick D. Miller*, ed. Brent A. Strawn and Nancy R. Bowen (Winona Lake, IN: Eisenbrauns, 2003), 101-112 (103), citing Claus Westermann, "Mensch, Tier und Pflanze in der Bibel," in *Gefährten und Feinde des Menschen: Das Tier in der Lebenswelt des alten Israel*, ed. Bernd Janowski, Ute Neumann-Gorsolke and Uwe Glebmer (Neukirchen-Vluyn: Neukirchener, 1993), 90-106.

131 Lucas, *DOTHB*: 697.

132 John P. Ross, "Some Notes on Miracles in the Old Testament," in *Miracles: Cambridge Studies in Their Philosophy and History*, ed. C. F. D. Moule (London: Mowbray, 1965), 43-60.

133 Ross, "Some Notes on Miracles in the Old Testament," 50.

the expression of the faithfulness of God who created and sustains the world. The continual sustenance of day and night cycle (Gen 1:16-18), the succession of seasons (Gen 8:22) are not just normal eventuality, but the acts of God. Miracles in the Old Testament are not perceived as what a modern mind acknowledges miracle, and are more inclined to the wonderful power of God, rather than the events themselves. McKenzie states that "the basis of wonder in the works of judgment and redemption is not the rare or the extraordinary, but the saving will of Yahweh towards His people; Yahweh is never more wonderful than when He appears as the helper and savior of Israel."[134]

## 3.5. God, Nature and Miracle within the Cosmological Worldview of Graeco-Roman Writers

Wendy Cotter in her *Miracles in Graeco-Roman Antiquity* distinguishes "miracle stories" from "nature's freakish wonders... genetic anomalies, or nature's strange and inexplicable phenomenon."[135] By following Bultmann, she divides miracle stories into four classes, such as healings, exorcisms, raisings from the dead, and nature miracles. Miracle stories according to her, are "those narratives in which a wonderful rescue or salvation of someone takes place by the overturning of 'the canons of the ordinary' through the intervention of a deity or hero."[136] The main problem in this sourcebook is the lack of definition for the phrase "Greco-Roman Antiquity" and the time span is more than 1300 years and come from various cultural and linguistic communities.[137] Therefore, the following is an attempt to look at specifically miracles that are associated with natural world or those that could be classified as nature miracles. Moreover, Cotter's third chapter which centre around four of Jesus' nature miracles will serve as a valuable entry point for further understanding of how nature is understood in relation to divine abilities in Graeco-Roman sources.

134 McKenzie, "God and Nature in the Old Testament," 139.

135 Wendy Cotter, *Miracles in Greco-Roman Antiquity: A Sourcebook for the Study of New Testament Miracle Stories* (London: Routledge, 1999), 1-2.

136 "The canons of the ordinary" is a phrase used by Harold Remus to express the system that holds within the cosmic order. Harold Remus, *Pagan—Christian Conflict Over Miracle in the Second Century*, PMS 10 (Cambridge, MA: The Philadelphia Patristic Foundation, 1983), 7-26, cited by Cotter, *Miracles in Greco-Roman Antiquity*, 2.

137 Robert Seesengood, review of Wendy Cotter, *Miracles in Greco-Roman Antiquity: A Sourcebook for the Study of New Testament Miracle Stories*, *Stone-Campbell journal* 4 (2001):140-142; see also Darrell L. Bock, review of Wendy Cotter, *Miracles in Greco-Roman Antiquity: A Sourcebook for the Study of New Testament Miracle Stories*, *BBR* 10 (2000): 313-314.

### *3.5.1. Nature and God*

The word "nature" (φύσις) is employed in a wide range of meanings. The meaning of the word has no single meaning among the pre-Socrates philosophers, in Plato, in Aristotle, in Epicurus, and among the Stoics, and thus carries with it various ideas.[138] Most frequently it means the essence of something, and less frequently the power or arrangement of nature, and infrequently it means the origin of something.[139] The Stoics used the term "nature" loosely and could connote a wide range of meaning, such as the whole of the universe, god, Zeus, the rational principle of the universe, the first cause, providence, a spirit or a fire.[140] They also speak of nature sometimes as embracing the universe and sometimes as producing things on earth, and also define it as "a self-moved condition (*hexis*) which follows inseminated rational principles and produces and preserves its products in definite periods of time, and produces effects which corresponds to their causes."[141]

What is significant in the development of the idea is the rise and gradual diffusion of the idea of cosmic "sympathy," a theory later became prominent among the astrologers who used it to explain the influence of the stars on the earth.[142] The later understanding dislocated the autonomies for both God and nature, and in the Hippocratic corpus the differentiation between nature, God and human beings is ambiguously understood.[143] This point of reference is crucial in this study because the Old Testament writers understand nature as enjoying autonomy, and also in Christian writings such identification of God and nature or even human beings without autonomous character in Graeco-Roman thought was impossible.[144] Therefore, the thesis is that the Gospel writers in particular understand nature in a sense that is much more connected and inclined to the Jewish roots rather than their contemporary Graeco-Roman thoughts.

---

138 Grant, *Miracle and Natural Law*, 4.

139 Grant, *Miracle and Natural Law*, 5.

140 Grant, *Miracle and Natural Law*, 8.

141 Grant, *Miracle and Natural Law*, 8.

142 Most famous example of "sympathy" is the iron which the magnet draws to itself. Cleomedes argues that the moon has greater "sympathy" for the earth because it is closer to the earth than the other stars. Under this framework of "sympathy" Cleomedes further argues that nature must control whatever exists, and tries to prove this with his five points: (1) There is order in the various parts of the universe, (2) there is order in the things which come into being, (3) there is "sympathy" among the various parts of the universe, (4) each part was made for some purpose, and (5) everything in the universe is useful and advantageous. Grant, *Miracle and Natural Law*, 9.

143 Grant, *Miracle and Natural Law*, 10-11.

144 Grant, *Miracle and Natural Law*, 18.

### *3.5.2. Nature Miracles of Heroes and Gods*

It was common for "divine men" of the Graeco-Roman world to "reveal their divinity through the miracles that accompany their births, and characterize their lives and make them triumph over death."[145] The tendency to customarily ascribed miracles to philosophical heroes is also evident in the rhetoric of Neoplatonism, and a biographer has to apologize when there is no miracle available for the person of concern.[146] The thought that miracles had to accompany the lives of great men was common and in Diogenes Laertius 4:64, the lunar eclipse at the death of Carneades was understood as reflecting the cosmic sympathy of the moon.[147] Therefore, the cosmological worldview within which the Graeco-Roman thinking revolves is quite similar in a sense that natural world, miracles and daily incidents were intermingled without much difficulty.

Cotter presents a list of gods and heroes of Graeco-Roman times who were capable of controlling nature.[148] Here the list will not be reproduced because the interest is already attained in the fact that the possibility to manipulate or control nature is not an unfamiliar idea and is not rejected in the framework of the Graeco-Roman thoughts, philosophical and scientifically accommodated. Therefore, without listing all the occurrences of miracle stories, it is best to understand that there is no or less tension when divine action and natural world are kept under a certain working methodology.

Moreover, the relevancy of Graeco-Roman miracle stories towards the study of Jesus' activity and the Gospel materials need serious consideration. Craig S. Keener, in his essay, "Jesus and Parallel Jewish and Greco-Roman Figures" states that miracles in Graeco-Roman world mostly fall into different classes, such as: direct intervention by deities, cures at healing shrines, stories about a distant mythical era, secretive magic, and occasional reports of the travelling sage-healer.[149]

The last figures of the list is being considered as most relevant for the study of historical Jesus, but Keener adds that these reports do not flourish

145 H. Windisch, *Paulus und Christus* (Leipzig: Hinrichs, 1934), 24-89; L. Bieler, *Theios Aner*, 2 vols. (Vienna: Höfel, 1935-1936); cited by Grant, *Miracle and Natural Law*, 165.

146 Eunapius (*Vit. Phil.* 471 ed. Boissonade) explains that a certain Antonius had no tendency to theurgy, perhaps because of imperial opposition to sorcery, cited by Grant, *Miracle and Natural Law*, 165.

147 Grant, *Miracle and Natural Law*, 165.

148 For the list, see Cotter, *Miracles in Greco-Roman Antiquity*, 130-172.

149 Craig S. Keener, "Jesus and Parallel Jewish and Greco-Roman Figures," in *Christian Origins and Greco-Roman Culture: Social and Literary Contexts for the New Testament*, ed. Stanley Porter and Andrew W. Pitts, vol. 1 of *Early Christianity in its Hellenistic Context*, vol. 9 in *Texts and Editions for New Testament Study* (Leiden: Brill, 2013), 85-111 (86).

widely till the third century CE. He further says that these reports may be a response to the growing Christian movement's account.[150] After carefully considering Graeco-Roman, Qumran, and Jewish sources, he came to the conclusion that miracle performers of Graeco-Roman period offer little basis for the understanding of the earliest Jewish tradition of Jesus.[151] He further argues that various Palestinian Jewish figures and the understanding of prophets, messiahs, and other exalted figures better inform how Jesus' earliest followers constructed Jesus' identity.[152]

Nina Henrichs-Tarasenkova, in her 2016 book *Luke's Christology of Divine Identity*, provides an interesting example for this argument, that the earliest followers of Jesus are not in need of Graeco-Roman miracle stories to construct Jesus' identity.[153]

> Luke encourages his readers (1) to construct Jesus' identity only in relation to YHWH, claiming for him the position of his Father YHWH, the Lord of heaven and earth, and presenting Elizabeth and John as models for any God-fearer to follow as they recognize Jesus' superior position through the Holy Spirit; (2) to attribute to Jesus responsibilities and functions of YHWH himself; and (3) to accept that Jesus carries out YHWH's responsibilities and functions successfully.[154]

Henrichs-Tarasenkova further shows that the way Luke characterizes Jesus and the Father God in such a way that they are impossible to be distinguished from one another. Therefore, it is more probable to accept that the Gospel writers adapted elements from Jewish Tradition and utilized it in such a way that is distinctive in presenting Jesus for their own theological and contextual purposes.

## 3.6. God, Nature and Miracle within the Cosmological Worldview of Second Temple Period Writers

The time frame for this period encompasses, before the destruction of the temple in 70 CE and the time after the destruction of the temple, when rival sectarian groups eventually disappeared.[155] They are the two distinct epochs in Jewish history, and the latter period of time witnessed the rise of

---

150 Keener, "Jesus and Parallel Jewish and Greco-Roman Figures," 86.

151 Keener, "Jesus and Parallel Jewish and Greco-Roman Figures," 110-111.

152 Keener, "Jesus and Parallel Jewish and Greco-Roman Figures," 110-111.

153 Nina Henrichs-Tarasenkova, *Luke's Christology of Divine Identity*, LNTS (London: T&T Clark, 2016),

154 Henrichs-Tarasenkova, *Luke's Christology of Divine Identity*, 194.

155 The period of second temple Judaism for Lester L. Grabbe starts from the Persian period 539 BCE. *An Introduction to the Second Temple Judaism: History and Religion of the*

rabbinic Judaism, the cessation of sacrificial worship, and the emphasis was shifted towards the synagogue and the Torah.[156] Martin Hengel emphasized that Hellenistic Judaism must be the designation for all Judaism in a strict sense from the time period of around the middle of the third century BCE.[157] However, the differences between Jewish and Hellenistic worldviews and the degree of Hellenization of the Jewish people inside Palestine and diaspora Judaism make it difficult to put them under a single framework.

There is no proper Christian form of miracle stories, because the essential characteristics found are similar to that of the corresponding miracle stories in Jewish and other ancient religions.[158] Therefore, rabbinic, Wisdom, Enochic and the book of *Jubilees* will be taken up in this next section to see how God and nature are understood within their working framework of cosmological worldview.

### *3.6.1. Rabbinic Literature*

In the Tannaitic period of early rabbinic Judaism, Honi the circle-drawer and Hanina ben Dosa were known for their miraculous abilities, and also for their compassion and piteous life. Honi was associated with nature miracle in a loose sense but Hanina was not ascribed any miraculous power except miraculous knowledge. According to Lidija Novakovic this type of miracle worker had received significant scholarly attention especially after the suggestion made by Geza Vermes that Jesus of Nazareth also belongs to this category.[159] As the context in which these two individuals worked their miracles is that of a lower socio-economic circumstance, it also seems appropriate to compare them with Jesus of Nazareth. Their piety and dependence to God are also evident from their stories being narrated. Though they were opposed by the priestly establishment and the Pharisaic teachers of the Law, their miracles were eventually "incorporated into and transmitted through the rabbinic literature."[160]

---

*Jews in the Time of Nehemiah, The Maccabees, Hillel and Jesus* (London: T&T Clark, 2010), xi.

156 Lidija Novakovic, "Miracles in Second Temple and Early Rabbinic Judaism," in *The Cambridge Companion to Miracles*, CCR, ed. Graham H. Twelftree, (Cambridge: CUP, 2011), 95-112.

157 Martin Hengel, *Judaism and Hellenism: Studies in their Encounter in Palestine during the Early Hellenistic Period* (London: SCM, 1974), 104.

158 Hendrickx, *The Miracle Stories of the Synoptic Gospels*, 7.

159 Geza Vermes, "Hanina ben Dosa: A Controversial Galilean Saint from the First Century of the Christian Era," *JSJ* 23 (1972): 28-50, cited by Novakovic, "Miracles in Second Temple,"110.

160 Novakovic, "Miracles in Second Temple," 103.

The rabbinic sages faced complex issue in regards to miracles that cannot be solved with ease. They cannot deny nor uncritically accept miracles because they would deny the saving power of God or invite chaos among them.[161] The reason is the sayings of the possibility of God's sending of false prophets in order to test them (Deut 13:2-4). The presence of various miracle workers in rabbinic literature cannot be encompassed here, but the lens is fixed to those that are in contact with natural world. Midrashic literature suggests that God made an arrangement during the six days of creation with the sea, the sun and the moon, the ravens, the fire, the lions, and the fish (*Gen. Rab.* 5.5; *Exo. Rab.* 21.6).[162] These are in connection with the Israelites passing through the sea, the sun and moon standing still for Joshua, the ravens were feeding Elijah, the fire did not harm Hananiah, Mishael and Azariah, the lions did not devour Daniel, and the fish swallow Jonah. These references of God making arrangement with natural elements make it clear that, the idea of nature as being autonomous and the interaction between God and nature is engulfed under the framework of their worldview on miracles.

The Mishnaic tractate *Chapters of the Father* also contains the origin of various entities of nature which occurred in the Old Testament narratives.

> Ten things were created on the eve of the Sabbath at twilight, namely: The mouth of the earth [that swallowed Korach], the mouth of the well [which furnished water in the desert], the mouth of the ass [that spoke to Balaam], the rainbow [which appeared after the flood], the manna, the shamir [used to cut the stones that were used to build the Temple], the shape of the written characters, the engraving instrument, and the tablets of stone (*m. PirqêAvôth* 5.8).[163]

The attempt to compromise the two poles of argument is evident in this kind of thinking, because the defending of the Old Testament nature miracles and that nature had been working as preordained is significant. The created order contains both normal forces and hidden or extraordinary forces are another attempt in answering the problem at hand. Thus, these Midrashic views made an attempt to preserve the idea of faithful God and an orderly world.[164] This also implies that the order of nature cannot be contained in the realm of what modern science could explain. This kind of synthesis may have contributed in much of the thrust of medieval philosophy where the role of miracles had to be justified.

---

161 Kenneth Seeskin, "Miracles in the Jewish Philosophy," in *The Cambridge Companion to Miracles*, ed. Graham H. Twelftree, CCR (Cambridge: CUP, 2011), 254-270.

162 Seeskin, "Miracles in the Jewish Philosophy," 255.

163 Quoted in Seeskin, "Miracles in the Jewish Philosophy," 255.

164 Seeskin, "Miracles in the Jewish Philosophy," 255-256.

During the Second Temple period, exorcism practices and demonology were steadily accommodated within the framework of God's relationship to the world.[165] But Eric Eve cautions that miracles were not a common theme in its literature, and that talk of exorcism, too, was rare; instead, the authors of such works "were more interested in keeping the law, in the history or prospects of the nation, or in wisdom and right living, or in the revelation of heavenly realities, or in promoting their own party."[166] An example can be seen in the *Mekhilta of R. Yismael* that uses the book of Exodus as the basic text for commentary, and it includes a great amount of miracle traditions. But, a closer look at this commentary shows that central biblical miracle texts do not receive an explanation. Thus, Michael Becker in his essay "Miracle Traditions in Early Rabbinic Literature: Some Questions on their Pragmatics" argues that "even if the early rabbis did understand the biblical events in a realistic manner and regarded them as the special signature of a divine intervention for the sake of Israel, miracles were not the object of their prominent interest."[167]

Miracles are according to Erkki Koskenniemi, only one piece of the picture a writer of Second Temple Judaism draws of a biblical hero.[168] There are writers who ignore Moses' miracles, but in Philo's and Josephus' texts Moses is a philosopher, general, statesman and miracle-worker. However, though Josephus gave the only complete account of a Jewish healer from Second Temple period, the overall view of miracles and magic in Josephus' writings is ambiguous according to Lidija Novakovic.[169] Novakovic further states that Josephus' narration of Israel's history is founded on "his belief in divine providence and the conviction that God intervenes in human affairs as revealed in sacred Texts, whose sanctity and inspiration Josephus vigorously defends (*Ag.Ap.* 1.42-3; 2.218-29)."[170] Eve remarks that "Josephus occasionally stresses that a miracle is outside the ordinary course of nature (e.g. *Ant.* 4.48-53). He occasionally suggests that a natural explanation can rob a sign of its

165 The justification of exorcistic practices is done by ascribing them to prominent biblical figures such as Abraham, David and Solomon. Examples are 1Qap Gen 20:16-29, 11Q5, 11Q11; LAB 16:3 (First Century CE document pseudonymously attributed to Philo). Novakovic, "Miracles in Second Temple," 97-98.

166 Eric Eve, *The Jewish Context of Jesus' Miracles*, JSNTSup 231 (New York: SAP, 2002), 244; see also J. R. Daniel Kirk, *A Man Attested by God: The Human Jesus of the Synoptic Gospels* (Grand Rapids, MI: Eerdmans, 2016), 486.

167 Michael Becker, "Miracle Traditions in Early Rabbinic Literature: Some Questions on their Pragmatics," in *Wonders Never Cease: The Purpose of Narrating Miracle Stories in the New Testament and its Religious Environment*, ed., Michael Labahn and Bert Jan Lietaert Peerbolte (London: T&T Clark, 2006), 48-69 (56).

168 Erkki Koskenniemi, *The Old Testament Miracle-Workers in Early Judaism*, WUNT 206 (Tübingen: Mohr, 2005), 14.

169 Novakovic, "Miracles in Second Temple," 99.

170 Novakovic, "Miracles in Second Temple," 99.

miraculous significance (*Ant.* 8.243-45)."[171] Therefore, it is to be understood that Josephus did not reject nature miracles of the Old Testament.

Apart from other miraculous acts, Josephus explicit mentioning of Moses' speech (*Ant* 2.286) makes it clear that in his attempt to distinguish between magic that comes from human trickery and genuine miracles that come from God, he identifies miracles performed by Moses as genuine.[172] It can be concluded that in similarity with the Gospel writers, Josephus also believed in nature miracles and regarded them as significant.[173] The matter of the fact is that the earlier writers do not really have in mind what modern science had imposed to modern writers and readers.

Josephus also recorded various accounts where individuals promised to perform certain miraculous signs which are similar to those of the events of the exodus and the conquest.[174] However, these are insignificant because Josephus did not report the actual performing of miracles, and thus there are scholars who question the understanding of these individuals as miracle workers.[175] From a different angle Novakovic convincingly points out that even if this is the case it is still important or worth exploring due to the fact that it points to the role of miracles and miracle workers in the context of the uprisings and resistance movements in Palestine during the first century CE.[176] However, the interest is on the nature miracles and the worldview, in which they were situated. The understanding of natural world as a created order and the actuality of an intervention by the creator is still at large under the working framework of the worldviews of both the Old Testament and the Second Temple Judaism (e.g. *1 En.* 72:1; and the expectations for the age to come is referred to several times – cf. *1 En.* 1:3-9; 5:6-9; 10:7; 10:16-11:2; 25:3-7).

---

171 Eve, *The Jewish Context of Jesus' Miracles*, 24.

172 Pharoah dismisses Moses' miraculous signs with the pretext that the Egyptian priests can also perform such spectacles. In his reply, Moses emphasizes that his own miraculous deeds "so far surpass their magic (*mageia*) and their art (*technē*) as things divine (*ta theia*) are remote from what is human (*ta anthrōpina*)." Novakovic, "Miracles in Second Temple," 100; see also George MacRae, "Miracles in the Antiquities of Josephus," in *Miracles: Cambridge Studies in their Philosophy and History*, ed. C. F. D. Moule (London: Mowbray, 1965), 129-147; Otto Betz, "Miracles in the Writings of Flavius Josephus," in *Josephus, Judaism, and Christianity*, ed. Louis H. Feldman and Gohei Hata (Detroit: Wayne State University Press, 1987), 212-235.

173 Eve, *The Jewish Context of Jesus' Miracles*, 52.

174 Paul W. Barnett, "The Jewish Sign Prophets – A.D. 40-70: Their Intentions and Origin," *NTS* 27 (1981): 679-697.

175 John P. Meier, *Rethinking the Historical Jesus: Mentor, Message, and Miracles*, vol. 2 of *A Marginal Jew: Rethinking the Historical Jesus*, ABRL (New York: Doubleday, 1994), 529.

176 Novakovic, "Miracles in Second Temple," 101.

Philo also resounds similar understanding when he asserts three things that are characteristic of his view of miracles. They are events that objectively occur; they are events that are sharply demarcated from the normal run of things as παράδοξα... παράλογα; and they are manifestly acts of God, for only God could perform them.[177] Both Josephus and Philo include miracles of provision in their narratives. Apart from creation, the plagues in Egypt, and miraculous supply of food and water in exodus event (*Vit. Mos.* 1.185-186, 199-200, 206, 210-212; 2.258-259; *Spec. Leg.* 2.199; 4.127-130; *Dec.* 16; *Congr.* 173), Philo also added creation and re-creation of nature: trees created ready-laden with fruit (*Op. Mund.* 40), plants created before the heavens were furnished (*Op. Mund.* 47), disposal of the flood waters (*Quaest. in Gen.* 2.28), and renewal of earthly flora after the flood (*Quaest. in Gen.* 2.47). Strengthening of the link between miracle and creation is further furbished in the narrative where the manna miracle is likened to the creation of the world (*Vit. Mos.* 2.267). Just as God called up the world out of nothing, God also called up plenty of manna in the wilderness.[178]

What is significant in Josephus is the scarcity of healing miracles, and more striking is the absent of healing miracles in Philo. Even the Old Testament does not contain many healing miracles, an even fewer in the Pentateuch. These can be analyzed from different perspectives, but the lack of healing miracles in these sources could be a pointer for the impact of contextual worldview that see God as creator and nature as constantly under God's control and instrument.

### 3.6.2. Wisdom Literature

The Ancient Israelites, similarly with their neighbouring Egyptians and Mesopotamians had a sense of awe in embracing the harmony and wonder of creation. The Old Testament is unique in seeing the creation as coming from Yahweh, the creator of heaven and earth. To them to live in a world created by God also means to live in relation and communion with the creator.[179] The Wisdom of Solomon and the book of Sirach also show this genuine awestruck sensation toward creation, and thus the interrelationship between God, nature and miracles are the interest in this study. This pin pointing of different themes from these literatures may shed light that will probably help in understanding the continuing trends of cosmological worldview in Jewish literature and also to situate the influence of this worldview in the New Testament, especially in the Gospels.

177 Eve, *The Jewish Context of Jesus' Miracles*, 55, citing Harry Austryn Wolfson, *Philo*, 2 vols. (Cambridge: HUP, 1947-1948), 1:354.

178 Eve, *The Jewish Context of Jesus' Miracles*, 78.

179 Craig G. Bartholomew and Ryan P. O' Dowd, *Old Testament Wisdom Literature: A Theological Introduction* (Downers Grove, IL: IVP, 2011), 15.

### *3.6.2.1. Wisdom of Solomon*

Though it is generally agreed that Greek was the original compositional language of Wisdom of Solomon, but the date and provenance are still ambiguous. The major witnesses for its original compositional language are Codices Sinaiticus, Vaticunus and Alexandrinus.[180] Since Wisdom of Solomon seems to be in contact with the Septuagint the earliest date could be around 200 BCE, and David Winston had identified a number of vocabularies from Wisdom of Solomon that was not attested elsewhere until the first century CE.[181] Therefore, Eve places Wisdom of Solomon in the early Roman period, and argues that it is impossible to be more precise than this dating.[182] Scholars however differ on the dating of Wisdom of Solomon, and the scope limits the study to thoroughly enquire the date and provenance.

Wisdom of Solomon lacks regular wording for the miracle stories, but the vocabularies used in connection with miracle includes *σημεῖον*, *τέρας*, *θαυμαστός* and *παράδοξος*, and none of these were used with frequency.[183] As with the other ancient sources briefly discussed, Wisdom of Solomon is also quite interested in the exodus events.[184] Especially, Wisdom of Solomon 11-19 portrays the exodus as a series of miracles in which natural elements changed their properties.[185]

According to Richard J. Clifford in his 1998 book *The Wisdom Literature*, these interests are the influences from Hellenistic religion that "a religion had to be old and for what was new needed validation by the old."[186] This is understandable when there was a need for accommodation under the framework of contemporary philosophy. This idea is implicit in Wisdom of Solomon 19:18, where it says: "For the elements changed places with one

---

180 David Winston, *The Wisdom of Solomon: A New Translation with Introduction and Commentary*, AB 43 (Garden City: Doubleday, 1979), 64-66; cited by Eve, *The Jewish Context of Jesus' Miracles*, 87; for the original language of the book, see also Ernest G. Clarke, *The Wisdom of Solomon*, CBC (Cambridge: CUP, 1973), 6-8; M. Gilbert, "Wisdom Literature," in *Jewish Writings of the Second Temple Period*, ed. Michael E. Stone (Philadelphia: Fortress, 1984), 283-324.

181 Winston, *The Wisdom of Solomon*, 22-23, cited by Eve, *The Jewish Context of Jesus' Miracles*, 87.

182 Eve, *The Jewish Context of Jesus' Miracles*, 87.

183 Eve, *The Jewish Context of Jesus' Miracles*, 89.

184 See Samuel Cheon, *The Exodus Story in the Wisdom of Solomon: A Study in Biblical Interpretation*, JSPSup 23 (Sheffield: SAP, 1997).

185 Richard J. Clifford, *Wisdom*, NCBC, ed. Daniel Durken (Collegeville: Liturgical Press, 2012), 1146.

186 Richard J. Clifford, *The Wisdom Literature*, IBT (Nashville: Abingdon Press, 1998), 137. Three ancient events were often cited as standards of antiquity in Hellenistic literature, such as Semiramis, the legendary founder of Assyria, The Trojan War, the oldest datable event in Greek history, and the Flood.

another, as on a harp the notes vary the nature of the rhythm, while each note remains the same."[187] The elements in this text are fire, earth and water, but air is not mentioned explicitly. The following verse makes reference to the interchanging of land and water creatures, each moving in other's environment. The allusion is regarded as the passing through the sea in exodus event, and presumably to the plague of frogs that had infested the land of Egypt. Verse 20 also discusses the rain that failed to quench the lightning (fire) in the plague of hail and also the fire that failed to destroy the manna that could be easily melted by the sun's rays. However, this imagery of the harp is ambiguous, and Winston argues that the reference is to the changing of the chords rather than the rhythm, but it does not change the underlying point.[188] Thus, the idea of God's ability to intervene in natural order and to control the elements is crystallized in the book.

#### *3.6.2.2. The Book of Sirach*

Yeshua Ben Sira is the Hebrew name of the author of the book of Ben Sira, and thus the Wisdom of Ben Sira is the Hebrew name, and Sirach in Greek (Sir 50:27). There are commentaries that employ the name Ben Sira for the author and Sirach for the book, and will also be followed here.[189] The author of Ben Sira may have been running some kind of educational school in the city (Sir 51:23), but scholars dispute on the exact time when schools arose in the ancient Israel.[190] As the description of the scribe in 39:1-11 provides some kind of self portrait of the author, Jeremy Corley states the possibility of the author as being one of the scribes of the Temple mentioned in Josephus (*Ant.* 12.3.3.142).[191] The dating claimed in the prologue is widely accepted. The statement, "For in the thirty-eight year, in the reign of Euergetes the king..." is understood as the reign of Ptolemy VII Physkon Euergetes II, who began to rule in 170 BCE, and thus the thirty-eight year would fall on 132 BCE, but the main body of work is mostly dated between 190-180 BCE.[192]

---

187 Eve, *The Jewish Context of Jesus' Miracles*, 91.

188 Winston, *The Wisdom of Solomon*, 330-331, cited by Eve, *The Jewish Context of Jesus' Miracles*, 91; see also J. P. M. Sweet, "The Theory of Miracles in the Wisdom of Solomon," in *Miracles*, ed. C. F. D. Moule (London: Mowbrays, 1965), 113-126.

189 Jeremy Corley, "The Book of Sirach," in *Old Testament*, ed. Daniel Durken (Collegeville: Liturgical Press, 2012), 1188-1254.

190 Corley, "The Book of Sirach," 1188.

191 Corley, "The Book of Sirach," 1188.

192 Richard J. Coggins, *Sirach* (Sheffield: SAP, 1998), 18-19; cf. Corley, "The Book of Sirach," 1188-1189.

Ben Sira is deeply impressed by the sense and significance of the order in the entire creation, and thus concerns himself with this topic variously.[193] In Sirach the cosmological interest is foremost evident in how Ben Sira signifies the virtue of modesty by saying that one cannot be successful without it while considering the order in creation (Sir 3:18, 20). As the natural order of the world is the miracle of the creation according to Ben Sira, and the miracles are so diverse that even God's holy ones cannot count them (Sir 42:17).

In Sirach 42:18 and 21, Ben Sira talks about the absolute sovereignty of God and how God does not need anyone for instruction. God oversees everything and no thoughts could escape God (Sir 42:20). For Ben Sira the result of the creation through the word (Sir 42:15) is a meaningful entireness locked in itself, and thus need no further additions: "How desirable are all his works, and how sparkling they are to see! All this things live and remain forever; each creature is preserved to meet a particular need. All things come in pairs, one opposite the other, and he has made nothing incomplete. Each supplements the virtues of the other. Who could ever tire of seeing his glory?" (Sir 42:22-25).[194]

Ben Sira narrates Elisha as performing miracles, during his lifetime, and also after death (Sir 48:13-14). These kinds of miracles come in contact with modern law of nature and negate the worldview of today's scientific world, but Ben Sira further emphasises the overcoming of death.[195] Isaiah's career in conjunction with Hezekiah is also mentioned, Sirach 48:20-21 talks about how God saved through Isaiah by smiting the Assyrian camp during the invasion by Sennacherib (Sir 48:20-21). Isaiah also lengthened the life of a king and the evidence was the sign of the reversing sun (Sir 48:23). The only prophetic activity attributed to Isaiah is the revelation of the things to come in the distant future, and showed the hidden things before they even happened (Sir 48:24-25).

Joshua is also included among these figures and the reason is mainly not by his words but because of his deeds. According to Koskenniemi, Joshua was considered as a bridge between Moses and Judges in Sirach.[196] The miraculous acting of Joshua in the event where the sun stood still and the

---

193 Friedrich Vincenz Reiterer, "The Interpretation of the Wisdom Tradition of the Torah within Ben Sira," in *Deuterocanonical and Cognate Literature Studies*, ed. Friedrich V. Reiterer, Beate Ego and Tobias Niklas, vol. 1 of *The Wisdom of Ben Sira: Studies in Tradition, Redaction, and Theology*, ed. Angelo Passaro and Giuseppe Bellia (Berlin: de Gruyter, 2008), 209-232 (211).

194 Reiterer, "The Interpretation of the Wisdom Tradition," 212-213.

195 Alon Goshen-Gottstein, "Ben Sira's Praise of the Fathers: A Canon-Conscious Reading," in *Ben Sira's God: Proceedings of the International Ben Sira Conference* (Durham – Ushaw College 2001), ed. Renate Egger-Wenzel, BZAW 321 (Berlin: Gruyter, 2002), 235-267 (255).

196 Koskenniemi, *The Old Testament Miracle-Workers in Early Judaism*, 28-29.

enemies were conquered by hail sent by God is recorded in Sirach 46:4-6. Joshua 10:8-15, than any other passages seem to inspire Ben Sira the most, because the parallels are quite transparent in Sirach 46:3-5.[197] It is certain that these parallels were not incidental in nature and scope. The miraculous acts of Joshua perhaps stimulated Ben Sira and thus count him among the prophets (cf. Sir 46:1). How Ben Sira understands the prophetic figures as being able to perform miracles is also embedded fairly in his inclusion of Joshua among his list.[198]

### 3.6.3. Early Enochic Writings and the Book of Jubilees

1 Enoch is a composite work and represents numerous periods and writers.[199] James C. VanderKam argues for a date between 161 and 152 BCE for the book of *Jubilees*, and the proposal is the outcome of the incorporation of certain battles of Judas Maccabeus, and the inclusion of other anti-Antiochian motifs.[200]

Josephus (*War* 2.137) reported that the Essenes "apply themselves with extraordinary zeal to the study of the works of the ancients," and from these

197 Marko Marttila, *Foreign Nations in the Wisdom of Ben Sira: A Jewish Sage between Opposition and Assimilation*, DCLS 13 (Berlin: de Gruyter, 2012), 183.

198 It may be plausible to say that Ben Sira includes Joshua in order to convey to his contemporary audience that battle was also inevitable to prevent the advance of Hellenism. Marttila, *Foreign Nations in the Wisdom of Ben Sira*, 184.

199 For the discussion on the date and provenance of 1 Enoch, see David W. Suter, "Enoch in Sheol: Updating the Dating of the Book of Parables," in *Enoch and the Messiah Son of Man: Revisiting the Book of Parables*, ed. Gabriele Boccaccini (Grand Rapids: Eerdmans, 2007), 415-443; see also Pierluigi Piovanelli, "A Testimony for the Kings and the Mighty who Possess the Earth: The Thirst for Justice and Peace in the Parables of Enoch," in *Enoch and the Messiah Son of Man: Revisiting the Book of Parables*, ed. Gabriele Boccaccini (Grand Rapids: Eerdmans, 2007), 363-379; Darrell L. Bock, "Dating the Parables of Enoch: A Forschungs bericht," in *Parables of Enoch: A Paradigm Shift*, ed. James H. Charlesworth and Darrell L. Bock (London: Bloomsbury, 2013), 58-113; Chad T. Pierce, *Spirits and the Proclamation of Christ: 1 Peter 3:18-22 in Light of Sin and Punishment Traditions in Early Jewish and Christian Literature*, WUNT 305 (Tübingen: Mohr Siebeck, 2011), 74; E. Isaac, "1 (Ethiopic Apocalypse of) Enoch: A New Translation and Introduction," in *Apocalyptic Literature and Testaments*, ed. James H. Charlesworth, vol.1 of *The Old Testament Pseudepigrapha*, ed. James H. Charlesworth (New York: Doubleday, 1983), 5-89, esp. 6-8.

200 James C. VanderKam, "Enoch Traditions in Jubilees and Other Second-Century Sources," in *The Society of Biblical Literature 1978 Seminar Papers*, SBLSP 13-14 (Missoula: Scholars Press, 1978), 229-251; see also James M. Scott, "The Division of the Earth in Jubilees 8:11-9:15 and Early Christian Chronography," in *Studies in the Book of Jubilees*, ed. Matthias Albani, Jörg Frey and Armin Lange (Tübingen: Mohr Siebeck, 1997), 295-296. L. Finkelstein and Nickelsberg leans toward earlier date of c.a. 168 BCE. Daniel A. Michiela, *The Dead Sea Genesis Apocryphon: A New Text and Translation with Introduction and Special Treatment of Columns 13-17* (Leiden: Brill, 2009), 15-17.

works "they study the healing of diseases, the roots offering protection and the properties of stones."[201] This list of subjects correlates with matters said to be revealed by the fallen angels in the *Book of Watchers* (*1 En.* 1-36), and also against which Noah is said to have received the knowledge of healing through "counter-revelation" (*Jub.* 10:10-14).[202] This attempt to distinguish between communities of Enochic tradition and Qumran is further forwarded while studying the findings at Masada by L. H. Schiffman in his *Reclaiming the Dead Sea Scrolls*.[203] Though the questions of date, authors and provenance cannot be ascertained, but it is commonly accepted now that these works originated in Judea and was in use in the Qumran community before the beginning of Christian period.[204] The link between Enochic writings and Matthew's Gospel will also be highlighted in the course of this study.

### *3.6.3.1. Early Enochic Writings (1 Enoch)*

1 Enoch was thought to have been lost but there are various ancient sources referring to it or even quoting parts of it. Then in 1773, after spending some years exploring the country of Ethiopia, James Bruce acquired three copies of it. Two main reasons for the writing of the book can be accessed from the text, and the reasons are that the Watchers instructed him to do it, and also to save his family from the flood (*1 En.* 81:5, 6).[205] Apart from the mythic nature of the text it is also appealing to understand the cosmological worldview of it. The interrelationship between spiritual entities and natural world is apparent and thus cemented the worldview where the word or idea of miracle in modern sense had no place assigned as such. The attempt here is not to narrate the

---

201 Todd S. Beall, by assembling a comprehensive list of the parallels between Josephus' description of the Essenes and the Qumran scrolls also concludes that "the sheer number of parallels is striking, and puts the burden of proof upon those who would insist that the Qumran community was *not* Essene." Todd S. Beall, *Josephus' Description of the Essenes Illustrated by the Dead Sea Scrolls*, SNTSMS 58 (Cambridge: CUP, 1988), 125. Despite attempts by some scholars to find another locale other than the Qumran for the Essenes, Qumran is the only site that accords with Pliny's and Josephus' descriptions of the sectarian group. Beall's conclusion is thus even more valid today, with the completed publication of the scrolls and additional archaeological information. Kenneth Atkinson and Jodi Magnes, "Josephus's Essenes and the Qumran Community," *JBL* 129 (2010): 317-342 (342).

202 David R. Jackson, *Enochic Judaism: Three Defining Paradigm Exemplars*, LSTS (London: T&T Clark, 2004), 7.

203 L. H. Schiffman, *Reclaiming the Dead Sea Scrolls: The History of Judaism, the Background of Christianity, the Lost Library of Qumran* (New York: Doubleday, 1995), 403.

204 Isaac, "1 (Ethiopic Apocalypse of) Enoch," 7-8.

205 Andy McCracken, introduction to *The Book of Enoch: A Modern English Translation of the Ethiopian Book of Enoch*, trans. of the Ethiopian text by Michael Knibb (Cedar Hill: LIEL, 2004), 5, http://www.scriptural-truth.com/stuff/BookOfEnoch.pdf.

myth in detail but to pin point the understanding of nature and what could be classified as miracle in the text.

The Watchers were imprisoned and latter slained, but evil persists because their offspring the giants become evil spirits (*1 En.* 15:8), and to be precise evil spirits proceed from their bodies (*1 En.* 15:9). Though their final destination is not stated, these evil spirits will remain upon the earth to oppress humanity and to corrupt the earth until the judgment day (*1 En.* 15:9-16:1).[206] As this kind of myth mostly originated due to the reality of social and political milieu, the origin of demons could also be considered in this line. The illicit sexual relation between angels and human women may represent concern about the Jewish priests taking unsuitable marriage partners.[207] The intertextuality between these stories and Matthew's Gospel will be dealt with later in the study.

The miracles of liberation in the exodus tradition, which is one of the factors that excited those who were interested in miracles among the Jews of antiquity is absent in 1 Enoch. This may well be related with the lack of interest in miracles in the Enochic tradition.[208] Another significant point of view could be drawn out from the fact that the angels rather than the evil spirits are assigned leading roles in the cosmic drama of the Book of the Watchers. Though the defeat of the evil spirits at the end times is presupposed, there is no emphasis embedded with it, because the emphasis is tied up with the final demise of the Watchers. Thus, Eve argues that the binding and ultimate defeat of the Watchers could not be understood as similar with the binding and ultimate defeat of the evil spirits, and the evil spirits were assigned only a minor part in the Book of the Watchers.[209] He further argues and concludes that "it would also be a mistake to read a significant eschatological defeat of evil spirits directly from the text of the *Book of Watchers*."[210] The main reason for this conclusion is the lack of exorcism in the Book of Watchers and 1 Enoch as a whole.

206 David W. Suter, "Fallen Angel, Fallen Priest: The Problem of Family Purity in 1 Enoch 6-16," *HUCA* 50 (1979): 115-135; George W. E. Nickelsburg, "Enoch, Levi and Peter: Recipients of Revelation in Upper Galilee," *JBL* 100 (1981): 575-600 (584-586).

207 David W. Suter, "Fallen Angel, Fallen Priest: The Problem of Family Purity in 1 Enoch 6-16," *HUCA* 50 (1979): 115-135; George W. E. Nickelsburg, "Enoch, Levi and Peter: Recipients of Revelation in Upper Galilee," *JBL* 100 (1981): 575-600 (584-586).

208 Eve, *The Jewish Context of Jesus' Miracles*, 153.

209 Eve, *The Jewish Context of Jesus' Miracles*, 153.

210 In the *Book of Watchers* there is no hope that is expressed for any repeat of miracles of liberation like those that took place in exodus event. The only solution to the evils described in the book is presented in terms of "a final judgment and cleansing of the earth." It is also the angels and not the evils that are given leading roles in the cosmic drama of this book; and the evil spirits play only a relatively minor role. The book does not contain exorcisms according to Eve, *The Jewish Context of Jesus' Miracles*, 153.

Though the direct connection on the subject of exorcism is not to be found, it is still significant because the identification of the role of the evil spirits may have been an influencing factor to Jesus' exorcisms and other miracles. The infliction of defeat on individual demons through exorcism would contribute to the final overthrow of evil cosmic powers is absent in the Book of Watchers, but according to Eve "it does provide a possible starting point for such ideas to develop" in the later New Testament writings.[211] Vander Kam argues that the most significant influence of Enochic tradition in the New Testament is ushered by the angelic reading of Genesis 6:1-4.[212]

Earlier than Vander Kam, E. Isaac in his essay, "1 (Ethiopic Apocalypse of) Enoch: A New Translation and Introduction," which is published in the first volume of *The Old Testament Pseudepigrapha* claims that 1 Enoch influences Matthew, Luke, John, Acts, Romans, 1 and 2 Corinthians, Ephesians, 1 and 2 Thessalonians, 1 Timothy, 1 John, Jude (*1 En.* 1:9 is directly quoted in Jude 14-15), and Revelation (having numerous points of contact).[213] Eve adds in this list 1 and 2 Peter, and shows his surprise in their omission in Isaac's list.[214] The presentation of God is in the same line with the Old Testament, and God is righteous and just, the creator of the world, the law giver, the dispenser of history, and the ultimate judge over all humanity and nature.

Another significant subject is how the Messiah in 1 Enoch (*1 En.* 45-57) is called the "righteous one" and "the son of man," and "is depicted as a pre-existent heavenly being who is resplendent and majestic, possesses all dominion, and sits on the throne of glory passing judgment upon all mortal and spiritual beings."[215] The parallelism between 1 Enoch 62:2 and Matthew 19:28 and also 1 Enoch 62 as a whole and Matthew 23:22 are strikingly interesting. All the verses affirm the throne of glory where the Son of Man will be sitting in order to pass judgment.[216]

Is this presentation of Messiah as possessing cosmic authority a vital point in the Christological framework of the New Testament writings, and most probably is it also the case for Matthew's Gospel? Many close similarities that

211 Eve, *The Jewish Context of Jesus' Miracles*, 153-154.

212 James C. VanderKam, "1 Enoch, Enochic Motifs, and Enoch in Early Christian Literature," in *The Jewish Apocalyptic Heritage in Early Christianity*, ed. James C. VanderKam and William Adler (Assen: Van Gorcum, 1996), 33-101 (100) quoted by Eve, *The Jewish Context of Jesus' Miracles*, 155.

213 Isaac, "1 (Ethiopic Apocalypse of) Enoch," 10.

214 According to Eve, the myth of the fallen Watchers is presupposed at 1 Pet 3:19-20; and 2 Pet 2:2-5 also appears to refer to the story of the rebel angels punished at the time of the flood. Eve, *The Jewish Context of Jesus' Miracles*, 154.

215 Isaac, "1 (Ethiopic Apocalypse of) Enoch," 9.

216 Daniel Assefa, "Matthew's Day of Judgment in the Light of 1 Enoch," in *Enoch and the Synoptic Gospels: Reminiscences, Allusions, Intertextuality*, ed. Loren T. Stuckenbruck and Gabriele Boccaccini (Atlanta: SBL, 2016), 199-214 (208).

exist between 1 Enoch and Matthew's Gospel in regards to the Son of Man could serve as a pointer to the understanding of cosmic Christ in Matthew's Gospel.[217] Few specific and detailed characteristic or feature shared by them that seem relevant for this study can be presented as below:[218]

1. Heavenly status - *1 En.* 46, 48:2-8, 62-63, 70-71.
   Matt 13:36-43, 16:24-28.
2. Judicial role - *1 En.* 46, 62-63, 69:26-29.
   Matt 13:36-43, 16:27, 19:28, 24:30, 25:31.
3. Seated upon throne of glory - *1 En.* 62:5, 69:27, 29.
   Matt 19:28, 25:31.

Therefore it can be seen that Matthew 13:37-43 and 25:31-46 contain the bulk of the traits attributed to the Son of Man, and suggest that Matthew's concept of the Son of Man was significantly influenced by 1 Enoch.[219] Though not as explicit as is found in John's Gospel, the heavenly origin of the Son of Man in Matthew's Gospel could also be drawn out from the fact that the mother of Jesus was "found to be with child of the Holy Spirit" (Matt 1:18; cf. *1 En.* 70:4). Jesus' miracles of healing are perhaps connected with 1 Enoch assertion of the wholeness of creation (*1 En.* 71:15-17). Matthew does not quote or reproduce stories from 1 Enoch, but Amy E. Richter makes an experimental comparison between them in her essay, "Unusual Birth: Enochic Traditions and Matthew's Infancy."[220] Richter argues that when the Book of Watchers and Matthew's infancy narrative are placed under one lens, the presence of motifs and themes from 1 Enoch is visible in Matthew's Gospel.[221] As Matthew

217 For example, both of them depict the Son of Man as sitting on the "throne of glory," with the authority to judge (*1 En.* 69:27, 29); the "throne of his glory" (Matt 25:31) may be a direct quotation. For a detail discussion, see Leslie W. Walck, "The Son of Man in the Parables of Enoch and the Gospels," in *Enoch and the Messiah Son of Man: Revisiting the Book of Parables*, ed. Gabriele Boccaccini (Grand Rapids, MI: Eerdmans, 2007), 299-337.

218 Walck, "The Son of Man," 330.

219 Walck, "The Son of Man," 330. The picture of Jesus as the eschatological Messiah who will vindicate the defenceless is not a new idea, but a typical Jewish portrait of Messiahship. William J. Dumbrell, *The Search for Order: Biblical Eschatology in Focus* (Eugene, OR: Wipf & Stock, 2001), 177; cf. Matthew V. Novenson, *Christ Among the Messiahs: Christ Language in Paul and Messiah Language in Ancient Judaism* (Oxford: OUP, 2012), 56-57.

220 Amy E. Richter, "Unusual Birth: Enochic Traditions and Matthew's Infancy," in *Enoch and the Synoptic Gospels: Reminiscence, Allusions, Intertextuality*, ed. Loren T. Stuckenbruck and Gabriele Boccaccini (Atlanta: SBL Press, 2016), 45-72; cf. Amy E. Richter, "The Enochic Watchers' Template and the Gospel of Matthew," (PhD diss., Marquette University, 2010), 252-254.

221 Richter, "Unusual Birth," 52.

operates with differing thrust, even when Enochic elements are utilized, it resulted in different ending in Matthew's Gospel.

The christological framework in which nature miracles are embedded must also be understood from the viewpoint of the traditions that influenced Matthew's Gospel because Enochic literature developed the identification of the Son of Man and the Messiah, and the expectations were then become transcendental in scope and nature.[222] Matthew's Christology thus encompasses the cosmological worldview that does not separate God and natural world but project them as being in an intimate interrelationship. Jesus as being pre-existent being and having the power to perform not only nature miracles but also the Son of Man responsible for the recreation and repairing of God's created world are the main thrusts of Matthew's Gospel when it is read by using 1 Enoch as one of the backdrops for the Gospel.

Richter's examination is significant especially in her comparison between the dreams of Enochic, Matthean, and Balaam stories.[223] The similarity in the languages between Balaam oracles in Numbers 23:7, 18, 24:3,15-17, 20, 21, 23 and the opening verse of 1 Enoch encourages Nickelsburg to assert that there is no way to ascertain what the author intended to achieve by the allusion to Balaam, but the similarities remain between the two dreamers and their reports.[224] The further comparison is made with a non-biblical text, an inscription from Deir 'Allā, dated 750 to 700 BCE[225] in which Balaam was mentioned as predicting a disaster to be inflicted upon the people due to the disruption of cosmic order. The gods had planned to unleash "final cosmic disaster in which the world will lapse into an all-encompassing gloom."[226] The description here is quite similar with that of Isaiah 13:14, Ezekiel 32:7-8, and Joel 2:10. Balaam's dream is both auditory message dream and a visual

---

222 Antti Laato, *A Star is Rising: The Historical Development of the Old Testament Royal Ideology and the Rise of the Jewish Messianic Expectations*, ISFCJ 5 (Atlanta: Scholars Press, 1997), 266, cited in Biju C., "Johannine Christology as an Intercultural Christology: A Quest for Hermeneutics in a Subaltern Indian Context," (DTh diss., Senate of Serampore College, 2016), 109.

223 Richter, "The Enochic Watchers' Template," 190-206.

224 George W. E. Nickelsburg notes that "The parallels to the Balaam oracles have been recognized by all commentators who have had access to the full and more accurate Greek text of this section." George W. E. Nickelsburg, *1 Enoch 1: A Commentary of the Book of 1 Enoch*, ed. Klaus Baltzer (Minneapolis: Fortress, 2001), 137-138, cited by Richter, "The Enochic Watchers' Template," 191.

225 Joseph Naveh, "The Date of the Deir 'Allā Inscription in Aramaic Script," *Israel Exploration Journal* 17 (1967): 256-258, cited by Richter, "The Enochic Watchers' Template," 191.

226 P. Kyle Jr. McCarter, "The Balaam Texts from Deir 'Allā: the First Combination," *Bulletin of the American Schools of Oriental Research* 239 (1980): 49-60 (57-58).

symbolic dream according to Robert Karl Gnuse.[227] Gnuse also states that the dreams in Matthew 1-2 follow this similar form of auditory message dream as described by A. Leo Oppenheim.[228] The form is also visible in 1 Enoch 13:7-16:4, in which Enoch receives auditory commands from the deity, and also receives a vision.[229]

Furthermore, in regards to the message of cosmic destruction Enoch's dream vision in 1 Enoch 83-84 bears more resemblance.[230] Thus, both Balaam (Deir ʻAllā) and Enoch's concerns are cosmic in scope and nature, and the presentation of the problem is in regards to the disruption of the intention of the divine over the order of the cosmos. The seer's job is to prevent the total annihilation of creation and humanity, and Richter sees this point as having connection with how Matthew presents the dreamer Joseph. Richter states that "it is clear that Matthew's intention is to identify the child who is protected by the dreamer Joseph as someone with cosmic and eschatological significance."[231] Richter's argument, especially in regards to the cosmic implications of Jesus according to Matthew opens up the scope of cosmic Christology in Matthew's Gospel.

### *3.6.3.2. The Book of Jubilees*

The book of *Jubilees* is peculiar among the apocalyptic literature because it retells the biblical account from creation to Sinai (Genesis to part of Exodus), and a prime example of the so-called "Re-written Bible."[232] There are differences to be found between 1 Enoch and *Jubilees*, there are also shared

---

227 Robert Karl Gnuse, *Dreams and Dream Reports in the Writings of Josephus: A Traditio-Historical Analysis*, (Leiden: Brill, 1996), 58; see also George M. Soares-Prabhu, *The Formula Quotations in the Infancy Narrative of Matthew: An Enquiry into the Tradition History of Mt 1-2*, Analectica Biblica 63 (Rome: Biblical Institute, 1976), 1-300, cited by Richter, "The Enochic Watchers' Template," 171.

228 This form also identifiable in the Hebrew bible narratives about Abram (Gen 15:12-21) Abraham (Gen 21:12-14), Abimelech (Gen 20:1-8), Hagar (Gen 21:16-20), Isaac (Gen 26:2-6, 24-25), Jacob (Gen 28:10-22, 31:10-17, Gen 46:1-7), Laban (Gen 31:24), Balaam (Num 22:8-13, 19-21, 24:2), Samuel (1 Sam 3:1-18), and Solomon (1 Kgs 3:4-15, 9:1-10, 2 Chr 1:6-12). Robert Karl Gnuse, "Dream Genre in the Matthean Infancy Narratives," *NovT* 32 (1990): 97-120.

229 Richter, "The Enochic Watchers' Template," 194.

230 Matthean vision of blood-drenched land and its cosmic sweep (blood of Abel – Matt 23:35-39; end times – Matt 24:1-26:1) is not readily evident in the biblical story of Cain and Abel, but an intriguing parallel could be found in the Book of the Watchers (*1 En.* 6-11), and particularly in 1 Enoch 9:1-2 the text is summed up in terms of blood poured out upon the land. Catherine Sider Hamilton, *The Death of Jesus in Matthew: Innocent Blood and the End of Exile*, SNTSMS 167 (New York: CUP, 2017), 47.

231 Richter, "The Enochic Watchers' Template," 195.

232 James C. VanderKam, *From Revelation to Canon: Studies in Hebrew Bible and Second Temple Literature* (Boston: Brill, 2002), 277; see also James C. VanderKam, *The Book of*

beliefs and practices. VanderKam highlights the common views of the writers, which are "the importance of the story about heavenly angels who descended and married women, the revealed character of 364-day solar calendar, and the firm conviction that there would be a time of ultimate reckoning."[233] The book of *Jubilees* is also called the Apocalypse of Moses due to its content, which is a revelation made to Moses at Sinai.[234] The revelation is in regards to the coming future which includes two eschatological scenarios and of the unseen world.[235]

In addition to the miracles from the history of Israel and those performed during their time, writers of the Second Temple period occasionally added miracles that are anticipated in the future. These kind of anticipated miracles or eschatological marvels are presented as the result of divine intervention into the natural world.[236] The ancient cosmological worldview permits them to think in such a way and they need no explanation of the possibility on the actuality of these miracles. One of the earliest descriptions of this kind of miracles is found in the book of *Jubilees*. In 23:26-30 the future age is envisioned "in terms of peace, spiritual renewal, gradual prolongation of the human life span, the slowing down and eventual disappearance of aging, and the restoration of health."[237] The gradual change of all life conditions and improvements in the quality of human life to God is significant because this working framework in which the interrelationship between nature, human beings, and God elucidates much of the cosmic motifs and themes in the New Testament writings.

In the book of *Jubilees* the biblical stories are reinterpreted and placed into a newer framework of a battle between good and evil powers.[238] The miracles performed by Moses and Abraham play an important role in this framework of the battle between powers. Moses and Abraham were living the ideal life that needs to be followed by the reader of the book of *Jubilees*.[239] The book of "*Jubilees* [also] has a tendency to eliminate elements of the biblical narrative that could suggest magical practices on the part of its heroes."[240] For example, Jacob's techniques for inducing spotted and speckled kids and lambs which the account of Genesis mentioned is omitted (*Jub.* 28:25-30; cf. Gen

---

*Jubilees* (Sheffield: SAP, 2001), 12; Frederick J. Murphy, *Apocalypticism in the Bible and Its World: A Comprehensive Introduction* (Grand Rapids: Baker, 2012), 164.

233 VanderKam, *From Revelation to Canon*, 277-278.

234 H. H. Rowley, *The Relevance of Apocalyptic*, 2nd ed. (London: Lutterworth, 1947), 64.

235 Murphy, *Apocalypticism in the Bible and Its World*, 164.

236 Novakovic, "Miracles in Second Temple," 106.

237 Novakovic, "Miracles in Second Temple," 107.

238 Koskenniemi, *The Old Testament Miracle-Workers in Early Judaism*, 62.

239 Koskenniemi, *The Old Testament Miracle-Workers in Early Judaism*, 62.

240 Martha Himmelfarb, *Between Temple and Torah: Essays on Priests, Scribes, and Visionaries in the Second Temple Period and Beyond*, TSAJ 151 (Tübingen: Mohr, 2013), 366.

30:25-43). The dexterity in the work of reinterpreting miracles in the book of *Jubilees* is significant and is remarkable because Pharaoh and his troops are no longer Moses' real opponents. Under this framework there are powerful masters behind the two parties; God supports the Israelites while Mastema sided with Pharaoh and his troops.[241] This kind of dualism is also common in other Jewish writings, especially in the Dead Sea Scrolls. Jörg Frey's differentiates ten different kinds of dualism in his essay, "Different Patterns of Dualistic Thought in the Qumran Library: Reflections on their Background and History."[242]

N. T. Wright without consulting Charlesworth, independently work out ten types: theological/ontological; theological/cosmological; moral; eschatological; theological/moral; cosmological; anthropological; epistemological; sectarian; psychological.[243] Though there are great varieties of dualisms, the term is indiscriminately applied regularly to one of them or all of them. He further suggests that we refer instead to "dualities" and save the term "dualism" only for specific types of dualities, such as the moral dualism of classic Zoroastrianism and Gnosticism, the cosmological dualism of Plato, and the anthropological dualism which divides the body and soul.

---

241 Koskenniemi, *The Old Testament Miracle-Workers in Early Judaism*, 59; see also VanderKam, *The Book of Jubilees*, 83; cf. Erkki Koskenniemi, "Miracles of the Devil and His Assistants in Early Judaism and Their Influence on the Gospel of Matthew," in *Evil and the Devil*, ed. Ida Fröhlich and Erkki Koskenniemi, LNTS 481 (London: T&T Clark, 2013), 84-97 (91).

242 (1) Metaphysical dualism – the opposition of two dominating causal powers of equal rank. (2) Cosmic dualism – the division of the world and of humanity into two opposing forces of good and evil, darkness and light. (3) Spatial dualism – the division of the world into two spatially divided parts such as heaven and earth, above and below, etc. (4) Eschatological dualism – the division of the world into two temporally divided parts… (5) Ethical dualism – the bifurcation of mankind into two mutually exclusive groups according virtues and vices. (6) Soteriological dualism – the division of mankind caused by faith/acceptance or disbelief/rejection in a saviour or by participation or not in a certain salvific act. (7) Theological dualism – the contrast between God and humanity or creator and creation. (8) Physical dualism – the absolute division between matter and spirit. (9) Anthropological dualism – the opposition of body and soul as distinct principles of being. (10) Psychological dualism – the contrast between good and evil is internalized and seen to be an opposition… between principles or impulses waging battle within human being. Jörg Frey, "Different Patterns of Dualistic Thought in the Qumran Library: Reflections on their Background and History," in *Legal Texts and Legal Issues: Proceedings of the Second Meeting of the International Organization for Qumran Studies Cambridge 1995*, ed. Moshe Bernstein et al. (Leiden: Brill, 1997), 275-335 (280-285); cf. J. H. Charlesworth, "A Critical Comparison of the Dualism in 1QS III, 13-IV, 26 and the 'Dualism' Contained in the Fourth Gospel," *NTS* 15 (1969): 389-418; see also, Jonathan T. Pennington, *Heaven and Earth in the Gospel of Matthew*, NovTSup 126 (Leiden: Brill, 2007), 332-333.

243 N. T. Wright, *The New Testament and the People of God: Christian Origins and the Question of God* (London: SPCK, 1992), 252-254.

The multidimensional pattern of the early Jewish theology of dualism is evident according to Frey, and especially the ethical and psychological elements were weakened or totally removed in the later texts in Qumran and all that was important then was to belong to the correct group or the community.[244] However, what is significant here is the retaining of cosmic element in Qumran. This cosmic element, which is the division of the world and of humanity into two opposing forces of good and evil, and darkness and light, is thus a working framework for the book of *Jubilees*, Qumran, and the Gospels.

The living condition as well as the political and religious tensions present in the Second Temple period is a test for the Israelites and consequently miracles became more relevant in those consequences. The idea of legitimization through miracles can also be seen in *Jubilees*; Moses' miracles are a manifestation of God's power. Abraham's prayer to the creator expelled the ravens which Mastem ahad sent after Tera was born to devour the land. This miracle manifests the truth of the new religion (*Jub.* 11:9-13; 18-24).[245] This act by Abraham is also understood in the sense of exorcism.[246]

The use of miracles as legitimization is another area where the Second Temple literature meets the Gospels. Such legitimization occurs in biblical and rabbinical sources as well as Graeco Roman sources.[247] In contrast, John P.

---

244 Frey, "Different Patterns of Dualistic Thought," 275-335; cf. Koskenniemi, *The Old Testament Miracle-Workers in Early Judaism*, 59.

245 Koskenniemi, *The Old Testament Miracle-Workers in Early Judaism*, 62; Koskenniemi, "Miracles of the Devil," 91.

246 Errki Koskenniemi, "Old Testament Figures as Miracle Workers," in *Religious and Spiritual Events*, ed. J. Harrold Ellens, vol. 1 of *Miracles: God, Science, and Psychology in the Paranormal*, ed. J. Harrold Ellens (Westport, CT: Greenwood Press, 2008), 77-86 (78).

247 When applied to deities miracles were meant to convince people to trust for themselves especially in the healing miracles. Mark's reports of healings and symbolic acts of Jesus functioned as an encouragement for the hearers, thus the disciples were reproved if their own faith for miracles is inadequate (Mark 4:38-40, 8:14-21, 9:18-29, 11:20-25). Miracles also possess propagandistic value among the Romans who employ those miracles of the Isis cult for political propaganda. Biblical and Jewish miracles also could legitimate persons, and both miracles performed directly by God and those performed by agents, certain kinds of prophets are reported in the Old Testament and other Jewish sources. Further, Christian miracles as authenticating Jesus were however become problematic for the later rabbis. Perhaps this is why the rabbis stressed that one should depend on the God of Abraham, not on Abraham as a miracle worker himself. However, the idea of the use of miracles as legitimization continues to be a subject of interest in Pauline epistles through rabbinic literature, Christians and others alike because they perceive Christian movement as confirming itself with signs like those of Jesus. Craig S. Keener, *Miracles: The Credibility of the New Testament Accounts*, 2 vols. (Grand Rapids: Baker, 2011), 1:58-65; cf. Novakovic, "Miracles in Second Temple," 95. According to Novakovic, in

Meier argues that unlike other miracle-workers of the time, Jesus had no need for legitimization by miracles.[248] Barry L. Blackburn also asserts that Jesus' performing of miracles is not "*in order to legitimate* his kingdom message," and "may not have healed and exorcised *in order to amass* crowds," but the effects and results upon those who witnessed them are very different.[249] These scholars may be right in their assessment of Jesus and his miracles. However as the study is interested in the theology or the worldview of the writer of a particular book who was in no doubt operated under the influences of the past and the contemporary sources, the argument that miracles serve as legitimization stands firm.

## 3.7. Nature Miracles within the Cosmological Worldview of the New Testament Writers

The New Testament writers are biased, so also all the writers or students of the past and also the present, and the future writers will also be biased. Due to the fact that there can never be a writing or exposition that is unbiased, because of the influences of traditional thoughts, present eco-political and contextual realities. Accordingly, the New Testament writers focus on the life and activity of Jesus of Nazareth. Bruce N. Kaye's observation in his 1977 book *The Supernatural in the New Testament* is noteworthy in this respect.[250]

The ethical monotheism that distinguished Israel's faith from that of other surrounding nations, and the ethical thrust is carried forward fully by the New Testament writers; the New Testament writers when they were confronted with nature miracles, they understood them to mean Jesus is Lord; the portrait of Jesus in the New Testament is a public figure, whose activity is open for public scrutiny.[251] Kaye further argues that Christianity in its origin did not welcome superstition and secret knowledge or secret experiences, but is open to public arena for scrutiny and examination.[252] Saying this does not negate what is already stated, because, especially the Gospel writers blended their own received traditions, experiences, thoughts, and concerns in the way they presented Jesus.

Gail R. O'Day in her 2012 essay, "Miracle Discourse and the Gospel of John," made an attempt to free herself from the agenda of redaction criticism

---

some instances miracles in Jewish literature also serve as the means of legitimization of a specifically Jewish perception of reality.

248 John P. Meier, *Matthew* (Collegeville, MN: Liturgical Press, 1980), 86.

249 Barry L. Blackburn, "The Miracles of Jesus," in *The Cambridge Companion to Miracles*, CCR, ed. Graham H. Twelftree (Cambridge: CUP, 2011), 113-130 (124).

250 Bruce N. Kaye, *The Supernatural in the New Testament* (London: Lutterworth, 1977).

251 Kaye, *The Supernatural in the New Testament*, 12-13.

252 Kaye, *The Supernatural in the New Testament*, 13.

and analyse miracle stories from rhetorical point of view.[253] Redactional study attempts to isolate sources, like miracle stories that predate the Gospels and dissected those sources to identify modification they went through. The focus about the placement they received in the Gospels in order to understand the theology of the Gospel writers, is another concern of redaction approach. However, rhetorical analysis is interested in the history, form, and theology of miracle stories, and often put them in different subjects as interrelated constitutive elements.[254]

Duane Watson, in his article "Miracle Discourse in Pauline Epistles" also notes that Paul's five times reference to his performance of miracle is found in the undisputed epistles.[255] Three times directly, to defend himself as a genuine apostle (2 Cor 12:11-12, to defend his gospel (Gal 1:1-5), and to legitimize his Gentile mission (Rom 15:17-19); and two times indirectly, when the recipients of the epistles were assumed to have knowledge of the miracles that accompanied his preaching (1 Cor 2:4-5, 1 Thess 1:4-5). Therefore, it is clear that significant topics and arguments are embedded in miracle stories of the New Testament writings, and especially the Gospel writings were capable of offering new frontiers for understanding miracles in newer contexts and environments.

## 3.8. Summary

The New Testament writers, especially the Gospel writers do not differ much in their cosmological worldview when put side by side with the Jewish writers, but differs from the Graeco-Roman writings which declined in giving autonomy to nature. The cosmological worldview within which God or divine, nature, and miracles were interrelated to each other runs in parallel lines. What is significant is that the peculiarity of traditional worldviews especially when considered under the same lens with modern science is evident. To study the ancient material from modern lens seems unpredictable and the degree of relative dissimilarities is acknowledged in today's biblical scholarship. Today's consensus inclines more towards situating miracle stories in their own cosmological worldview and theological framework. Therefore, to interpret miracle stories, it is more relevant to rely on the ancient cosmological worldview than to commence the discussion from modern historical point of view.

253 Gail R. O'Day, "Miracle Discourse and the Gospel of John," in *Miracle Discourse in the New Testament*, ed. Duane F. Watson (Atlanta: SBL, 2012), 175-188.

254 Duane F. Watson, introduction to *Miracle Discourse in the New Testament*, ed. Duane F. Watson (Atlanta: SBL, 2012), 1-16 (11).

255 Duane F. Watson, "Miracle Discourse in the Pauline Epistles: The Role of Resurrection and Rhetoric," in *Miracle Discourse in the New Testament*, ed. Duane F. Watson (Atlanta: SBL, 2012), 189-196.

As it is evident, modern science is more interested in the actuality and possibility of nature miracles. The writers of the Old Testament, the Graeco-Roman, the rabbinic literature and the New Testament give little or no concern for modern question of the possibility of nature miracle. This is mainly due to the starting point of their working framework; the framework which is related to cultural, contextual, scientific, economic and political milieu. Therefore, to locate the Jewish roots of miracle stories in Matthew's Gospel, it is unnecessary to look beyond the cosmological worldview espoused by the Jewish tradition. To give importance to the modern understanding of natural world during the study of Matthew's Gospel is also out of the scenario. As Eve notes that in striking events God was "believed to act, either directly or through an intermediary," and goes on to asserts that, "all creation is thought to be under God's control; a miracle occurs when God chooses to exercise that control in an unusual fashion."[256] Therefore, with this worldview in mind the re-evaluation of Christology from sociological point of view is in need. This will serve as a working framework to study the nature miracles in Matthew's Gospel, and will become a lens of reference to identify how Matthew understands and utilizes the idea of cosmic Christology in his Gospel. Matthew's interest in nature miracles probably points to his theological purposes, and these purposes need reconsideration and reconstruction in order to reinterpret nature miracles as the basis for the development of cosmic Christology.

256 Eve, *The Jewish Context of Jesus' Miracles*, 1-2.

Chapter 4

# Cosmic Christology in Other New Testament Writings

## 4.1. Introduction

Thomas R. Schreiner rightly points out that what David Wenham says about Luke's Gospel could also be said about all the other Gospels: "Luke's first and foremost theme is Jesus. This may be stating the obvious, but it is still worth saying."[1] To communicate the richness and comprehensive picture of Jesus, the study cannot be restricted to the titles ascribed to Jesus. Even parables of Jesus provide implicit Christology, and miracle stories and Gospel narratives also provide rich resources to formulate and develop Christology of the Gospels.[2] Public debate on the identity of Jesus was commonly represented by the Gospel writers. Jesus' miracles and words stirred up serious debate even among the disciples.[3] Here in this section, the study will make an attempt to survey and trace the texts that could be interpreted under the umbrella of cosmic Christology.

## 4.2. Synoptic Gospels

In terms of cosmic Christology in other Synoptic writings, the presentation of Jesus as preexistent and divine is the interest given in this study. Luke's

---

1 Thomas R. Schreiner, *New Testament Theology: Magnifying God in Christ* (Grand Rapids: Baker, 2008), 169, quoting David Wenham, "The Purpose of Luke-Acts: Israel's Story in the Context of the Roman Empire," in *Reading Luke: Interpretation, Reflection, Formation*, SHS 6, eds. C. G. Bartholomew, J. B. Green, and A. C. Thiselton (Grand Rapids: Zondervan, 2005), 79-103 (83).

2 For parables of Jesus as suggesting implicit Christology, see Craig L. Blomberg, *Interpreting the Parables* (Downers Grove, IL: IVP, 1990).

3 Schreiner, *New Testament Theology*, 169.

recorded that Jesus while he was still in his mother's womb is acknowledged by other. Jesus' uniqueness is manifested when Mary is called by Elizabeth as "the mother of my Lord" (Luke 1:43). Darrell Bock rightly says that by using the term "Lord" here Luke does not emphasize Jesus' lordship.[4] He sees that the term here and in Luke 2:11 is a foreshadowing of the nature of high Christology in Luke-Acts.[5] In Luke 7:6-7, Jesus' authority over sickness or natural circumstances is portrayed. The centurion without assigning any title to Jesus recognizes that he is unworthy to receive Jesus in his house (Luke 7:6-7; Matt 8:8), which is another pointer to Jesus' uniqueness.[6] Luke frequently uses "the Lord" without modifier in his narrative. Even though the vocative use is found in earlier tradition, Rudolf Bultmann argues that it proves nothing. He further says that "it is only a translation of the Aramaic title of address used by a pupil ("disciple") to his teacher ("master")."[7] However, Bock argues that "Lord" in Luke 2:11 "suggests that absolute sovereignty and divine relationship which Jesus possesses in his role as salvation-bringer" is a pointer for Jesus' unique authority.[8] He further notes that by drawing on Old Testament ideas, Luke declares and interprets the saving events of the tradition. Thus seeing how Bock arguments run, the preexistent nature of Jesus and the all authority he possesses could simply fall under cosmic christological interpretation.

Jesus' sovereign freedom in forgiving sins is seen in the account of the healing of the paralytic (Matt 9:2-8 par.), and this demonstrate divine actions and an allusion to Psalm 103:3, where Yahweh is the one who forgives sins and heals diseases (cf. Isa 33:24).[9] It is important here to note how Jesus response to the accusation, which is "only God can forgive sins" (Matt 9:6). Instead of protesting that he was not forgiving sins by his own authority, he establishes his own virtue. Jesus' divine authority in healing, and sovereign authority to forgive sins is presented clearly, and in Mark 14:61-64, this incident is again taken up, and Jesus is condemned for arrogating to himself divine prerogatives. For Otfried Hofius, there is no notion here in this passage that one action is more difficult than the other under the sovereign power of God.[10] Jesus' pronouncement of the forgiveness of sin and the corresponding question from the audience in Luke 7:49, "Who is this, who even forgives sins?" amplified

4 Darrell L. Bock, *Proclamation from Prophecy and Pattern: Lucan Old Testament Christology*, JSNTSup 12 (Sheffield: JSOT Press, 1987), 69-82.

5 Bock, *Proclamation from Prophecy and Pattern*, 80.

6 Schreiner, *New Testament Theology*, 188.

7 Rudolf Bultmann, *Theology of the New Testament: Complete in One Volume*, trans. Kendrick Grobel (New York: Charles Scribner's Son, 1951), 51.

8 Bock, *Proclamation from Prophecy and Pattern*, 81.

9 Schreiner, *New Testament Theology*, 189.

10 Otfried Hofius, *Neutestamentliche Studien*, WUNT 132 (Tubingen: Mohr Siebeck, 2000), 43, 46-47, cited in Schreiner, *New Testament Theology*, 189.

Jesus' identity as being more than a prophet.[11] Luke further testifies Jesus' cosmic status by including Jesus' declaration of who will be forgiven, which is solely a divine prerogative (Luke 18:14).[12]

When reading the ending part of Luke's Gospel, one cannot ignore the fact that Jesus is exalted as forgiveness of sin to all the nations and should be proclaimed in Jesus' name (Luke 24:47). Luke 24:49 further reveals the close association between the Father and Jesus, because Jesus will send "the promise of the Father" the Spirit. The Father's promised gift is to be bestowed by Jesus, and the exalted position is conveyed by Jesus' ascension to heaven and his blessing of the followers (Luke 24:50-51).[13] All this indication of Jesus' divine stature could be rightly taken as a pointer to the cosmic christological significance, but Luke does not make a clear cut path toward the same. Jesus' divinity as seen in Luke's Gospel may not be easily interpreted as cosmic Christology, but at least there are hints that suggest Jesus' authority over the creation, which cannot be ignored when cosmic Christology is considered.

Jesus' acknowledgement of ignorance about the final day in Matthew 24:36 and Mark 13:32 raises question about Jesus' preexistence. The reason and explanation may vary on Jesus' unawareness, but what is still clear is that Jesus places himself in the heavenly hierarchy, with the heavenly beings, such as angels, rather than with human beings.[14] In Luke 22:31-32, Jesus is also portrayed as a heavenly intercessor, and Jesus' prayer for the disciples secures their belief and helps them to not commit apostasy.[15] Even though Jesus' preexistence stature is not recognized by other human beings, the spiritual figures, the demons and the unclean spirit acknowledge that Jesus is God's holy one and Son (Mark 1:24; 3:11-12; Luke 4:1-37). During Jesus' baptism, a voice from heaven, as recorded by Mark and Luke says "You are my Son" (Mark 1:11; Luke 3:22), denoting how the Father places authoritative approval of Jesus as Son of God.[16]

---

11 Darrell L. Bock, *Luke 1:1-9:50*, BECNT (Grand Rapids: Baker Academic, 1994), 706-707; cf. Simon J. Gathercole, *The Pre-existent Son: Recovering the Christologies of Matthew, Mark, and Luke* (Grand Rapids: Eerdmans, 2006), 58. Other parallel verses are also found in Matt 9:2; Mark 2:5; Luke 5:20-21. The questioners in these episodes more or less made an attempt to frame Jesus as speaking blasphemies.

12 Arland Hultgren, *The Parables of Jesus: A Commentary* (Grand Rapids: Eerdmans, 2000), 125.

13 Schreiner, *New Testament Theology*, 189.

14 Schreiner, *New Testament Theology*, 192-193.

15 Schreiner, *New Testament Theology*, 193.

16 Schreiner, *New Testament Theology*, 193.

Jesus' preexistence may be implied in Matthew's Gospel by the claim Jesus made that he sent the prophets and other emissaries.[17] "I send you prophets, sages, and scribes, some of whom you will kill and crucify, and some you will flog in your synagogues and pursue from town to town" (Matt 23:34). As in the Old Testament the Lord is the one who sends the prophet to the people, what Jesus' made claim is an astonishing one. This means that for Jesus to say that he sends the prophet is being an alignment to Yahweh rather than human beings; and there is no evidence to be found where wisdom teacher makes this kind of self-claim.[18] The alternative view could be put forward in a sense that Jesus is referring to his previous visits to Jerusalem, but in Matthew's Gospel up to this point, "Jesus has neither been to Jerusalem, not expressed any feeling about the city in his ministry..."[19] Furthermore, Jesus uses a metaphor where he compares himself to a hen in his lament over Jerusalem: "How often have I desired to gather your children together as a hen gathers her brood under her wings, and you were not willing!" (Matt 23: 37b). This could be seen as an allusion to the Old Testament where God offers protection to the people (e.g., Deut 32:11; Ruth 2:12; Pss 17:8; 36:7; 57:1; 61:4; 63:7; 91:4).[20] Concrete reasons could be established that Jesus is making a divine claim here in these verses.

In Luke 5:8, Peter's reaction in Jesus' presence is very similar with that of Isaiah's reaction in the presence of the Lord (Isa 6:5). These similar reactions made Schreiner to conclude that "The account intimates that Jesus is like Yahweh, in whose presence a sinful person cannot abide."[21] The claim that Jesus is "sunrise or dawn (ἀνατολή) from on high" in Luke 1:78 could also be taken as a depiction of Jesus' preexistence because of these evidences: that the term is associated with the Messiah in Jewish tradition (cf. Zech 3:8; 6:12 LXX; *y.Ber* 2:4; Philo, *Confusion* 62), and the sunrise or dawn will come "from on high," in contrast to what is written in Zechariah, where the branch comes from the earth (Zech 6:12 LXX). The phrase "coming from on high" indicates that the sunrise hails from heaven, from God's realm, and the language of visitation also points to Jesus as deity. The sunrise thus came to shed light on his people (Luke 1:79), and is fitting with the messianic prophecy in Isaiah

17 Robert M. Bowman Jr. and J. Ed Komoszewski, *Putting Jesus in His Place: The Case for the Deity of Christ* (Grand Rapids, MI: Kregel, 2007), 94.

18 Schreiner, *New Testament Theology*, 193; cf. Gathercole, *The Pre-existent Son*, 71.

19 Gathercole, *The Pre-existent Son*, 214; see also Bowman Jr. and Komoszewski, *Putting Jesus in His Place*, 94.

20 Craig S. Keener, *A Commentary to the Gospel of Matthew* (Grand Rapids: Eerdmans, 1999), 558; cf. John Nolland, *The Gospel of Matthew: A Commentary on the Greek Text*, NIGTC (Grand Rapids: Eerdmans, 2005), 950-951.

21 Schreiner, *New Testament Theology*, 193-194.

9:1, 5-6.[22] The interrelationship between God, Jesus Christ and the cosmos is closely intertwined here.

Jesus' transcendence could be implicitly hinted in Jesus' answer "I am" in Mark 14:61-62 where the chief priest asks Jesus "Are you the Christ, the son of the Blessed One." There is a possibility to allude the answer to the self-descriptive language of God in the Old Testament (e.g. Is 43:10, 13).[23] Mark's Christology is first and foremost royal in character, and the major titles for Jesus are "Messiah," "Son of David," "King of the Jews (Israel)," and "Son of God." Though these titles are related and overlap with one another in meaning to some extent, Kingsbury argues "Mark draws distinction among them which the reader dare not to ignore."[24]

## 4.3. Johannine Writings

John reaffirmed his source's Christology, but deepened it and enhanced it.[25] R. Alan Culpepper argues that in order to defend the claim that "no one has ascended into heaven except the one who descended from heaven, the Son of Man" (John 3:13) John probably drops the report "We have found Elijah" in John 1:43.[26] The use of Logos in the prologue of John's Gospel could be understood as a means to communicate the cosmic nature of Jesus' identity. For the evangelist "the beginning lies in the pre-existence of Jesus, which directs our attention to the absolute beginning of all things."[27] The use of the term Logos in Greek philosophy in Heraclitus and Stoics too speak of logos concept as a part of the beginning but Johannine Logos differs because it is the cosmic law which rules the universe and at the same time present in the human intellect.[28] James D.G. Dunn also notes that the Logos poem of Johannine Prologue is where the Wisdom and Logos speculation of Alexandrian Judaism

---

22 Schreiner, *New Testament Theology*, 194.

23 L. W. Hurtado, "Christ," *DJG* 106-117, (110-111).

24 Jack D. Kingsbury, *The Christology of Mark's Gospel* (Philadelphia: Fortress, 1983), 140. Karl Kertelge also notes that though Jesus' intention to remain hidden is seen in the phrase "they [the demons] should not make him known" (Mark 3:12), but Mark makes it clear that the true identity of Jesus cannot in fact remain hidden. Karl Kertelge, "The Epiphany of Jesus in the Gospel," in *The Interpretation of Mark*, 2nd ed. SNTI, ed. William R. Telford (Edinburgh: T&T Clark, 1995), 105-124.

25 R. Alan Culpepper, "The Christology of the Johannine Writings," in *Who Do You Say that I Am? Essays on Christology*, ed. Mark Allan Powell and David R. Bauer (Louisville: Westminster John Knox Press, 1999), 66-87.

26 Culpepper, "The Christology of the Johannine Writings," 67.

27 Oscar Cullmann, *The Christology of the New Testament* (London: SCM, 1963), 249.

28 Cullmann, *The Christology of the New Testament*, 251; see also Leon Morris, *Studies in the Fourth Gospel* (Grand Rapids: Eerdmans, 1969), 116-117.

reach their climax.[29] John's explicit statement that the Logos, God's creative and revelatory utterance from the beginning of time, has become flesh is a concept of cosmic Christology. Therefore, the presence of cosmic Christology in Johannine writings is a much complex thought than that of the Synoptic Gospels.

The prologue does not itself provide a developed Christology because once John identifies the Logos (made flesh) with "the only Son" in 1:14, the concept of Logos is discarded.[30] T. E. Pollard argues that while the Prologue can stand by itself, John's "intended the Logos of the Prologue to be interpreted in the light of Jesus the Christ, the Son of God, whose earthly life is the theme of the Gospel."[31] The Prologue is a pointer to the two stark paradoxes of Christian faith: Firstly, the Trinitarian paradox on the nature of the relationship between the Father and the Son, distinct yet one in the unity of Godhead that is "the paradox of distinction-within-unity." Secondly, the paradox of the humanity and divinity of Jesus Christ, the word made flesh.[32] Both these cases become more explicit in the body of the Gospel itself. The only interest here is the cosmological language and cosmic christological concept present in the Prologue.

The high Christology and the centrality of Jesus in Johannine writings are long recognized by scholars.[33] Robin Scroggs comments "High Christology!

29 James D. G. Dunn, *Christology in the Making: A New Testament Inquiry into the Origins of the Doctrine of Incarnation*, 2nd ed. (Grand Rapids, MI: Eerdmans, 1989), 256. There are various interpretations of the Johannine source for Logos: The Philosophical or Hellenistic concept, The Gnostic concept, the Philonian source, the "Special Guidance of the Spirit" view, and the Hebrew "Wisdom" source. For details, see Edgar J. Lovelady, "The Logos Concept: A Critical Monograph on John 1:1," *GTC* (1963): 15-24.

30 T. E. Pollard, *Johannine Christology and the Early Church*, SNTSMS 13 (Cambridge: CUP, 1970), 12-13.

31 Pollard, *Johannine Christology and the Early Church*, 13.

32 Pollard, *Johannine Christology and the Early Church*, 13.

33 Ernst Käsemann argues that the Johannine Jesus is "a god striding on the earth," *The Testament of Jesus: A Study of the Gospel of John in the Light of Chapter 17*, trans. G. Krodel (Philadelphia: Fortress, 1968), 73. Käsemann was building up his argument from F. C. Baur, W. Wrede, G. P. Wetter and E. Hirsch, all of whom reject that the picture of Jesus as being that of a human being in John's Gospel. Cf. C. F. Evans, "The Passion of John," in *Explorations in Theology*, 9 vols. (London: SCM Press, 1977), II: 50-66 (62), argues that "One may legitimately ask with respect to this gospel as a whole whether its Christ ever really has his feet firmly on the earth." Anthony T. Hanson, *The Prophetic Gospel: A Study of John and the Old Testament*, SE (London: T&T Clark, 1991), 62, expressed similar view "the Jesus of the Fourth Gospel cannot possibly be a historical representation: he is divine figure, the eternal Word appearing as a man but retaining all the attributes of God except invisibility and omnipresence." Hans Windisch, "John's Narrative Style," in *The Gospel of John as Literature: An Analogy of Twentieth Century Perspectives*, trans. D. Orton, ed. Mark Stibbe (Leiden: E. J. Brill, 1923), 25-64 (62),

Jesus Christ is completely divine, is God. This is the judgement universally held of the thought of the Gospel of John."[34] This high Christology has led many scholars to doubt the veracity of John's portrait of Jesus, but the purpose here is not to defend the accuracy, the focus is on cosmic Christology in Johannine writings. John's purpose of writing is to persuade his readers to believe that Jesus is the Christ, God's Son (John 20:31). John's credentials are those of an eyewitness, and he wishes to pass on the truth he acquired about the union he has found with God the Father and Jesus Christ (1 John 1:1-4).[35]

The Prologue establishes the eternal preexistence of the Logos, and John is trying to make clear the role of the Logos, not only in human salvation but also in the entire cosmos.[36] In other words, it can also be said that the whole cosmos has life in the Logos, because "All things came into being through him, and without him not one thing came into being. What has come into being in him was life, and the life was the light of all people" (John 1:3-4).[37] Elizabeth Harris rightly points out that John's emphasis in the Gospel is consistently theocentric.[38] Jesus in John's Gospel speaks and acts as having divine origin throughout the Gospel (e.g., John 8:42; 17:3). At the very beginning of time when the material world came into existence the Logos was already in full existence. The contrast between the changing, becoming of material and finite world to that of the ever existing divine being, the Logos is clear in the very first words of the Prologue.[39] John's Gospel portrays Jesus as the Son of Man and the one who came down from heaven, and the Son of Man is identified with the preexistent heavenly being who came down on earth (John 3:13; 6:62). Barnabas Lindars thus observes that "...in John's concept of pre-existence, Jesus carries no implication that he is anything less than fully and

---

argues that the Johannine Jesus is "*the new Christ-type, detached from the earth and from history... a divine Christ from heaven.*"

34 Robin Scroggs, *Christology in Paul and John*, Proclamation Commentaries (Philadelphia: Fortress, 1988), 63; see also Helen C. Orchard, *Courting Betrayal: Jesus as Victim in the Gospel of John*, JSNTSup 161 (Sheffield: SAP, 1998), 17-18; see also Richard Cassidy, *John's Gospel in New Perspective: Christology and the Realities of Roman Power* (Maryknoll, NY: Orbis Books, 1992), 29.

35 George A. Maloney, S. J., *The Cosmic Christ: From Paul to Teilhard* (New York: Sheed & Ward, 1968), 72.

36 Maloney, S. J., *The Cosmic Christ*, 75; cf. T. W. Manson, *On Paul and John: Some Selected Theological Themes*, SBT 38, ed. Matthew Black (London: SCM, 1963), 134-135.

37 Maloney, S. J., *The Cosmic Christ*, 75.

38 Elizabeth Harris, *Prologue and Gospel: The Theology of the Fourth Gospel* (London: T&T Clark, 2004), 11.

39 Maloney, S. J., *The Cosmic Christ*, 75.

truly human."[40] It is also argued that the prologue of John's Gospel affirms the preexistence of Christ in an absolute manner.[41]

This same concept of preexistent Logos is also seen clearly from the statement that Christ is "the origin of God's creation" (Rev 3:15), and Christ is "the Alpha and Omega, the beginning and the end" (Rev 21:6; 22:13; cf. 1 John 2:13-14).[42] 1 John 5:19 tells that human beings are all born of God, but the whole cosmos is under the influence of the Evil One. The use of Logos shows the interrelationship between God, Jesus Christ and the created world. The Logos is preexistent and is abiding with God, and is of the same nature as God, thus "the Word was God."

George A. Maloney suggests that this is to show the reader the unique function of the Logos as a creating being.[43] It is thus the Logos that brings the universe from its existence in the mind of God into actual existence. For John, Jesus Christ is through whom the whole universe is created. Therefore, the role of the Logos is not static but wherever created beings are coming into existence or moving into various degree of existence, there the Logos is operative. Maloney deals with three central aspects of John's portrait of Jesus that relates with cosmic Christology: Logos, Light and Life. He sees that John's perspective is quite peculiar to that of the Synoptic Gospels and Paul. John's writing is simple but seems removed from present reality, and alarms the reader as mystical.[44] For John, Jesus Christ is the Logos, the light and the life whose mission is to bring about eternal salvation for humanity. Jesus Christ is the beginning and is the source and principle of all finite existence, and the Omega towards whom reality is moving and through whom it will attain its fullness.

The christological tone for the whole book of Revelation is situated in the first chapter itself, and thus begins with the assertion that this is "the revelation of Jesus Christ," and the title Jesus Christ appears three times in this chapter.[45] According to Donald Guthrie, "The first Christian readers would need to be led from Jesus Christ to the Lamb, the name which dominates the second part of the book."[46] The opening chapter made it clear that Jesus is the faithful witness, the first born from the dead, the ruler of the kings of the earth (Rev

40 Barnabas Lindars, *John* (Sheffield: JSOT Press, 1990), 75.

41 Robert Kysar, *Voyages with John: Charting the Fourth Gospel* (Texas: BUP, 2005), 30.

42 Manson, *On Paul and John*, 134-135.

43 Maloney, S. J., *The Cosmic Christ*, 76.

44 Maloney, S. J., *The Cosmic Christ*, 94.

45 Cf. Ben Witherington, *Revelation,* CBC (Cambridge: CUP, 2003), 28.

46 Donald G. Guthrie, "The Christology of Revelation," in *Jesus of Nazareth: Lord and Christ: Essays on the Historical Jesus and the New Testament Christology*, eds. J. B. Green and Max Turner (Grand Rapids, MI: Eerdmans, 1994), 397-412 (398). Also quoted in Witherington, *Revelation,* 28.

1:5), and the one who will come on the clouds in the future for judgment (Rev 1:7). In verse 13 we have the first of the only two references in this book to Jesus as one being like a Son of Man, and the context clearly portrayed Jesus' divine status. "It was the Ancient of days in Dan. 7 that has such raiment, whereas here it is Christ who is both divine and one like a Son of Man."[47]

Elisabeth Schüssler Fiorenza finds it "remarkable" not to find the "Son of man" title in Rev 1:13 and 14:14 (as these verses have the term "like"), because her brief comparison between the book of Revelation and the Synoptic Apocalypse shows interesting resemblance between them. She even suggests that a careful study of the book of Revelation "might show more affinities to the apocalyptic discourse of the Synoptics."[48] The phrase constitutes an allusion to Daniel 7:13. Υἱὸς του ἀνθρώπου could mean "the son of man," "the human being," or simply "the man."[49] The phrase here in this expression is without the article and thus lacks such specificity. David E. Aune takes the expression as an allusion to Daniel 7:13 and not to "the son of man" in gospel traditions (e.g., Mark 8:31; 9:12).[50] However, G. K. Beale takes the phrase "son of man" as definite and involving allusions to Daniel 7:13 and "the son of man" in gospel traditions.[51] The trend of applying Old Testament images and names used for Yahweh is seen in the book of Revelation, and are applied to Christ or to both the Father and Christ.

Though it is clear in Revelation 1:17-18 and 22:13 that the person referred to as the Alpha and Omega is Christ, but according to Ben Witherington, the person referred to as Alpha and Omega in Revelation 1:8 is ambiguous.[52] However he admits that "It is worthwhile to consider the significance of calling both God and Christ the Alpha and Omega."[53] Richard Bauckham also

47 Witherington, *Revelation,* 28.

48 As it is long been acknowledged, the first sevenfold series of the seals shows remarkable parallelisms to the Synoptic Apocalypse. The word of Christ in Rev 1:7 is closely related to the announcement of the Parousia of the "Son of Man" in Matt 24:30. Other allusions are also to be found in Mark 13:35, 37 and Matt 25:13 where there is an exhortation to watch as Christ or the Parousia will come like a thief (Rev 3:2-3; 16:5; cf. Matt 24:42; Luke 12:39-40). Rev 5:3b and Matt 24:50; 12:8 are especially close. Elisabeth Schüssler Fiorenza, *The Book of Revelation: Justice and Judgment, 2nd ed.* (Minneapolis: Fortress, 1998), 102-104.

49 BDAG 1026.

50 David E. Aune, *Revelation 6-16*, WBC 52B (Grand Rapids, MI: Zondervan, 1998), 800-801.

51 G. K. Beale, *Revelation*, NIGTC (Grand Rapids: Eerdmans, 1999), 771-772.

52 Witherington, *Revelation,* 28, sees the title as referring probably to God, but the absence of a clear cut portrayal as is found in Rev 1:17-18 (the one who was dead but is now alive forever and has in his hands the keys of Death and Hades) made it more difficult to identify whom the author is referring to, God or Christ.

53 Witherington, *Revelation,* 29.

suggests that this title conveys that the idea of the person in question "precedes and originates all things, as their Creator, and he will bring all things to their eschatological fulfillment."[54] He further argues that "the titles cannot mean anything else when they are used of Christ in 22:13."[55] This identification of Jesus as the first and the last may be an allusion to Isaiah 44:6 and 48:12, where this is a divine self-designation of Yahweh.[56] All these point forward to the idea of the preexistence of Christ in the book of Revelation. Witherington thus seems right when he argues that in the book of Revelation "First and Last probably does not mean anything different from Alpha and Omega."[57] Revelation 19:11 and 13 talk about the coming of Jesus Christ at the end; the overcoming of Satan and also the establishment of the kingdom of God. Cosmic Christology in Johannine writings could not be missed by a careful reader, and especially the cosmic christological significance found in John's Gospel is far more complex to the Synoptic writings.

Christ as seen in the Prologue to John's Gospel, Revelation also portrayed Christ as "the origin of God's Creation (Rev 3:14 – ἡ ἀρχὴ τῆς κτίσεως τοῦ θεοῦ).[58] This is a cosmic christological language which is also found in other parts of New Testament writings (esp. Col 1:15-20). For the Mediterranean society conceptualizes "the first in any social ranking has precedence and prominence, eminent worth if only because this first being allows all that follow to exist."[59] According to Witherington, this does not likely means that Christ "is the first created being or the first-born from the dead (for which John uses other terminology) but rather is another way of saying about Christ what is said clearly in Rev. 22:13."[60] It is made clear in Revelation 5 that Christ who is the Lamb is an object of worship. Revelation 5:8 talks about "the Lamb who has triumphed through his death and resurrection" and who "is the focus of the

54 Richard Bauckham, *The Theology of the Book of Revelation* (Cambridge: CUP, 1993), 55; see also Witherington, *Revelation,* 29.

55 Bauckham, *The Theology of the Book of Revelation*, 55.

56 Witherington, *Revelation,* 29.

57 Witherington, *Revelation,* 29.

58 Though this statement does not precisely echo any of the Old Testament passage, it may perhaps be related to Isa 65:61. Commentators generally accepted this background, but R.H. Charles observes and concludes that John was directly or indirectly acquainted with the Colossian epistle. For more discussion on the background and parallel, see Collin J. Hemer, *The Letters to the Seven Churches of Asia in their Local Setting*, JSNTSup 11 (Sheffield: JSOT Press, 1986), 184-186; cf. R. H. Charles, *A Critical and Exegetical Commentary on the Revelation of St. John*, 2 vols. (Edinburgh: T&T Clark, 1920), 1:94-95.

59 Bruce J. Malina and John J. Pilch, *Social-Science Commentary on the Book of Revelation* (Minneapolis: Fortress, 2000), 63.

60 Witherington, *Revelation,* 29.

circle of worship in heaven that includes the worship of the living creatures and the elders, the representatives of all creatures both animal and human."[61] This line of thought may not be taken as an explicit pointer to cosmic Christology, but the relationship between Christ and creation or the cosmos cannot be ignored. Thus, it is appropriate to consider it as an evidence of the presence of what we now called cosmic Christology in the minds of the earliest Christians.

## 4.4. Pauline Writings

The task here is to highlight the presence of the theology and idea that prompted the reader to see the interrelationship between God, Christ and the cosmos. The discussion of the elements of the cosmos in Galatians 4:3-10 and the subject of 1 Corinthians 15:23-28 which indicates the eschatological submission of the cosmic principles and powers to Christ are significant. It is to say that for Paul, "Christ is accorded a cosmic role in God's dealing with the Cosmos."[62] The appearance of some important cosmological terms in Colossians 1:16; 2:8-10, 15 and 20 (elements of the cosmos, principles, and powers) are already found in Paul's authentic writings. This line of thinking dominates not only the authentic letters but also the deutero-Pauline letters to the Colossians and the Ephesians. For example, the principal theme in Colossians 1:15-20; though regarded as being a hymn quoted and used by the writer is already seen in 1 Corinthians 8:6. Thus, Dunn argues that this "can be regarded as an expression of Pauline Theology.[63]

Paul equates those who are under the elements of the cosmos with those who are under the law.[64] Paul's writing in Galatians affirms high Christology in its development. Jesus is more than a human being can be chalked out from Paul's own saying that his apostleship is not "sent neither by human commission nor from human authorities, but through Jesus Christ and God the Father" (Gal 1:1). The Father is the one who raised Jesus from the dead (Gal 1:1). While other dead people await their resurrected bodies (cf. 1 Cor 15:23), Jesus received a glorified body. When Paul says "Grace to you and peace from God our Father and the Lord Jesus Christ" (Gal 1:3), he equates Jesus to God, and implies that Jesus is the source of grace and peace. He sees the union between God and Jesus in purpose, and his authority came from Jesus and the Father, and grace and peace to humanity came from Jesus and the Father, and Jesus died for salvation of human beings in obedience to the Father's will

61 Witherington, *Revelation,* 29.

62 George H. van Kooten, *Cosmic Christology in Paul and the Pauline School,* WUNT 2 (Tübingen: Mohr Siebeck, 2003), 1.

63 James D. G. Dunn, *The Theology of Paul the Apostle* (Grand Rapids, MI: Eerdmans, 1998), 266.

64 van Kooten, *Cosmic Christology in Paul and the Pauline School,* 74-75.

(Gal 1:1-4). Therefore, cosmic Christology is seen from the very first chapter of Galatians, which talks about the interrelationship between God, Jesus and creation.

While it is understood in recent analysis that the concepts of mystery and revelation in Pauline literature assert wisdom to be his hermeneutical key, it is significant to see how Paul equates Jesus with God and how he asserts Jesus as "the key for the understanding of all revelation: whether in the gospel, in scripture, or in creation."[65] It cannot be ignored that the pre-Christian Paul drew from the theme of wisdom, and thus the sapiential influence also need not be neglected.[66] This further strengthens the fact that Paul understood Jesus as divine agent coming into the cosmos to represent God and to redeem those under the law.

The redemption and glorification of human beings are intimately tied up with that of the cosmos as a "total unit."[67] The fall of human beings had cosmic repercussions and the glorification into the "new human being" would also touch the cosmos. "All creation" thus includes not only human beings but also the cosmos as a whole, and will participate in the glorification of human beings.[68] Human beings and the material world are conceived as a unit, thus the whole of creation moved together in the attainment of fulfilment or destruction. The end toward which all creation is moving is that of Christ's victory, and the final attainment of glorification will be at the parousia. Paul's cosmic Christology is formulated in this line so that Christ's coming to the cosmos is not only for humanity but for the cosmos in all its totality. Paul's summary on the relation of all things to Christ and of Christ to God is clearly seen in First Corinthians 15:28: "When all things are subjected to him, then the Son himself will also be subjected to the one who put all things in subjection under him, so that God may be all in all."

Ralph P. Martin considers Philippians 2:6-11 to be a "carmen," which is "a Christological ode devoted to praise of the Church's Lord and hailing him in confession."[69] In accordance with the Jewish tradition of Psalmody Martin believes that it is an offering of praise by the primitive church to its "cultic God" Jesus Christ. Thus, he understands the passage as a hymn, a christological confession that proclaims the Christ as preexistent, incarnate,

65 Markus N. A. Bockmuehl, *Revelation and Mystery in Ancient Judaism and Pauline Christianity*, WUNT 2 (Tübingen: Mohr Siebeck, 1990), 153.

66 C. Marvin Pate, *The Reverse of the Curse: Paul, Wisdom, and the Law*, WUNT 2 (Tübingen: Mohr Siebeck, 2000), 190.

67 Maloney, S. J., *The Cosmic Christ*, 39-40.

68 Maloney, S. J., *The Cosmic Christ*, 40.

69 Ralph P. Martin, *Carmen Christi* (New York: CUP, 1967), 20.

and exalted.[70] Ernst Kasemann also believes that this hymn deals with a divine being's incarnation and exaltation, and the content is mythical.[71] For James D. G. Dunn, the hymn exemplifies Adam Christology, and is structured "both to reflect God's intention in creating humankind (Adam), and to contrast the traditional understanding of Adam's failure."[72]

It is always accurate to consider the text in its context rather than isolating the christological ideas from it. Philippians 2:6-11 is also situated by its preceding chapter of ethical exhortation in which Paul exhorts his readers to humility. Paul first explains how his imprisonment helped him to spread the gospel (1:12), and his desire that Christ is proclaimed in every way (1:18). Paul again exhorts them to live their live "worthy of the gospel of Christ," (1:27), and to live in unity and not to be intimidated by the opponents (1:27-29). After giving another words of encouragement, comfort and exhortation to act with humility (2:1-4), Paul started illustrating the example of the true and supreme humility set by Christ Jesus. Though the message of ethical exhortation is clear, the christological emphasis embedded in the passage cannot be ignored. The christological emphasis that asserts that Christ was equal in status with God and humbled oneself through incarnation is a pointer to the preexistent status of Christ. The text painted a clear picture of the preexistent Christ as equal with God not simply, and "as clothed in the garments of divine majesty and splendor. He was in the form of God, sharing God's glory" (Phil 2:6).[73] The use of ὑπάρχων here instead of the simpler verb "to be" (εἰμι), in its full lexical meaning may perhaps point to the idea of "to exist (really)."[74] The

---

70 Martin, *Carmen Christi*, 21-23.

71 Robert Morgan, "Incarnation, Myth, and Theology: Ernst Kasemann's Interpretation of Philippians 2:5-11," in *Where Christology Began: Essays on Philippians 2*, eds. Ralph P. Martin and Brian J. Dodd (Louisville: Westminster John Knox Press, 1998), 43-73.

72 James D. G. Dunn, "Christ, Adam, and Preexistence," in *Where Christology Began: Essays on Philippians 2*, eds. Ralph P. Martin and Brian J. Dodd (Louisville: Westminster John Knox Press, 1998), 74-83 (74).

73 P. T. O'Brien, *The Epistle to the Philippians*, NIGTC (Grand Rapids, MI: Eerdmans, 1991), 210-211; see also Richard Bauckham, *Jesus and the God of Israel: God Crucified and Other Studies on the New Testament's Christology of Divine Identity* (Grand Rapids, MI: Eerdmans, 2008), 42; for a more detailed discussion on "form" see, Gerald F. Hawthorne, "In the Form of God and Equal with God (Philippians 2:6)," in *Where Christology Began: Essays on Philippians 2*, eds. Ralph P. Martin and Brian J. Dodd (Louisville: Westminster John Knox Press, 1998), 96-110.

74 The present participle ὑπάρχων stands in temporal contrast with the aorist participle λαβών in 2:7b, and thus indicating that before this person described by ὑπάρχων took the formof a slave (2:7) and was already existed in the form of God. ὑπάρχων also stands in sharp contrast to the participle, γενόμενος (having being born/having been made in the likeness of human beings – ἐν ὁμοιώματι ἀνθρώπων γενόμενος). See Hawthorne, "In the Form of God," 96-97.

language here thus provides a kind of presupposition which the rest of the sentence assumes, that is the preexistent being, the one who emptied oneself.

This idea of sharing God's glory also corresponds well with John 17:5 "The glory I had in your presence before the world existed" and Hebrews 1:3 "He is the reflection of God's glory and the exact imprint of God's very being." For Paul and the reader, Christ preexistent state as a person, and God's exalting and bestowing him "the name that is above every name" which means the sharing of the name by Christ and God create no tension in their theologizing.[75] Yet sharing the same name does not nullify the distinctness between them. The belief that in his preexistent state Christ possessed equality with God carries with it the idea of Christ being an agent of creation of "all things" (1 Cor 8:6; Col 1:15).

There are significant similarities to be found in 1 Corinthians 15 and Philippians 2:6-11. Both passages assert the risen Christ as the centre of faith, due to the reason that Christ did not remain in the preexistent state as the Son, but took on the flesh and dwell among human beings to bear their sins for their salvation. This christological emphasis is also to be found in Colossians as well.

## 4.5. Deutero Pauline Writings

The christological hymn found in Colossians 1:15-20 is not treated properly as suggested by Larry L. Helyer in the article "Cosmic Christology and Col 1:15-20."[76] He argues that "the actual theological affirmations about the relationship between Christ and the cosmos" is given minimum regard.[77]As rightly stated by Helyer, the prima facie reading of the text yields "a portrait of Jesus as the preexistent agent of creation, the regent of creation, and the reconciler of creation – creation being understood as the universe, including spiritual beings and powers."[78] This Christology became the traditional understanding of the Church until the post-Enlightenment and modern eras. The impact of modern scientific worldview resulted in the confinement of Paul's cosmic Christology inside the sphere of soteriology.[79]

There is another approach that simply understands the cosmic language as incidental to Paul's thought. According to this argument, Paul's cosmic Christology is included in his theologizing only due to the Colossian errorists

75 Cf. Brendan Byrne, "Christ's Pre-existence in Pauline Soteriology," *TS* 58 (1997): 308-330.

76 Larry L. Helyer, "Cosmic Christology and Col 1:15-20," *JETS* 37 (1994): 235-246.

77 Helyer, "Cosmic Christology and Col 1:15-20," 235.

78 Helyer, "Cosmic Christology and Col 1:15-20," 235.

79 Helyer, "Cosmic Christology and Col 1:15-20," 236.

who were advocating astrological and cosmological doctrines.[80] However, by citing Paul's earlier letters such as Galatians 2:15-4:31 (esp. 4:4-5) and a close parallel Romans 8:3, it is quite clear that the language of preexistence is employed while referring to the coming of Jesus Christ or the sending of the Son by the Father (Christ coming under the constraints of law). It is important to see that there was a prior existence of a form of cosmic Christology which is dated earlier than Colossians.[81] As John G. Gibbs rightly asserts in his article "Pauline Cosmic Christology and Ecological Crisis" that the author of the Colossians "was primarily carrying further what Paul and some pre-Pauline communities, namely that Christ was Mediator in the work of Creation" hinted the presence of tradition behind the Colossian hymn.[82] The train of thought begins with God and the Lord, Jesus Christ, and proceeds toward both the creation and redemption. It conceives God to be the source and goal of both creation and redemption, and the Lord of the Mediator of both creation and redemption.[83]

The imagery of the Colossian hymn may be ambiguous, but the christological aspect is quite intriguing. Firstly, the hymn moves towards the direction of the image of God, and then hovers around other themes such as, authority, rule, creation, crucifixion, resurrection, and reconciliation. While the first part or the main part of the hymn focuses on the cosmology of creation, the later part emphatically reflects on the cosmology of reconciliation. According to Dunn, the focus shifts "from the divine purpose that shaped creation in the beginning to the divine purpose that retrieves creation for its intended end, from first creation to re-creation beyond death."[84] The linguistic

80 Helyer, "Cosmic Christology and Col 1:15-20," 236; Cf. J. Becker, *Paul, Apostle to the Gentiles* (Louisville: Westminster, 1993), 380.

81 1 Cor 8:6 suggests a pre-Pauline confession: "Yet for us there is but one God, the Father, from whom all things came and for whom we live; and there is but one Lord, Jesus Christ, through whom all things came and through whom we live." Cf. Helyer, "Cosmic Christology and Col 1:15-20," 237-238.

82 H. Hegermann argues that there was a Christology of Christ as Mediator of creation in Palestinian kerygma, and maintains that Paul combated erroneous cosmic speculations in Colossae by refereeing to the confession of faith in 1 Cor 8:6 witnesses. H. Hagermann, *Die Vorstellung vom Schöpfungsmittler im hellenistischen Judentum und Urchristentum*, TU 82 (Berlin: Akademia-Verlag, 1961), 135, 169, cited by John G. Gibbs, "Pauline Cosmic Christology and Ecological Crisis," *JBL* 90/4 (1971): 466-479 (469). To answer the question "from where does the tradition come from?" Dunn argues that it came from an already formed hymn, and apart from Wisdom tradition he suggests that another source of possible inspiration is the contemporary Stoic philosophy. James D. G. Dunn, *The Epistles to the Colossians and to Philemon*, NIGTC (Grand Rapids, MI: Eerdmans, 1996), 83-104.

83 Gibbs, "Pauline Cosmic Christology and Ecological Crisis," 470-471.

84 Dunn, *The Epistles to the Colossians and to Philemon*, 97.

nuances in phrases "in him/through him/for him" emphasizes the "coherence and continuity" of divine purpose which is now recognized in Christ from the beginning and to the end.[85] Thus, the conviction is that the original state of creation has been subdued under the authority of darkness and the need to be reinstated. In this line of thought the need to articulate or rearticulate cosmic Christology is relevant.

The resurrection of Christ and its consequences for creation is significant in cosmic Christology found in the Colossian hymn. "That he might be in all things preeminent" is the immediate outcome of the resurrection, which is in tension with the first part of the hymn where the emphasis was given on the "*primordial* primacy."[86] The cosmic Christology integrates both Adam Christology and Wisdom Christology, that give much emphasis to "the divine purpose of creation and Christ's supremacy over (the rest of) creation."[87] While Wisdom Christology emphasizes creation in the beginning, Adam Christology delves into the realm of creation redeemed.[88] The cosmic significance of Jesus Christ is thus clearly to be seen in the Colossian hymn, though it is impossible to grasp the full dimension of it. In the human Jesus, there is the incarnation Son of God: the one in, through, and for whom all things were created in the beginning, and who, by means of the cross and resurrection has brought into existence a new beginning.[89]

In her article "In Him all Things Hold Together," Teresa Okure looks into the text of the hymn in Colossians 1:15-20, and states that the invisible God who acts in creation is "visible and touchable in the person of Jesus."[90] She further argues that the "fullness of the deity" which dwells in Jesus Christ is the foundation for human beings to hear, see, and touch God. This relationship with divinity could be accessed through baptism, and the baptized is incorporated into the same body of Christ.

---

85 Dunn, *The Epistles to the Colossians and to Philemon*, 97.

86 The Wisdom motifs in Col 1:15 emphasized Christ's "*primordial* primacy" according to Dunn, but in Col 1:18 they emphasize Christ's primacy as a result of resurrection, and particularly his work of reconciliation as the last Adam. Dunn argues that resurrection's immediate result is "that he might be in all things preeminent" and also "that he might come to have first place in everything." Dunn, *The Epistles to the Colossians and to Philemon*, 98-99.

87 Dunn, *The Epistles to the Colossians and to Philemon*, 99.

88 Dunn, *The Epistles to the Colossians and to Philemon*, 99; cf. James D. G. Dunn, "Pauline Christology: Shaping the Fundamental Structures," in *Christology in Dialogue*, ed. R. F. Berkey and S. A. Edwards (Cleveland: Pilgrim, 1993), 96-107.

89 Helyer, "Cosmic Christology and Col 1:15-20," 246.

90 Teresa Okure, "In Him all Things Hold Together: A Missiological Reading of Colossians 1:15-20," *IRM* xci/360 (2002): 62-72.

Vincent A. Pizzuto argues that the Colossian hymn is written to serve as "a unifying creedal statement over and against heretical views that were threatening to seep into the faith life and practice of his [sic] young Christian audience."[91] He further remarks that "this hymn serves foundation to the epistle," and the epistle itself is an exegesis of the hymn to show how "the cosmic Christology proclaimed... is to be lived in the daily lives of the baptized."[92] Therefore, cosmic Christology does not only assert Christ's preexistent state of being but also how Christ could be encountered in the daily life of the believers. This in turn explains how significant it is for the earliest Christian to come to grasp with a knowledge of God's will in their lives, and the mere cosmic speculation is now dissolved in Christ.[93] Colossians 3:1 thus says, "So if you have been raised with Christ, seek the things that are above, where Christ is, seated at the right hand of God."

As Christ is portrayed in a number of ways as being superior to "all things," the Christology in Ephesians may also be interpreted as cosmic Christology. The idea of the ascension and exaltation of Christ receives significant emphasis in this epistle. A. van Roon remarks, "The exalted kurios is central to this epistle."[94] He further argues that this central theme is "organically" connected with particular attention to the cosmos, and also to that of supernatural spirits and forces.[95] Van Kooten also argues that Ephesians "was presented as the twin letter of *Col* and is in fact a commentary on *Col* with, as its main purpose, a critical modification of its cosmology and cosmic Christology."[96] He further suggests that, the introductory prayer itself makes it clear that the author of Ephesians understands Christ as being given to the church as head of the cosmos. Though the church is totally filled with Christ, "the cosmos outside the church is in the process of being filled with Christ."[97] The connection between soteriology and the "cessation of baleful chaos which exists up to the highest reaches of the cosmos," is another interest of this epistle.[98]

The intention of the author of Ephesians is clearly seen in the attempt being made to establish firmly the Lordship of Christ to the readers' understanding.

91 Vincent A. Pizzuto, *A Cosmic Leap of Faith: An Authorial, Structural, and Theological Investigation of the Cosmic Christology in Col 1:15-20*, BET 41 (Paris: Peeters, 2006), 42.

92 Pizzuto, *A Cosmic Leap of Faith*, 42.

93 Cf. Pizzuto, *A Cosmic Leap of Faith*, 42.

94 A. van Roon, *The Authenticity of Ephesians* (Leiden: E.J. Brill, 1974), 259.

95 van Roon, *The Authenticity of Ephesians*, 259.

96 van Kooten, *Cosmic Christology in Paul and the Pauline School*, 148-149.

97 van Kooten, *Cosmic Christology in Paul and the Pauline School*, 168.

98 van Roon, *The Authenticity of Ephesians*, 259.

The traditional conflation of Psalm 110:1 and Psalm 8:6 which emphasizes both an enthronement and a cosmic Christology is given a prominent place in the summary of the prayer in Ephesians 1:20-22.[99] The exaltation theme is heightened by listing expansively the enemies conquered at the resurrection (1:21). The influx of Christianity brought numerous individuals to the church, and is safe to assume that their previous means of protection from hostile powers are not completely forsaken. The most pressing question for the Ephesians according to Clinton E. Arnold is thus "where does Christ stand in relation to the hostile "powers"?"[100] More specifically "Is Christ alone sufficient, or there is a need for additional protection from the attacks and influences of these powers?" Therefore, as described by most interpreters, Ephesians presents cosmic Christology, where Christ is portrayed in numerous ways as being superior to all things.[101]

The theme of exaltation is taken up again in the identification of believers with Christ in his ascension in 2:6; and in rather different terms, in the preface of the description of Christ as the giver of gifts to the church in 4:8-10. This strongly suggests that the relationship of Christ to the powers and that of the cosmos was "a live issue to the readers of the epistle."[102] It is thus important to see that it is the author's task to establish firmly the Lordship of Christ. In contrast to contemporary deities such as Magna Mater and Hekate, who were claimed to possess power over the underworld and the cosmos, the author of the Ephesians introduces "the sole and supreme Lordship of Christ."[103] The idea of the exaltation of Christ also has significant implication to Christ's relationship to the powers in other New Testament writings, and is not new to Paul (1 Cor 15:24, 27; Phil 2:9; cf. 1 Pet 3:21-22). Colossians presents Christ as Lord, who "disarmed the rulers and authorities and made a public example of them, triumphing over them in it" (Col 2:15). The Philippian hymn also portrays the same thought that "God has highly exalted him and bestowed on him the name which is above every name" (Phil 2:9). 1 Peter is also explicit in stating the exaltation theology: "[Christ] has gone into heaven and is at the right hand of God, with angels, authorities, and powers made subject to him" (1 Pet 3:22).

Ephesians clearly presents cosmic Christology by saying that God intended to sum up all things in heaven and on earth in Christ (Eph 1:10), and

99 Clinton E. Arnold, *Ephesians: Power and Magic: The Concept of Power in Ephesians in Light of its Historical Setting*, SNTS 63 (Cambridge: CUP, 1989), 124.

100 Arnold, *Ephesians*, 123.

101 Cf. Arnold, *Ephesians*, 123-124.

102 Arnold, *Ephesians*, 125.

103 Arnold, *Ephesians*, 125.

also says that Christ is the one who fills everything (1:23; 4:10).[104] Ephesians highlights clearly the supremacy of Christ to "all things" and especially the malignant angelic powers.[105] The epistle attempts to communicate to the reader that these hostile powers are now under their control because the believers are now identified with the cosmic Christ, and thus power and authority are shared. Cosmic Christology of Ephesians presents the relationship between Christ, believers and the forces of the cosmos. Christ's fulfilment of all things could not be separated from Christ's fulfilment of the church. Christ permeates the cosmos and also the church with his dominion and blessings, but the epistle is however more interested in Christ's relationship with the church than to the cosmos.[106] While the cosmos receives cosmic changes through the blessing, the church receives "the eschatological pneumatical gifts or the pleroma."[107]

## 4.6. Hebrews

Philip Church in his article "Hebrew 1:10-12 and the Renewal of the Cosmos" compares Hebrews 1:10-12 and the quoted text of Psalms 102:25-27, which is generally understood as a prediction of dissolution.[108] By using the quotation in Hebrews as a proof, he argues that Isaiah predicts not dissolution but restoration. Hebrews 1:3 also claims that the exalted upholds all things, and also is active in a discussion about the dominion of the coming world (Heb 2:5-9). The author of the Hebrews utilizes the Psalm text and applies it in the discussion of the exaltation of the Son of God in the world to come.[109] Christ is portrayed as the changeless one who founded the cosmos, and though the cosmos deteriorated and decayed, Christ will roll it up like a cloak and will transform it (Heb 1:10-12) in the "coming world" (Heb 2:5).

Edward Adams in his essay "The Cosmology of Hebrews" argues that the author's use of ὀικουμένη (inhabited earth) in 2:5 rather than αἰών (age or era) as in 6:5 makes it clear that there is a new world in view, not merely a new era.[110] The new world in view is thus "a new worldly environment to

---

104 Frank J. Matera, *New Testament Christology* (Louisville: Westminster John Knox Press, 1999), 157.

105 Arnold, *Ephesians*, 125.

106 Matera, *New Testament Christology*, 157.

107 van Roon, *The Authenticity of Ephesians*, 259.

108 Philip Church, "Hebrews 1:10-12 and the Renewal of the Cosmos," *TynBul* 67.2 (2016): 269-286. After a careful exegesis on both the texts, and considering the context of the quotation in Hebrews, he concludes that this text in Isaiah "indicates not dissolution, but renewal after the destruction resulting from the exile."

109 See also Church, "Hebrews 1:10-12 and the Renewal of the Cosmos," 285-286.

110 Edward Adams, "The Cosmology of Hebrews," in *The Epistle to the Hebrews and Christian Theology*, ed. Richard Bauckham et al. (Grand Rapids: Eerdmans, 2009), 122-139 (137).

be populated by the people of God, i.e., a new created order." The Hebrew's worldview proposed by Adams inclines toward a cosmology that is not easily identified as the kind of Platonic cosmology, which James W. Thompson seeks to connect with the text.[111] However, there is no evidence that is strong enough to say that Hebrews embrace the anti-materialist dualism, and the idea of creation as being inherently negative is also absent in the epistle.[112]

Even though the religious background for Hebrews is as elusive as it is important, "no less than four different types of literature/systems of thought have been suggested as providing the milieu in which the homily is grounded: (i). Philo, (ii). Qumran, (iii). Gnosticism, and (iv). Apocalyptic and Rabbinical Judaism."[113] George W. MacRae in his article "Heavenly Temple and Eschatology in the Letter to the Hebrews," argues that there are two concepts in regards to the relationship between heaven and the heavenly temple in Hebrews.[114] The conception of heaven as a temple inclines more toward a Philonic or Platonic cosmology and the concept of a temple in heaven is associated more to apocalyptic cosmologies.[115]

No apocalyptic Jewish authors such as Philo and Josephus "hold the view that the cosmos is God's temple complex – with heaven itself being

---

111 James W. Thompson, *The Beginnings of Christian Philosophy: The Epistles to the Hebrews* (Washington DC: The Catholic Biblical Association of America, 1982), esp. 152 162. Thompson argues that Hebrews 12:27 made a contrast between the sense-perceptible world (the material world) from the intelligible world (the non-material world). James W. Thompson, "That which cannot be shaken: Some Metaphysical Assumptions in Heb 12:27," *JBL* 94 (1975): 580-587.

112 Cf. David M. Moffitt, "Serving in the Tabernacle in Heaven: Sacred Space, Jesus' High-Priestly Sacrifice, and Hebrews' Analogical Theology," in *Hebrews in Contexts*, ed. Gabriella Gelardini and Harold W. Attridge (Leiden: Brill, 2016), 259-279 (267).

113 Mikeal C. Parsons, "Son and High Priest: A Study in the Christology of Hebrews," *EvQ* 60 (1988): 195-216 (196); cf. F. F. Bruce, "Recent Contributions to the Understanding of Hebrews," *ExpTim* 80 (1969): 260-264. The most forceful and detailed argument regarding the influence of Philo on Hebrews was to be seen in C. Spicq's work *L'Epitre aux Hebreux*, 2 vols. (Paris: J. Gabalda, 1952), and for the assessment of this work, see J. C. McCullough, "Some Recent Developments in Research on the Epistle to the Hebrews," *IBS* 2 (1980): 141-165 (143). For the relationship between Hebrews and Qumran, see Yigael Yadin, "The Dead Sea Scrolls and the Epistle to the Hebrews," *Scripta Hierosolymitana* 4 (1958): 133-143. For Hebrews and Gnosticism, see T. W. Manson, "The Problem of the Epistle to the Hebrews," *BJRL* 32 (1949-1950): 1-17. For Hebrews and Judaism, see Gershom G. Scholem, *Major Trends in Jewish Mysticism* (New York: Schocken Books, 1961), 40-79.

114 George W. MacRae, "Heavenly Temple and Eschatology in the Letter to the Hebrews," *Semeia* 12 (1978): 179-199; for the distinction of these two conceptions, see also Jonathan Klawans, *Purity, Sacrifice, and the Temple: Symbolism and Supersessionism in the Study of Ancient Judaism* (Oxford: OUP, 2006), 111-144.

115 See also Moffitt, "Serving in the Tabernacle in Heaven," 268-269.

the cosmic sanctuary/temple," and also use the singular οὐρανός that agrees with Greek philosophical speculation about the nature of the cosmos.[116] However, Hebrews seems to have stand in contrast with this notion, especially due to the use of plural and singular forms of οὐρανός that fit well with the practice and thought of contemporaries who believed in multiple heavens. In Jewish apocalyptic cosmology, the highest heaven is where the tabernacle or temple structure is located, and this space is exactly where Jesus had entered according to Hebrews. References made to angels, and also to God and Jesus who thus dwell in the innermost sanctuary are to be understood as recalling and presupposing the cosmology of the Jewish apocalyptic literatures.[117]

David A. deSilva in his 2000 book *Perseverance in Gratitude: A Socio-Rhetorical Commentary on the Epistle "to the Hebrews,"* remarks how the author contrasts Jesus with Levitical priests on different points such as "mortal versus immortal, subject to sin versus not subject to sin."[118] This is to heighten the advantages that could be accumulated by the reader, who are according to the author of Hebrews are able now to approach God through "another priest arising according to the order of Melchizedek" (Heb 7:11). DeSilva also states that this emphasis is not just on the superiority of Christ, but also magnifies "the value of the access to God made possible by Jesus – an access never before made possible to God's covenant people."[119] As Jesus is the one who entered the Holy of Holies he became the eternal priest who has effected a better covenant (Heb 7:16-17, 22). Therefore, as Grant R. Osborne also states, that "The High Christology of the book begins in the first chapter, where we see (in a near Johannine sense) that God's revelation through his Son transcends the OT revelation through the prophets because he is "heir of all" as well as both Creator and sustainer of the universe (1:1-3)."[120] C. F. D. Moule in his 1977 book *The Origin of Christianity*, also had previously argued that "Hebrews starts with a fully 'cosmic' Christology, in which the Son of God is associated with creation and so is preexistent.[121]

In regards to the Christology of Hebrews, firstly Logos Christology needs attention. Though an explicit Logos Christology could not be read out from Hebrews, as is found in the prologue to John's Gospel, there are

116 Moffitt, "Serving in the Tabernacle in Heaven," 273.

117 Cf. Joy A. Barnard, *The Mysticism of Hebrews: Exploring the Role of Jewish Apocalyptic Mysticism in the Epistle to the Hebrews*, WUNT 2/331 (Tübingen: Mohr Siebeck, 2012), 209.

118 David A. DeSilva, *Perseverance in Gratitude: A Socio-Rhetorical Commentary on the Epistle "to the Hebrews"* (Grand Rapids: Eerdmans, 2000), 264.

119 Cf. DeSilva, *Perseverance in Gratitude*, 55.

120 Grant R. Osborne, "The Christ of Hebrews and other Religions," *JETS* 46/2 (2003): 249-267 (258).

121 C. F. D. Moule, *The Origin of Christology* (Cambridge: CUP, 1977), 101.

verses like Hebrews 1:2-4 (the dignity of the speech in the Son) that suggest Hellenistic Jewish conceptions of Logos and Sophia.[122] Ronald Williamson initially recognized a "rudimentary form of a Logos Christology,"[123] and later wrote: "My own earlier hesitations about the propriety of speaking of a Logos-doctrine in Hebrews have now been abandoned... to do justice to the Christology of Hebrews it is necessary to speak of it as a doctrine of the incarnation of the Logos in Jesus of Nazareth."[124]

In regards to the preexistent nature of Christ in Hebrews, there are significant passages that need to be discussed, which are Hebrews 1:5-13; 2:12-13; 5:5-6; 7:17, 21; and 10:5-9.[125] Though there are scholars who see these passages as undefined address by God to the earthly Jesus, there are others who see references to preexistence in these dialogues.[126] Along with Anthony T. Hanson, in his article "'Plurality of Divine Persons' and the Quotations in Hebrews 1.6ff," T. F. Glasson, also sees these references as a clue for the preexistent of Christ in Hebrews.[127] However, Gathercole is careful to accept these texts as being a proof for Hrebrews' preexistence of Christ, as there are other text where there is a speech between God and the Christian believer (Heb 13:5-6).[128]

George B. Caird is very careful in insisting the argument that Psalm 8 in Hebrews 2:6-8 control the argument found in Hebrews 1 and thus come to the conclusion that one cannot find the literal preexistence of Christ in Hebrews 1:1-14.[129] Likewise, L. D. Hurst sees that the interpretation of Hebrews 1 must be done in the light of the humanity of Christ in Hebrews 2.[130] Thus, Hurst

122 Jonathan I. Griffiths, *Hebrews and Divine Speech*, LNTS 507, ed. Mark Goodacre (London: Bloomsbury, 2014), 42.

123 Ronald Williamson, *Philo and the Epistle to the Hebrews*, Arbeiten zur Literatur und Geschichte des hellenistischen Judentums 4 (Leiden: Brill, 1970), 410.

124 Ronald Williamson, "The Incarnation of the Logos in Hebrews," *ExpTim* 95 (1983-1984): 4-8 (4).

125 Anthony T. Hanson comments on chapter one and two: "in 1.5, 1.7-13 we have the Father addressing the Son in Psalms. In 2.12, 13 we find the Son addressing the Father."

126 George B. Caird, *New Testament Theology*, ed. L. D. Hurst (Oxford: Clarendon, 1994), 64, argued that in these passages "God addresses the man Jesus." He goes on to argue that Heb 10:5 is not about Jesus' birth but about the beginning of his adult ministry (67). However, Simon J. Gathercole argues that the subject is "a body prepared" and is therefore specifically incarnational. *The Preexistent Son*, 44, n. 4.

127 T. F. Glasson, in his article "'Plurality of Divine Persons' and the Quotations in Hebrews 1.6ff," *NTS* 12 (1966): 270-272.

128 Gathercole, *The Pre-existent Son*, 44-45.

129 George B. Caird, "Exegetical Method of the Epistle to the Hebrews," *CJT* 5 (1959): 49.

130 L. D. Hurst, "The Christology of Hebrews 1 and 2," in *The Glory of Christ in the NT: Studies in Christology in Memory of George Bradford Caird*, ed. L. D. Hurst and N. T. Wright (Oxford: Clarendon, 1987), 151-164.

came to the conclusion that the Son in Hebrews 1 is not to be understood as a unique privileged, divine being who became human being, but to be termed as a human figure that attains to an exalted status.[131]

In contrast to these views Victor Rhee in his article "Christology in Hebrews 1:5-14: The Three Stages of Christ's Existence," argues that "a careful study of Hebrews 1 reveals that the author of Hebrews considered Jesus as the preexistent Son, not in a metaphorical but in a literal sense, before the stage of incarnation."[132] Further, Rhee convincingly argues that instead of reading chapter 1 with the background of humanity in chapter 2, Hebrews 1:5-14 and the rest of the epistle is to be understood in light of Hebrews 1:1-4.

Accordingly, the Son's three stages of existence is first introduced in the exordium (1:1-4), where God's communication in the Son stands in continuity with that speech in the prophets. Verses 2b-4 "presents the Son in terms used elsewhere to depict God's personalized 'wisdom' and 'word'" and thus affirms that "God's speech in the Son comprises the Son's being and action, not simply his words."[133] As the concept of preexistence may be found in Wisdom literature, the Logos in Philo, the Son of Man in 1 Enoch, the Torah of the Rabbis, the Logos of the Stoics, and also the myths of the Gnostics, references to Christ's preexistence would not pose much question to the author and the reader of Hebrews.[134]

## 4.7. Summary

As this chapter shows, it is evident that there are various texts and passages in the New Testament that could be accommodated or interpreted under the

131 Hurst, "The Christology of Hebrews 1 and 2," 163.

132 Victor (Sung Yul) Rhee, "Christology in Hebrews 1:5-14: The Three Stages of Christ's Existence," *JETS* 59 (2016): 717-729 (718); see also Victor (Sung Yul) Rhee, "The Role of Chiasm for Understanding Christology in Hebrews 1:1-14," *JBL* 131 (2012): 341-362 (360); cf. Paul Ellingworth, The Epistle to the Hebrews: A Commentary on the Greek Text, NIGTC (Grand Rapids: Eerdmans, 1993), 111.The uniqueness of Christ's origin is clearly portrayed, and is appointed as the "heir of all things" and through Christ God "made the world. First, Christ unique origin made him the very figure of the Father. Second, as Christ is the heir of all things, the magnitude of his dominion over the cosmos is indicated. Third, Christ is not a created instrument, but through Christ God created the worlds, and this shows the power of Christ's operation, which may be put forth in other words "according to his divine operation." Cf. Daniel Keating, "Thomas Aquinas and the Epistle to the Hebrews: The Excellence of Christ," in *Christology, Hermeneutics and Hebrews: Profiles from the History of Interpretation*, LNTS 423, ed. John C. Laansma and Daniel J. Treier (London: Bloomsbury, 2012), 84-99.

133 Griffiths, *Hebrews and Divine Speech*, 42.

134 For a detailed discussion of how preexistence functions in these ancient writings, see Fred Craddock, *The Pre-Existence of Christ in the New Testament* (Nashville: Abingdon, 1968), 31-76.

framework of cosmic Christology. The stages of development may differ, but the presence of cosmic Christology in many passages of the New Testament cannot be ignored.

The survey portrays that though the presentation of Jesus' divinity in Synoptic Gospels may not be easily interpreted as cosmic Christology, but hints that suggests Jesus' authority over the creation cannot be ignored. It is conceivable that there are accounts in the Synoptic Gospels that portray Jesus as God rather than human beings. Jesus' preexistent nature in some of the passages of the Synoptic Gospels is important to understand and develop cosmic Christology. The interrelationship between God, Jesus and human beings or the cosmos are closely woven together.

The chapter also shows that Johannine writings provide a more developed cosmic Christology than the Synoptic Gospels. Cosmic Christology can be read out from the use of the term Logos in the prologue of John's Gospel. The role of the Logos is however made clear that it is not only in human salvation but also in the entire cosmos. Jesus in John's Gospel speaks and acts as having divine origin throughout the Gospel (e.g. John 8:42; 17:3). The statement that Christ is "the origin of God's creation" (Rev 3:15), and Christ is "the Alpha and Omega, the beginning and the end" (Rev 21:6; 22:13; cf. 1 John 2:13-14) reaffirms the cosmic significance of Jesus' being. The use of Logos in Johannine writings shows the intimate interrelationship between God, Jesus Christ and the cosmos.

Christ is associated with cosmic role in God's dealing with the cosmos in Paul's writings. By implying Jesus as the source of grace and peace, Paul equates Jesus to God, and sees the union between God and Jesus in purpose (Gal 1:1-4). Cosmic Christology guided the discussion of the first chapter of Galatians. Paul understood Jesus as divine agent coming into the cosmos to represent God and to redeem those under the law. Paul also asserts Jesus as the key for the understanding of all revelation. Paul's Christology is framed under the understanding that Christ's coming to the cosmos is for all creation, and not only for humanity. First Corinthians 15:28, sums up well the cosmic significance of Christ's intervention in the cosmos. The idea that Christ, who humbles oneself through incarnation is a portrayal of his preexistence (Phil 2:6); the preexistent being who emptied oneself. The sharing of the name by Christ and God "the name that is above every name" does not create much tension in Paul's thought.

The Colossian hymn portrays the significance of resurrection of Christ and its consequences for creation. The invisible God who acts in creation is visible and touchable in the human Jesus, and he is the foundation for human beings to hear, see, and touch God. The cosmic Christology proclaimed by the Colossian hymn is to be lived in the daily lives of the baptized. Cosmic Christology does not only assert Christ's preexistent state of being but also how Christ could be encountered in the daily life of the believers, and in the relationship with the cosmos.

The Christology in Ephesians also represents cosmic Christology. The idea of the ascension and exaltation of Christ receives significant emphasis in this epistle. The intention of the author of Ephesians is clearly seen in the attempt made to establish firmly the Lordship of Christ to the readers' understanding. The exaltation theme is heightened (Eph 1:21), and the pressing question is where does Christ stand in relation to the hostile powers? Christ is thus portrayed in numerous ways as being superior to all things, and is alone sufficient from the attacks and influences of other powers. To this theologizing Ephesians employs cosmic Christology. God intends to sum up all things in heaven and on earth in Christ (Eph 1:10), and Christ is the one who fills everything (Eph 1:23; 4:10). Cosmic Christology of Ephesians presents the relationship between Christ, believers and the forces of the cosmos.

The Epistle to the Hebrews also claims that the exalted upholds all things (Heb1:3), and also is active in a discussion about the dominion of the coming world (Heb 2:5-9). Christ is portrayed as the changeless one who founded the cosmos, and though the cosmos deteriorated and decayed, Christ will roll it up like a cloak and will transform it (Heb 1:10-12) in the "coming world" (Heb 2:5). Though not as explicit as John's Gospel, Logos Christology is also found in Hebrews (e.g. 1:2-4). The preexistent status of Christ is also to be found in several passages (Heb1:5-13; 2:12-13; 5:5-6; 7:17, 21; 10:5-9). Hebrews portrayal of Jesus as immortal and not subject to sin is to place Jesus in contrast with Levitical priests who are mortal and subject to sin. Jesus is "another priest arising according to the order of Melchizedek" (Heb 7:11) and thus the believers are now able now to approach God through him. Jesus who is the heir of all and both the Creator and sustainer of the universe (Heb 1:1-3) is portrayed through cosmic Christology in Hebrews.

Chapter 5

# Cosmo-Christological Framework

## 5.1. Introduction

Christology occupies the core of New Testament theological discussion. This section of the study will look at the contribution and influences of different themes and concepts to the development of Christology. The fragmented and scattered christological throughout the writings of the New Testament reflect the nature and function of communities of different times and places. This will in turn help the study to grasp the basic features of early communities of faith, and how they conceptualized and developed Christology. Thus, the analysis will re-evaluate Christology in general from sociological point of view and proceed to contextual understanding of Christ, so as to provide a framework designed to highlight the cultural-eco-cosmic christological focus and significance on nature miracles in Matthew's Gospel.

## 5.2. Proclamation and Christology

Edwin K. Broadhead in his 1992 book *Teaching with Authority*, argues that the Gospels are "strategic narratives" of proclamation, and the main focus is on the subject of Christology.[1] To understand how Jesus was presented in the writings of the Gospels is to discern the authors' Christology. In the study of Christology, C. I. David Joy in his 2007 book *Christology Re-Visited*, states that Christology and Jesus movement cannot be separated.[2] The importance of examining the socio-political world of Palestine, and sources such as Josephus,

1 Edwin K. Broadhead, *Teaching with Authority: Miracles and Christology in the Gospel of Mark*, JSNTSup (Sheffield: SAP, 1992), 13.

2 C. I. David Joy, *Christology Re-Visited: Profiles and Prospects* (Bangalore: Asian Trading Corporation, 2007), 12.

Philo and many other non-canonical texts in relation to Christology must be understood. Therefore, it is significance to study how Jesus was proclaimed in a particular socio-cultural and religious milieu.

Questions like, "Who was or who is Jesus of Nazareth?" have been posed since the beginning of Christianity. The message and the person of Jesus of Nazareth receive much more attention in scholarly debate. The historicity of Jesus is well attested now in the scholarship but still there is no consensus on the significance of the person or the content of his teaching.[3] Rudolf Bultmann claims "He who formerly had been the *bearer* of the message was drawn into it and became its essential *content. The proclaimer became the proclaimed* – but the central question is: in what sense?"[4] Thus, the study of Christology is an attempt to answer the question – in what sense did the different writers of the Gospels present and portray Jesus.

Bultmann's assertion that, "*the message of Jesus* is a presupposition for the theology of the New Testament rather than a part of that theology itself" makes it clear that there would be no New Testament theology without the message of Jesus.[5] New Testament is thus an expression of the identity of Jesus, and is not a mere collection of his actions and sayings. The opening accounts of the Gospels make the connection apparent between history and theological reflection.[6] Matthew and Mark open their Gospels in a similar way, by representing Jesus as Christ or Messiah – "The book of the genealogy of Jesus Christ, the son of David, the son of Abraham" (Matt 1:1), and "The beginning of the gospel of Jesus Christ, the Son of God" (Mark 1:1).[7] Though Luke was trying "to write an orderly account" (Luke 1:3) but basically to make known "the truth concerning" (Luke 1:4) Christian faith. Therefore, these documents may have lack biographical interest as one might have expected, and the reason might be their recognition of Jesus as the Christ.

## 5.3. Jesus' World – Milieu, Archaeology and Christology

Biblical scholarship is mainly literary studies and text-centred, and the text of the Bible was the primary object and exegesis. Archaeology plays a role to assist exegesis or to discover new written materials. This trend is now blurred with the realization of the significance of archaeological findings and positive interaction began to emerge. New discoveries of documents, inscriptions,

3 Hans Schwarz, *Christology* (Grand Rapids: Eerdmans, 1998), 1.

4 Rudolf Bultmann, *Theology of the New Testament*, trans. K. Grobel, 2 vols. (New York: Charles Scribner's Sons, 1951), 1:33.

5 Bultmann, *Theology of the New Testament*, 1:3.

6 Schwarz, *Christology*, 2.

7 Scripture translations here and throughout the study are from RSV, if not mentioned otherwise.

papyri, especially from Qumran strengthened this interaction. However, nonverbal materials and symbols need to be interpreted more carefully, and this area is where biblical scholars are lacking. Jonathan L. Reed in his 2000 book *Archaeology and the Galilean Jesus*, reckons this as a lack of interaction between New Testament scholars and archaeologists, and shows his suspect and says it is akin to Rorschach test.[8]

According to Seán Freyne, the initial focus of archaeological exploration in the region was on the origins of Israel, and also the development of synagogue art and architecture in the Byzantine period.[9] Early attempts made by Gustav Dalman's reports on Palestinian archaeology and topography, or Joachim Jeremias' archaeological and ethnographic studies generated interest to find the real world of Jesus.[10] Shirley Jackson Case's article "Jesus and Sepphoris" is another interesting earlier work that attempts to draw a clearer picture of Jesus, especially the life before ministry.[11] Craig A. Evans in his 2012 book *Jesus and His World*, argues from archaeological findings that Jesus cannot be a Cynic, as some scholars had suspected.[12] He also remarks the importance of archaeological findings in Galilee in general and in Sepphoris in particular. These findings make the student of the New Testament to re-evaluate many things, and it is no longer tenable to think of Jesus as having grown up in isolated village. These discoveries made it clear that Jesus grew up in a village with a large urban centre at its immediate vicinity. Archaeology opened up new insights and prospects to better understand Jesus and his ministry.

To situate Jesus in Galilean context, an analysis of the specific social conditions of Galilee under Roman rule, especially during the reigns of Herod the Great and Herod Antipas is mandatory. The discussion of social resistance in the form of various movements in and around the area during this time is also important. Morten Høerning Jensen in his 2010 book *Herod Antipas*

---

8 Jonathan L. Reed, *Archaeology and the Galilean Jesus: A Re-examination of the Evidence* (Pennsylvania: Trinity Press International, 2000), 1-2. Rorschach test is a type of projective test used in psychoanalysis, in which a standard set of symmetrical ink blots of different shapes and colours is presented one by one to the subject, who is asked to describe what they suggest or resemble. According to the subject's psychological state of being, the ink blots could be seen and described with various different meanings.

9 Seán Freyne, *Jesus, A Jewish Galilean: A New Reading of the Jesus-Story* (London: T&T Clark, 2004), 13.

10 Gustav Dalman, *Orte und Wege Jesu*, 3rd ed. (Gütersloh: Bertelsmann, 1924), cited in Reed, *Archaeology and the Galilean Jesus*, 6; Joachim Jeremias, *Jerusalem in the Time of Jesus: An Investigation into Economic and Social Conditions during the New Testament Period*, trans. F. H. and C. H. Cave (Philadelphia: Fortress, 1969).

11 Shirley Jackson Case, "Jesus and Sepphoris," *JBL* 45 (1926): 14-22.

12 For details, see the chapter "In the Shadow of Sepphoris: Growing up in Nazareth." Craig A. Evans, *Jesus and His World: The Archaeological Evidence* (London: SPCK, 2012), 13-37.

*in Galilee*, identifies four major issues that are associated with Galilee that can be related to historical Jesus: (1) The nature of the political situation, and particularly whether the population had revolutionary tendencies, (2) the origins of the Galileans, (3) the nature of the relationship between cities and villages, and (4) the cultural milieu.[13] The first and the last issues are important in relation to the understanding of Christology in New Testament.

There are scholars who argue for a healthy economy in Galilee, and general prosperity for the general populace. They also argue for a mutually beneficial or close relationship between the cities and the surrounding rural areas.[14] There are also other scholars who argue that even if the broader economy was healthy, due to the inherent structures present in the agrarian societies, the people at the lowest end of the social spiral did not gain much.[15] Consequently, the relationship between cities and villages was based on the exploitation of the resources of the rural poor by the urban elite. Therefore, the relation between the cities and rural areas surrounding them was leech-like characters rather than symbiotic in nature. These works paint the general picture of the geo-political realities of Jesus' world. The socio-political context of Jesus plays significant roles in shaping the Christology of the Gospels in particular and other New Testament writings in general.

---

13 Morten Hørning Jensen, *Herod Antipas in Galilee: The Literary and Archaeological Sources on the Reign of Herod Antipas and its Socio-Economic Impact on Galilee*, 2nd ed. (Tübingen: Mohr, 2010), 5-9.

14 Douglas Edwards, "The Socio-Economic and Cultural Ethos of Lower Galilee in the First Century: Implications for the Nascent Jesus Movement," in *The Galilee in Late Antiquity*, ed. Lee I. Levine (New York: The Jewish Theological Seminary of America, 1992), 53-73; Mark Chancey, *Greco-Roman Culture and the Galilee of Jesus* (Cambridge: CUP, 2005); Jensen, *Herod Antipas in Galilee*, 9-34.

15 Cf. Amanda Witmer, *Jesus, the Galilean Exorcist: His Exorcisms in Social and Political Context*, LNTS (New York: T&T Clark, 2012), 61; Richard A. Horsley, *Bandits, Prophets, and Messiahs: Popular Movements in the Time of Jesus* (Harrisburg: Trinity Press International, 1999); Richard A. Horsley, *Galilee: History, Politics, People* (Valley Forge: Trinity Press International, 1995); William E. Arnal, *Jesus and the Village Scribes: Galilean Conflicts and the Setting of Q* (Minneapolis: Fortress, 2000); William E. Arnal, "The Parable of the Tenants and the Class Consciousness of the Peasantry," in *Text and Artifact in the Religions of Mediterranean Antiquity: Essays in Honour of Peter Richardson*, ed. Stephen G. Wilson and Michael Desjardins, vol. 9 of *Studies in Christianity and Judaism/Études Sur Le Christianisme et Le Judaïsme* (Waterloo: WLUP, 2000), 135-157; Reed, *Archaeology and the Galilean Jesus*, 108-114; John Dominic Crossan and Jonathan L. Reed, *Excavating Jesus: Beneath the Stones, Behind the Texts: The Key Discoveries for Understanding Jesus in his World* (San Francisco: Harper SanFrancisco, 2001); Freyne, "Archaeology and the Historical Jesus," 64-83; John S. Kloppenborg, *The Tenants in the Vineyard: Ideology, Economics, and Agrarian Conflict in Jewish Palestine* (Tübingen: Mohr Siebeck, 2006).

Freyne also changed his overall view of the political and economic situation of Galilee due to his further access of archaeological data. Especially in his article "Urban-Rural Relations in First-Century Galilee." He states that it is an exaggeration to describe the rural-urban relationship as "uniformly hostile" but he still argues "that the rural animosities toward the cities were deep-seated and permanent"[16] Jesus therefore lived in a cultural context that witnesses the continuous growing control of colonialism. According to Joy, the healings of the Lepers and demon possessed individuals (Mark 1:40-44; 3:7-12), or the calling of the tax collector (Mark 2:13-17) indicate the commitment Jesus of Galilee had, to usher the people of the margin into the fullness of life. The increasing gap between the urban and rural villages in Galilee was the result of colonialism; it creates isolation of the rural areas both politically and culturally.[17]

In addition to this rural-urban relation, the conditioning effects of Alexander's Hellenization pose another difficult situation in a wider context of Palestine.[18] The living condition of Jesus thus includes the unwanted presence of foreign troops and rulers, and various revolts and attempts to agitate against foreign oppressive groups must have moulded and conditioned much of the writings of the Gospels. Jesus' movement also move along the line of resistance of the crowd to Roman colonialism and Jerusalem authoritarianism.[19]

Jesus addressed the challenge to the social and religious values of the world he was living in. Though social issues could be separated by modern readers, it was not possible in the culture which was pervasively religious. It is thus fruitless to argue whether Jesus' concerns were social or religious. Jesus cannot be understood apart from his culture which was shaped by religious traditions. His learning will include mostly of the stories and traditions contained in the Jewish Scriptures; and he was taught certainly in his home by his parents and in the synagogue school by elders.[20] Especially as a Jew, his history was explicitly embedded with the relationship with God, whose name they do not even pronounce because of reverence. Jesus' education had to be primarily religious.

16 Seán Freyne, "Urban-Rural Relations in First-Century Galilee: Some Suggestions from the Literary Sources," in *The Galilee in Late Antiquity*, ed. Lee I. Levine (New York: The Jewish Theological Seminary of America, 1992), 75-94 (83).

17 Joy, *Christology Re-Visited*, 23.

18 Joy, *Christology Re-Visited*, 21.

19 Joy, *Christology Re-Visited*, 23.

20 "The hypothesis of some formal education in the local synagogue is well grounded." John P. Meier, *The Roots of the Problem and the Person*, vol. 1 of *A Marginal Jew: Rethinking the Historical Jesus*, ABRL (New York: Doubleday, 1991), 277.

## 5.4. Infancy Narratives and Christology

Matthew and Luke reserve approximately five chapters for the infancy materials, and Joy argues the significance of these materials for the Gospel writers in their endeavour to define and describe their Christology.[21] The concept of messiah and messianic expectation provides special pertinence for the infancy narratives. As the infancy narratives reflects a Christology of the presence of God (Emmanuel – Matt 1:23), it is an appropriate inclusion in this discussion.[22]

David R. Bauer, in his 1995 article "The Kingship of Jesus in the Matthean Infancy Narrative," also reveals that little attention is given to the kingship of Jesus in Matthean Christology.[23] He argues that Matthew gives prominence to the kingship of Jesus in the infancy narrative by developing Jesus' kingship "by means of a double contrast."[24] These contrasts are presented through Herod versus Jesus, and Herod versus Magoi. Therefore, it is clear that Matthew's treatment of infancy narratives is significant for his Christology. These christological elements in Matthew's Gospel are so vital to examine the later christological passages.[25]

As both the structures of the infancy narratives of Matthew and Luke are woven around Jesus' birth there are no arguments that could seriously doubt that the person of Christ is the centre in these infancy narratives. Without much consideration of what actually exist in the text, one could have easily construct eschatology as a focal point in these narratives. The writer of the Gospels first and foremost understood the person of Jesus in eschatological terms, which proceeds to soteriology. Jesus is pictured as an eschatological fulfilment of God's promise to Abraham. The articulation and personification of the eschatological event is the person of Jesus.

Kingsbury, after a thorough examination of the structure of Matthew's Gospel concludes that it is "focusing as it does on the person, ministry and death

21 Joy, *Christology Re-Visited*, 15.

22 Cf. Joy, *Christology Re-Visited*, 17. Raymond E. Brown argues that the relationship between "Son of David" and "Son of God" which exists in the Matthean account of the ministry is to be found in his infancy narrative. Raymond E. Brown, *The Birth of the Messiah: A Commentary on the Infancy Narratives in the Gospels of Matthew and Luke* (New York: Doubleday, 1993), 135. However, J. Nolland argues that no Son of God Christology is to be found in Matthew's infancy narratives. See J. Nolland, "No Son-of-God Christology in Matthew 1:18-25)," *JSNT* 62 (1996): 3-12.

23 David R. Bauer, "The Kingship of Jesus in the Matthean Infancy Narrative: A Literary Analysis," *CBQ* 57 (1995): 306-323.

24 Bauer, "The Kingship of Jesus in the Matthean Infancy Narrative: A Literary Analysis," 307.

25 Joy, *Christology Re-Visited*, 17.

and resurrection of Jesus Messiah, is thoroughly Christological in tenor."[26] By placing Matthew's infancy narrative in the context of the whole Gospel, it can be affirmed that Jesus is the central figure of it. Kingsbury analysis states that Matthew's Gospel in structured firstly around the three major headings (1:1; 4:17; 16:21), secondly around the five ending formulae (7:28; 11:1; 13:53; 19:1 & 26:1), and thirdly around two sets of three-fold summary passages (4:23-25; 9:35; 11:1b & 16:21; 17:22-23; 20:17-19).[27] Significantly, Kingsbury indicates how the name Jesus predominates in all these vital passages. Krister Stendahl in his article "Quis et Unde?" also indicates the centrality of Christology in the infancy narrative.[28] Brown suggests an expansion of Stendahl's formula (who and where) by adding how and where as a basic approach for Matthew 1-2.[29] Thus, this is how it looks with an expansion:

i. Who? The genealogy of Jesus (1:1-17)
ii. How? The legal adoption of Jesus (1:18-25)
iii. Where? Visiting the birthplace of Jesus (2:1-12)
iv. When? From Bethlehem to Nazareth (2:13-23)

### *5.4.1. Davidic Messiahship*

Not as prominent as in Matthew's Gospel, the theme of Davidic Messiahship is also clearly evident in Luke's infancy narrative. The emphasis on the theme is given on the same level Κύριος, υἱὸς, and σωτέρ. The concept of Christ as ἅγιον and as the revelation of God is another christological concept in Luke's infancy narrative. After perusing the two narratives, differences and contrasting ideas appear. It has to be noted that Matthew's genealogy seems to present Jesus as a true Israelite, and in particular of Davidic descent, while Luke seems to be more interested to show the true humanity of Jesus.[30] This might be the main reason for differences in form and content between the two genealogies. However, the focal point in both the genealogies is not to identify the ancestors, but to identify to the audience who Jesus is. Passages like Matthew 2:4 and Luke 1:69; 2:26 and 3:15 contain some significant evidence of the early-century Jewish messianic hopes. Though there are diversities in

---

26 Jack D. Kingsbury, *Matthew: Structure, Christology, Kingdom* (Philadelphia, PA: Fortress, 1975), 36.

27 Kingsbury, *Matthew*, 7-36.

28 Krister Stendahl, "Quis et Unde? An Analysis of Matt.1-2," in *Judentum, Urchristentum, Kirche*, ed. W. Eltester (Berlin: Topelmann, 1964), 94-105.

29 Raymond E. Brown, *The Community of the Beloved Disciple* (New York: Paulist, 1979), 53-54.

30 Ben Witherington, "Birth of Jesus," *DJG*: 60-74.

Jewish views of messianism, there is no doubt that they held strikingly similar views concerning the coming of the Davidic Messiah.[31]

At the outset one needs to understand the transition of Christology from a Christology of Jesus to a Christology of the early church. One clear point of transition is seen in the use of the title "Christ or Messiah." The term Messiah gradually became associated with the kings of Judah, but not exclusively. It was customary in the Ancient Near East to anoint people as they assumed important new positions in the community (βασιλεύς, ἱερεύς, προφήτης). Anointing had a wide range of meanings, but usually it served as a marking of divine protection, health, and mission. The term "messiah" gradually became associated with the kings of Judah, though not exclusively. Following the Babylonian Exile (586-539 BCE) the use of the title connotes the futuristic hope of Israel for restoration and deliverance from oppression.

The most prominent christological motif in Matthew's infancy narrative is the Davidic Messianic theme, and serves as Matthew's predominant Christology. The genealogy traces the history of Davidic monarchy throughout the entire history of Israel. The threat and protection of the royal line in the infancy narrative of Matthew's Gospel parallels the history of Israel.[32] W. D. Davies, after a careful examination on the gematria of the name David, concludes that the three fourteens in the genealogy follow the numerical value of the name David.[33]

The greeting of the angel to Joseph, the title Son of David, and the confirmation of Joseph as having legal Davidic heirship all confirm the centrality of Davidic Covenant in Matthew's infancy narrative. However, as I. Howard Marshall maintains that in regard to the subject of Jesus' Messiahship, "Luke's usage is basically that of his sources, and he does not show any independent development of it."[34] Though Marshall does not regard the idea of kingship as Luke's primary concern, A. R. C. Leaney and Earle E. Ellis regard it as a central theme in Luke's Gospel.[35] When we look at the Acts of the Apostles, a great deal of the usage of Χριστός can be found which is in connection with Davidic Messianic theme. Though there are places where

31 Cf. Graham Stanton, "Messianism and Christology: Mark, Matthew, Luke and Acts," in *Redemption and Resistance: The Messianic Hopes of Jews and Christians in Antiquity*, ed. Markus Bockmuehl and James C. Paget (New York: T&T Clark, 2007), 78-96 (80).

32 Derek Jeffery Morphew, "A Critical Examination of the Infancy Narratives in the Gospels according to Matthew and Luke," (Ph.D. diss., The University of Cape town, 1980), 225.

33 W. D. Davies, *The Setting of the Sermon on the Mount* (Cambridge: CUP, 1963), 74-77.

34 I. Howard Marshall, *Luke, Historian and Theologian* (Exeter: Paternoster, 1970), 168-169.

35 A. R. C. Leaney, *A Commentary on the Gospel According to St. Luke* (London: Adam & Charles Black, 1966), 34-37; Earle E. Ellis, *The Gospel According to Luke*, CB (Edinburgh: T. Nelson & Sons, 1966), 10.

Luke's explicit emphasis of Davidic Messiahship could be found, it is still safe to say that Luke emphasizes it lesser than Matthew.[36]

### *5.4.2. Saviour*

Bultmann and others assume that the term σωτέρ was adapted from the Hellenistic mystic religion. Bultmann states "The general sense of the mysteries may be defined as the imparting of "salvation" (σωτερία), hence the deities are called "Saviour" (σωτέρ)."[37] However scholars are less certain whether σωτέρ title is of fundamental significance for the mystery cults, and its influence to the Christian use of the title is more questionable. Apart from the Imperial cultus, the evidence affirms that σωτέρ was not a common terminology in the later mystery cults. Due to this evidence Oscar Cullmann concludes that the use of σωτέρ in the Gospels is a derivation from the Old Testament, and also from the Christian response to the use of κύριος for Jesus. He believes there is "reason to assume that this christological designation is an Old Testament title of honour for God transferred to Jesus," and that: "the name "Saviour" (like all the Divine attributes) was ascribed to Jesus in connection with his dignity as Kyrios."[38]

In the Old Testament, only Othniel and Ehud were called saviour (Judg 3:9, 15), and the title was not in common usage for the Messiah. Though the title was usually ascribed to God in the Old Testament, the New Testament uses it for God and almost as much as for Jesus.[39] When the title Saviour is ascribed to Jesus, it is often found in conjunction either with Jesus as κύριος (Luke 2:11) or as God (Titus 2:13-14). Therefore Cullmann's conclusion makes sense; he states "Primarily we are concerned here with the transfer to Jesus of an Old Testament divine attribute. Jesus is the σωτέρ because he will save his people from their sins. This is how Matthew 1:21 explains the name Jesus. This proper name is one of the Hebrew forms of the title "Saviour" applied to God in the Old Testament."[40]

What is observed here in Luke's use of σωτέρ and σωτερία in the infancy narrative corresponds well enough to that of Matthew's infancy narrative. Matthew's infancy narrative contains three tiers of christological teaching: Jesus is understood to be the Messianic king of the lineage of David, and he is understood as the Saviour, and also as Emmanuel. The title Emmanuel in the

---

36 Morphew, "A Critical Examination," 230-231.

37 Reginald H. Fuller, *The Foundations of New Testament Christology* (London: Collins, 1965), quoting Rudolf Bultmann, *The New Testament and Mythology and Other Basic Writings* (Minneapolis: Augsburg, 1984), 157-158.

38 Oscar Cullmann, *The Christology of the New Testament* (London: SCM, 1963), 238-239.

39 Examples are 1 Tim 1:1; 2:3; 4:10; Titus 1:3; 2:10; 3:4; Jude vs. 25; Luke 1:47.

40 Cullmann, *The Christology of the New Testament*, 242.

infancy narrative of Matthew's Gospel reflects the significance of the presence of God (1:23), and thus provide a key word for locating Christology in the Gospel.[41]

## 5.5. Baptism of Jesus and Christology

Though baptism is in no way unique to the early Christians or Jewish practices, the writer of the Gospels utilize the practice to formulate their Christologies, particularly a christological title namely the Son of Man. The practice of baptism is widespread, it can be grouped in the same place with that of Hindu rituals in the Ganges river, the purification ritual in the Babylonian cult of Enki, the Egyptian practices of purifying new-born children and also the symbolic revivification rites performed on the dead. Even the term βαπτίζω and related terms were used to define ritual practices by different religious communities of early century.[42]

The suggestion that Jewish proselyte baptism or Qumran washings (cf. 1QS 3:4–9; 4:18-22; 6:14–23) was a precursor of John's baptism looks plausible at first, but the differences found among these rituals are significant enough to set apart John's baptism. The major distinction is that the Jewish proselyte baptism was for Gentiles, and Qumran washings unlike John's baptism were not a one-time initiation rite.[43] Andreas J. Köstenberger in his article "Baptism in the Gospel" also makes it clear that it is impossible to know when proselyte baptism was initiated.[44] Thus, the absence of evidence makes it unfair to assume it as an antecedent of John's baptism and also the Christian baptism.

Unlike the Jewish proselyte baptism where Gentiles were convert to Judaism, John's baptism was for the Jews, and not for the Gentiles. Ben Witherington asserts that heredity is considered by John the Baptist as an inadequate safeguard from the coming of God's wrath, and thus Israel on the same level with the Gentiles was lost. They all need to repent and receive God's forgiveness to receive safety from the wrath of God.[45] Köstenberger also points out that "John's baptism and Jewish proselyte baptism both harken back to Jewish ritual cleansing and bathing practices."[46] Therefore, like other Jews

---

41 Joy, *Christology Re-Visited*, 17.

42 The term and other related terms were associated with the Early Cretan religion, Thracian religion, Eleusinian mystery religions and in several Gnostic groups and cults. David S. Dockery, "Baptism," *DJG*: 55-58.

43 Dockery, "Baptism," 56-57.

44 Andreas J. Köstenberger, "Baptism in the Gospel," in *Believer's Baptism: Sign of the New Covenant in Christ*, NSBT (Nashville: B&H Academics, 2006), 11-34 (11).

45 Ben Witherington, "John the Baptist," *DJG*: 388-389.

46 This suggestion receives support from mishnaic passages such as m. Pesah. 8:8, where it says "If a man became a proselyte on the day before Passover he may immerse himself

who receive John's baptism at the time, so also Jesus did (Mat 3:15 - "Let it be so now; for it is proper for us in this way to fulfill all righteousness"). The account of Jesus' baptism is important and significant for the Gospel writers. All the Synoptic Gospels recorded it, but in John' Gospel it is not directly described (Matt 3:13-17; Mark 1:9-11; Luke 3:21-23; cf. John 1:29-33).

In search for the right place to locate the framework of baptism, Joy in his 2007 book *Christology-Revisited*, draws upon an argument from Dieter Zeller, who sees elements of Hellenism and Orientalism in the baptism narratives.[47] Joy also states that "The mentioning of Heracles (descent from gods) and divine man concept of Hellenism are reflected in the baptism narratives (Mark 1:9-11)."[48] He further argues that "Ideas such as messianic secret, distinctiveness of the kingdom of God and identity of Jesus are inseparable part of this episode."[49] Therefore he emphasizes the importance of placing baptism event "in the wider and deeper framework of Hellenism and Judaism," but he insists that "Hellenism and similar religio-cultural schools need to be brought into the forefront of discussion."[50]

Mark uses the event of Jesus' baptism to initiate his christological moment in the life of Jesus, but Matthew and Luke did it in their infancy narratives. Having said this, it has to be understood that Jesus' Lordship which is recognized mainly in the resurrection is being transferred to different parts of Jesus' life in the Gospels. This is why Brown used the expression "christological moment" to refer to those scenes taken from the life and ministry of Jesus that became the vehicle for the expression of a post-resurrectional Christology.[51] Thus, the shift in the development of Christology is made clear that the eschatologically oriented resurrection is transformed into Jesus being anointed with the Spirit on baptism event, and consequently the title Son of God is asserted.

The Son of God is often utilized to signify important christological moments in the Gospels (e.g., Mark 15:39). Modern minds must be cautious not to read late doctrinal development back into biblical texts, and since the doctrine of the Trinity is not defined until the fourth century CE, it ought not to be read into the pages of the New Testament. Larry W. Hurtado stresses the importance of Jewish monotheistic background to discuss early Christian

---

and consume his Passover-offering in the evening." This text is a discussion of Jewish proselyte baptism "in the context of Levitical cleansing in preparation for the Passover." Köstenberger, "Baptism in the Gospel," 12.

47 Joy, *Christology Re-Visited*, 18, citing Dieter Zeller, "New Testament Christology in its Hellenistic Reception," *NTS* 46 (2000): 312-333.

48 Joy, *Christology Re-Visited*, 18.

49 Joy, *Christology Re-Visited*, 18.

50 Joy, *Christology Re-Visited*, 18-19.

51 Raymond E. Brown, "Gospel Infancy Narrative Research From 1976 to 1986: Part II (Luke)," *CBQ* 48 (1986): 677-678.

devotion to Christ.[52] He provides two characteristics of ancient Jewish religiousness:

> (1) a remarkable ability to combine a genuine concern for God's uniqueness with an interest in other figures with transcendent attributes which are described in the most exalted terms and which we may call "principal agent" figures who are even likened to God in some cases; and (2) an exhibition of monotheistic scruples, particularly and most distinctively in public cultic/liturgical behaviour.[53]

According to Hurtado, phrases having links with adjectives such as one, only, sole, alone and others are significant; God being pictured as monarch over all; divine title linked with the term such as living or true; positive confessional formulas "Yahweh is God"; God's glory defined as not transferable; God described as without rival; God referred to as incomparable; and scriptural passages used as expressions of monotheism.[54] The narratives of Jesus' baptism contain implicit christological motif which is monotheistic in nature.[55]

## 5.6. Ministry of Jesus and Christology

The people whom Jesus administered are referred in the Gospels by various terms: the poor, the blind, the lame, the crippled, the lepers, the hungry, the miserable, sinners, prostitutes, tax collectors, demoniacs, the persecuted, the downtrodden, the captives, all who labour and are overburdened, the rabble who know nothing of the law, the crowds, the little ones, the least, the babes, the lost sheep of the house of Israel.[56] Jeremias observes that Jesus generally refers to them as the poor or the little ones, while these same people are referred by the Pharisees as sinners or the rabble, who know nothing of the law.[57]

This authoritative presentation of Jesus is reflected in many of the christological passages. Jesus thus prophesied that the divine political power

52 Larry W. Hurtado, *How on Earth Did Jesus Become a God? Historical Questions about Earliest Devotion to Jesus* (Grand Rapids, MI: Eerdmans, 2005), 111.

53 Hurtado, *How on Earth Did Jesus Become a God*, 111.

54 Joy, *Christology Re-Visited*, 19, citing Hurtado, *How on Earth Did Jesus Become a God*, 119-120.

55 Joy, *Christology Re-Visited*, 20.

56 Examples are Mark 1:23, 32-34, 40; 2:3, 15, 17; 3:1; 9:17-18, 42; 12:40, 42; Luke 4:18; 5:27; 6:20-21; 7:34, 37, 39; 10:21; 11:46; 14:13, 21; 15:1-2; 18:10, 13, 22; Matt 5:10-12; 8:28; 9:10, 14; 10:3, 15, 42; 11:28; 15:24; 19:30; 20:16; 21:31-32; 25:40, 45; John 7:49; 9:1-2, 8, 34.

57 Joachim Jeremias, *New Testament Theology: The Proclamation of Jesus*, trans. John Bowden (New York: Scribner's, 1971), 112.

of the future would be in the hands of the weaker section of the social strata (e.g. Luke 6:20; 12:32; 22:29, 30; 'poor in spirit' in Matt 5:3). The comparison between the rich and the poor and the mighty and the lowly is evident in the Gospels, and the reversal of these fortunes is what Jesus' words partly implied. However, Jesus' prediction does not connote only the changing of places but the new way of life. The Christology of authority is again reflected in these passages and the authority is understood in terms of solidarity, justice and reconciliation. The structure of the kingdom is here without oppression and power of domination, but of the mutual and spontaneous responsibility to another (Mark 10:42-45).

In Jesus' correspondence to the law, the opposition is not to the law as such, but the attitude of the practitioners. Again the authoritative control by the religious leaders had made the law into burden, whereas the true intention is to be a service. Jesus' opposition towards the leaders of his time largely arise from the fact that those who enslaved themselves to the law impose oppressive burdens to others, especially the low ranking public.[58] Jesus is not interested in abolishing the law (Matt 5:17-18), and do not intend to make addition or subtraction or emendation (Matt 5:18). Jesus does not oppose the law itself but authoritatively opposes the authority that continuously makes imposition to the people, and thus Christology of authority is ascertained through Jesus' attitude to the law.

Jesus' proclamation of the salvation of God shows how he understands the signs of the times. It is clear that Jesus' understanding of the signs involves his own successful ministry among the marginalized.[59] The liberating praxis present in Jesus' ministry moulds the Christology of New Testament.

Jeremias states that "The use of the everyday word "abba" as a form of address to God is the most important linguistic innovation on the part of Jesus" and is unique when compared with the contemporary.[60] The way Jesus approached God was contrastingly different with that of the tradition. Jesus addresses God as abba, and teaches others to do the same (Luke 11:2), but no one had taught this to others before. The intimacy Jesus had with the Father and the intimacy which he urged on his disciples; was scandalous for the Jewish leadership during the time.[61] Jesus' use of abba as an address to God shows and expresses the core of the relationship between Jesus and the Father.

58 Nolan, *Jesus before Christianity*, 86-87.

59 Nolan, *Jesus before Christianity*, 95.

60 Jeremias, *New Testament Theology*, 36.

61 Kenan B. Osborne, *Sacramental Theology: A General Introduction* (New York: Paulist Press, 1988), 121. However, Joseph A. Fitzmyer argues that "There is no evidence in the literature of pre-Christian or first-century Palestinian Judaism that abba was used in any sense as a personal address for God by an individual – and for Jesus to address God as abba or Father is therefore something new." Joseph A. Fitzmyer, "'Abba and Jesus'

## 5.7. Jesus' Death and Resurrection and Christology

Since there are numbers of canonical and non-canonical references to the crucifixion, it is best to understand the event as historical.[62] The portrayals of Jesus' death and resurrection in the Gospels are impressively similar. The similarities found among the Synoptic Gospels are understandable, but John's Gospel also shows remarkable similar patterns. The interesting fact is that, "out of the approximately six percent of material in John's Gospel that is paralleled in the Synoptic Gospels, almost all of it occurs in the fourth evangelist's account of Jesus' sufferings and death in Jerusalem."[63] After a careful consideration between the passion narratives of the Gospels, Brown thinks that John did not rely on Mark and also on Matthew. He states that Matthew's separate material is not reflected in John's Gospel. He agrees with other scholars who maintain that Luke and John drew from earlier traditions that had "certain similarities and cross-fertilization."[64] These resemblances can be taken as pointers to understand the event as historical, as had been already stated. The suggestion that the writers of the Gospels shared and drew from an earlier stereotyped oral tradition or an earlier connected written account is either useless or meaningless supposition. It is also affirmed that there are more christological fragments in the passion narratives than any other parts of the Gospels.[65]

---

Relation to God," in *A cause de L'Evangile*, Lectio Divina 123 (Paris: Cerf, 1985), 28. However, the discovery of 4Q372 that contains writing in which God is called abba, is mentioned by Eileen M. Schuller in her article, "The Psalm of 4Q372 1 within the Context of Second Temple Prayer." Eileen M. Schuller, "The Psalm of 4Q372 1 within the Context of Second Temple Prayer," *CBQ* 54 (1992): 75-79. Thus, there is an argument that says, in *b. Ta'an.* 23b, God is referred to as abba, but Jeremias convincingly argues that this is not an exception mainly because the word abba is applied to God in almost a mocking manner, and the one address in this text is not God but the "Master of the world." Donald A. Hagner, *The Jewish Reclamation of Jesus: An Analysis and Critique of Modern Jewish Study of Jesus* (Eugene: Wipf & Stock, 1984), 212; Jeremias further states that "With the help of my assistants I have examined the whole later Jewish literature of prayer, and the result was that in no place in this immense literature is this invocation of God to be found." Joachim Jeremias, "The Lord's Prayer in Modern Research," in *New Testament Issues*, ed. Richard Batey (New York: Harper & Row, 1970), 95.

62 Joy, *Christology Re-Visited*, 34.

63 Richard N. Longenecker, "Christological Materials in the Early Christian Communities," in *Contours of Christology in the New Testament*, ed. Richard N. Longenecker (Grand Rapids: Eerdmans, 2005), 47-78 (51).

64 Raymond E. Brown, *The Death of the Messiah: From Gethsemane to the Grave*, vol. 1 (New York: Doubleday1994), 77-93.

65 Joy, *Christology Re-Visited*, 34.

Jeremias in his 1996 book *The Eucharistic Words of Jesus*, sets out generally the agreements and disagreements among the passion narratives.[66] He suggests a four-stage development of the passion narrative: an early kerygmatic confession – as now appears in First Corinthians 15:3b-5; a short account – which began with the arrest of Jesus; a long account – which included the triumphal entry, the cleansing of the temple, the question about Jesus' authority, the Last Supper with the announcement of betrayal, Gethsemane, arrest of Jesus, trial before the Sanhedrin, denial of Peter, the condemnation by Pilate, the crucifixion, the empty grave; and expansions of the then existing narrative – by the addition of particular incidents and blocks of traditional material into the forms which we now have in the four gospels.[67]

The context in which passion material formed and first used is a matter of significance. Barnabas Lindars remarks "One of the first tasks which the Church had to undertake in defence of its claim was to explain the suffering and death of Jesus the Messiah."[68] We find in the various passages of the book of Acts and First Corinthians 15 that the earliest Christians understood themselves as witnesses of the resurrection of Jesus and proclaimer of the most startling event in history.[69] Marcus J. Borg's understanding of the transition of the pre-Easter Jesus to the post-Easter Jesus in his article "From Galilean Jew to the Face of God: The Pre-Easter and Post-Easter Jesus," in *Jesus at 2000*, could play significant role here.[70] As the disciples continued to experience Jesus as a living reality and in a radical way after his death, the Christology of the earliest Christians now acknowledged and defined Jesus as Lord, King, and God incarnate. The heralding of a victory over death, and God's raising of Jesus to glory is a vindication of "both the origin and the truth of the authority/power that he had claimed and manifested."[71] Brown states that after seeing the risen Jesus the disciples realized that Jesus' identity was much more than they had understood during his ministry.[72] Therefore it is significant that the preexistence of Jesus dominates the christological discussion right from the initial stages of developments.

---

66 Joachim Jeremias, *The Eucharistic Words of Jesus*, trans. Norman Perrin, NTL (London: SCM, 1966), 89-96.

67 Jeremias, *The Eucharistic Words of Jesus*, 96.

68 Barnabas Lindars, *New Testament Apologetic: The Doctrinal Significance of Old Testament Quotations* (London: SCM, 1961), 75.

69 Longenecker, "Christological Materials," 54.

70 Marcus J. Borg, "From Galilean Jew to the Face of God: The Pre-Easter and Post-Easter Jesus," in *Jesus at 2000*, ed. Marcus J. Borg (Oxford: Westview, 1997), 7-20.

71 Raymond E. Brown, *An Introduction to New Testament Christology* (New York: Paulist Press, 1994), 105.

72 Brown, *An Introduction to New Testament Christology*, 105.

Borg further argues that the metaphorical and conceptual development is important to be understood, in order to sketch how a multiplicity of metaphors became the subject of intellectual reflection.[73] The metaphors that arises within the Jesus movement were abstracted and systematized into a conceptual framework in the course of time, and became the essential fabrics of the New Testament writings, especially for the Gospels. Borg also explains how Son of God could be understood during the time of Jesus. The Hebrew word could be used in various senses (Ps 2:7; Hos 11:1). The truth embedded in all the uses of the Son of God signifies a relationship of intimacy with God. Initially, to call Jesus Son of God is to identify the intimate relationship between Jesus and God. However, the title developed in the Christian tradition "from being a relational metaphor to being a biological metaphor in the birth stories of Matthew and Luke."[74]

## 5.8. Miracles and Christology

The redactional work of the writers of the Gospels in selecting their own collection of miracle stories is significant. Instead of creating their own miracle stories and fashioning them after Hellenistic miracle workers, it is more probable that they made a selection according to their theological purpose and narrative framework.

Broadhead asserts the vital role played by the miracle stories in the narrative framework of the Gospels, and how they emphasize various christological portraits of Jesus.[75] William Wrede was the one who made a decisive link between miracles, Christology and the nature of the Gospels.[76] Wrede's analysis of miracle traditions paved a new route for the theological discussion of the christological impact of miracles in the Gospels, rather than the previous interest in the historicity of the events. Martin Dibelius and Bultmann continued to take up the linkage between miracles and Christology.[77] By picking up Wrede's portrait of "Jesus as the supernatural Son of God," Bultmann linked the idea with the concept of θεῖος ἀνήρ, which was articulated by Ludwig Bieler.[78]

73 Borg, "From Galilean Jew to the Face of God," 13.

74 Borg, "From Galilean Jew to the Face of God," 13.

75 Broadhead, *Teaching with Authority*, 13.

76 William Wrede, *The Messianic Secret*, trans. J. C. G. Greig, LTT (Cambridge: James Clarke, 1971).

77 Martin Dibelius, *From Tradition to Gospel*, trans. Bertram Lee Woolf (New York: Charles Scribner's Sons, 1967); Bultmann, *Theology of the New Testament,* 2 vols.

78 Bultmann, *Theology of the New Testament*, 1: 130-133; Ludwig Bieler, *Theios Anēr: Das Bild des 'Göttlichen Menschen' in Spätantike und Frühchristentum*, 2 vols. (Darmstadt: Wissenschaftliche Buchgesellschaft, 1967), 73-122, cited in Broadhead, *Teaching with Authority*, 15.

Going backward to Josephus, he calls Jesus a wise man who also "worked startling deeds" and the more ancient non-Christian sources, the rabbis and Celsus approved the performing of miracles by Jesus.[79] There is an inclination towards the positive reception of miracle stories among modern scholars. Craig S. Keener argues that there is a lack of substantial contemporary evidence to affirm the Jewish expectation of a miracle-working messiah and non-messianic figures like Paul were also believed to be miracle workers (2 Cor 12:12).[80] He further argues that christological interest may have played significant role in the shaping and interpretation of miracle accounts.

It is unnecessary to assume that Christology later led the church to invent many accounts of Jesus' ministry, as there was little reason to invent miracle stories for christological reasons. Keener suggests that the already claims of Jesus' miracles and other significant claims about Jesus combined, contributed to "apologetic for higher Christology."[81] However, from the point of form criticism the form of miracle stories when compared with that of ancient accounts reveal a number of common motifs.[82]

The writers of the Gospels do not include every miracle stories they acquired, partly due to the limitation of their writing material and theological purposes. The tendency to summarize miracles is evidence in the Gospels; examples are Mark 1:34; 3:10; 6:5, 56; Matthew 11:5; Luke 7:22.[83] This limitation of the number of miracle stories is itself significant and eclectic. John the latest of the Gospels recorded only seven miracle stories, and each of the stories acts as an introduction to a longer discourse. As all the writers of the New Testament do not just report whatever miracle stories they come across, every miracle stories need serious scrutiny to find out their purpose in the narratives. Every miracle story might serve one major purpose, and perhaps embedded with different sub-categories of meaning.

The understanding that the writers of the Gospels invented miracle stories and projected Jesus as miracle worker of the first century Graeco-Roman world attracts much attention. Barry Blackburn expresses this position clearly by stating that the "study of Gospel miracle stories has long been heavily influenced by the belief that early Greek-speaking Christians, whether Jewish or Gentile, formulated these accounts so as to assimilate Jesus to the typical miracle-working divine man (theios aner) with which the Hellenistic world

79 Craig S. Keener, *Miracles: The Credibility of the New Testament Accounts*, 2 vols. (Grand Rapids: Baker, 2011), 1:25.

80 Keener, *Miracles*, 1:27.

81 Keener, *Miracles*, 1:27.

82 For more information on common motifs, see Werner Kahl, *New Testament Miracle Stories in their Religious-Historical Setting: A Religionsgeschichtliche Comparison from a Structural Perspective*, FRLANT 163 (Göttingen: Vandenhoeck and Ruprecht, 1994).

83 Keener, *Miracles*, 1:29.

was familiar."[84] Among Blackburn's division of miracle workers "seers" are most common.[85] The common type of their miraculous power is some form of divination, and itinerant priests who were not unknown during the time also seem to have specialized in divination.[86] However, these figures are not relevant to this discussion because the idea of divination which is the most prevalent power "plays a comparatively minor role in the miracle traditions associated with Jesus in the Gospels."[87] The more relevant category is that of healers, and Blackburn listed thirteen of them.[88]

However, many of these figures are quasi-mythological and use medicinal herbs. Apart from Asclepius, there is no evidence that they impart healing more than once and thus the assumption that miracles are quite common in the first century CE needs serious revision. Blackburn makes it clear that even Asclepius' healings are not that relevant to be compared with Jesus' miracles in the Gospels. He states:

> Given the modern connotation of 'miracle,' it might appear misleading to so describe Asclepius's healings since he employed herbs (drugs and salves) and sometimes performed surgery. Moreover, Homer and Pindar say that Asclepius was educated in the healing arts by his centaur teacher, Chiron. Nevertheless the degree to which Asclepius' medicine is intertwined with magic and miracle is illustrated in Ovid's account of the healing of Hippolytus: "Straightaway he drew from an ivory casket simples that before had stood Glaucus' ghost in good stead... Thrice he touched the youth's breast, thrice he spoke healing words: then Hippolytus lifted his head."[89]

However, Wendy Cotter in her 1999 book *Miracles in Greco-Roman Antiquity: A Sourcebook for the study of New Testament Miracle Stories*,

---

84 Barry Blackburn, '*Theios Aner*' *and the Markan Miracle Traditions: A Critique of the Theios Aner Concept as an Interpretive Background of the Miracle Traditions Used by Mark*, WUNT 2.40 (Tübingen: Mohr Siebeck, 1991), 185.

85 Blackburn divides the Hellenistic "human-plus" miracle workers into three categories: seers, healers, and workers of other miracles.

86 Fritz Graf, *Magic in the Ancient World*, trans. Franklin Philip (Cambridge: HUP, 1997), 49.

87 Barry Blackburn, "'Miracle Working *THEIOI ANDRES*' in Hellenism (and Hellenistic Judaism)," in *The Miracles of Jesus*, vol. 6 of *Gospel Perspective*, ed. David Wenham and Craig Blomberg (Sheffield: JSOT Press, 1986), 185-218 (190).

88 Asclepius, Machaon, Podalirius, Polemocrates, Nicomachus, Gorgasus, Alexanor, Aristomachos, Amunos, Iatros Hros, Oresinios, Menecrates of Syracuse, and Pyrrhus.

89 Blackburn, '*Theios Aner*,' 25; For the use of medicine in Graeco-Roman antiquities see Howard Clark Kee, *Medicine, Miracle and Magic in New Testament Times* (Cambridge: CUP, 1986), 27-66.

describes at the outset how plentiful the miracle stories are in the Graeco-Roman world.[90] A chapter named "Heroes who Heal" consists of names like Pythagoras, Empedocles the Pythagorean, King Pyrrhus, Augustus/Vespasian, Apollinius of Tyana, the Physician Asclepiades, and biblical heroes Moses, Elijah, and Elisha.[91] In the chapter named "Exorcists and Exorcisms" she listed Apollonius of Tyana as the only example of non-Jewish exorcist.[92] The third chapter "Gods and Heroes who control nature," contains Orpheus, Pythagoras, Empedocles the Pythagorean, Apollonius of Tyana, Julius/Augustus, Abaris, Xerxes, Alexander/Caligula.[93] Contrasting to her statement, after omitting names of heroes that came from post-Jesus sources the numbers that came up is lesser than expected.

## 5.9. Geopolitics and Christology

The promises in the New Testament to become a citizen of the Kingdom of God do not involve rule or agriculture. According to the evidence in the Book of Acts, earlier Christian community had not much interest in accumulation of wealth and land. The majority does not belong to a ruling class, and later turn into an egalitarian society. Apart from an Ethiopian minister in Acts 8:27, there are no conversion story of high ranking person in the early Christian history. Peter Brown convincingly argues that early Christians did not have access to politic of the time, and thus made no claims about political structures.[94] The community comprises mostly of people without ranks who were urbanites. Lack of social and political power among the community members is evidence from the writings of New Testament.

Michael S. Northcott in his 2013 book *A Political Theology of Climate Change*, argues that the development of a more settled approach to agriculture and politics is encouraged by the delay of the parousia and the success of mission in the early history of Christianity.[95] He observes that their political theology involved no geopolitical claims apart from apocalyptic ones – the end of the world and the revelation of the true Lord instead of the Emperor. As the expectation of Christ's return got delayed, the idea that Christ will not return until the gospel is being preached throughout the world (Matt 28:19). Consequently, "If the world was to be Christianised, it was inevitable that

90 Wendy Cotter, *Miracles in Greco-Roman Antiquity: A Sourcebook for the Study of New Testament Miracle Stories* (London: Routledge, 1999), 1.

91 Cotter, *Miracles in Greco-Roman Antiquity*, 35-53.

92 Cotter, *Miracles in Greco-Roman Antiquity*, 75-130.

93 Cotter, *Miracles in Greco-Roman Antiquity*, 131-174.

94 Peter Brown, *Through the Eye of a Needle: Wealth, the Fall of Rome, and the Making of Christianity in the West, 350-550 AD* (Princeton: Princeton University Press, 2013), 56.

95 Michael S. Northcott, *A Political Theology of Climate Change* (Grand Rapids: Eerdmans, 2013), 35.

this would involve also a new cosmology, a new politics, a new spirituality of earth, its depths, and its heavenly realms."[96] This is evident in some passages of the later New Testament writings. Christ rising into the heaven to be seated at the right hand of God (Mark 16:19) to rule the world, and the imaginary communion of the saints, the "cloud of witnesses" that surrounds the living Christians (Heb 12:1) present a new geopolitical relation between souls and bodies, of heaven and earth.

A meteorologist, R. R. Kelkar's 2010 e-book *Bible Meteorology* is an interesting analysis of the synthesis between the Bible's presentation of meteorology and science.[97] He himself affirms that he is not capable to attempt to theologize the meteorological significance. He has stated two purposes of the book: Firstly, it is to show that the science of meteorology and how the Bible speaks about weather are not in conflict. Secondly, it is also to show that there are no suggestion in the Bible that the elements of nature are God-like or worthy of adoration and worship.[98] The scientific insights in a simple language could serve as an interpretative tool. For example, how he explains the four winds in the Bible is uncomplicated. The east wind brought a swarm of locusts, right after the seventh plague that is the hailstorm of the ten plagues of Genesis. The hailstorm provide wet sandy soil, a most favourable breeding ground for locusts, and the next day a strong west wind caught up the locusts and they disappeared.

Thunderstorm has been used as a metaphor for life's struggles in ancient times and today, but in the Old Testament it connotes the visible appearance of Yahweh. The thunderstorm is a vital element in theophany of the Old Testament and to some extent to the Christology of the New Testament. John L. McKenzie observes that the thunderstorms, in some instances accompanied by earthquakes are in the Old Testament writings a common trait to describe theophanies.[99]

---

96 Northcott, *A Political Theology*, 35.

97 R. R. Kelkar, *Bible Meteorology* (2010), E-book edition, https://rrkelkar.wordpress.com/books/bible-meteorology-by-prof-r-r-kelkar.

98 Kelkar, Bible Meteorology, 3.

99 John L. McKenzie, "Theophany," DB, 884; cf. Theodore Hiebert, "Air, the First Sacred Thing: The Conception of רוח in the Hebrew Scriptures," in Exploring Ecological Hermeneutics, eds. Norman C. Habel and Peter Trudinger (Atlanta: SBL, 2008), 9-20 (14), who states, "It is the storm wind (הרצס; as in Ps 107:25 and Ezek 1:4) after all, not a modest "whirlwind," from which God speaks to Job about the magnificence of creation (Job 38:1)." Hiebert also states that "The most common natural form of divine appearance in Israelite literature is the thunderstorm… The thunderstorm is the predominant form of theophany in Israel's older literature, the early poetry and epic (J/E) sources, and in the psalms. While not as frequent or explicit, it also lies behind the major theophanies in the literature of Israel's later historians, prophets, and apocalyptic writers." See also, Theodore Hiebert, "Theophany in the OT," ABD 6:505-511 (509).

Cloud has also played significant role in indicating divine presence in both the Old Testament and the New Testament. For McKenzie it is "an almost universal element of the theophany."[100] The earliest appearance of cloud in connection with divine presence could be seen in the Exodus-Sinai event, where the pillar of cloud acts as a guidance and protection for the Israelites in the wilderness. The setting for the first encounter between the Israelites and their God starkly involves cosmological dramatic setup, and thunders, lightning and thick cloud occupy the stage (Exod 19:16). Therefore McKenzie states, "The presentation of YHWH in the theophany of the storm is striking (Ps 18:8-16; Hab 3:3-15; Judg 5:4-5; Exod 19:16, 19; Ezek 1). The theophany is an Israelite confession of the power of YHWH in nature; but this power is not a blind, irrational force."[101] It is the manifestation or an appearance of God in "character and attributes" where God's divinity and power is revealed. Thus according to McKenzie, theophany is to be distinguished from other appearances of God where God is known as the revealer.[102]

The theological significance of theophany is not limited to a terrifying portrait of authority, but also to exhibit the power of God and the sovereignty over the elements of the cosmos. William Propp states that "the storm theophany... situates the divine in meteorological phenomena. The thunderstorm has both beneficent and frightening aspects. Even at a physiological level, intense, subsonic sound waves provoke terror in all animals, ourselves included."[103] This meteorological phenomena makes the narrator to bypass the need to elaborate or explain the authority and sovereignty of God. The dramatic staging of the elements of the cosmos therefore acts as a literary device and prepare the plot well enough to the minds of the audience.

The convulsion of nature is also seen in the narration of Jesus' ministry. The Synoptic Gospels had Jesus calming the storm (Matt 8:23-27, Mark 4:35-40, Luke 8:22-25). It also describes that at the death of Jesus, darkness came over the land (Matt 27:45, Mark 15:33, Luke 23:44). In the book of Acts Jesus was taken by the cloud from their sight (Acts 1:9). Sovereignty over nature and the inter-connecting features of Jesus with cosmic elements introduces the reader into cosmic Christology.

---

100 McKenzie, *DB*, 885.

101 John L. McKenzie, "Aspects of Old Testament Thought," in *The New Testament and Topical Articles*, JBC 2 (Englewood Cliffs: Prentice-Hall, 1968), 1285-1287.

102 McKenzie, *DB*, 884.

103 William Propp, *Exodus 19-40*, AB 2A (New York: Doubleday, 2006), 164.

## 5.10. Framework for Cosmic Christology in Matthew's Gospel: Contextual and Ecological Concerns

Teilhard de Chardin thinks that "The cosmic sense must have been born as soon as humanity found itself facing the frost, the sea and the stars. And since then we find evidence of it in all our experience of the great and unbounded: in art, in poetry, and in religion."[104] Thus, it is not difficult to assume that every culture has its form of understanding their place in the cosmos, the sense of their journey, the relativity of time, the destiny for humankind and how everything is connected to the divinity or in primal religions, the Supreme Being. The consciousness is being portrayed by the language of myth and the symbolism of the imagination. It is a known fact that every culture has its own cosmology, its own body of knowledge and practices, beliefs, customs and rituals. Each cosmology possesses its own structure and processes, rules and principles, and these are defined by the person presenting their particular view of the world. It can be regarded as a picture of the world that human beings carried inside their head. Accordingly, cosmology has become a science, and more precisely a speculative science.[105] Therefore, to read and understand the theology of the biblical writers in their own speculative cosmological worldview is essential.

Matthew must be analysed not from today's cosmological perspective but from his time and cosmological worldview. Jesus' utterance of these words, "Every one then who hears these words of *mine* and does them will be like a wise man who built his house upon the rock" [emphasis added] (Mat 7:24) precedes in Matthew's Gospel the nature miracles. A messenger speaking with God's own authority is not found in other sources of first-century Judaism. Due to this fact Larry R. Helyer called Jesus at the very least as God's personal emissary or agent, and further states that the extensive collection of the stories of healing miracles in the Synoptic Gospels testify Jesus' extraordinary powers, but fell short of cosmic Christology.[106] John K. Riches also mentions that, while Matthew allegorizes the story of the Stilling of the Storm, "he weaves motifs associated with the final cosmic battle into the description of the coming of the Son of Man in chapter 24."[107]

However, way back in 1909, Charles W. Waddle in his article "Miracles of Healing" significantly surveys from psychological perspective, the

---

104 Matthew Fox, *Meister Eckhart: A Mystic Warrior for our Times* (California: New World Library, 2014), 15.

105 Alan P. Lightman, *Ancient Light: Our Changing View of the Universe* (Cambridge: HUP, 1991), 1-2.

106 Larry R. Helyer, *The Witness of Jesus, Paul and John: An Exploration in Biblical Theology* (Downers Grove, IL: IVP, 2008), 284.

107 John K. Riches, *Conflicting Mythologies: Identity Formation in the Gospels of Mark and Matthew*, SNTW (Edinburgh: T&T Clark, 2000), 264.

development of the understanding and conception of diseases and sickness and the means of healings in ancient civilizations.[108] He states that "With the prophets and seers of the olden time *cosmic miracles* were more numerous than healing miracles. In New Testament times the reverse is true" [emphasis added].[109] It is not quite clear what he means by cosmic miracles, but a hint is to be found when he argues that Jesus' statement "to the disciples that by faith they might move mountains may be taken as evidencing His belief in their ability to perform cosmic miracles..."[110] It is clear that Waddle recognizes nature miracles as cosmic miracles. In nature miracles Jesus does something that is contrary to the known laws of nature, and deals with the realm of creation and providence. These miracles are the sources for Helyer to find "a key building block of cosmic Christology," but according to him one has to first "embrace supernaturalism and assumes the essential reliability and authority of the Gospel tradition."[111] He points out that these nature miracles on a face-value reading portray Jesus Christ who possessed power over the created order.

It is convincing to understand that the writers of the Gospels eclectically choose certain miracle stories from a wide range of sources to emphasize their christological or theological interest, be it in an oral form or in a written form. The transfiguration scene depicts Jesus' radiance like the *shekinah* glory of the God of Israel (Matt 17:1-13; Mark 9:2-8; Luke 9:28-36). In Mark's Gospel Jesus predicts his own death at the hands of the elders, chief priest and scribes, and also his resurrection (Mark 8:31; 9:31; 10:33-34).

This threefold repetition is also found in the other synoptic writings (Matt 16:21; 17:22-23; 20:18-19; Luke 9:22, 44; 18:31-33). It is significant that the Synoptic Gospels are careful not to directly attribute Jesus' resurrection as his own inherent power. Here, Matthew's use of passive voice has to have deeper understanding of the identity of Jesus. Even though John's Gospel explicitly mentions the ability of the Son to come back from the dead (John 10:18), the synoptic writers make it apparent that the resurrection was not an independent act.[112] On the one hand, the transfiguration evidently suggests the belief that Jesus was more than a mere mortal being, and was also divine. On the other hand the resurrection narratives in the Synoptic Gospels project that for the writers of the Gospels, "Jesus Christ is a unique individual standing in a unique category."[113] Therefore, how cosmic Christology attains its formulation

108 Charles W. Waddle, "Miracles of Healing," *AJP* 20 (1909): 219-268.

109 Waddle, "Miracles of Healing," 244.

110 Waddle, "Miracles of Healing," 244.

111 Helyer, *The Witness of Jesus*, 284.

112 Helyer, *The Witness of Jesus*, 284.

113 Helyer, *The Witness of Jesus*, 284.

and the relationship with ecological concern with contextual thrust will be the main focus in this section.

### *5.10.1. Cosmic Christology*

Cosmological understanding of the Old Testament is often assumed in the New Testament.[114] Thunder is metaphorically identified as the voice of God in the Old Testament (Ps 18:13; 29) and is too powerful to understand (Job 24:14). John also identifies the thunderous voice as coming from God, and can be interpreted. John however says that there are others who think of it as voice of an angel (John 12:29). Mark's report that Jesus disallow the demons to speak because they knew who Jesus was (Mark 1:34), and later in the Gospel these unclean spirits confessed that he was the Son of God (Mark 3:11-12). Mark's presentation of Jesus and the unclean spirits implies that the common knowledge of cosmic event is shared between them. Matthew also wrote a passage where these spirits confessed Jesus as Son of God, and asked him if he is coming to torture them before the appointed time (Matt 8:29). These spirits are the ones Jesus will disarm (Col 2:15) and the powers in heaven, on earth and under the earth will ultimately bow to Jesus (Phil 2:10).

Christopher M. Tucket is right when he states that "Matthew is famous (or infamous!) among the evangelists for presenting elements that appear at times to be in considerable tension with each other on key issues such as Jesus' attitude to the Jewish Law, or Jesus' attitude to Gentiles."[115] Thus he argues that a neat and coherent Christology may not emerge in Matthew's Gospel.[116] It is also important to note that Matthew's indebtedness to his source Mark's Gospel makes him to reproduce many of Mark's christological passages.

According to Riches, "Matthew tends to emphasize both the forensic and the cosmic dualist strands of Jewish eschatology."[117] David C. Sim in his 1996 book *Apocalyptic Eschatology in the Gospel of Matthew*, argues that the elements of dualism and determinism are dominant in Matthew's treatment of eschatology.[118] He further argues that this is to be "explained in terms of the critical situation that Matthew was facing in relation to Judaism, the Gentile world and indeed to other groups within the church."[119]

114 "Cosmology," *DBI*: 169-174.

115 Christopher M. Tuckett, *Christology and the New Testament: Jesus and His Earliest Followers* (Louisville, KY: Westminster John Knox Press, 2001), 119.

116 Tuckett, *Christology and the New Testament*, 119.

117 Riches, *Conflicting Mythologies*, 263.

118 Sim, *Apocalyptic Eschatology in the Gospel of Matthew*, 75-87.

119 Riches, *Conflicting Mythologies*, 265, citing David C. Sim, *Apocalyptic Eschatology in the Gospel of Matthew* (Cambridge: CUP, 1996), 35-41.

Ilia Delio in her article "Cosmic Christology in the Thought of Zachary Hayes" argues that Bonaventure's cosmic Christology, developed by Zachary Hayes offers a rich theological lens to explore the significance of cosmic Christology in an evolutionary world.[120] Although, Bonaventure sees that there is no absolute necessity for an incarnation of the Word, "he does discern congruity between the mode of Incarnation [the divine Word] and the mystery of creation."[121] This congruity means for Bonaventure, "factual, positive inner relation between the inner divine reality of the Word, the extra divine reality of the Word and the reality of the incarnation."[122]

Bonaventure, in a unique synthesis of philosophy and theology argues that the true nature of reality can be known by beginning at the centre of reality, and the centre is Christ, the Word of God.[123] For him, the mystery of Christ becomes paradigmatic for the understanding of all reality, and the principle of created reality is thoroughly relational.[124] The Franciscan theologian from Alexander of Hales to Scotus, including Bonaventure "did not limit the discussion of the meaning of Christ to the reality of the cross" but they expand it to the widest possible horizon.[125] They held that "a world without Christ is an incomplete world," that means that the whole world is structured christologically.[126] Thus, this world is not merely a plurality of unrelated things but is to be conceived as a true unity, a cosmos that is centred in Christ.[127]

As Christianity was exposed to the new cultural and intellectual reality of wider worldview, the challenge to adaptation and for recognition became more burdensome. The Jewish/Christian worldview contains the emphasis of salvation, historical schema and the eschatological difference between the present age and the future age that is to come. On the other hand the wider worldview mainly focuses on the instinct of cosmology, "that made an ontological distinction between the immutable, eternal world of the divine and

120 Ilia Delio, "Christology in the Thought of Zachary Hayes," *FS* 65 (2007): 107-120 (108).

121 Delio, "Christology in the Thought of Zachary Hayes," 111, citing Zachary Hayes, "Incarnation and Creation in the Theology of St. Bonaventure," in *Studies Honoring Ignatius Brady, Friar Minor*, ed. Romano Stephen Almagno and Conrad Harkins (St. Bonaventure, NY: The Franciscan Institute, 1976), 309-329 (311).

122 Hayes, "Incarnation and Creation in the Theology of St. Bonaventure," 311.

123 Delio, "Christology in the Thought of Zachary Hayes," 112.

124 Zachary Hayes, "The Meaning of *Convenientia* in the Metaphysics of St. Bonaventure," *FS* 34 (1974): 74-100 (100).

125 Zachary Hayes, "Christ, Word of God and Examplar of Humanity," *Cord* 46.1 (1996): 3-17 (6).

126 Hayes, "Christ, Word of God and Examplar of Humanity," 6.

127 Cf. Delio, "Christology in the Thought of Zachary Hayes," 113-114.

the changing, transient world of humanity."[128] Jürgen Moltmann observes this worldview as cosmocentric because "Human beings saw themselves and their civilisation as embedded in the orders of the cosmos which wrapped them round."[129]

It is generally stated that in the fourth century the cosmic significance of Christ receives more interest than before and dominates the christological concerns of early apologists.[130] Various texts of the New Testament also show that there is a shift in the understanding of the meaning of faith in the early Christian communities. Explicit texts such as the prologue of John's Gospel, 1 John 1:1-3, Colossians 1:15-20, and Ephesians 1:3-14 highlighted the earliest interest of cosmic Christology among the writers of the New Testament.

Christology developed with the expansion of Christianity, and it can be said that it moved from a predominantly Jewish, historical and eschatological way of thinking into a Greek worldview. David Bosch states that:

> The "low" Christology of the early Jewish Christians, who had put a high premium on the historical Jesus, gave way to Hellenistic Christianity's preoccupation with the exalted Christ, who became identified with the timeless Logos, an approach which led to a radical spiritualization of the Christ event. The interest shifted from eschatology to protology, to Christ's eternal pre-existence, his relation to God the Father, and the nature of his incarnation. It became more important to know *whence* Christ came than *why*."[131]

Christological development that took place after Jesus' death and resurrection is primarily encouraged by "A cluster of memory, events, and experiences."[132] The memory of Jesus as Messiah; the Easter experiences of the disciples; an ongoing religious experience and visions of the risen Jesus; and reflection on Scripture in light of those experiences, all contribute in early church's understanding of Jesus. Sean M. McDonough in his 2009 book *Christ as Creator: Origins of a New Testament Doctrine*, argues that "For the early Christians the Messiah was not an afterthought, a kind of cosmic bandage to bind up a broken world, he was God's mode of self-communication to the world

128 Colin J. D. Green, *Christology in Cultural Perspective: Marking Out the Horizons* (Grand Rapids: Eerdmans, 2003), 31.

129 Jürgen Moltmann, *The Way of Jesus Christ: Christology in Messianic Dimensions*, trans. Margaret Kohl (Minneapolis: Fortress, 1993), 46.

130 Green, *Christology in Cultural Perspective*, 30-31.

131 David J. Bosch, *Transforming Mission: Paradigm Shifts in Theology of Mission* (New York: Orbis, 1991), 197.

132 Michael F. Bird, *Jesus the Eternal Son: Answering Adoptionist Christology* (Grand Rapids, MI: Eerdmans, 2017), 30.

from the beginning."[133] He further states that this same Messiah is the one who willingly bought back the creation, and also the one who brought it into being in the first place.[134] Richard Bauckham also argues on the development of Christology:

> To include Jesus also in the unique creative activity of God and in the uniquely divine eternity was a necessary corollary of his inclusion in the eschatological identity of God. This was the early Christians' Jewish way of preserving monotheism against the ditheism that any kind of adoptionist Christology was bound to involve. Not by adding Jesus to the unique identity of the God of Israel, but only by including Jesus in that unique identity, could monotheism be maintained.[135]

Scholars generally restricted Paul's cosmic statements to the sphere of soteriology. Bultmann and others are accepted Paul's cosmic Christology as not really focussing to the actual cosmos in all its vastness, but had to do with the salvation of human beings.[136] T. E. Pollard's concludes that "the cosmology, if it is cosmology, is totally subservient to soteriology, and by making it thus Paul runs true to form."[137] The cosmic languages are understood as merely providing the cover-up for the real significance of salvation and thus cosmic Christology is reduced to anthropology and soteriology.

There are others who simply refer to cosmic language as incidental to Paul's thought. They argue that if those Colossian errorists did not advocate

---

133 Sean M. McDonough, *Christ as Creator: Origins of a New Testament Doctrine* (Oxford: OUP, 2009), 235.

134 McDonough, *Christ as Creator*, 236.

135 Richard Bauckham, "Paul's Christology of Divine Indentity," in *Oxford Handbook of Pauline Studies*, ed. R. Barry Matlock (Oxford: OUP, forthcoming), quoted by Bird, *Jesus the Eternal Son*, 31, n. 61.

136 Larry R. Helyer, "Cosmic Christology and Col 1:15-20," *JETS* 37 (1994): 235-246. According to Helyer, the following scholars are representative of those who hold that Pauline theology is essentially soteriological and not really interested in cosmological concerns Rudolf Bultmann, *Theology of the New Testament: Complete in One Volume*, trans. by Kendrick Grobel (New York: Charles Scribner's Son, 1951), 227-232, 254-259; J. M. Robinson, "A Formal Analysis of Colossians 1:15-20," *JBL* 76 (1957): 270-287; H. Hegermann, *Die Vorstellung vom Schopfungsmittler im Hellenistischen Judentum und Urchristentum*, TU 82 (Berlin: Akademie, 1961); E. Kasemann, "A Primitive Christian Baptismal Liturgy," in *Essays on New Testament Themes*, SBT 41 (Naperville: Allenson, 1964), 149-168; H. J. Gabathuler, *Jesus Christus Haupt der Kirche-Haupt der Welt*, ATANT (Stuttgart: Zwingli, 1965); E. Lohse, *Colossians and Philemon* (Philadelphia: Fortress, 1971); T. E. Pollard, "Colossians 1:12-20: A Reconsideration," *NTS* 27 (1981): 572-575.

137 Pollard, "Colossians 1:12-20," 573.

astrological and cosmological doctrines, Paul would have never included cosmic Christology in his theologizing.[138] Another approach insists to interpret Paul in the light of the struggles to explain the significance of Christ in the earliest period. Helyer argues that "cosmic Christology is a pointer to the salvific intentions of God" and is not to be kept at the periphery of Paul's theology.[139] The reading of the text may also support cosmic Christology as traditionally understood to be a significant part of Paul's theological articulation.[140]

If Paul's usage of cosmic language could be understood and signified, then the argument that there was an early cosmic christological framework makes sense. The earliest documents of the New Testament provides clue to understand other cosmic languages to be found especially in the Gospels. Here it is also important to note the relation between cosmic Christology and the personified Wisdom of the Old Testament. Moltmann argues that "Logos Christology is originally Wisdom Christology, and is as such cosmic Christology."[141] Though this is said in relation to the prologue of John's Gospel, which is dated later than the other Gospels, but Pauline epistles especially First Corinthians pre-dated the Synoptic Gospels.

The manner in which Paul identifies Christ as the σοφία ἡμῖν ἀπὸ θεοῦ (wisdom from God) in First Corinthians 1:30 is interesting. Denis Edwards in his 1995 book *Jesus the Wisdom of God*, argues that this phrase is a major basis for Wisdom Christology.[142] However, scholars differ in their acceptance of what Paul means by wisdom here. There are scholars who think that Paul was simply picking up his opponents' wisdom language,[143] but there are others who think that Paul characterizes Jesus as the new Torah.[144] Does Paul identify Jesus as the personified wisdom, is still a debate in process.[145] However, the similarity of this understanding with how the preexistent Wisdom and Torah

138 Helyer, "Cosmic Christology," 236-237, representatives of this view would be F-W Eltester, *Eikon im Neuen Testament*, BZNW 23 (Berlin: Alfred Topelmann, 1958); J. Becker, *Paul: Apostle to the Gentiles* (Louisville: Westminster, 1993).

139 Helyer, "Cosmic Christology," 237.

140 For Cosmic Christology in Pauline and Deutero Pauline epistles, see Chapter Four.

141 Moltmann, *The Way of Jesus Christ*, 33; Ben Witherington, *The Christology of Jesus* (Minneapolis: Fortress, 1990).

142 Denis Edwards, *Jesus the Wisdom of God: An Ecological Theology* (New York: Orbis, 1995), 38.

143 Ulrich Wilckens, "Sophia," *TDNT* 7: 465-528.

144 Martin Hengel, "Jesus und die Tora," *ThB* (1978): 152-172; W. D. Davies, *Paul and Rabbinic Judaism: Some Rabbinic Elements in Pauline Theology*, 4th ed. (Philadelphia: Fortress, 1980).

145 For detail discussion see Aquila H. I. Lee, *From Messiah to Preexistent Son: Jesus' Self-Consciousness and Early Christian Exegesis of Messianic Psalms* (Eugene: Wipf & Stock, 2005), 285-296.

were described in Intertestamental Judaism is worth noting. The suggestion that Paul transferred to Christ the attributes which he formerly ascribed of Wisdom/Torah, is still a strong candidate to explain striking similarities found between them.

In the context of food offerings to idols, Paul states "yet for us there is one God, the Father, from whom are all things and for whom we exist, and one Lord, Jesus Christ, through whom are all things and through whom we exist" (1 Cor 8:6). This confessional statement suggests a pre-Pauline confession, a material which could be commonly accessed by the contemporary writers of the New Testament. Gordon D. Fee sees that the formula is constructed in such a way that one cannot deny the Trinitarian implications.[146] He further explains the absence of tension in Paul's mind while on the one hand affirming monotheism and on the other hand making distinction between the Father and Jesus Christ.[147] This makes it clear that Paul's comic Christology embraces the preexistence of Jesus and the idea is also found in other New Testament writings.

### *5.10.2. Joining of Traditions in Paul's Thought and the Development of Cosmic Christology in Later New Testament Writings*

Paul interpreted the phrase "image of God" in light of his diverse conceptual milieu. It has been noted that Paul collected and renovated the various ideas and concepts of his time. Through the lens of the incarnate and risen Christ, Paul formulates his Christology which is a merging of Wisdom tradition and Jewish first-human being speculation.[148] Paul understands Jesus as the historical Christ in which the concrete reality of God made human being is evident (Phil 2:6-11; Col 1:15-20). The cosmic Christology in Pauline writings is the result of eclectic but cautious choosing from the existing traditions. Paul's reinterpretation of these traditions in the light of the resurrection of Jesus is becoming apparent in recent scholarship of Paul's doctrine of the image of God.[149]

---

146 Gordon D. Fee, *The First Epistle to the Corinthians*, NICNT (Grand Rapids: Eerdmans, 1987), 375-376.

147 Fee, *The First Epistle to the Corinthians*, 376.

148 James D. G. Dunn, *The Theology of Paul the Apostle* (Grand Rapids: Eerdmans, 1998), 204-205; Seyoon Kim, *The Origin of Paul's Gospel*, WUNT 2, ed. Martin Hengel and Otfried Hofius (Tübingen: Mohr, 1984), 137; cited in Eric Montgomery, "The Image of God as the Resurrected State in Pauline Thought," *Bible.org.*, https://bible.org/article/image-god-resurrected-state-pauline-thought.

149 In the early mid-twentieth century, Paul's Adam-Christ typology was attributed to a Gnostic redeemer myth or Urmensch theory. In recent scholarship, it has been convincingly shown that this attribution do not suffice the explanation of the origin of Pauline thought. It is more appropriate to see Paul as basing his ideas on Jewish traditions around the

Paul's thought within the broader spectrum of Second Temple conceptions of the image of God has to be taken seriously, due to the fact that during this period the phrases "image of God" and "likeness of God" were interpreted in various ways.[150] Not later than the sixth century BCE, it is plausible that the legendary developments of the tradition of the first human being emerged in Jewish literature.[151]

Philo describes the first human being in terms of perfection in both body and soul, and compared the original human being to all those coming afterwards and asserts that the first human being was "the most beautiful of beings."[152] The image of God is thus identified as a manifestation of the radiance of God's glory (1QS IV, 19-23).[153] During the second century BCE these stories had been developed and gained significant place in the Jewish concept of creation.

Sirach 49:16 that states the glory of Adam above all other created thing is one example of the development of Adam tradition. 1 Enoch 69:11 mentions the creation of human beings as originally intended to be like angels, and to live in an eternal state of purity and righteousness. Wisdom 2:23-24 states that "God created the man in immortality and he made him an image of his own eternity." In these understanding, it is clear that the original human being was intended to live forever, and not to experience death. These examples demonstrate the presence of the idea and belief that the first human being was created by God in a perfect and ideal state, and to live without experiencing death.

---

creation accounts. Kim, *The Origin of Paul's Gospel*, 163-183; Jarl E. Fossum, *The Image of the Invisible God: Essays on the Influence of Jewish Mysticism on Early Christology*, NTOA (Freiburg: Universitts verlag Freiburg, 1995), 13; A. J. M. Wedderburn, "Philo's 'Heavenly Man'," *NovT* 15 (1973): 160-177.

150 The word εἰκών has a fairly broad lexical range. In Koinē Greek it was used for bills of sales, portrait pictures, statues, coin impressions, and even human rulers who represented a god. "εἰκών," *TDNT* 2:388-90. It was also used for abstract concepts, such as ideas, thoughts, and dreams (e.g. Philo, *Conf. Ling*. 97), as well as Platonic ideas, such as the cosmos as an image of God (*Corp. Herm*. 8:2-5; 11:15). In general, εἰκών should be defined as something which resembles the form, appearance, or characteristics of something else.

151 Dexter E. Callender, "The Primal Man in Ezekiel and the Image of God," in *SBL Seminar Papers*, 1998, SBLSP 37 (Atlanta: Scholars Press, 1998), 2:606-625.

152 The mind according to Philo is the aspect of human being in which the image of God consists, and the primary distinction between animals and human beings is explained in terms of the degree to which they partake of soul. Walter T. Wilson, *Philo of Alexandria: On Virtues: Introduction, Translation, and Commentary*, PACS 3 (Leiden: Brill, 2011), 321.

153 In CD A III, 20 we see "Those who remained steadfast in it will acquire eternal life, and all the glory of Adam is for them"; and in 4Q504 VIII, 4 we also have "[...Adam] our father, you fashioned in the likeness (תומד) of [your] glory [...]." The concept of the physically perfect and glorious first man became more fully developed in the first few centuries CE. (*Hist. Rech*. 5:4; 7:2; 12:1-3; *Apoc. Ab*. 23:5; *Poimandres* 12-14).

Three significant strands of the concept of the image of God are relevant here. As stated earlier, Paul's choosing and synthesizing of the available ideas of his time could be projected briefly in this way. Firstly, it is probable that the image of God was initially interpreted as a reference to the invisible form of God to the visible semblance of the human body.[154] The life of Adam and Eve and the Sibylline Oracles made implicit references to the human body as the image of God (*Sib. Or.* 1:23; *L.A.E.* 13:3).[155] The Testament of Isaac is more explicit when Isaac before his death commands his son Jacob to carefully preserve his body so that the image of God is not defiled (*T. Isaac* 6:33-35). In the following centuries some rabbinic writings like the Babylonian Talmud – *Baba Batra* and *Sanhedrin* and the *Genesis Rabbah*,[156] which is a midrashic source, and Gnostic writings became more explicit in associating the image of God with the physical form of the human body.[157]

Secondly, as Judaism infused with the Hellenistic world and thought, the image of God took on another connotation of humanity's inner being. The idea that God possess a physical form faded and to come in terms with it the image of God was then applied not to the physical body of human beings. The prominent concept that emerged from this shift of understanding is that a person's immortal soul that represented the image of God is housed within a temporal body (Ps.-Phoc. 105-108).[158]

Thirdly, the divine Wisdom tradition also utilized the phrase "image of God" in their line of thought. While dealing with the Second Temple understanding of Wisdom, Anthony C. Thiselton asserts that "…the figure of Wisdom manifests, radiates, and mediates the otherwise inaccessible, transcendent reality of God."[159] Though the Second Temple literature rarely used explicit image terminology to refer to divine Wisdom, it is still probably

154 Walther Eichrodt, *Theology of the Old Testament*, trans. J. A. Baker, 2 vols. (London: SCM, 1964), 2:122-24; D. J. A. Clines, "The Image of God in Man," *TynBul* 19 (1968): 53-103.

155 L.A.E. seems more explicit, which asserts that the face and likeness of Adam were made in the image of God. It is also possible that the description of Christ in Heb 1:3 is meant to convey the idea of Jesus as a physical representative of God (χαρακτὴρ τῆς ὑποστάσεως αὐτοῦ). Dave Steenburg, "The Worship of Adam and Christ as the Image of God," *JSNT* 39 (1990): 95-109.

156 A religious text from 300-500 CE is a midrash comprising a collection of ancient rabbinical homiletical interpretations of the book of Genesis.

157 Cf. *b. B. Bat.* 58a; *b. Sanh.* 38a-b; *Gen. Rab.* 8:9-12; 24:2; *Poimandres* 12-14. See Alon Goshen Gottstein, "The Body as Image of God in Rabbinic Literature," *HTR* 87 (1994): 171-195.

158 In *Hist. Rech.* 15:10 the disembodied soul, which ascends to God after death, is described as "the likeness of a glorious light."

159 Anthony C. Thiselton, *The First Epistle to the Corinthians: A Commentary on the Greek Text*, NIGTC (Grand Rapids: Eerdmans, 2000), 834.

significant to probe them so as to understand how this thought could relate with Paul's idea of Christ as the image of God.[160] In this strand of understanding Wisdom tradition as the background for New Testament Theology and especially for Paul, James D. G. Dunn argues:

> It is clear therefore that the tradition of (pre-existent) Wisdom has been influential at many points in NT christology. In some of the earlier (i.e. Pauline) passages it may be no more than that language or exegesis has been prompted by specific language or some particular exegesis used in Wisdom tradition. But, in other cases there can be little doubt that the role of Wisdom is being attributed to Christ.[161]

Wisdom of Solomon 7:26 describes Wisdom as "a reflection of eternal light, a spotless mirror of the working of God, and an image of his goodness." Here the writer further describes Wisdom as the one who is more beautiful than the sun and who envelops the earth in its entirety; the authoritative character who holds the capabilities to create and perform all things, and to renew all things. Wisdom was also understood by Philo as "the beginning, and the image, and the sight of God." He also understands that when a person displays wisdom with his mind and wise virtue by his action, then that person could be seen as an image of God.[162] Therefore, it is clear that the Wisdom tradition identifies Wisdom as the image of God and also identifies human beings as the image of God when they possess wisdom and virtue. Wisdom is also found in Proverbs 8:22-31 as God's Personified Wisdom:

> The LORD created me at the beginning of his work, the first of his acts of old. Ages ago I was set up, at the first, before the beginning of the earth. When there were no depths I was brought forth, when there were no springs abounding with water. Before the mountains had been shaped, before the hills, I was brought forth; before he had made the earth with its fields, or the first of the dust of the world. When he established the heavens, I was there, when he drew a circle on the face of the deep, when he assigned to the sea its limit, so that the waters might not transgress his command, when he marked out the foundations of the earth, rejoicing in his inhabited world and delighting in the sons of men.

---

160 James D. G. Dunn, *Christology in the Making: A New Testament Inquiry into the Origins of the Doctrine of the Incarnation* (London: SCM, 1980), 167; see also Steenburg, "Adam and Christ," 102.

161 Dunn, *Christology in the Making*, 167.

162 Philo, *Leg*. 1.43-55.

This is a significant passage for the articulation of Christology in the early Church's thought.[163] Wisdom figures as a primordial being who sits besides God's throne as his consort in the Wisdom of Solomon from the Old Testament apocrypha (9:4). Moreover, according to this passage (Prov 8:22-31) Wisdom participates with God in the creation of the world.[164] This might have helped the early century writers to express the doctrine of Trinity, with Jesus Christ portrayed as the agent through whom all things were created.[165] Christopher M. Tuckett in his 1996 book *Q and the History of Early Christianity: Studies in Q*, notes that these ideas were "heavily exploited in early Christianity where the texts concerned were applied to Jesus."[166] B. Metzger and M. D. Coogan argue that "Christology of pre-existence and incarnation is generally agreed" to "have developed from the identification of Jesus with the wisdom of God."[167] In the Pauline and deutero-Pauline epistles Jewish statements about Wisdom in connection to Jesus are to be found. Christ is "the power of God and the Wisdom of God" (1 Cor 1:24). In him "are hid all the treasures of Wisdom and knowledge" (Col 2:3), and like Wisdom, Jesus assisted God in the creation of all things (1 Cor 8:6). Moreover, George A. Wells argues that Jesus like the Jewish Wisdom figure, sought acceptance on Earth but was rejected and returned to heaven.[168]

Paul introduced Wisdom Christology by connecting and synthesizing various traditions he was in contact with. Paul took up the attributes of Wisdom and incorporated it into cosmic Christology, and to this according to Helyer, Paul added another Christology of "second Adam."[169] Helyer further argues that "Paul's diction thus displays a melding of Wisdom and second-Adam motifs," and also suggests that "the actual structure of Colossians 1:15-

---

163 For discussion of how Patristic Christology makes use of the personification of Wisdom found in this passage, and discussion of this theme in Judaism as well as the New Testament, see Maurice Dowling, "Proverbs 8:22-31 in the Christology of the Early Fathers," *Perichoresis* 8 (2010): 47-65.

164 George A. Wells, *Cutting Jesus Down to Size: What Higher Criticism Has Achieved and Where It Leaves Christianity* (Illinois: Open Court, 2009), 211.

165 Bruce K. Waltke, *The Book of Proverbs: Chapters 1-15*, NICOT (Grand Rapids, MI: Eerdmans, 2004), 129.

166 Christopher M. Tuckett, *Q and the History of Early Christianity: Studies in Q* (Edinburgh: T&T Clark, 1996), 169.

167 "Jesus Christ," in *Oxford Companion to the Bible*, ed. B. Metzger and M. D. Coogan (New York: OUP, 1993), 356-366 (356).

168 Wells, *Cutting Jesus Down to Size*, 211.

169 Helyer, *The Witness of Jesus,* 286.

20 probably highlights the midrashic exposition of Genesis 1:1 by means of Proverbs 8:22 using the technique of *gezera shawa*."[170]

As is previously stated Wisdom tradition is also to be found in Matthew's Gospel and later in the letter to the Hebrews. It developed into a "genuine incarnational Christology" in the New Testament and a more developed form of which is "explicitly articulated... near the end of the first century CE"[171] According to Carl R. Holladay, "one finds for the first time 'a full blown concept of Christ's personal pre-existence and a clear doctrine of incarnation.'"[172] Therefore, it is not an assumption to state that the incarnational Christology in the framework of Wisdom tradition is already prominent in the thought and theology of Matthew. Here, it is now clear that Paul's usage of traditional wisdom material helps him to articulate cosmic Christology in a more comprehensive way, and Matthew must also be read in this line of thought.

### *5.10.3. Wisdom Christology in Matthew's Gospel*

The lack of cosmic Christology in the synoptic Gospels led earlier generation of New Testament scholars to assume that it developed at a later period. Contrastingly, as mentioned earlier, Paul's drawing of the available traditions of his time and the presence of Wisdom tradition in Matthew's Gospel indicates its early development.[173] There is a strong influence of Wisdom to be found in the Gospels of Matthew and John, but other parts of New Testament also could bear fruitful results with serious search. The use of Wisdom language by Jesus and identifying Jesus as the wisdom of God are two varying discussions seen in this sphere of study. Arguing from the feminine status of Wisdom, this development of Wisdom Christology is to be appreciated.

Celia M. Deutsch points out passages in Matthew's Gospel where Wisdom and Jesus are identified.[174] The passage without concealment is Matthew 11:19 – in which Jesus says, "Yet wisdom is justified by her deeds." This is taken as an implication of addressing his own deeds as to those of

---

170 Helyer, *The Witness of Jesus*, 286. The Jewish interpretative principle of *gezera shawa* takes into account from two or more separate passages that contain the same word, and the interpretation assumes that this provides sufficient reason for explaining the one text in the light of the other.

171 Carl R. Holladay, "New Testament Christology: Some Considerations of Method," *NovT* 25 (1983), 257-278.

172 Holladay, "New Testament Christology," 262.

173 Rosemary Radford Reuther, *Godesses and the Divine Feminine: A Western Religious History* (London: University of California Press, 2006), 130; see also Jann Aldredge-Clanton, *In Search of the Christ-Sophia: An Inclusive Christology for Liberating Christians* (Mystic, Conn.: Twenty-Third Publications, 1995), 23.

174 Celia Deutsch, "Wisdom in Matthew: Transformation of a Symbol," *NovT* 32 (1990): 13-47.

Wisdom, or even that he himself is Wisdom. In Luke's Gospel, the verse leave some gap between Jesus and Wisdom – "Yet wisdom is justified by all her children" (Luke 7:35).[175] Matthew does not leave such distance but connects Wisdom's and Jesus' deeds. The context in both the Gospels makes it clear that these are the concluding remarks made by Jesus to the parable. The parable had been applied to John and Jesus.

Deutsch argues that Luke's version here is closer to the original due to the presence of "children" in the text, and Wisdom corresponds to the children in the parable.[176] She further argues that Matthew changed it to "her deeds" so as to create a parallel with "deeds of the Christ" in v. 2.[177] Matthew's redactional work makes sense when we compare it with Luke's Gospel in the references made by Jesus toward John. Luke has "none is greater than John" (Luke 7:28) while Matthew has "there has risen no one greater than John the Baptist" (11:11).

In Matthew the tension between revelation and concealment shared by Jesus and Wisdom come to light. Jesus' use of parables to proclaim "what has been hidden since the foundation of the world" (13:35), and Jesus' thanking God in prayer "that thou hast hidden these things from the wise and understanding and revealed them to babes" (Mat 11:25) are clear example of the tension between revelation and hiddenness. Jesus' use of parables and beatitudes are in line with the typical wisdom discourse, and particularly similar with the blessing of Wisdom in Proverbs 8.[178]

### *5.10.4. Ecological Christology*

The methodological problem in constructing ecological Christology lies in the fact that the Gospel writers thematically present Jesus' interaction with nature as dominion over nature. Jesus was explicitly understood by the first followers as being concerned with illness, injustice, and religio-political

175 Deutsch, "Wisdom in Matthew," 33.

176 Deutsch, "Wisdom in Matthew," 34.

177 Deutsch, "Wisdom in Matthew," 34; see also "The disappearing gap between Wisdom and Jesus emphasizes their common roles of prophet, teacher, host, and also the rejection they receive when their hearers reject them. One such rejection of Jesus is witnessed in Matthew 13:54 (Mark 6:2), where the people ask, "Where did this man get this wisdom and these mighty works?" and refuse to believe his words." Silvia Schroer, *Wisdom Has Built Her House: Studies on the Figure of Sophia in the Bible*, trans. Linda M. Maloney and William McDonough (Collegeville: Michael Glazier, 2000), 122.

178 Sharon H. Ringe, *Wisdom's Friends: Community and Christology in the Fourth Gospel* (Louisville: Westminster John Knox Press, 1999), 59, and Leo D. Lefebure, *Toward a Contemporary Wisdom Christology: A Study of Karl Rahner and Norman Pittenger* (New York: University Press of America, 1988), 26, 28. Lefebure also identifies Jesus' superiority to Solomon in Matthew 12:42 as a link to the wisdom tradition, but not to Wisdom outright. Lefebure, *Toward a Contemporary Wisdom Christology*, 26, 28.

oppression. Though it is obvious that the word environmentalist was unheard and irrelevant to the Gospel writers, Jesus was not presented even implicitly according to modern connotation of this term. Therefore, the huge amount of published materials on ecotheology relatively imparts little attention to Christology in proper manner. Ecotheology arrives later than the gender issues, cultural interactions, interreligious dialogue, political and economical liberation in the main discussion of Christology. It has found its hold mainly in the conversation of liberation theology. Christological questions are rarely to be found in the writings of ecothelogical scholars.[179]

There are scholars who are interested in developing ecologically sensitive Christology. Elizabeth Johnson develops a wisdom interpretation of Jesus, which is further taken in an explicitly ecological direction.[180] Another perspective is initiated from the christological hymn of Colossians. This perspective "focuses on the Cosmic Christ and attempts to go beyond the exclusive link between Christ and human redemption."[181] It has been developed by Joseph Sittler, and Matthew Fox popularizes it, and Jürgen Moltmann also utilizes this perception as a link between Christology and ecotheology.[182] Sally McFague's 1993 book *The Body of God: An Ecological Theology*, and Sue Patterson's 1998 essay "Creation and Postmodernity," are other noteworthy attempts to develop eco-Christology.[183] All these and other recent attempts brought the subject of eco-Christology into a new

179 There are writings that give much attention to the relation between ecology and Christology, and some of the notable ones are: Edwards, *Jesus the Wisdom of God: An Ecological Theology*; Sallie McFague, "An Ecological Christology: Does Christianity Have It?" in *Christianity and Ecology*, ed. Dieter Hessel and Rosemary Radford Ruether (Cambridge: HUP, 2000), 29-45.

180 Duncan Reid, "Enfleshing the Human: An Earth-Revealing, Earth-Healing Christology," in *Earth Revealing – Earth Healing: Ecology and Christian Theology*, ed. Denis Edwards (Minnesota: The Liturgical Press, 2001), 69-84, citing Elizabeth Johnson, *She Who is: The Mystery of God in Feminist Theological Discourse* (New York: Crossroad, 1992); Edwards, *Jesus the Wisdom of God: An Ecological Theology*.

181 Reid, "Enfleshing the Human," 80.

182 Reid, "Enfleshing the Human," 80, citing Steven Bouma-Prediger, *The Greening of Theology: The Ecological Models of Rosemary Radford Reuther, Joseph Sittler, and Jürgen Moltmann* (Atlanta: Scholars Press, 1995); Matthew Fox, *The Coming of the Cosmic Christ: The Healing of Mother Earth and the Birth of a Global Renaissance* (Melbourne: Collins Dove, 1988); Jürgen Moltmann, *The Way of Jesus Christ: Christology in Messianic Dimensions*, trans. Margaret Kohl (Minneapolis: Fortress, 1993). For the discussion of the significance of Joseph Sittler, Jürgen Moltmann, and Matthew Fox, see also Deane-Drummond, *Eco-Theology*, 103-107.

183 Sallie McFague, *The Body of God: An Ecological Theology* (London: SCM, 1993); Sue Patterson, "Creation and Postmodernity," in *The Task of Theology Today: Doctrines and Dogma*, ed. V. Pfitzner and H. Regan (Adelaide: Australian Theological Forum, 1998), 84-111.

dimension where the discussion of Cosmic Christ no longer neglects the quest of historical Jesus.

Douglas John Hall's critique of Western ecclesiastical influence becomes crucial in the present understanding of the link between the Cosmic Christ and ecology.[184] By rejecting the common assumption of conventional understanding of humanity as above the nature, he constructs an ecological reading of Jesus which is not separated from the historical Jesus. Hall's reinterpretation of the image of God carries with it the responsibility to care for creation. Thus, he sees Christ the image of God as the pre-existent being that comes to serve all of creation in humility and gives humanity a model of stewardship.[185]As Larry L. Rasmussen asserts, "Imaging God is acting in a godly way toward one another and other creatures. Imaging God is loving earth fiercely, as God does."[186] Therefore, in this line of discussion, the problem of the uneasy tension between the preexistence notion of Cosmic Christ and the historical Jesus of Nazareth could be contained.

### 5.10.5. Contextual Christology

Every Christology is contextual in a sense that it emerges out of a particular social need and condition. The author of Hebrews states that "Jesus Christ is the same yesterday and today and for ever" (Heb 13:8). It seems that the study of Jesus is inexhaustible, and a single category of Christology nor a specific creedal formula cannot encapsulate or define the true meaning of Jesus and his ministry presented by the Gospel writers, and also their theological purposes while they portrait Jesus in such a peculiar manner. The New Testament itself portrays Christ in context, and four Gospels had been canonized. Each of the Gospels and other New Testament writings reflect distinctive situation in which it was written and read. Christology is formulated in a specific context with focus to answer particular questions and to dissolve issues that urgently required attention, thus it is safe to say that it is always contextual.

Daniel I. Migliore, in his article "Christology in Context: The Doctrinal and Contextual Tasks of Christology Today," argues that there are "two concerns – the doctrinal concern for the unity of faith in Christ and the contextual concern for expressions of that faith appropriate to particular situations-stand in tension with each other..."[187] He further describes how New Testament presents various Christologies, and how they reflect the distinctive milieu in which they were

184 Douglas John Hall, *Imaging God: Dominion as Stewardship* (Grand Rapids: Eerdmans, 1986), 53-59.

185 Hall, *Imaging God*, 21-26.

186 Larry L. Rasmussen, *Earth Community, Earth Ethics* (Geneva: WCC Publications, 1996), 280.

187 Daniel I. Migliore, "Christology in Context: The Doctrinal and Contextual Tasks of Christology Today," *Int JBT* 49 (1995): 242-254.

written and read.[188] While speaking of Christology in context, it is important to understand how various liberation theologies signify the relevance of Jesus Christ today "to empower the marginalized and the despised in the society."[189] These expressions of one's life situation in relation to Christology need better recognition. As the centre of Christianity swiftly shifted towards the periphery from the West, the emerging Christologies from the peripheral contexts are gaining significance.

Contextual theology does not tackle with the traditional issues like the question of the natures of Jesus and does not have as its task to uncover the historical personality of Jesus. While dealing with the Asian perspective, R. S. Sugirtharajah in his 1993 essay "Prologue and Perspective" of *Asian Faces of Jesus*, mentions that "The Asian profiles of Jesus found here seek to perceive Jesus in a different way – from the side."[190] This is to come in terms with the most significant proponent of liberation theology, Gustavo Gutiérrez's idea of openness to others as the foundation of liberation.[191]

Gutiérrez defines liberation theology as "a critical reflection on historical praxis."[192] Historical praxis means according to him, is not any kind of action but a "transforming action." The transforming action of history is to be understood as transformation of nature, as the relationship of the person to nature, and as the relationship of the persons among themselves. It also means a transforming action initiated by the poor, humiliated, despised races, and the marginalized themselves.[193] Therefore, the focus of liberation Christology is mainly to understand and reinterpret Jesus from the concrete experiences and perspective of the poor and marginalized of the Third World.

Jon Sobrino in his 1993 book *Jesus the Liberator: A Historical-Theological Reading of Jesus of Nazareth*, focuses on the historical life of Jesus of Nazareth, and he sees Jesus of Nazareth as the central figure in liberation Christology.[194] This observation sounds valid because the Gospels generally portray Jesus is a person who was mostly found associated with the subaltern people in the community. Jesus was found regularly among the

188 Migliore, "Christology in Context," 243.

189 Joy, *Christology Re-Visited*, 125.

190 R. S. Sugirtharajah, "Prologue and Perspective," in *Asian Faces of Jesus*, FCS, ed. R. S. Sugirtharajah (Maryknoll: Orbis, 1993), viii-xii.

191 Gustavo Gutiérrez, *A Theology of Liberation: History, Politics, and Salvation*, trans. Sister Caridad Inda and John Eagleson (Maryknoll: Orbis, 1973), 36.

192 Gutiérrez, *A Theology of Liberation*, 6-15.

193 Gustavo Gutiérrez, "Statement," in *Theology in the Americas*, ed. Sergio Torres and John Eagleson (Maryknoll: Orbis, 1976), 310-311 (310).

194 Jon Sobrino, *Jesus the Liberator: A Historical- Theological Reading of Jesus of Nazareth*, trans. Paul Burns and Francis McDonagh (New York: Orbis, 1993), cited in Joy, *Christology Re-Visited*, 128.

marginalized people and the Gospels' portrayal contains with it an indication that Jesus favoured the poor.

Liberation Christology argues that Christ's presence is to be found among the poor. The poor became the criterion for Christology in an inclusive way.[195] This is not exclusive and means that Christ is present at least among the poor. Jesus' regular presence among the poor in his time signifies Jesus' attitude to the poor, and is significant for liberation theology. Jesus' preaching of the kingdom of God made it clear that the kingdom is good news for the poor (Luke 4:18). The kingdom is also made up of the poor (Luke 6:20). Jesus had to lose his security, dignity, and life during his mission, and thus sets an example of the kingdom of God and the manner in which it should be ushered into existence. All these portrayal of Jesus is an important tool for the development of liberation Christology.

Liberation Christology is impressive mainly due to its ecclesial setting and its praxis, which is among the people. Due to this praxic nature, liberation Christology continues with the same information about Jesus as classical Christology, but employs differing interpretations. It focuses on the suffering poor as the contextual lens and paves a way "to arrive at ways of seeing the Christ and his salvific power not only in human Jesus but in every human person."[196] The Christology of liberation theology recognizes that every New Testament document was written with christological intent that could not be divorced from the text.[197] Though the European quest for historical Jesus approaches Jesus as an "object of investigation," liberation Christology sees Jesus as the "criterion of discipleship."[198]

The initiation of Dalit theology is put forwarded by Arvind P. Nirmal with his lecture at Carey Society's valedictory function in April of 1981.[199] Christology plays a central role in Dalit theology, and the hermeneutic principle is rooted deeply in the life, death and resurrection of Jesus. Dalit theology also has a fundamental concern for liberation at its core. For Dalit theologians, Christology offers "the essential paradigm for liberating existence, involving

---

195 Jon Sobrino, "Christ as Liberator" in *Christology: A Global Introduction: An Ecumenical, International, and Contextual Perspective*, ed. Veli-Matti Kärkkäinen (Grand Rapids: Baker, 2003), 237-244 (241-242).

196 Thomas Bohache, *Christology from the Margins* (London: SCM, 2008), 87.

197 Jon Sobrino, *Christology at the Cross Road* (Maryknoll: Orbis, 1978), 13.

198 Julio Lois, "Christology in the Theology of Liberation," in *Mysterium Liberationis: Fundamental Concepts of Liberation Theology*, trans. Robert R. Barr, ed. Ignacio Ellacuria and Jon Sobrino (Maryknoll: Orbis, 1993), 168-193 (174).

199 The title of the paper is "Towards a Sudra Theology" and the valedictory program is organized by Carey Society, United Theological College, Bangalore. Sathianathan Clarke, *Dalits and Christianity: Subaltern Religion and Liberation Theology in India* (Delhi: OUP, 1999), 56, quoted in Joy, *Christology Re-Visited*, 130.

a transformative movement from dehumanization to humanization."[200] Nirmal remarks, "We are not just Dalits. We are Christian Dalits. Something has happened to us. Our status has changed. Our Exodus from Hinduism – which was once imposed on us – to Christianity or rather to Jesus Christ is a valuable experience – a liberating experience."[201]

The question on the preexistence of Christ is not important for these cultural Christologies, as is previously stated, Jesus as an object of investigation becomes irrelevant. Instead, the struggle of God in the human Jesus is acknowledged and understood as a struggle for the liberation of humanity from "whatever dehumanizes it."[202] According to K. P. Kuruvila, God in Jesus Christ embraces the world and also the physical things in life.[203] God incarnates in the midst of humanity and God in Jesus Christ shares the agonies with them. He further asserts that "God has shared the conditions of our lives in the life of Jesus."[204] Kelly B. Douglas states that in every generation, the Christian communities "have to discern the significance of Jesus Christ for their own lives, because their affirmations of Jesus Christ are contextual."[205] The historical, cultural, social, and political milieu inevitably shape and develop the community's Christology. God's interaction with humanity and nature and God's salvific motive are culminated in the person of Jesus within a particular culture and society.

Therefore, the main interest is not to unearth historical data but to "recover the praxis of historical Jesus as the hermeneutical key for the liberative praxis of the Christian church."[206] Christology in this respect is to recover historical dimension of the mystery of Jesus Christ and to relate it with the cultural and sociological realities in a particular milieu.

### *5.10.6. Contextual Tribal Christology in Mizoram*

Renthy Keitzar in his 1995 book *In Search of a Relevant Gospel Message*, provides ten points summary of the main features of missionary theology in

---

200 Adrian Bird, "M.M. Thomas: Theological Signposts for the Emergence of Dalit Theology," (Ph.D. diss., University of Edinburgh, 2008), 50.

201 Arvind P. Nirmal, "Towards a Dalit Christian Theology," in *Frontiers in Asian Christian Theology: Emerging Trends* (Maryknoll: Orbis, 1994), 27-40 (34).

202 K. P. Kuruvila, *The Word Became Flesh: A Christological Paradigm for Doing Theology in India* (Delhi: ISPCK, 2002), 194.

203 Kuruvila, *The Word Became Flesh*, 51.

204 Kuruvila, *The Word Became Flesh*, 51.

205 Kelly B. Douglas, Carter Heyward and Francine Cardman, "Dictionary of Feminist Theologies," in *The Strength of Her Witness: Jesus Christ in the Global Voices of Women*, ed. Elizabeth A. Johnson (Maryknoll, NY: Orbis, 2016), 78-85 (78).

206 Kuruvila, *The Word Became Flesh*, 53.

North East India.[207] He argues that "our academic discipline in biblical or theological studies has not made any breakthrough in this hangover of the missionary religion of theology."[208] Even with the emergence of various denominations, the legacy of the earlier missionary movements and the theology they espoused continues to get hold of the theology of the churches especially in Mizoram. The reproduction of their own theology by the missionaries which was rooted in their tradition and culture witnesses the Christologies mainly of Christ as a saviour from sin, and Christ as a conqueror of evil spirits.

The Tribal theology in the context of the Northeast Indian is not to be treated as a single articulation as there are differences in socio-cultural settings, worldviews and cultural and traditional practices. K. Thanzauva, a prominent proponent of Tribal Theology asserts "In our effort to construct tribal theology, we have been pointing out 'what theology is not' in Northeast India... Today we are confronted with a new question of 'what tribal theology is or should be.'"[209] Thanzauva asserts that tribal theology needs a synthetic-praxis model, which is a combination of two models.[210] He opines "combination of the two is necessary in a society like ours, suffering as it does from a crisis of identity,

---

207 Renthy Keitzar, *In Search of a Relevant Gospel Message* (Guwahati: CLC, 1995), 38-39, quoted in L. H. Lalpekhlua, *Contextual Christology: A Tribal Perspective* (Delhi: ISPCK, 2007), 90. Here are the points: (1) The inerrancy and the authority of the Bible, including the plenary inspiration of Scripture and Christo-centric interpretation (2) The deity of Christ (3) The virgin birth of Christ (4) The creation of man in the image of God and an historical fall into sin, including the universality of sin as inherited (5) The substitutionary atonement of Christ and the belief that solely the blood of Christ achieves salvation (6) Salvation by faith alone through the grace of God in Jesus Christ (7) The necessity of every believer to have an assurance of salvation (8) The doctrine of the Trinity, and the presence of the Holy Spirit as a person with believers for spiritual generation (9) The universality (Catholicity) and spirituality of the church which rises above sectarian prejudices (10) Christ's physical resurrection and bodily return to earth (i.e. in His second coming) for judgment and the millennial reign, with the believers to enjoy bliss with God and the unbelievers to endure torment in hell until the final judgment, when they will be punished with everlasting destruction.

208 Keitzar, *In Search of a Relevant Gospel Message*, 91, quoted in Lalpekhlua, *Contextual Christology*, 91.

209 K. Thanzauva, "Issues in Tribal Theology" in *Tribal Theology: A Reader,* ed. Shimreingam Shimray (Jorhat: Eastern Theological College, 2003), 17; see also K. Thanzauva, "Tribal/Indigenous Interpretation of the Bible: A Keynote Address," in *Tribal Theology and the Bible: A Search for Contextual Relevance,* ed. Yangkahao Yashum (Jorhat: Eastern Theological College, 2011), 13-25.

210 For brief explanation of models of inculturation (contextualization), see Khayaipam Khamrang, "The Tangkhul Naga Tribe (India) between Tradition and Modernity," in *Inkulturation zwischen Tradition und Modernitat*, ed. Fritz Frei (Fribourg: Presses Universitaires de Fribourg, 2000), 35-72 (67).

at the same time struggling for liberation from all forms of alienation."[211] The struggle to identify oneself as an Indian or to see the inclusion in India as an unwilling participation still controls the discourse and expressions of many of the Northeast thinkers and writers, and especially the nationalist movement.

A methodological shift in tribal theology is initiated by Wati Longchar whose articulation moves towards a creation-centric approach.[212] He contends that the main concerns of the indigenous people are overlooked by the missionaries and biblical scholarship. He criticizes the introduction of anthropocentric reading which emphasizes the revelation of God through the bible and through the person of Jesus. According to him this kind of reading undermines the divine revelation through the natural created order.[213] He also criticizes the mainstream Asian scholars who are more interested in relating the biblical texts to the religious text of Hindus, Buddhists and Sikhs for the clarification and building of communal harmony. Thus, he thinks that mainstream Asian interpreters lack interest towards indigenous peoples' earth-centred religion, culture and ethics.[214] The sense of injustice experience among the indigenous peoples arose out of economic poverty, unemployment, or disease, and these are all a result of alienation from the land. Therefore, the starting point for reading the Bible is the land, which is "the point of reference and key to understanding human self-hood, God and spirit."[215] This interest in the significance of land for the tribals made him to understand that land is the foundation of history, existence and identity. Land does not only "sustains and nourishes all beings... [it also] gives them an identity and selfhood."[216] This identification of land as a giver of identity and selfhood has been so true especially to the Mizos.

Bendangla Longkumer's article "Weaving Christology from Tribal Women Perspective: An Ao- Naga Reading" is from the perspective of women to formulate tribal Christology.[217] This article is quite significant because of its peculiar approach in utilizing her tribal heritage to propose *Arasentur*, an Ao-Naga women shaman as her working model. This formulation according to her is not limited to women and she sees it as an inclusive view that includes

211 Thanzauva, "Issues in Tribal Theology," 19.

212 Wati A. Longchar, "Reading the Bible from the Perspective of Indigenous People's Experience: A Methodological Consideration," *MIT Journal of Theology* 4 (2003): 41-58.

213 Longchar, "Reading the Bible," 51.

214 Longchar, "Reading the Bible," 51.

215 Longchar, "Reading the Bible," 54.

216 Wati A. Longchar, "Indigenous People's Theologies in Asia: Methods and Perspectives," *Issues in Theological Research: A Methodological Exploration*, ed. Wati A. Longchar (Bangalore: BTESSC/SATHRI, 2010), 147-169 (160).

217 Bendangla Longkumar, "Weaving Christology from Tribal Women Perspective: An Ao-Naga Reading," *JTS* 15 (2010): 29-45.

the whole humanity and their experiences.[218] Takatemjen, in his 1998 book *Studies on Theology and Naga Culture*, also makes an attempt to articulate a contextual tribal Christology from the folktale of Ao-Naga tradition "*Lijaba and the two sisters*."[219] In his comparison between the Lijaba tradition and Gospel's accounts of Jesus teachings and ministry, he comes up with two important themes: Jesus as *Lijaba* co-suffers with the poor and Jesus as *Lijaba* liberates the oppressed.[220]

Another attempt to formulate contextual tribal Christology is to be found in Hemkhochon Chongloi's 2008 book, *Indoi*.[221] The relationship between Kuki Christology and the *Indoi* symbolism is drawn in this study and the concept of *Pathen* is utilized.[222] According to Chongloi, as it is familiar with other primal religions, the Kuki also believes in the existence of Supreme Being, but the prevalence of *Indoi* symbol suggests that the Kuki religiosity also implicitly affirms the concept of *Pathen* as an idle god. After the initial creation *Pathen* has become unavailable to the people, but this remoteness is overcome by the

---

218 *Arasentur* is Feminine and *arasentner* is masculine. The person is known as having the abilities to achieve ecstasy and communicate with spirits, heal, act as mediator between the transcendence and immanence, and also act as intercessor and counsellor in a social group. The comparison and relation is made between Jesus and *arasentur* mainly on the act of healing others. The healing which both of them impart is a holistic reconciliation and restoration of the individual with the spirits and the environment around them.

219 Takatemjen, *Studies on Theology and Naga Culture* (Delhi: ISPCK, 1998), 55-68.

220 The story is about the meeting between *Lijaba* (believed to be the creator and the God of the fields) and the two poor orphan sisters who lived in the outskirts of a village in a small hut. *Lijaba* who annually visits the village to bless his people came at night disguising oneself, and did not find a place to stay for the night was warmly welcomed in their home by the two sisters. *Lijaba* fed them that night and latter blessed their insignificant field with harvest and cursed all the fields owned by other villagers. By observing the social setting of the folktale and the actions of *Lijaba,* Takatemjen compares Jesus' teachings and actions with that of *Lijaba* tradition and formulate theological reflections from them (especially, Matt 25:31-46, Luke 14:12-24; John 4:1-28).

221 Hemkhochon Chongloi, *Indoi: A Study of Primal Kuki Religious Symbolism in the Hermeneutical Framework of Mircea Eliade* (Delhi: ISPCK, 2008), 284-287. Yangkahao Vashum's model of Jesus Christ as the Ancestor and Elder Brother is not considered because it is found not relevant in the Mizo context. However, it is still another significant articulation of contextual Christology. Yangkahao Vashum, "Jesus Christ as the Ancestor and Elder Brother: Constructing a Relevant Indigenous/Tribal Christology of North East India," *Journal of Tribal Studies 13* (2008): 21-36.

222 *Pathen* means Supreme Being, and *Indoi* is a symbol that is made out of a bundle of several articles taken from parts of animals and plants ("a slanted mother pig skull, a piece of he-goat's curved horn, bracelet, dao, a jar made from gourd, etc."), which is bound together bound together by a single thread made out of *khaopi* plant and is hung on the front porch of every Kuki house. The parts of animals and plants separately inspired with sacred characteristics. This symbol is used to concretize the presence of *Pathen* in every household. Chongloi, *Indoi*, 5.

*Indoi* symbol. Therefore, the relationship between *Indoi* and *Pathen* resembles the Christ-God relationship which is conceptualized in the incarnation. The institution of *Indoi* which awaited the sacred manifest in the material objects thus relates with the Christ-event as a living experience of God.

Now to come to the Mizos, L. H. Lalpekhlua in his 2007 book *Contextual Christology*, states that the series of revival movements throughout the history of Christianity in Mizoram evidently "have become a springboard for the further development of Christology in Mizo Christian thought."[223] Since the first revival movement in 1906, there are four major movements, in 1906, 1913, 1919 and 1930.

The first revival movement in Mizoram came from Wales through the Khasi Church, and is sparked by the receiving of the news about the revival movement that took place at the Khasi Hills in 1905. Great expectation is built up among the Mizos for a similar revival, which is witnessed in the writings J. Meirion Lloyd.[224] In 1906, both Welsh and Baptist missionaries in Mizoram jointly sent ten delegates to attend the assembly of the Khasi Presbyterian Church at Mairang in the Khasi Hills (presently Meghalaya State), in the hope of sharing the revival. After their return at Aizawl (Mizoram), 9th April 1906, the first revival movement broke out during their farewell prayer meeting for the southern delegates of Mizoram.[225] The main christological emphasis during the first revival movement according to Lalpekhlua was the work of Christ on the cross, which was seen as forgiveness of sin.[226] The Christology that presupposes the sin of human beings reaffirmed the western Christology, Christ as the saviour from sin.

In the second revival movement of 1913, the main theme was the second coming of Christ, and was expected to happen in the very near future. As Mangkhosat Kipgen pointed out, among the minority Baptist churches in the southern part of Mizoram, the theological emphasis was upon the crucifixion of Christ.[227] Lalpekhlua argues that "Christ's second coming must be understood also within the framework of the understanding of Jesus Christ as the way to heaven."[228] The christological concern of the third revival movement of 1919

223 Lalpekhlua, *Contextual Christology*, 99.

224 He cites D. E. Jones who says "We used to receive newspapers giving accounts of the miracles of grace occurring in Wales and had letters from friends naming some of our acquaintances who had known the power of the Spirit. We gave a resume of these in weekly meetings and it roused in us a deep desire to see something of this nature in Mizoram." J. Meirion Lloyd, *History of the Church in Mizoram* (Aizawl: SPB, 1991), 89.

225 For details see Lalsawma, *Revivals the Mizo Way: Forty Years of Revival Movements in Mizoram* (Aizawl: Lalsawma, 1994), 31-54.

226 Lalpekhlua, *Contextual Christology*, 102.

227 Mangkhosat Kipgen, *Christianity and Mizo* (Aizawl: MTC, 1997), 258.

228 Lalpekhlua, *Contextual Christology*, 111.

was again on the emphasis of the cross of Christ and his redemptive suffering, which is for salvation.[229] The Christology of the suffering of Christ became real and personal and became a basis of hope for salvation in the context of their great suffering from "the plague" and impoverished condition of life.[230] Lalpekhlua rightly observes that this kind of individualistic approach to Christology neglect the corporate structure of the tribal society and had little significance for the community as a whole.[231] The fourth revival movement of 1930 emphasizes on the work of the Holy Spirit and spiritual gifts, such as ecstatic dancing, healing through prayer, laying on of hands, speaking in tongues, transference of the Spirit by touch, symbolic gestures, trances and visions.[232]

Generally, the christological emphasis seen in these movements do not provide a shift from the Christology of the missionaries. Apart from the reintroduction of traditional drums in worship and the emergence of indigenous Mizo Christian songs, these revival movements can be seen as reaffirming the adopted Christology, and also as reestablishment of the dominion power of the British Empire. Due to natural disasters and difficulty in daily living, the Mizos are in no condition to oppose or to even contextualize their way of worship or even their Christologies. Those who continue to indulge in indigenous way of merry-making with rice-beer and traditional drums are all seen as sins, and in need of repentance. Every indigenous awakening is suppressed with authority and the introduction of drums in Mizo worship services were rejected for decades in both the Mission station churches of the Northern and Southern regions.[233] However, many Mizo indigenous Christian songs were composed during these times, and many of them are still used widely to this day.

Having this foundation, the Presbyterian Church of Mizoram and the Baptist Church of Mizoram articulates their doctrinal confessions. The ten doctrines are published in a small booklet by the Presbyterian Church of

---

229 Lalpekhlua, *Contextual Christology*, 115.

230 As this revival is preceded by the First World War and a severe influenza epidemic, the death of Christ on the cross and his sufferings became more vivid and real, thus to symbolize crucifixion some people stood against the wall or lay on the floor, stretching their arms out as if they were being crucified.

231 Lalpekhlua, *Contextual Christology*, 115.

232 J. Meirion Lloyd, *On Every High Hill* (Liverpool: CMFMO, 1956), 56; Lalsawma, *Revivals the Mizo Way*, 155-70.

233 Lalpekhlua, *Contextual Christology*, 116. There were two Mission stations in Mizoram, Mission Veng, Aizawl and Serkawn, situated in the northern and southern regions respectively.

Mizoram, probably in 1961.[234] And in 1988 the Baptist Church of Mizoram also came up with the confession.[235] The contents are mostly derived from the christological confessions of the Apostolic and the Nicene Creeds.

The lack of documentation of the theological ideas and worldviews, especially in relation to Christology in Mizo contextual theology is a major concern and resulted in a long dependent on the Christologies of unfamiliar cultures. The missionaries shown no interest to contextualize Christology and rather condemned any upcoming contextual thought. This is one of the reasons why there are a number of sects emerging in a short period of the history of Christianity in Mizoram. Some prominent sectarian groups are "Tlira pawl" (Tlira's sect) and "Khuangtuaha Pawl" (Khuangtuaha's sect), but do not produce sources that could be scrutinized, and the only available sources are the production of persons who are not associated with them. However, it is still significant to come to a group of people who are in constant struggle to define Christ in their own setting of socio-cultural tradition. Lalpekhlua rightly asserts that "Despite a number of their limitations, the life and the views of these movements reflect a strong desire for the indigenization of the gospel."[236] The sectarian movements in Mizoram are not free from misinterpreting or misusing of the Bible, and those outside their boundary see them as living their own desired way of life.[237]

One visionary experience by Tlira is especially revolutionary, because the people he sees in the vision is trapped in a python's belly. He also realizes that if the big python closes its mouth, everyone will be trapped and only the Son of Man is able to open it in his second coming.[238] After telling this to the congregation in his preaching, the meeting was abruptly closed at the request of certain church leader who declared the presence of Satan.[239] According to Tlira, the python of his vision was the church formed and fashioned in Western perspective. The Christology advocated in this sect differs from the contemporary churches in Mizoram. The physical return of Jesus Christ is rejected and also the rapture of the saints and the resurrection of the dead. They

234 Saiaithanga, *Thurin Zirna* [*A Study of the Doctrine*], rev. ed. (Aizawl: SL&PB, 1965), iii. It is mentioned here in this book that the doctrine has been in use since 1961.

235 Baptist Church of Mizoram, *Zoram Baptist Kohhran Thurin Puanchhuah* (*Baptist Confession*) (Serkawn: BCM, 1988).

236 Lalpekhlua, *Contextual Christology*, 136.

237 B. B. Goswami, "Hill Tribesmen of Northeast India: The Impact of Christianity," in *The Tribal World and its Transformation*, ed. Bhupinder Singh and J. S. Bhandari (New Delhi: Concept, 1978), 123-129.

238 Lalsawma, *Revivals the Mizo Way*, 63; James Dokhuma, *Zoram Kohhran Tualṭo Chanchinte* (Histories of the indigenous Churches of Mizoram) (Aizawl: D. Buanga, 1975), 2.

239 Lalsawma, *Revivals the Mizo Way*, 63.

prefer to speak of the second coming of Christ as the coming of Christ's spirit into the life of believers.

The sect that followed Khuangtuaha's teachings was the other significant sect that had been previously mentioned. The sect propels the idea of the millennial reign of Christ, and this will take place in the near future with the second coming of Christ on earth. They believe that after God abandoned the Israelites, they became the "new Israel."[240] The hope to witness and attain the millennial reign of Christ without tasting death and the expectation of this reality to be inaugurated in Mizoram looms large in their teachings. The expectation of Christ return on earth and the establishment of millennial reign here on earth and not in heaven is a significant eschatological articulation. Apart from these the emphasis on Christology is not much to be found, but their reaction to Western forms of Christian worship songs is to be highly appreciated. Instead of adapting to westernized hymns and choruses, they compose their own by utilizing the traditional Mizo tunes.[241] They also rejected the banning of rice beer by the church and they opine that there is no reason why God should not allow human being to enjoy the fruit of blessings:

> Oh! How strange it is the spirit's way!
> Some of us are going back to beer drinking,
> At the root of all is Lord Jesus.
> You did say drinking was unlawful!
> But when I enquired afresh from Calvary,
> "Take it if you will" he said to me.[242]

The differentiation between true believers and carnal persons is the key to understand their permission to indulge in drinking rice beer and singing traditional songs and dancing, and merry making. The intentions of the true believers are pure and thus cannot be compared with others who indulge in self-enjoyment, because for carnal persons these all became unclean, banned and immoral.[243]

Lalpekhlua thus come up with the presentation of Christology in the framework of the Mizo concept of *pasalṭha*.[244] This is a synthetic task of applying the results of investigations in order to formulate Christology based

240 Vanlalchhuanga, *An Zirtirnate* (*Their Teachings*) (Aizawl: Goshen, 1984), 50; Z. T. Sangkhuma, *An Danglamna te* (*Their Distinctives*) (Aizawl: Rinzawna, 1991), 86; for a detail theology of Khuangtuaha pawl, see Lalpekhlua, *Contextual Christology*, 143-148.

241 Lalpekhlua, *Contextual Christology*, 147.

242 Lalsawma, *Revivals the Mizo Way*, 118.

243 Lalsawma, *Revivals the Mizo Way*, 187; Dokhuma, *Zoram Kohhran Tualṭo Chanchinte*, 49-50.

244 Lalpekhlua, *Contextual Christology*, 201-235.

on the concept. He proposes four reasons to validate the choosing of the concept of pasalṭha as a model to interpret Jesus Christ in Mizoram:

> 1) It is integrally rooted in Mizo cultural consciousness; 2) It incorporates both practical and theoretical implications for Mizos; 3) it is able to be used in a systematic theological framework; and 4) Even though it has some limitations, it lends itself particularly to the construction of a uniquely Mizo Christology.[245]

The liberative value and cultural rootedness are significant in the christological articulation of this thesis. As Sallie McFague asserts, "There is no model able to encompass the riches and complexity of the divine-human relationship."[246] Lalpekhlua also affirms the relevancy of other models, and in no way claim that this model also suffers the inadequacy common to other various models of contextual Christologies. He further highlights two limitations in this pasalṭha model: Firstly, its lack of universality because the Mizos in the past lived in isolated small villages and are politically independent of each other. Secondly, pasalṭha occasionally showed intense reserve about themselves, and would tell others that he feel no pain even at the verge of death.[247] Another important addition to this model is the use of the concept of *tlawmngaihna*.[248] It is very interesting and stimulating to see how the christological passages of the Bible are interpreted in the framework of this model. As "… any theology which claims to be Christian theology… must maintain close and positive relation with the Bible," Lalpekhlua's Christ as pasalṭha does not venture away from the Bible, and also provides a praxis-oriented Christology.[249]

However, especially when speaking of the incarnation as an act of tlawmngaihna it is clear that, as has been said before in the context of contextual theologies, the notion of the preexistence of Jesus Christ is adapted freely. Therefore this present study also is not an attempt to study the possibility or the mystery of the pre-existent nature of Jesus Christ in modern cosmological sense, but mainly to identify cosmic Christology in Matthew's Gospel and to relate it with the contextual understanding of the correlation of cosmic Christ and created orders.

245 Lalpekhlua, *Contextual Christology*, 202.

246 Sallie McFague, *Metaphorical Theology: Models of God in Religious Language* (Philadelphia: Fortress, 1982), 144, quoted in Lalpekhlua, *Contextual Christology*, 203.

247 Lalpekhlua, *Contextual Christology*, 203-204.

248 Tlawmngaihna means selfless service for others, humility, kindness, patience, honesty, hard work, and trustworthiness. However, this is the ideal lifestyle of not only pasalṭha but for all the Mizos, and thus a person who is not identified as pasalṭha could be classified as "mi tlawmngai" (use in noun).

249 John Macquarrie, *Principle of Christian Theology* (London: SCM, 1977), 10.

## 5.11. Summary

It is clear that the Christologies we have in the Gospel writings and various literatures that came from all over the globe are all contextual and are relevant and at the same time irrelevant to a particular socio-cultural context. The question Dietrich Bonhoeffer asked in his letters from the Nazi prison of Tegel in 30th April 1944 bears the same significance then and now: "'Who was Jesus when he lived two-thousand years ago?' but 'Who is Jesus today?'"[250] More precisely the question could mean, 'Who is Jesus here and now, at this point in history, and in this time and place?' This question thus encompasses and probe into the identity of Jesus, the condition of this present earth, and the local reality of a person.

As Stephen B. Bevans puts it "doing theology contextually is not an option", but a "theological imperative."[251] To this it can be added that it is not only imperative, it is an exegetical envelope that cannot be escaped by anyone during the process of theologizing. Bevans further states that there are external and internal factors that necessitate contextualization of theology. The dissatisfaction with classical approaches to theology is the external factor, and the incarnational nature of the Gospel is the internal factor.[252] These factors make it clear that Christology that arises out of a particular culture and context is not readily adapted or accommodated by another. However, as in the case of the Mizos, the lack of education in general, and the fear of the colonial power in particular are few factors that led to the uncomfortable adaptation of Western Christology. The shackles that need to be broken down, but even to this day the churches due to unawareness became partly the colonial instrument to defy and resist any contextual Christology in Mizoram. This does not mean that, any christological interest must be acknowledged, but those that are not contradictory with the Bible must be given room to develop and prosper.

As liberational and contextual Christologies often utilize the traditional Christology for foundation, especially the preexistent nature of Jesus, it does not pose a threat to the doctrinal teachings but helps to develop what is at hand to make it relevant to the mass. Paul probably synthesizes traditions around him in order to articulate a more complex image of God concept. The concept which took a hold on to the thoughts of other New Testament writers, and became prominent in the early church and continues to dominates even the present churches. The cosmic Christology developed partly from Wisdom tradition involves ecological interests, and also pushes forward the significance

---

250 Joel Lawrence, *Bonhoeffer: A Guide for the Perplexed* (New York: T&T Clark, 2010), 33.

251 Stephen B. Bevans, *Models of Contextual Theology* (Maryknoll: Orbis, 1992), 1.

252 Bevans, *Models of Contextual Theology*, 5-10, cited in Lalpekhlua, *Contextual Christology*, 3-4.

of contextual understanding in order to formulate a Christology for today in any given context.

Acceptance of the dogma of the Incarnation became the basic starting point within traditional Christology and also for tribal contextual Christology. For the tribals of Northeast India, the idea of incarnation and the relation of Supreme Being with nature are concepts that had been acknowledged from time immemorial. As a result the Messiahship, the divinity, and the preexistence of Jesus undoubtedly took a stronghold in the thoughts of the Mizos. However, as Lalpekhlua observes, the inherited Christology is in another perspective an individualistic and otherworldly, and focuses mainly to the death of Christ on the cross, but neglects Jesus' life and ministry.[253] The focus needs adjustment, instead of the emphasis on the salvation of individual soul, and the call to individual for repentance, Christology needs to address the socio-economic, ecological and political problems of contemporary Mizo society. The missionaries projected the traditional culture of the Mizos as evil or a mere preparatory for the coming gospel, and thus undermined the values of the culture, and this is the dilemma where Christology has to revive the traditional ecological concerns and cultural and religious identity. Therefore, cosmic Christology with ecological thrust could serve as an exegetical tool to study nature miracles in Matthew's Gospel and the outcome would probably provide a foundation to do a contextual Christology with an emphasis to liberate the Mizo traditional thought of the mutual interrelationship between Supreme Being and nature.

253 Lalpekhlua, *Contextual Christology*, 5-6.

Chapter 6

# Exegesis of Select Passages

## 6.1. Introduction

It is important to understand the phrase "nature miracles" at this point because the classification of miracle stories cannot be ascertained to this point of time. The fact is that the phrase is still a contested phraseology. An alternating phrase "anomalous miracles" used by Eric Eve is helpful but as it can also include the miracles of the raising of the dead, it encompasses even some of the healing miracles.[1] John P. Meier's suggestion that these nature miracles could be termed as "gift miracles" is also misleading according to Graham H. Twelftree, mainly because the category contains only the stories of water being turned into wine and multiplication of food, and the other miracles that has to do with natural order of the world were excluded.[2] Thus, to call these miracle stories that are to be considered in this section as nature miracles can be justified, mainly due to the absence of a better phrase.

It is also noteworthy to observe that each Gospel writer uses these stories to convey various theological points, but according to Twelftree "despite their different perspectives, the Gospel writers present a remarkably similar view of the nature miracle stories."[3] Walking on the water and stilling of the storm in the Synoptic Gospels present similar view that Jesus, like God acts to rescue

1 For the discussion on the phrase "anomalous miracles," see Eric Eve, *The Healer from Nazareth: Jesus' Miracles in Historical Context* (London: SPCK, 2009), 145-160.

2 John P. Meier, *Rethinking the Historical Jesus: Mentor, Message, and Miracles*, vol. 2 of *A Marginal Jew: Rethinking the Historical Jesus*, ABRL (New York: Doubleday, 1994), 877-880; Graham H. Twelftree, "Nature Miracles and the Historical Jesus," in *The Nature Miracles of Jesus: Problems, Perspectives, and Prospects*, ed. Graham H. Twelftree (Eugene, OR: Wipf & Stock, 2017), 1-40 (5).

3 Twelftree, "Nature Miracles and the Historical Jesus," 8.

people, able to walk on water and still the storm. In feeding the crowds, Jesus is acting as the Lord of the elements, and is greater than Moses or Elisha. Apart from this, the lacking of faith in the part of the disciples or the lesson of faith is seen in different nature miracles. Twelftree further argues that "the stories are used to identify Jesus and provide followers with a basis for their faith in him."[4] He also points out that all the Gospel writings perceive nature miracles as a basis of faith, and thus states "for they point beyond the supposed event to their agent: God himself in Jesus acting on earth to identify himself and, often indirectly, meet human needs."[5] Matthew's employment of nature miracles in his Gospel to identify Jesus is in coherence within his cosmological worldview and christological framework.

## 6.2. Nature Miracles and Matthew's Cosmological Worldview

At this juncture, it is important to look at the reality and conception of miracle stories within Matthew's cosmological worldview. Errki Koskenniemi, in his article "Miracles of the Devil and His Assistants in Early Judaism and their Influence on the Gospel of Matthew" investigates the miracles performed by evil powers and the reaction they caused among Jewish theologians and Matthew.[6] He argues that exorcisms and demons were not that problematic to Matthew, as he may have easily omitted them in his writing. Matthew could also distance Jesus from common exorcists by not narrating how Jesus sent the disciples and told them to drive out demons (10:7).[7] Therefore, it is a tough task to claim that miracles were somehow problematic to Matthew. A number of Old Testament references that play significant role in Matthew's Gospel appear in the context of miracle stories (1:18-24, 2:1-15, 8:16-17, 12:18-21).[8]

To cement this point of argument, Koskenniemi further states that Matthew chapter 8-9 that contains a chain of miracle stories, records almost all of Mark's miracle stories, but mostly abridges them with a skillful redactor's hand.[9] Matthew also gives different version that contains the theological elements of Mark's stories, perhaps an editing style to abbreviate them and make them short and brief (e.g. Mark 2:1-12 and Matt 9:1-8; Mark 5:1-20 and Matt 8:28-34; Mark 5:21-43 and Matt 9:18-26; Mark 9:14-29 and Matt

4 Twelftree, "Nature Miracles and the Historical Jesus," 8.

5 Twelftree, "Nature Miracles and the Historical Jesus," 9.

6 Errki Koskenniemi, "Miracles of the Devil and His Assistants in Early Judaism and their Influence on the Gospel of Matthew" in *Evil and the Devil*, ed. Ida Fröhlich and Errki Koskenniemi, LNTS 481 (London: T&T Clark, 2013), 84-97.

7 Koskenniemi, "Miracles of the Devil," 96-97.

8 Koskenniemi, "Miracles of the Devil," 94.

9 Koskenniemi, "Miracles of the Devil," 94.

17:14-21).[10] Matthew could have omitted altogether some of Mark's miracle stories, remove certain features, or make some clear changes. This seems to come in terms with early Jewish doubts or struggle concerning miracles which is already discussed in the previous chapter (3.6) under the heading "God, Nature and Miracle within the Cosmological Worldview of Second Temple Period Writers." According to Koskenniemi, Matthew follows this tradition in his Gospel and do not fall too far from his predecessors in dealing with miracle stories.[11] Therefore, Matthew did not reject miracle claims, and like the early rabbis Matthew also is careful in dealing with miracle stories. Though miracles were a reality for Matthew, he also warns the readers about the misleading miracles especially that are to appear in the end times. The thrust of the matter is thus the possibility or actuality of miracles in general or nature miracles is not in question in Matthew's cosmological worldview.

Though miracle stories pose problematic issue in some sense during the early first century thinkers, but for Matthew these nature miracles provide foundational ground to articulate and develop his christological motif. This is clear in his utilization and employment of the stories of nature miracles where Jesus expects his disciples to trust in God for material provision (6:25-34), and for safety (10:29-31).[12] Due to this understanding, Craig S. Keener argues against Günther Bornkamm who focuses on the theme of discipleship in the miracle story of the stilling of the storm. Keener holds that the primary function of the miracle story is christological in nature.[13] It was Heinz

10 For the passage and comparison, see Ulrich Luz, *Das Evangelium nach Matthäus*, EKK 2 (Zürich: Benziger, 1985), 8-11, 343-348, cited by Koskenniemi, "Miracles of the Devil," 94.

11 Koskenniemi, "Miracles of the Devil," 97.

12 Early Christians probably continued to trust God for nature miracles when needed (Jas 5:16-18, Mark 11:23), but they do not see their authority in such situations as Jesus would have encountered it, duc to the fact that they perceive Jesus as being authoritative in performing miracles, but they view their own authority in inferior ways. This shows that their conception of Jesus as having cosmic authority or divine authority is continued even in the later writings of the New Testament. Craig S. Keener, *The Gospel of Matthew: A Socio-Rhetorical Commentary* (Grand Rapids: Eerdmans, 2009), 279.

13 Keener, *The Gospel of Matthew*, 279, citing G. Bornkamm, "The Stilling of the Storm in Matthew 8:23-27," in *Tradition and Interpretation in Matthew*, eds. G. Bornkamm, G. Barth and H.J. Held, trans. Percy Scott (Philadelphia: Westminster, 1963), 52-57. According to Bornkamm, by positioning the story right after the two sayings of Jesus about discipleship (Matt 8:19-22), and by adding the Jesus saying, "Why are you afraid, you of little faith?" (Matt 8:26), Matthew reinterprets the tradition and made it addresses the theme of discipleship. He observes the addition of "disciples" in the introduction of Matt 8:23. He also highlights the shift of disciples' cry for help from their criticism of Jesus to their confession of confidence in Jesus (Matt 8:25), using "Lord" as a divine designation rather than a human title of respect. Matthew has taken the story out of its biographical setting in Mark and Luke, placed it in a different context in his gospel, and

J. Held, in his essay "Matthew as Interpreter of the Miracle Stories," who thinks that Matthew often redacted Mark to present a more christological and other theological interpretation of miracle stories.[14] What is also noteworthy in Matthew's Gospel is that the expectations of Jesus' contemporaries were repeatedly exceeded in the presentation of Jesus' identity and deeds (7:28, 9:9, 12:23, and 22:33).[15] Therefore, the employment of nature miracles by Matthew mainly pointed towards the christological motif, and specifically the identity and authority of Jesus. By saying this it does not however mean that other embedded themes are minor agenda.

R. T. France argues that the theme that best summarizes the whole of Matthew's message is the fulfilment of the Old Testament, and labels fulfilment as "the special trademark" of this Gospel.[16] Way back in 1952 this theme has already been identified by C. H. Dodd in his book *According to the Scriptures: The Substructure of New Testament Theology*.[17] The theme of fulfilment in Matthew's Gospel was further explored by B. Lindars in his 1961 book, *New Testament Apologetic: The Doctrinal Significance of the Old Testament Quotations*.[18] Another influential article on fulfilment theme is to be found in C. F. D. Moule's article "Fulfilment words in the New Testament: Use and abuse."[19] These studies clearly show that the Christian writers of the first century are in some way or another interested in the theme of fulfilment, and they indicated Jesus as the one who fulfilled the Old Testament hopes. While other New Testament writers quoted a few obvious texts as fulfilled in Jesus, Matthew, in his Gospel explored this motif extensively.[20]

R. B. Hays' observation that the presentation of Jesus by Gospel writers are mainly focus to show that Jesus' teachings, actions, death and vindication

---

adds edited works in a characteristic way so as to make it serve a new motive. The new role is thus a kerygmatic model of "the danger and glory of discipleship." Bornkamm, "The Stilling of the Storm in Matthew 8:23-27," 53-56.

14 Heinz J. Held, "Matthew as Interpreter of the Miracle Stories," in *Tradition and Interpretation in Matthew*, eds. G. Bornkamm, G. Barth and H. J. Held, trans. Percy Scott (Philadelphia: Westminster, 1963), 242-245.

15 Keener, The Gospel of Matthew, 279.

16 For a discussion on the fulfilment of Old Testament, see R. T. France, *Matthew: Evangelist and Teacher* (Downers Grove: IVP, 1989), 167.

17 C.H. Dodd, *According to the Scriptures: The substructure of New Testament Theology* (London: Nisbet, 1952).

18 Barnabas Lindars, *New Testament Apologetic: The Doctrinal Significance of the Old Testament Quotations* (London: SCM, 1961).

19 C. F. D. Moule, "Fulfilment words in the New Testament: Use and abuse," *NTS 14* (1967/8): 293-320.

20 W. D. Davies and D. C. Allison, *Matthew 1-7*, ICC (London: T&T Clark, 2004a.), 1:211; J.P. Versteeg, *Evangelie in viervoud: Een karakteristiek van de vier evangeliën* (Kampen: Kok, 1980), 23.

constituted the continuation and climax of the Old Testament.[21] The ancient biblical stories were "the *generative milieu* for the gospels, the original environment in which the first Christian traditions were conceived, formed and nurtured."[22] Particularly, Matthew also shows conscious dependence upon the language and themes found in the book of Genesis.[23]

Though there are studies that uncover typological connection between Genesis, Exodus and Matthew, the most obvious connection between Matthew and Genesis according to Jonathan T. Pennington is the opening statement of Matthew's Gospel: Βίβλος γενέσεως Ἰησοῦ Χριστοῦ υἱοῦ Δαυὶδ υἱοῦ Ἀβραάμ (Matt 1:1).[24] Pennington further argues that this opening statement puts Jesus "in the context of three of the most important realities of Jewish history and identity – the book of Genesis, the king David, and the Patriarch Abraham."[25]

The observation by commentators that the phrase Βίβλος γενέσεως bears correlation with Genesis is not uncommon.[26] Warren Carter's argument in his article "Matthew and the Gentiles: Individual Conversion and/or Systematic Transformation" takes the understanding further by stating that the opening verse of Matthew's Gospel did not evoke for the reader only the name of the book of Genesis in the LXX and the reference in Genesis 2:4 and 5:1, but also points toward the larger Genesis accounts.[27] He suggests that Matthew alludes intentionally to the book of Genesis to call to mind "the story of God's creative

---

21 R. B. Hays, "The Canonical Matrix of the Gospels," in *The Cambridge Companion to the Gospels*, ed. Stephen C. Barton (Cambridge: CUP, 2006), 53-75 (53).

22 Hays, "The Canonical Matrix of the Gospels," 53; see also Jonathan T. Pennington, "Heaven, Earth, and a New Genesis: Theological Cosmology in Matthew," in *Cosmology and the New Testament Theology*, ed. Jonathan T. Pennington and Sean M. McDonough, LNTS (London: T&T Clark, 2008), 28-44.

23 Pennington, "Heaven, Earth, and a New Genesis," 35-36. The NA27 appendix of references list four quotations and 23 allusions to Genesis.

24 Pennington, "Heaven, Earth, and a New Genesis," 36; Dale C. Allison, *The New Moses: A Matthean Typology* (Eugene, OR: Wipf & Stock, 1993) provides a detail discussion of this typological connection. Michael D. Goulder also utilizes Genesis and Exodus allusions in Matthew 1-5 as an example to justify typological interpretation. Michael D. Goulder, *Type and History in Acts* (London: SPCK, 1964), 1-13,

25 Pennington, "Heaven, Earth, and a New Genesis," 36. The opening verses of Mark's Gospel and John's Gospel could also be taken as connecting with Genesis due to their use of the word ἀρχὴ.

26 W. D. Davies and D. C. Allison, *A Critical and Exegetical Commentary on the Gospel According to Saint Matthew*, 3 vols. (Edinburgh: T&T Clark, 1998-1999), 1:149-154; Dale C. Allison, *Studies in Matthew: Interpretation Past and Present* (Grand Rapids: Baker, 2012), 157-162.

27 Warren Carter, "Matthew and the Gentiles: Individual Conversion and/or Systematic Transformation," *JSNT* 26 (2004), 259-282 (262), cited in Pennington, "Heaven, Earth, and a New Genesis," 36-37.

and sovereign purposes for the whole world as the initial context of hearing the story of Jesus."[28] It seems obvious that Matthew's allusion to Genesis is intentional, but care must be taken in regards to the understanding of how a partial citation stimulates a larger text.

Carter's use of John Foley's work on "traditional referentiality" is convincing because the larger text is well-known for the author and the readers.[29] It is also important to note that scholar like Jeannine K. Brown argues against this understanding. The main reason for this understanding is the resonance of covenantal motifs in this chapter, where the genealogy begins with Abraham but not Adam. The inclusion of Gentile figures woven into God's covenant and the emphasis of the exile as a threat to God's covenantal promises (1:11-12, 17) could be taken as deemphasizing the allusion to creation.[30] However, Brown did not fail to observe how Matthew draws upon certain Genesis persons, places and texts for various purposes. Brief summary of Brown's observations is as follows:[31]

> 1. Gen 38:8 is alluded in Matt 22:24 to signal the story of Onan and Tamar as a backdrop to Deuteronomy legislation of the levirate marriage.
>
> 2. Most of the Genesis persons in Matthew's genealogy highlight covenantal themes of the story of Israel.
>
> 3. The story of Cain and Abel provides for Matthew a meta-narratival theme of sin and restoration (cf. Matt 5:21-24; 18:23; 23:35).
>
> 4. Matthew uses story in the service of paraencsis by referencing Noah and the flood to warn of judgment and to exhort toward readiness, and Sodom and Gomorrah to announce and warn of judgment (Matt 19:4-5).
>
> 5. Matthew draws upon certain Genesis persons and texts to highlight his Christology. The martyrdom of the "righteous Abel" (Matt 23:35) offers an analogy for the death of the innocent Jesus. It may also be the case that Isaac is referenced or evoked at a number of points in Matthew's Gospel to provide a pattern for Jesus' own faithful and willing participation in the plan of God.

---

28 Carter, "Matthew and the Gentiles," 262.

29 Carter, "Matthew and the Gentiles," 262; cf. Pennington, "Heaven, Earth, and a New Genesis," 37.

30 Jeannine K. Brown, "Genesis in Matthew's Gospel," in *Genesis in the New Testament*, ed. Maarten J. J. Menken and Steve Moyise (London: T&T Clark, 2012), 42-59 (49).

31 Brown, "Genesis in Matthew's Gospel," 59.

The intertextual relationship between Matthew's Gospel and Genesis is observable in the first words through the first section of the Gospel, and this pattern progresses.[32] Matthew's genealogy contains introductory verse that says "An account of the genealogy of Jesus the Messiah, the son of David, the son of Abraham" (Matt 1:1). Matthew makes theological claims from the start about "the main protagonist within the story; he is the Messiah."[33] He further identifies Jesus within the sphere of the ongoing history of Israel; that Jesus is a Jew and the son of Abraham. Matthew continues the claim that Jesus is of royal descent, the son of David, a Davidic Messiah.[34] E. Anne Clements in her 2014 book *Mothers on the Margin*, also notes that the opening words of Matthew's Gospel Βίβλος γενέσεως, a parallel phrase from Genesis 2:4 and 5:1 create an intermediate intertextual links between Matthew's Gospel and Genesis.[35]

Among other allusions, Matthew 1:1 as highlighting the role of Abraham, and Matthew 28:19 as a reference to all nations are clear connection to Genesis 11-12 where Abraham was the one through whom God will bless "all the families of the earth shall be blessed" (Gen 12:3 NRSV).[36] The connection becomes significant to understand Matthew's Christology and also his cosmological worldview. In Genesis, God's authority as creator of

---

32 For a discussion on the imprint of Genesis in Matthew's Gospel, see Pennington, "Heaven, Earth, and a New Genesis," 37-39. It is also to be noted that the idea of using the term "heaven" for God out of reverential circumlocution is where the Second Temple Judaism and Matthew meets. However, Pennington argues that this reverential circumlocution is not that convincing in Matthew's Gospel. Due to a source provided by Gustaf Dalman's thesis, scholars explain heaven in Matthew's Gospel as merely a reverential circumlocution. The connection or interrelationship between Matthew's Gospel and Second Temple Judaism is still clear due to the presence of this kind of metonymy also in Rabbinic literature. Ephraim E. Urbach, *The Sages: Their Concepts and Beliefs, trans. Israel Abrahams*, 2 vols. (Jerusalem: Magnes, 1975), 1:70-71, cited by Jonathan T. Pennington, *Heaven and Earth in the Gospel of Matthew*, NovTSup 126 (Leiden: Brill, 2007), 36-37; cf. Gustaf Dalman, *The Words of Jesus*, trans. D. M. Kay (Edinburgh: T&T Clark, 1902).

33 E. Anne Clements, *Mothers on the Margins: The Significance of the Women in Matthew's Genealogy* (Eugene, OR: Pickwick, 2014), 22.

34 Clements, *Mothers on the Margins*, 22.

35 Matthew's genealogy also follows the same pattern of the genealogies in Genesis, that is A begat B, B begat C, and so on. However, Matthew differs in one important respect. The genealogies in Genesis are normally introduced with the forefather from whom the descendants follow: "These are the descendants of Noah's Sons, Shem, Ham, and Japheth" (Gen 10:1). Unlike this pattern, Matthew's genealogy starts at its end point "Jesus Christ," and is not called "book of the genesis of Abraham" but rather "book of the genesis of Jesus Christ." Thus, the line of descendants starts with Jesus Christ (Matt 1:1) and also ends with Jesus, the one called Christ (Matt 1:16). Clements, *Mothers on the Margins*, 22-23.

36 Pennington, "Heaven, Earth, and a New Genesis," 38.

heaven and earth is the basis for the redemption for all the nations through Abraham. Matthew's motif of redemption is also enveloped within his cosmological worldview and also his theme of heaven and earth, and the culmination in Jesus' own authority over heaven and earth (28:18), and the disciples are to go and bring blessing to all the nations.[37]

This kind of intertextuality is not limited to Genesis alone because it is also widely recognized that Matthew 28:16-20 also refers to Daniel 7:13. There is another contestant for this intertextual connection in 2 Chronicles 36:23 where Cyrus king of Persia announced "The LORD, the God of heaven, has given me all the kingdoms of the earth, and he has charged me to build him a house at Jerusalem, which is in Judah. Whoever is among you of all his people, may the LORD his God be with him. Let him go up."[38] All these convincingly points Matthew's Gospel as not being removed distantly from the Old Testament and the Second Temple literatures. It is thus appropriate to consider Matthew's Gospel as having been influenced and largely framed within the boundary of the ancient Jewish cosmological worldview.

## 6.3. The Stilling of the Storm (8:23-27)

### *6.3.1. Narrative Framework*

Jesus' stilling of the storm is not a unique material for Matthew's Gospel, and is found also in other Synoptic Gospels (Matt 8:23-27, Mark 4:35-41, Luke 8:22-25), but distinctive in Matthew's choice of words. In regards to the structure of Matthew's Gospel,[39] this story is found in the second cycle of miracles clusters around the Sea of Galilee (8:2-9:34). According to Anthony J. Saldarini, the emphasis in this cycle is the responses of Jesus' audiences.[40] These responses are seen in terms of faith, discipleship and gentile mission.[41] The reason for this understanding is that the cycle consists a set of three miracle stories that are interwoven with another two sets of two discipleship stories and is followed by a pericope that stresses the need for more messengers of the kingdom (9:35-38).[42]

---

37 Pennington, "Heaven, Earth, and a New Genesis," 38.

38 Bruce J. Malina, "The Literary Structure and Form of Matt. xxviii. 16–20," *NTS* 17 (1970): 87-103.

39 For a chiastic structure, see W. D. Davies and D. C. Allison, *A Critical and Exegetical Commentary on the Gospel According to Saint Matthew*, 3 vols. (Edinburgh: T&T Clark, 1998-1999), 2:68.

40 Anthony J. Saldarini, "Matthew," in *Eerdmans Commentary on the Bible* (Grand Rapids: Eerdmans, 2003), 1000-1063 (1021).

41 David L. Turner, *Matthew*, BECNT (Grand Rapids: Baker, 2008), 227.

42 Turner, *Matthew*, 227. As the healing story of the synagogue official's daughter in 9:18-26 actually enveloped another healing story of the woman with blood issue (9:20-22), the number of miracle stories can be counted as ten. Consequently, the number is compared

Bornkamm was the one who initiates the redactional study of Matthew's Gospel in a short article in 1948, "The Stilling of the Storm in Matthew."[43] In this article he emphasizes and illustrates how Matthew interpreted earlier tradition. Matthew is not to be seen only as a presenter of earlier tradition but is to be seen also an editor who was making use of the sources that he acquired. When comparing Matthew's Gospel with that of Luke, one can easily determine the editing works embedded in them. Bornkamm's hypothesis is driven by an initial methodological assertion: Kerygmatic faith in Jesus served as the foundation of the gospel tradition.[44] The biographies of Jesus are not available but a proclamation of his words and deeds drawn from primitive Christian tradition which are shaped to serve kerygmatic concerns are available in the Gospels.[45] Therefore, Jesus had to be understood from the perspective of the faith in Jesus proclaimed by the early church.

The writers of the Gospels had freedom to alter traditions in the light of pragmatic interests, even in their endeavour to record factual traditional data. Bornkamm sees that this methodology is confirmed by the pericope found in Matthew 8:23-27, "the stilling of the storm." His first contextual observation argues that this miracle story is placed by Matthew in a different place when compared with Mark and Luke. He posits that the story is taken out of its biographical setting by Matthew, and placed it in a context of a series of miracles (chaps. 8-9), and Matthew's purpose is to portray Jesus as the "Messiah of deed" after portraying him as the "Messiah of the word" in the previous section of his Gospel "the sermon on the mount" (chaps. 5-7).[46]

Bornkamm points out that the utterance of ejaculatory prayer by the disciples (Κύριε, σῶσον, ἀπολλύμεθα) is found only in Matthew's Gospel. He argues that the disciples in their desperate cry address Jesus as Κύριε here in Matthew's Gospel, rather than Διδάσκαλε in Mark 4:38 or Ἐπιστάτα in Luke 8:24. Bornkamm sees this as Matthew's redactional work to portray the desire

---

to the ten plagues of Moses and scholars like Erich Klostermann suggests that that these chapters are planned to picture Jesus as the new Moses or the church as a new exodus. Cf. Erich Klostermann, *Das Matthäus evangelium* (Tübingen: Mohr, 1927), cited by D. A. Carson, "Matthew," in *Matthew-Mark*, 2nd ed. EBC 9 (Grand Rapids: Zondervan, 2010), 23-670; cf. Howard M. Teeple, *The Mosaic Eschatological Prophet* (Philadelphia: SBL, 1957), 82; W. D. Davies, *The Setting of the Sermon on the Mount* (Cambridge: CUP, 1966), 86-93; Allison, *The New Moses*, 208; George Wesley Buchanan, *The Gospel of Matthew*, NTS 1 (Eugene, OR: Wipf & Stock, 1996), 363.

43 Günther Bornkamm, "The Stilling of the Storm in Matthew 8:23-27," in *Tradition and Interpretation in Matthew*, ed. G. Bornkamm, G. Barth and H. J. Held, trans. Percy Scott (Philadelphia: Westminster, 1963), 52-57.

44 Bornkamm, "The Stilling of the Storm in Matthew 8:23-27," 52.

45 Paul Frederick Feiler, "The Stilling of the Storm in Matthew: A Response to Günther Bornkamm," *JETS* 26 (1983): 399-406 (399).

46 Bornkamm, "The Stilling of the Storm in Matthew 8:23-27," 53.

of the disciples to follow Jesus at all costs. He further notes that Matthew was the only one who kept Jesus' rebuke of the disciples before the miracle. He also suggests that the phrase "little faith" conveys a symbol of the hard road of the disciple. As difficult as it may be, the disciples can depend on the word of Jesus that overcomes the storm.[47] "This is characteristic of paradigmatic narratives and provides Matthew's audience and likewise, us with an opportunity to imitate and follow Christ."[48] The miracle story is thus an illustration of the costs and rewards of discipleship. As the disciples are rocked by the storm, so also "the little ship of the church" stands against severe persecution. But the person of Christ, who as a human being "with no place to lay his head," is capable to calm the tempest and vindicate his followers with words, because he is the majestic Lord. Therefore, the story is "a description of the dangers against which Jesus warns anyone who over thoughtlessly presses to become a disciple. At the same time it shows him as one who… is able to reward the sacrifice of abandoning earthly ties. The story becomes a kerygmatic paradigm of the danger and glory of discipleship."[49]

Bornkamm, Held and others situated the stilling of the storm (8:23-27) in the second miracle section of Matthew 8-9, and unanimously identified it under the theme of discipleship. William G. Thompson also follows this and analyses each pericope through composition techniques such as repetition of keywords, verbal contacts, similar styles and vocabulary in supporting Held's second theme, which is discipleship (8:18-9:17). He observes that each of the three sections uses its own particular repetitions in order to identify its theme and grouping.

Heinz J. Held seeks to bring clarity to the Matthean miracle stories that engaged much of chapters 8 and 9 with a thematic approach, and also focuses the investigation completely through the lens of form criticism.[50] Under the influence of his mentor Bornkamm, he approaches miracle stories in Matthew's Gospel as paradigms.[51] He analyses how Matthew rewrites Mark's miracle stories through abbreviation and expansion. He prefers the proposal of Martin Dibelius that the stories of Jesus' miracles were either "paradigms" or "tales," rather than that of Rudolf Bultmann's identification of the miracle

---

47 Bornkamm, "The Stilling of the Storm in Matthew 8:23-27," 57.

48 Feiler, "The Stilling of the Storm in Matthew," 400.

49 Bornkamm, "The Stilling of the Storm in Matthew 8:23-27," 57.

50 Held finds Matthew's miracle stories similar to the concepts of Dibelius' paradigm and Bultmann's apothegm. Here he concludes that Matthew's miracle stories are given an illustrative meaning. Heinz J. Held, "Matthew as Interpreter of the Miracle Stories," in *Tradition and Interpretation in Matthew*, ed. G. Bornkamm, G. Barth and H. J. Held, trans. Percy Scott (Philadelphia: Westminster, 1963), 242-245.

51 Held, "Matthew as Interpreter," 178.

story as, a "form" unfamiliar to the ordinary person of the first century.[52] Held concludes that Matthew's miracle stories assumed brevity, focus, and special Jewish message that characterized the Dibelius paradigm form.[53] He also indicates that there is a systematic nature in Matthew's editorial plan, and thus sees a careful arrangement of miracle stories in chapter 8-9, which came right after a meaningful redactional work in chapter 5-7. He observes that this "reveals Matthew's intention to show Jesus' mission as involving both word and deed."[54]

What is significant in Held's analysis is his division of chapter 8-9 into three sections, under one overarching theme. He identifies a theme for each one of them: Prophecy fulfilment of God's Servant/Christology (8:1-17), Discipleship (8:18-9:17) and Faith (9:18-31).[55] It is also noteworthy because even when he identifies the stilling of the storm under the theme of discipleship, he still holds that these three sections are mutually exclusive, but the overarching theme is Christology.[56]

By comparing Matthew and in particular Mark's Gospel, Held concludes that the abridgements of Matthew's sources were applied to serve the interests of his own interpretation.[57] In an extended discussion on the miracle stories, he puts forward the idea that these collection of miracle stories of Jesus carries with it christological functions.[58] Apart from the christological function, miracle stories also serve "to highlight the themes of faith and discipleship."[59] Evert-Jan Vledder in his 1997 book *Conflict in the Miracle Stories: A Socio-Exegetical Study of Matthew 8 and 9*, argues that "Matthew re-interpreted his source in such a way that these three themes [Christology, faith, and discipleship] in particular come to the fore."[60] Therefore we see the blending of rhetorolects in this miracle stories, where different rhetorical dialects are blended together to create discourse.

Thompson's analysis shows that the miracle stories relate both Jesus' words and his deeds. How Thompson presupposes Matthew as possessing a much intelligent writing skills is evident in his concluding remarks of his

---

52 Held, "Matthew as Interpreter," 241-246.

53 Held, "Matthew as Interpreter," 242.

54 Held, "Matthew as Interpreter," 246, cited by Mark R. Saucy, "Miracles and Jesus' Proclamation of the Kingdom of God," *BiblioSac* 153 (1996): 281-307 (283).

55 Held, "Matthew as Interpreter," 245-246, 248-249.

56 Held, "Matthew as Interpreter," 248.

57 Held, "Matthew as Interpreter," 167.

58 Held, "Matthew as Interpreter," 246-247.

59 Evert-Jan Vledder, *Conflict in the Miracle Stories: A Socio-Exegetical Study of Matthew 8 and 9*, JSNTSup 152 (Shefield: SAP, 1997), 31.

60 Vledder, *Conflict in the Miracle Stories*, 31.

article.[61] Another presupposition of Thompson is that Matthew's interest in the person of Jesus (i.e., Jesus' word and deed) which is reflected in the verbal contact between the set of miracle stories is another compositional technique.[62] The first division (Matt 8:1-17) shows Jesus' power in word and work, and Thompson sees this in the repetition of the same keyword. In the leper's healing story, the word "cleanse" is repeated (8:2, 3a, 3b). In the second story of the cure of the centurion's servant, the centurion believed the power of Jesus' word (8:8, 9) and Jesus' word cured the servant (8:13).[63] Other examples are that, "touching" occurs in 8:3 and 8:15; "Lord" is used in 8:2 and 8:5-6. For Thompson some styles and vocabularies reveal the redactor's intention to utilize these pericopae into a single unified composition. The example Thompson has given is the genitive-absolute construction and the word order (8:1, 5) or a coherent setting of these episodes (8:1, 5, 14, 16).[64]

### 6.3.2. Analysis of the Passage

*[23]And when he got into the boat, his disciples followed him. [24]And behold, a great earthquake arose in (under) the sea, so that the boat was being covered by the waves. But he was sleeping. [25]And they came to him and woke him, saying, "Lord, save (us), we are perishing." [26]And he said to them, "Why are you afraid, you of little faith?" Then when he got up, he rebuked the winds and the sea, and there was a great calm. [27]And the men marvelled, saying, "What kind of a person is this that even the winds and the sea obey him?"*

The structure of the passage is simple and direct, despite the mixing of the two concerns of discipleship and Christology: (1) The occasion (v. 23; cf. v. 18); (2) the dire need of the disciples with the added note about Jesus' sleeping (v. 24); (3) the appeal for help (v. 25), which stands at the centre of the passage; (4) the response of Jesus in word and deed (v. 26); and (5) the disciples' amazement expressed in a question (v. 27).

Using Mark 4:36-41 as a source, Matthew adapted the story for his own purpose. Perhaps Luke did the same in his Gospel (Luke 8:22-25). The role of abbreviation in Matthew's compositional technique needs no further explanation because there are a number of substantial and significant changes even in this passage. In Mark's Gospel the disciples "took him" with them in the boat, but in Matthew's Gospel, in keeping with his theme, Jesus get into the boat first and then adds ἠκολούθησαν αὐτῷ οἱ μαθηταὶ αὐτοῦ "his disciples

61 "Somewhere between these two extremes we find the evangelist, an intelligent man who not only reacted to the material inherited from his sources, but also created a new interpretation of the Gospel tradition for the community he served." Thompson, "Reflections on the Composition," 388.

62 Thompson, "Reflections on the Composition," 370.

63 Thompson, "Reflections on the Composition," 369.

64 Thompson, "Reflections on the Composition," 370.

followed him."[65] Scholars often point out the catechetical value in this story by understanding the boat as the church. Bornkamm's focus on the difference between the pericope in Matthew 8:23-27 and its parallels in Mark 4:35-41 and Luke 8:22-25 could be classified as a pioneering work and he provides an illustration of how Matthew achieved new meaning by placing the pericope in different context than where it is situated in Mark.[66]

According to Bornkamm, by positioning the story right after the two sayings of Jesus about discipleship (Matt 8:19-22), and by adding the Jesus saying, "Why are you afraid, you of little faith?" (Matt 8:26), Matthew reinterprets the tradition and made it addresses the theme of discipleship.[67] He also cites the addition of "disciples" in the introduction of Matthew 8:23 to strengthen his argument. He also highlights the shift of disciples' cry for help from their criticism of Jesus to their confession of confidence in Jesus (Matt 8:25), using "Lord" as a divine designation rather than a human title of respect.[68] Matthew has taken the story out of its biographical setting in Mark and Luke, placed it in a different context in his gospel, and adds edited works in a characteristic way so as to make it serve a new motive.[69]

According to Bornkamm, the new role is thus a kerygmatic model of "the danger and glory of discipleship."[70] As Matthew replaces "disciples" with "men" to the question of who Jesus is in Matthew 2:27, one can identify the typical "choral ending" of a paradigm.[71] Bornkamm does not explain in his article why this pericope is paradigmatic, but acknowledges that the theological intention of Matthew here is the emphasis on the theme of discipleship.

Matthew added the word *ἰδοὺ* "behold/look" in v. 24 and substitutes Mark's (followed by Luke) *λαῖλαψ μεγάλη ἀνέμου* "great storm" by *σεισμὸς μέγας ἐγένετο ἐν τῇ θαλάσσῃ* "great earthquake in the sea." Matthew's favourite word *ἰδοὺ* is an indication and to call attention to the reader that something exceptional is going to happen.[72] Matthew did not just say that there is a great storm in the sea, but peculiarly talks about *σεισμὸς μέγας*. Matthew uses the

65 Donald A. Hagner, *Matthew 1-13*, WBC 33a (Dallas: Word Books, 1993), 220; see also John P. Meier, *Matthew* (Collegeville, MN: Liturgical Press, 1980).

66 Bornkamm, "Stilling of the Storm," 53.

67 Bornkamm, "Stilling of the Storm," 55.

68 Bornkamm, "Stilling of the Storm," 54-56.

69 Feiler, "The Stilling of the Storm in Matthew," 399.

70 Bornkamm, "Stilling of the Storm," 57.

71 Bornkamm, "Stilling of the Storm," 56; Martin Dibelius, *From Tradition to Gospel*, trans. Bertram Lee Woolf (New York: Charles Scribner's Sons, 1967), 57-58.

72 Hagner, *Matthew 1-13*, 221.

word σεισμός five times in his Gospel (24:7, 27:51 - σείω, 54, 28:2), but the other Synoptics use it only once in each Gospel (Mark 13:8, Luke 21:11).[73]

Using this data, Grant R. Osborne argues that it is true that this word σεισμὸς literally means earthquake but is commonly used of a violent storm on the sea with huge waves.[74] When Mark has the word "windstorm," what is the need for Matthew to change it into a more unfamiliar description of the storm? Donald A. Hagner is right in saying that the introduction of earthquakes here stands in some tension with Matthew's later references in his Gospel.[75] Matthew's alteration and omission of Mark's material cannot be easily sidelined as a simple editorial work, but could yield significant understanding of Matthew's working framework.

Donald Senior in his 1985 book *The Passion of Jesus in the Gospel of Matthew*, observes that in Matthew's Gospel earthquakes happen "when divine power makes itself felt."[76] While Matthew utilizes a word that share the identical root with the word used to describe the shaking of the earth, Mark uses an ordinary word for storm or squall.[77] Another great earthquake is mentioned in Matthew 28:2 when "the angel of the Lord" rolled back the stone at the entrance of Jesus' tomb. Therefore, Senior states that "Jesus then displays his own divine power over storm and sea and rescues the disciples from the threatening chaos"[78] in this miracle story.

John F. O'Grady also argues that the use of earthquake "implies an apocalyptic overtone to the whole episode."[79] Mark Goodacre further suggests that this utilization of earthquake may indicate that Matthew also has other things in mind, not only the drowning at the sea but also the various afflictions that the disciples will face in the future.[80] What is already stated has to be

73 This utilization of the word shows Matthew's interest in earthquakes. It is also a fact that earthquakes are the cause of enormous tidal waves, and there is evidence in Greek literature that earthquakes were at times associated with winds and heavy seas. Cf. Hagner, *Matthew 1-13*, 221; BAGD, 746. Adrian M. Leske states that "earthquake was seen as a symbol of God breaking into his ordered universe to bring judgment on evildoers and justice for the righteous." See Adrian M. Leske, *The Prophetic Vision and the Real Jesus: Growth of the Prophetic Vision and its Impact on the Mission of Jesus in Matthew's Gospel* (Eugene: Wipf & Stock, 2017), 177.

74 Grant R. Osborne, *Matthew*, ECNT (Grand Rapids: Zondervan, 2010), 313.

75 Hagner, *Matthew 1-13*, 221.

76 Donald Senior, *The Passion of Jesus in the Gospel of Matthew* (Collegeville, MN: Liturgical Press, 1985), 144.

77 Senior, *The Passion of Jesus*, 144.

78 Senior, *The Passion of Jesus*, 144; cf. Bornkamm, "Stilling of the Storm," 56.

79 John F. O'Grady, *The Gospel of Matthew: Question by Question*, QQBSC (New York: Paulist, 2007), 61.

80 Mark Goodacre, "Redaction Criticism," in *Searching for Meaning: An Introduction to Interpreting the New Testament*, ed. Paula Gooder (Louisville: SPCK, 2008), 38-42.

repeated here because this is the reason why Bornkamm argues that the story becomes a "kerygmatic paradigm of the danger and glory of discipleship"[81] in Matthew's Gospel.

Matthew's presentation of this miracle story encompasses the idea of Jesus' divinity and cosmic authority, and thus the Christology that can be chalked out in this story is cosmic Christology. A dimension of Jesus' majesty is revealed and the capability of Jesus in handling any crises, even from natural order is clearly propounded.[82] As the Lake of Galilee is situated six hundred feet below the sea level, in the steep-sided rift valley of the Jordan, it is subjected to sudden, violent squalls.[83] The argument is that a regular storm could not have frightened these seasoned fishermen.[84] However, Matthew reports that they were frightened, and is understandable due to the use of the term "earthquake." The intensity of the situation is accomplished by the term "earthquake" and the term also indicates a catastrophic proportion. Therefore, it can be said that a catastrophic storm which is described with the use of the term "earthquake" and not a regular term is employed by Matthew to emphasize Jesus' divinity and cosmic authority.

It can also be seen that it is not so clear how Jesus can stay asleep. The exhaustion due to rigorous ministry may be the reason for Jesus' sleeping even during the storm. The nature of the boat is also not clearly depicted. Jesus' sleeping under such circumstances could also encourage the question in which the passage ends "what kind of a person?" The similarity with the Old Testament character Jonah is also interesting, and the mentioning of Jonah in the context of Jesus as being the "one greater than Jonah" (12:41) makes the similarity of the two stories more convincing. O. Lamar Cope and W. D. Davies and Dale C. Allison see Jonah as the major background motif and believe that this sleeping episode is an allusion to Jonah.[85] However, Osborne argues that "the most that can be said is that Jesus' stilling the storm may echo God's stilling the storm in Jonah 1:15-16."[86] The situations are too different and the parallels are ambiguous, and Jonah was travelling in a much larger ship and probably is exhausted in his fleeing from the presence of the Lord.[87] The Old Testament's assertion that such sleep is an evidence of a trust in God's

81 Bornkamm, "Stilling of the Storm," 57.

82 Larry Chouinard, *Matthew*, TCPNC (Joplin, MO: College Press Publishing Co., 1997), 161.

83 Osborne, *Matthew*, 313; R. T. France, *The Gospel of Matthew*, NICNT (Grand Rapids: Eerdmans, 2007), 336.

84 Chouinard, *Matthew*, 161.

85 O. Lamar Cope, *Matthew: A Scribe Trained for the Kingdom of Heaven* (Washington: CBAA, 1976), 96-98; Davies and Allison, *A Critical and Exegetical Commentary*, 2:72.

86 Osborne, *Matthew*, 313.

87 Osborne, *Matthew*, 313; Hagner, *Matthew 1-13*, 221.

protection is a more suitable explanation in this situation (cf. Job 11:18-19; Ps 3: 5-6, 4:8; Prov 3:24-26).[88] Moreover, Jonah's prayer to God and the disciples' plea to Jesus in Matthew are quite similar.

Matthew's insertion of one of his favourite words προσελθόντες "coming to him," at the beginning of verse 25 is another interest.[89] Jack D. Kingsbury, in his 1969 book *The Parables of Jesus in Matthew 13: A Study in Redaction Criticism*, argues that the word προσέρχομαι (προσελθόντες – verb part.) "to approach, to draw near," in Matthew's Gospel carries cultic overtones of coming before the deity and thus ascribes to Jesus a "lordly dignity" that demands reverence.[90] "Thus, in forty-nine instances Matthew utilizes the verb προσέρχομαι ('to come to,' 'to approach'), which in the LXX is cultic in coloration and in Josephus is used of stepping before a king, in order to portray persons as approaching Jesus with the same reverence that would be due to a deity or king."[91] Crispin H. T. Fletcher-Louis also argues that historically there was a precedent for the worship of human beings within ancient Judaism, and he considers that the worship of Jesus is not unthinkable or insurmountable.[92] It seems that Matthew is influenced by his environment of a larger literary community in which such conceptions were current.

Similarly, James R. Edwards in his article "The use of Προσερχεσθαι in the Gospel of Matthew" studies the background of the word and argues that "this term, particularly in the Pentateuch, though to a lesser extent elsewhere in the LXX and Hellenistic literature, reveals that προσερχεσθαι (προσέρχομαι)

---

88 Osborne, *Matthew*, 313; Hagner, *Matthew 1-13*, 221.

89 James R. Edwards, "The use of Προσερχεσθαι in the Gospel of Matthew," *JBL* 106 (1987): 65-74 (67). Edwards provided a detail list of all the occurrences of the verb: Of the approximately 90 occurrences of προσέρχομαι and its variants in the New Testament, Matthew has 52 of them. Matthew's usage is all the more striking when compared with the individual New Testament authors: Mark (5 times), Luke (10 times), John (1 time), Acts (12 times), 1 Timothy (1 time), Hebrews (7 times), and 1 Peter (1 time). In nearly three-fourths of Matthew's uses of προσέρχομαι, Jesus is the object of the verb as the one who is being approached (4:3, 11, 5:1, 8:2, 5, 19, 25, 9:14, 18, 20, 28, 13:10, 36, 14:15, 15:1, 12, 23, 30, 16:1, 17:14, 19, 18:1, 21, 19:3, 16, 20:20, 21:14, 23, 22:23, 24:1, 3, 26:7, 17, 49, 50, 60 [2 times], and 28:9 – a total of 38 instances). Most frequently, the disciples approach Jesus in order to inquire of him (8:25; 13:10, 36; 14:15; 15:12, 23; 17:19; 18:1, 21; 24:1, 3; 26:17), but others too approach Jesus either to inquire of him (8:19, 9:14, 19:16, 20:20), or to ask for help (8:2, 8:5, 9:18, 9:20, 15:30, 17:14, 21:14).

90 Jack D. Kingsbury, *The Parables of Jesus in Matthew 13: A Study in Redaction Criticism* (Richmond: John Knox Press, 1969), 40-41.

91 Jack D. Kingsbury, *Jesus Christ in Matthew, Mark, and Luke* (Eugene: Fortress, 1981), 76.

92 Crispin H. T. Fletcher-Louis, "The Worship of Divine Humanity as God's Image and the Worship of Jesus," in *The Jewish Roots of Christological Monotheism: Papers from the St. Andrews Conference on the Historical Origin of the Worship of Jesus*, JSJSup 63 (Leiden: Brill, 1999), 112-128 (113).

carries unmistakable cultic connotation... now transferred to Jesus."[93] While analyzing the Sermon on the Mount, Hagner, in the same line with Edwards, also affirms that the word itself points to the messianic character of Jesus.[94]

Jae Hun Lee, in his application of Bornkamm's redactional method to Matthew 17:14-20 in "Günther Bornkamm and Redaction Criticism," also comes close to identify this term as having cultic connotation.[95] He observes that Matthew also changes "teacher" in Mark 9:17 into "Lord," and the disciples' questioning in Mark 9:28 into their προσελθόντες "coming to him" in Matthew 17:19.[96] He argues that Matthew, in the previous verse (Matt 17:14) used προσελθεν "come" and γονυπετῶν "kneeling down" to describe the father of the epileptic boy as worshiper.[97] This does not negate the significance of προσέρχομαι in Matthew's Gospel, rather helps to concretize what Kingsbury and Edwards had put forth. Lee comes short to improve Bornkamm's redactional observation on the passage and also on the significance of the use of προσελθόντες in Matthew 17:19, perhaps his scope of study restricted him.

For Mark's διδάσκαλε "teacher," Matthew substitutes κύριε "Lord" (Luke has the repeated ἐπιστάτα ἐπιστάτα "master, master," a Lukan favourite and used only in Luke). Therefore, the wording of the disciples' cry for help comes closer to a prayer than Mark's abrupt "Teacher, don't you care if we drown?"

---

93 Of its approximately 45 occurrences in the Pentateuch, προσερχεσθαι and is used variously, and some examples are: to describe the bringing of offerings to God (Lev 21:17, 18, 21; Num 17:5, Deut 21:5); or approaching God (Exod 16:9, 22:7, Lev 9:5, Deut 5:27), the tabernacle (Lev 10:4, 5, 22:3, Num 18:22), the altar (Lev 9:7, 8, 21:23, Num 18:3), the Passover (Exod 12:48 [2 times], 49, Num 9:14), Mt. Sinai (Deut 4:11), the elders of Israel (Deut 25:9), or Moses (Exod 34:32, Num 9:6, 10:4, 27:1, 31:48, 32:2, 16, 36:1, Deut 1:22, 5:23) and Aaron (Num 18:4), both of whom were seen as representatives of God (Exod 7:1, Num 12:7). Note that all references to LXX are to the 8th ed. of *Septuaginta, id est vetum testamentum graece iuxta*, ed. Alfred Rahlfs (Stuttgart: Württembergische Bibelanstalt, 1935). Edwards, "The use of Προσερχεσθαι in the Gospel of Matthew," 65-66.

94 Hagner, *Matthew 1-13*, 86.

95 Jae Hun Lee, "Günther Bornkamm and Redaction Criticism," in *Prevailing Methods before 1980*, ed. Stanley E. Porter and Sean A. Adams, vol. 1 of *Pillars in the History of Biblical Interpretation* (Eugene, OR: Pickwick, 2016), 321-340 (327).

96 Lee, "Günther Bornkamm and Redaction Criticism," 327. Matthew's healing story of the epileptic boy (Matt 17:14-16) and the following passages are another example of Matthew's alteration of his source (Mark's Gospel) in wording and phrasing.

97 Lee, "Günther Bornkamm and Redaction Criticism," 327. Edwards also has pointed out that Matthew's usage of auxiliary terms in conjunction with προσέρχομαι heighten the respect or reverence of those who approach Jesus. Some examples are: προσκυνεῖν (8:2; 9:18; 20:20; 28:9) and κύριε (8:2, 5, 25; 13:27; 17:14; 18:21; 25:20), but also παρακαλείν (8:5), διδάσκαλε (8:19; 19:16), γονυπετείν (17:14), ἐλεεῖν (17:14), αἰτεῖν (20:20), προσφέρειν (25:20), and ῥαββί (26:49). Edwards, "The use of Προσερχεσθαι in the Gospel of Matthew," 67.

(Mark 4:38 NIV).[98] Osborne also argues that the use of κύριε here points "to the authority of Jesus as Lord of all."[99] He also warns the reader not to read too much into the language and insists that the disciples did not mean this kind of understanding.[100]

Matthew's employment of the key word σῶσον "save" is seen by many interpreters as the message that dealt with spiritual "salvation" in light of spiritual "death," but Osborne argues that "Save us, we're about to die" reflects their fear in a near death experience and not a soteriological message.[101] Again the question "why would Matthew insert a new word here?" is answered by Keener's observation that the term is sometimes used to address the deities at sea (cf. Matt 14:30, Acts 27:20, 31, Diod. Sic. 4.43.1, Ach. Tat. 3.5).[102] The terms σῴζω and σωτηρία first refer to salvation (human or divine) from serious peril. These terms can mean "deliverance" or "preservation." It is used for a person's safe return to one's own home or one's own country after an absence or a journey. It can also mean a "guarantee of safety" or a "security against danger."[103]

"Save" and "perish" perhaps initially refer to the disciples' physical welfare, but according to Blomberg, in the time of the writing of Matthew's Gospel the terms become the standard terminology for spiritual salvation and destruction. Thus he opined that Matthew may have intended a "double entendre here."[104] Contemporary understanding of this term simplifies the narrative and focuses primarily on the lesson about Jesus' stilling the storm of our lives.[105]

As noted earlier, and as Blomberg also asserts, the main focus of this passage is christological. The question answered in this story has less to do with what Christ will do for us, but the major concern is the identity of Jesus Christ and the authority he possesses.[106] The reverential terminology and the liturgical form of request are pointers to the understanding of the divinity of Jesus and his cosmic relationship with natural orders.

---

98 France, *The Gospel of Matthew*, 336.

99 Osborne, *Matthew*, 313.

100 Osborne, *Matthew*, 313.

101 Osborne, *Matthew*, 313.

102 Keener, *The Gospel of Matthew*, 280.

103 W. Foerster, "σῴζω, σωτηρία," *TDNT* 7: 965-969.

104 Craig L. Blomberg, *Matthew*, NAC 22 (Nashville: Broadman, 1991-2014),149; cf. F. W. Beare, *The Gospel According to Matthew: Translation, Introduction and Commentary* (San Francisco: Harper & Row, 1982), 215, who notes that "Lord, save" may have been a liturgical form in Matthew's church like the later "Lord, have mercy."

105 Blomberg, *Matthew*, 150.

106 Blomberg, *Matthew*, 150; cf. Feiler, "The Stilling of the Storm in Matthew," 340-342.

In Matthew's Gospel, verse 26 a is transposed from its later position in Mark's narrative (4:40), and thus unlike Mark's Gospel Jesus' rebuke is placed before the miracle. Again, Matthew employs another favourite terminology ὀλιγόπιστοι "you of little faith" and helps to soften Mark's unsympathetic phrases of separate question "Do you not have faith?"[107] Even though Matthew's narrative reads more naturally, Blomberg is not convinced by the suggestion that Matthew is trying to present the disciples in a more positive way.[108]

This suggestion is often held by scholars since the seminal study of Bornkamm's "The Stilling of the Storm." "Little faith" may have no significant improvement over Mark's "no faith."[109] Davies and Allison argue that "In Matthew's mind, the story of the stilling of the tempest is instruction for the faithful. It is a call not to come to faith but rather to exercise the faith one already has."[110] Perhaps the change occurs due to the difference in perspective and the theology of the writer of the Gospels.

Unlike Mark, Matthew (so also Luke) omits the words spoken by Jesus to the elements, σιώπα, πεφίμωσο "peace, be still" (Mark 4:39). In Matthew's story, Jesus speaks to the winds and sea as though they were conscious beings. Instead of Mark's "peace, be still" Matthew's Jesus rebukes nature elements (ἐπιτιμάω).[111] How Matthew may have pictured the natural elements as being subject to supernatural or demonic powers is not clear, but the hint is quite vivid that the evangelist did not see them as lifeless elements.[112]

As already noted in the previous chapter Matthew's cosmological worldview, like the Old Testament and the Second Temple Judaism, is capable to accommodate this kind of anthropomorphizing of the natural elements. Enochic tradition clearly depicted that the celestial bodies and natural elements and phenomena were commonly anthropomorphized by ancient Jews and also

---

107 Hagner, *Matthew1-13*, 221.

108 Blomberg, *Matthew*, 149.

109 Blomberg, *Matthew*, 149; for arguments on the improvement of the picture of the disciples in Matthew, see Ulrich Luz, *Studies in Matthew*, trans. Rosemary Selle (Grand Rapids, MI: Eerdmans, 2005), 121-122; cf. Meier, *Matthew*, 89-90; Richard A. Burridge, *Imitating Jesus: An Inclusive Approach to New Testament Ethics* (Grand Rapids, MI: Eerdmans, 2007), 219-220.

110 Davies and Allison, *A Critical and Exegetical Commentary*, 2:74.

111 With the exception of the simple command "go" in 8:32, Matthew never records Jesus' direct commands to demons. According to Davies and Allison, the likely reason is that Matthew desires "to separate Jesus from any taint of magical method, or from a desire to prevent Christian exorcists from using Jesus' words as though they were magical formulae." Davies and Allison, *A Critical and Exegetical Commentary*, 2:74.

112 Davies and Allison, *A Critical and Exegetical Commentary*, 2:74.

thought of as ruled by heavenly or supernatural creatures (1 En. 72-82).[113] Especially in 3 Enoch 14, the names of the princes in charge of the different natural elements and other facets of nature are listed.[114]

France rightly argues that Matthew's use of the word "rebuke" here is not to be taken as a suggestion to regard the storm as a demonic force.[115] Rather, Jesus' confident rebuke to the storm expects the recognition of his authority, and according to France, "the immediate calm which resulted, show that he wields the Creator's power."[116] Davies and Allison also argues that there is no period in Matthew's narrative that the storm get progressively ceases, but the great calm is established instantaneously.[117]

Hagner also comments that this phrase "refers to more than simply the cessation of the storm."[118] Instead, he argues "there was a mysterious, supernatural calm that testified to the sovereign power of Jesus," and there is a strong contrast with the σεισμὸς μέγας "great earthquake" (8:24).[119] Alfred Plummer rightly stated that, "a sudden drop in the wind is possible, but that would not at once calm the sea," and naturally, the immediate calm is unanticipated.[120] Thus, it can be claimed that the sea may not calm at once,

---

113 Davies and Allison, *A Critical and Exegetical Commentary*, 2:74; cf. Ps 77:18, 104:7; 1 En. 60:11-25, 2 En. 19, Rev 14:18 (where there are the mentioning of "the angels who are over rivers and sea").

114 Davies and Allison, *A Critical and Exegetical Commentary*, 2:74; for the wind spirit see Jub. 2:2, and for the sea spirit see 1 En. 60:16 and 69:22 (cf. 2 Bar. 10:8; PGM 3:226-228).

115 Keener argues that "Jesus rebukes the sea (8:26) just as he would any spirit (17:18)." He also notes that though the suggestion to regard the storm as demonic force need not imply that Jesus addressed the angel over the sea as is seen in Jub. 2:2, 1QM 10:11-12, 1 En. 66:2, 2 En. 19:3-4, b. Pesah 118b, it is interesting to see that later in the tradition God slew that angel during exodus (b. B. Bat. 74b, Num. Rab. 18:22). He also observes that the term for "rebuke" here expresses authority in a different manner in 12:16, and negatively in 16:22, and 20:31. Hagner also suggests that the idea of rebuking may presuppose evil spirits as expressing themselves in the storm. However, France, observes that the verb ἐπιτιμάω occurs frequently in Matthew's Gospel with no demonic connotations, and there is nothing else except in 17:18 (where the verb occurs in an exorcism account) that supports such a suggestion. For France, "the choice of the verb here may be ascribed not only to dramatic anthropomorphism, but more significantly to the OT usage." Keener, *The Gospel of Matthew*, 280; Hagner, *Matthew 1-13*, 222; France, *The Gospel of Matthew*, 337; cf. The idea of "rebuke" having a connection with exorcism, see also Blomberg, *Matthew*, 149-150.

116 France, *The Gospel of Matthew*, 337; Debra Scoggins Ballentine, *The Conflict Myth and the Biblical Tradition* (New York: OUP, 2015), 175-176.

117 Davies and Allison, *A Critical and Exegetical Commentary*, 2:74.

118 Hagner, *Matthew 1-13*, 222.

119 Hagner, *Matthew 1-13*, 222.

120 Alfred Plummer, *An Exegetical Commentary on the Gospel According to St. Matthew* (New York; Stock, 1909), 131.

but the disciples' question after the calm (ὅτι καὶ οἱ ἄνεμοι καὶ ἡ θάλασσα αὐτῷ ὑπακούουσιν; "that even winds and sea obey him?") discourages this interpretation of the text. The only possible explanation is to interpret the phrase in the light of Matthew's christological framework, that Jesus' power works it complete effect immediately, as also found in Matthew's healing stories.

To continue further with the healing stories, Matthew's christological framework could also be chalk out from his omission of Mark's healing story of two-stage cure of the blind man at Bethsaida. It is being explained as the fear of the Gospel writers to misrepresent Jesus' power, because Jesus performs more difficult miracles.[121] It is a curious observation that Matthew and also Luke omit the only story in which Jesus makes more than a single attempt to heal a person.[122] Steven A. Galipeau argues that the story is omitted probably because the use of spittle (another example is Mark 7:31-37 where Jesus use spittle to help loosen the man's tongue) can depict Jesus as using shamanistic technique.[123]

Coming back to the present schema, this immediate calming of the storm is significant because the way their prayer is answered surpassed what they expected and contrary to all their experience of the lake.[124] Though the disciples had witnessed healings of different sorts, "this was a miracle on their own element, and their amazement and fear (Mk.) were in proportion."[125] Therefore, what can be deduced from the instant calm, the omission of a two-staged healing and healings that involve shamanistic procedure is that they do not fit Matthew's christological framework.

Again, Matthew abbreviated and altered Mark's ἐφοβήθησαν φόβον μέγαν (Mar 4:41) "they were afraid with a great fear," and simply has ἐθαύμασαν "they marveled" (v 27). As miracles over nature are not as common as other miracle stories in Jewish and Christian history, it is appropriate for "the disciples to wonder aloud about the identity of the man," and Matthew brings

121 James R. Edwards, *The Gospel According to Mark*, PNTC (Grand Rapids, MI: Eerdmans, 2002), 244; Ian Boxall, *Discovering Matthew: Content, Interpretation, Reception* (Grand Rapids, MI: Eerdmans, 2014), 35.

122 Steven A. Galipeau, *Transforming Body and Soul: Therapeutic Wisdom in the Gospel Healing Stories*, rev. ed. (Carmel, CA: Fisher King Press, 2011), 16.

123 Galipeau, *Transforming Body and Soul*, 16. The writing of Suetonius in the early second century about the healing of a blind man by the Emperor Vespasian spittle may well be considered here, as Vespasian ruled during the period 69-79 CE. Vespasian's healing and John 9:6-7 are remarkably paralleled. Daniel Lynwood Smith, *Into the World of the New Testament: Greco-Roman and Jewish Texts and Contexts* (London: Bloomsbury, 2015), 98.

124 Plummer, *An Exegetical Commentary on the Gospel According to St. Matthew*, 131.

125 Plummer, *An Exegetical Commentary on the Gospel According to St. Matthew*, 131.

"the narrative to its Christological climax."[126] Matthew makes it more vivid when he uses the word "marveled" because it enhances his narrative and a key word to tackle the identity of Jesus.

Matthew is unique to have οἱ ἄνθρωποι "the men" as the subject of the verb "marveled." It is unusual and there are scholars like Ulrich Luz who suggest that these "men" are not in the story at all, and the intended subject is the member of Matthean church.[127] Hagner differs to Luz and argues that, as Matthew omitted Mark's reference to "other boats" (Mark 4:36), there are no other alternatives to apply the object to, and even more unlikely that the men are those who heard the story.[128] France also differs to Luz, and argues that Luz's suggestion calls for an "unparalleled literary technique" in Matthew's Gospel.[129] He further argues that "the disciples are the natural referent in the story, and the context suggests a good theological reason for characterizing them precisely as ἄνθρωποι."[130]

Hagner's and France's arguments carry significance for this study. Especially, France's suggestion is noteworthy, that the designation ἄνθρωποι "human beings" set apart the disciples and Jesus, who is depicted in this passage as more than a human being.[131] Yet again Matthew abbreviates Mark's "to one another" and simply has λέγοντες "saying" and uses the word ποταπός "what kind of a person" against Mark's and Luke's τίς ἄρα οὗτός "who then is this." This further heightens the significant nature of the person of Jesus from other human beings in this context.

This rhetorical question: ποταπός ἐστιν οὗτος ὅτι καὶ οἱ ἄνεμοι καὶ ἡ θάλασσα αὐτῷ ὑπακούουσιν thus calls for an understanding that has to be enveloped under the Old Testament passages already mentioned above; the passages that make the control of winds and water the special and sole prerogative of Yahweh.[132] Matthew's presentation of Jesus by his reworking of Mark's material sheds much light on his christological interest and also his cosmological worldview.

---

126 Blomberg, *Matthew*, 150. For God's rebuke of the sea cf. Pss 18:15, 104:7, 106:9, Isa 50:2; Nah 1:4.

127 According to Luz, "the evangelist steps out of the story as it were and lets the people to whom his church proclaims the gospel speak as if they were reacting to Jesus' miracles." Ulrich Luz, Matthew 8-20: A Commentary, trans. James E. Crouch, *Hermeneia* (Minneapolis: Fortress, 2001-2007), 21.

128 Hagner, *Matthew 1-13*, 222.

129 France, *The Gospel of Matthew*, 337.

130 France, *The Gospel of Matthew*, 337.

131 France, *The Gospel of Matthew*, 337.

132 France, *The Gospel of Matthew*, 337; cf. Ballentine, *The Conflict Myth and the Biblical Tradition*, 175-177.

### *6.3.3. Cosmic Christology in the Passage*

As highlighted in the analysis of the passage, Matthew has eliminated details that are inessential in his christological framework. Mark and Matthew focus on Jesus' unique identity, and Matthew in a heightened way retouch the story, and thus the disciples in Matthew's Gospel address Jesus as Lord. Matthew's redaction of Mark's story consists of the following:

> (1) moving the pericope out of its position in Mark (where it follows the parables pericopes) to a much earlier place; (2) deleting "On that day, when evening had come"; (3) changing the direct speech of Jesus' instruction to go across to the other side into indirect speech; (4) moving Mark's reference to Jesus' "leaving the crowds" to the beginning of the story, so that the crowds become the reason for Jesus embarking the boat: "Now when Jesus saw great crowds around him"; (5) changing the emphasis on the disciples' concern for Jesus ("they took him with them in the boat, just as he was") into rather different "And when he got into the boat, his disciples followed him"; and (6) deleting the reference (Mark 4:36b) to other boats being with him. This is *very* extensive redaction by Matthew; there is no part of Mark 4:35-36 that is not affected by it.[133]

Without striding away from Mark's christological focus, Matthew reworks the miracle story. Matthew's other agenda is set out first in the narrative block of Matthew 8-9, that is the theme of discipleship. Luke places the cost of discipleship elsewhere in his Gospel and is not associated with the stilling of the storm (Luke 9:57-62). In contrast to Luke, Matthew situates the miracle story right after setting it clear the cost of discipleship in 8:19-22.

Consequently, Matthew skillfully utilizes the word "follow" as a link word.[134] When Mark has παραλαμβάνουσιν αὐτὸν "they took him" (Mark 4:36), Matthew has the disciples ἠκολούθησαν αὐτῷ "followed him" onto the boat (Matt 8:23). Matthew uses these links to set the miracle story in an environment that calls for total discipleship.[135] Therefore, redaction-critical approach makes it clear that Matthew has adapted Mark's story, but brings out vibrantly the theme of Jesus' authority over the cosmos, and also introduces the theme of discipleship.[136]

---

133 B. Ward Powers, *The Progressive Publication of Matthew: An Explanation of the Writing of the Synoptic Gospels* (Nashville: B&H Publishing Group, 2010), 533-534.

134 David Wenham and Steve Walton, *Exploring the New Testament: A Guide to the Gospels and Acts*, vol. 1 of *Exploring the New Testament*, 2nd ed. (Downers Grove, IL: IVP, 2011), 81.

135 Wenham and Walton, *Exploring the New Testament*, 81.

136 Wenham and Walton, *Exploring the New Testament*, 81.

It is evident that Matthew refocuses the story in its original context, and adds editorial works so as to amplify the unique authority of Jesus' works. First by using the word "behold," Matthew calls attention to the reader to expect something that is extraordinary to happen. After which, Matthew carefully chose the word "earthquake" to describe the storm, perhaps to intensify the perilous situation. This word has eschatological overtones of God's action, particularly in earth-shaking situations.[137] Jesus performing God's action is a pointer to the divinity of Jesus and the concept of cosmic Christology. Jesus who is capable of controlling even the natural phenomena, and the one who acts as Yahweh did in the Old Testament, is clearly revealed in this miracle story.

As already hinted, Yahweh's victory over the cosmic sea is the coming ἔσχατον in the Old Testament, and the victory over the nations in the last days is compared with the victory over the sea (Ps 46, Isa 17:12-14).[138] The last conflict between Yahweh and the adversary in the future is also communicated in a similar language (Isa 50:2-3; cf. Rev 13:1, 21:1).

The cosmological understanding of the Old Testament and the Second Temple Judaism as a backdrop for this miracle help to define more clearly the description of the sea, the fear and the awestruck of the disciples, and the action of Jesus. Therefore, according to Davies and Allison, the implicit Christology is that "The cosmic forces of evil that threaten the order of creation are brought under the control of one who has authority over them, and who, in the latter days, exercises the sovereign power of God... In his sovereign word the elements have found their master."[139] This Christology cannot be defined better by any other words, except the phrase cosmic Christology.

### *6.3.4. The Rhetorical Purpose of the Passage*

The miracle stories in Matthew 8-9 are usually grouped into three because there are nine separate miracle stories that comprise ten individual miracles. There are two miracles of healing that are intertwined in one unit (9:18-26). These three groups of stories contain three miracles each (8:1-17, 8:23-9:8, 9:18-34) and are arranged in such a way by utilizing narrative interludes between them (8:18-22, 9:9-17). Each group focuses on the call of discipleship, and the response to that challenge by a variety of individuals. This focus is sharply situated against the backdrop of the unique authority of the one who called them for discipleship, and the addition of the stilling of the storm in these

137 Wenham and Walton, *Exploring the New Testament*, 81.

138 Davies and Allison, *Matthew 8-18*, 75.

139 Davies and Allison, *Matthew 8-18*, 75.

narratives is a pointer.[140] It is difficult to understand which theme is more important for Matthew, and does not necessarily need dissecting.[141]

All that can be said with certainty is that Matthew adapts Mark's miracle story, and without losing the focus, blends it brilliantly with his other theme. However, depending on the lenses and methodologies applied, the result may vary. There is no doubt that in this study, the christological significance is kept at the forefront and the theme of discipleship at the periphery. Subsequently, it is important to look at the rhetorical purpose and result of it within the christological framework of Matthew.

In this narrative block Matthew does not offer peculiar materials except the formulá-quotation that concludes the first set of stories.[142] Matthew's skill in bringing together of two narrative sequences (rhetorolects) that occur separately in Mark's Gospel is crucial for his purpose. Matthew has not only interwoven these narratives but also altered the sequence by moving the story of the leper (Mark 1:40-45) to the beginning of his first group. The work of abbreviating stories is evident in this miracle story. Matthew has only seven verses (8:28-34), while Mark has twenty verses (5:1-20). The nine verses in Matthew 9:18-26 is also much shorter than the twenty-three verses in Mark 5:21-43. Therefore, in Matthew's Gospel these stories are not recorded for their own sake, but "serve a more disciplined function within an overall framework setting out Jesus' acts of power."[143]

The unique authority that is expressed in 7:28-29, and 9:8 is the same authority that is expressed in the healing of centurion's servant in 8:9. Matthew develops Jesus' authority further in the realm of cosmological elements by using the miracle of the stilling of the storm. This is a theological thrust that point toward Jesus as the Son of God who is above creation. As the use of the phrase "Save, Lord" takes the form of a prayer, perhaps the situation may be associated with the Christian worship. The word "rebuked" may also be explained with cosmological significance, as a graphical indication of "the personal authority of Jesus, as master of the created order."[144]

---

140 For the grouping of miracles, see France, *The Gospel of Matthew*, 300-302.

141 J. Andrew Overman, *Church and Community in Crisis: The Gospel According to Matthew*, NTC (Pennsylvania: Trinity Press International, 1996), 125, argues that the story is about "following" and is made explicit by Matthew in verse 23. He also sees the cry of the disciples as a unison prayer or exclamation "Lord save!" (Matt 8:25). It is important to see that even though Matthew may have given importance to the theme of discipleship, but this does not restrict him to blend his christological concern. In other words, the miracle story does not necessarily need to carry one theme alone.

142 France, *The Gospel of Matthew*, 300.

143 France, *The Gospel of Matthew*, 301.

144 France, *The Gospel According to Matthew*, 162.

The redactional work of Matthew in these narratives is evident in the omission "of the less essential (though interesting) narrative details provided by Mark."[145] This peculiar structure in Matthew 8-9, and especially in the stilling of the storm, thus heightens the emphasis on the uniqueness and the authority of Jesus. The main rhetorical significance of the stilling of the storm in this context (Matt 8-9) is the phrase "even winds and sea obey him" (Matt 8:27).

The theme of discipleship and the trial of the disciples' faith could be understood as sub-plot, as is also seen in Matthew's blending of similar themes in the previous miracle story (the healing of the centurion's servant in 8:5-13). As France also argues, it is important to be sure that Matthew's primary concern, as also for Mark and Luke is a record of Jesus' supernatural power.[146] Therefore, the passage carries both the thematic (discipleship) and theological (cosmic Christology) significances.

As the expression "This was done in order that what was written in the prophets might be fulfilled," is unique to Matthew, and this miracle story could perhaps be included under this expression. In this methodology, Matthew consistently interprets Jesus on the basis of the Old Testament messianic expectations.[147] Thus, this story portrays the identity of Jesus. Especially, an ironic ending of the story "even the wind and the sea obey him" shows how difficult it is to comprehend who Jesus is. Paul Frederick Feiler also concludes that "Having suffered the rejection of mainstream Judaism, Matthew's church needed to hear this message. The true Israel is composed of all those who understand Jesus as Messiah and live, having been delivered."[148]

The argument is that cosmic Christology is not incompatible with Matthew's Gospel. The miracle stories of Matthew 8-9 and particularly the nature miracle of the stilling of the storm provide essential evidence for cosmic Christology. Even the earliest Christians sensed the significance of Jesus' life that surpassed his earthly ministry (cf. John 1:1-18, 1 John 1:1-3, Col 1:15-20, and Eph 1:3-14).[149] This nature miracle is a pointer to the progression of faith in the early Christian community. The concept of faith apparently relocates its connotation from the following of the teachings of the historical Jesus to a state of confidence that God revealed in and through Jesus. The cosmic significance of this passage cannot be ruled out easily, and what is embedded in this miracle

145 France, *The Gospel According to Matthew*, 151.

146 France, *The Gospel According to Matthew*, 161.

147 Matt 3:3; 4:14; 8:17; 11:10; 12:17, 40; 13:14, 35; 15:7; 21:4.

148 Feiler, "The Stilling of the Storm in Matthew, 406.

149 Peter Callaghan, "Cosmic Christology and the Reclamation of Christ's Relevance in the 21st Century," *Graduate Annual* 3 (2015): 1-10 (3), http://digitalcommons.lasalle.edu/graduateannual/vol-3/iss1/5.

story points to a Christology that is molded within the cosmic christological conceptual framework of Matthew's Gospel. The stilling of the storm is not a developed statement of cosmic Christology, but an exhibition of the cosmic significance of Christ and the true identity of the human Jesus, who performed miracle attributed to Yahweh's prerogative.

## 6.4. The Feeding of the Multitudes (14:13-21)

### *6.4.1. Narrative Framework*

Matthew's narrative after recounting the beheading of John the Baptist now turns to Jesus' compassion to the sick and healing, but the main subject for Matthew is another nature miracle, the feeding of the five thousand.[150] This is the only miracle story of Jesus that appears in all the Gospels, which can be understood as an indication of the significance attached to this story by the early Christians who live in different localities.[151] The existence of the parallel formations shows that this story cannot be viewed in isolation but receives its interpretation in part from its context.[152] Again, Matthew seems to depend on the material provided by Mark (Mark 6:32-44; cf. Luke 9:10b-17, John 6:1-15), and this redactional work will be discussed later. Another feeding miracle is also found in Mark (8:1-10) and Matthew (15:32-39), and is accepted generally as a doublet narrative because there is generally a consensus that both the miracle stories shared a founding narrative.[153]

---

150 This study will use the number five thousand as the size of the crowd with the understanding that the women and children that were present, and the actual number would certainly much bigger than recorded. Actually it is interesting to note that sociologists say that when you gather a crowd of men, women, and children, the ratio of women and children to men can be as high as five or six or more. With this calculation the story is perhaps a feeding of the thirty-five thousand. For the case for women and children in the story read Megan McKenna, *Not Counting Women and Children: Neglected Stories from the Bible* (New York: Maryknoll, 1994).

151 Joseph Rhymer, *The Miracles of Jesus* (Middlegreen, UK: St. Paul Publications, 1991), 36-37.

152 E. Bummel, "The Feeding of the Multitude," in *Jesus and the Politics of His Day*, ed. E. Bummel and C. F. D. Moule (Cambridge: CUP, 1984), 211-240 (212).

153 The feeding of the four thousand (Matt 15:32-39) differs from the feeding of the five thousand notably only in that Jesus is the one who initiates the feeding and not the disciples as in this present miracle story. Other differences are found in the use of numbers: the crowds have been with Jesus for three days, seven loaves are multiplied, seven baskets of leftovers collected, and four thousand are fed. Harold Riley however rejects this understanding as doublet, and his argument is based on Matthew's priority over Mark. Harold Riley, *The First Gospel* (Georgia: Mercer University Press, 1992), 28-29; cf. Latourelle, *The Miracles of Jesus and the Theology of Miracles*, 72-73; Roger David Aus, *Feeding the Five Thousand: Studies in the Judaic Background of Mark 6:30-44 par. and John 6:1-15*, SJ (Maryland: University Press of America, 2010), 74-75.

The episode commences with Jesus withdrawing from the crowd by a boat to a deserted place of privacy. Jesus was followed by the crowds on land, and he reached the place before them. Later Jesus is ἐξελθὼν "going out" (14:14) to the crowds.[154] Matthew vividly tells that Jesus felt compassion for a large crowd and healed the sick. In the evening, the disciples came to Jesus and asked him to send the crowd away to go into villages so they would not have to feed them. Jesus, however, disagreed with the disciples and told them to give the crowd something to eat. The disciples ironically informed Jesus about their inventory, which was "only five loaves and two fish." Jesus directed them to bring the available food and also ordered the crowd to sit down on the grass. Taking the food, Jesus looked up to heaven and blessed and broke the loaves and gave it to the disciples for distribution. At the end of the episode, not only were the crowd satisfied with the amount of food they received, but there were twelve baskets leftovers.

The similarities between the four Gospels' accounts are remarkable.[155] The amount of the available food supply (five loaves of bread and two fish) to feed the crowd of five thousand is similar in every Gospels. All the Gospels have the disciples initially asking whether there will be enough food for the crowd. The gathering of twelve baskets of leftovers after everyone had been satisfied is also included in each of the Gospel's account.

Blomberg argues against the understanding of the miracle as simply an illustration of Jesus' compassion for human need, due to the lack of urgency in Matthew's setting, and states that the disciples' suggestion to send them for food "offered a realistic alternative."[156] As Jewish tradition holds that the miracle of abundant provision of food during the exodus event (manna in the wilderness) will be repeated by the Messiah even in a grander scale.[157] As John in his Gospel develops spiritual import of the story by placing Jesus' discourse on "the bread of life" (John 6:26-59), the application in Matthew must also point to spiritual sustenance, and the focus must be on Christology.[158] Hagner also argues that this feeding story has unmistakable messianic implications.[159]

154 Cf. Robert H. Gundry, *Matthew: A Commentary on his Handbook for a Mixed Church under Persecution*, 2nd ed. (Grand Rapids, MI: Eerdmans, 1994), 290-291.

155 For a discussion of the similarities between the synoptic gospel accounts of the feeding, see Ivor Buse, "The Gospel Accounts of the Feeding of the Multitudes," *ExpTim* 74 (1963): 167-170.

156 Blomberg, *Matthew*, 233.

157 Blomberg, *Matthew*, 233; cf. Peder Borgen, *Bread from Heaven: An Exegetical Study of the Concept of Manna in the Gospel of John and the Writings of Philo* (Leiden: Brill, 1965).

158 Blomberg, *Matthew*, 233.

159 Donald A. Hagner, *Matthew 14-28*, WBC 33b (Dallas: Word Books, 1995), 415.

### 6.4.2. Analysis of the Passage

*[13]When Jesus heard this, he withdrew from there in a boat to a deserted place*
*by himself. But when the crowds heard it, they followed him on land from the*
*towns. [14]As he came out (of a boat) he saw a great crowd, and he had compassion*
*on them and healed their sick. [15]When evening came, the disciples came to him*
*and said, "This is a deserted place, and the hour is now late. Send the crowds*
*away, so that they go to the villages and buy food for themselves." [16]He (Jesus)*
*said to them, "They do not need to go away, you give them something to eat."*
*[17]They said to him, "We have nothing here except five loaves of bread and two*
*fish." [18]And he said "Bring them here to me." [19]Then he ordered the crowds*
*to sit down (recline) on the grass, and taking the five loaves and the two fish,*
*looking up to heaven, blessed[160] and broke the loaves, and gave them to the*
*disciples, and the disciples gave them to the crowds. [20]They all ate and were*
*satisfied, and they picked up twelve full baskets[161] of what was left over of the*
*broken pieces. [21]And there were about five thousand men, apart from women*
*and children. [22]And immediately he made the disciples to get into the boat and*
*go before him to the other side, while he sent the crowds away.*

While in the Mark and Luke, Jesus withdraws with his disciples in order to rest after the mission in Galilee, Matthew's narration says that Jesus withdraws for safety from Herod Antipas, and probably alone. Before this time, John's imprisonment also led Jesus to leave Jordan Valley (Matt 4:12). Therefore, the phrase "When Jesus heard" may chronologically follow 14:13-14, and vv. 3-12 could be read as a flashback about the fate of John the Baptist.[162] Though the sequence is awkward and rightly pointed out by Terence L. Donaldson in his article "'For Herod had arrested John' (Matt. 14:3): Making sense of an unresolved flashback," but since Matthew had already used the sending forth of the disciples in chapter 10, it is not suitable for him to use the disciples'

---

160 There are few textual variants in the two feeding miracles of Matthew's Gospel. The feeding of five thousand had Jesus blessed (εὐλογέω) the food, but in the feeding of four thousand Jesus gave thanks (εὐχαριστέω). Εὐχαριστέω, as the table benediction which is a Semetism is interchangeable with εὐλογέω. H. Patsch, "εὐλογέω," *EDNT* 2:79-80; see also "εὐχαριστέω," *EDNT* 2:87-88.

161 The term for baskets here is κόφινος, but Matthew uses σπυρίς in the feeding of four thousand. The latter term is also used in Mark 8:8, 20 par. Matt 15:37 and 16:10. In Acts 9:25, Paul was let down over the wall out of the city of Damascus in σπυρίς. See H. W. Kuhn, "σπυρίς," *EDNT* 3:267. Another difference is the number of baskets of the leftover, 12 in the first miracle and 7 in the second miracle.

162 Blomberg, *Matthew*, 231; Daniel J. Harrington, *The Gospel of Matthew*, vol. 1, SPS (Collegeville, MN: The Liturgical Press, 1991), 219; cf. O. Lamar Cope, "The Death of John the Baptist in the Gospel of Matthew," *CBQ* 38 (1976): 515-519; Camille Focant, *The Gospel According to Mark: A Commentary*, trans. Leslie Robert Keylock (Eugene, OR: Pickwick, 2004), 254.

return at this juncture.[163] Jesus being geographically distancing himself from hostility is a recurrent pattern in Matthew's Gospel. Chapters 14-16 are dominated by Jesus going in and out of the province of Galilee, especially by means of several lake crossings.[164]

Scholars observed the motif of withdrawal as a feature of Matthew's Gospel. Each time the verb "withdrawal" appears in chapter 2, it was a response to a dangerous situation. The Magi who withdrew to their country in 2:12 were warned not to return to Herod. Joseph withdrew to Egypt after being warned about Herod's intentions (2:14). When Joseph was returning to Israel, again he was warned that Archelaus, Herod's son, was in power, and thus withdrew to Galilee (2:22). The motif continues when Jesus withdrew to Galilee after hearing that John the Baptist had been arrested (4:12). When Jesus heard that the Pharisees conspire to destroy him over a Sabbath controversy, again he withdrew (12:14). Here also in this miracle story the same motif occurs over again in the report of the murdering of John the Baptist. Jesus again withdraws, to a deserted place by a boat.

Deirdre Good argues that "This motif however is part of a three-fold pattern of hostility/withdrawal/prophetic fulfilment Matthew seems to have created."[165] Her analysis shows that this pattern runs throughout the Gospel, and is used by Matthew to move his narrative along. Matthew specifically mentions Joseph and Jesus as moving from one region to another. She also draws attention to passages that contain the elements of hostility followed by withdrawal from LXX and 1 and 2 Maccabees. The LXX translation of Exodus 2:15 where Moses "withdrew (ἀνεχώρησεν) from Pharoah and dwelt in the land of Midian" is significant, especially when it is read with the idea of Matthew's interest in Moses typology.[166]

Another significant suggestion made by Good is that "the theme of the withdrawal of Wisdom in apocalyptic sources is the more immediate background for the hostility/withdrawal/fulfillment of prophecy pattern in Matthew, especially when the subject of pattern is Jesus."[167] The seven instances

---

163 Terence L. Donaldson argues that the flashback remains puzzlingly incomplete and the grammatical structure (a participle form of "to hear") without a direct object is used regularly in Matthew's Gospel. He argued that the report brought to him by the disciples of John (v. 12) was clearly what Jesus "heard." However, this may not make much difference to the present study. Terence L. Donaldson, "'For Herod had arrested John' (Matt. 14:3): Making sense of an unresolved flashback," *SR* 28 (1999): 35-48; Harrington, *The Gospel of Matthew*, 219; cf. Davies and Allison, *A Critical and Exegetical Commentary*, 2:463; Hagner, *Matthew 14-28*, 417.

164 Blomberg, *Matthew*, 231.

165 Deirdre Good, "The Verb ΑΝΑΧΩΡΕΩ in Matthew's Gospel," *NovT* 32 (1990): 1-12 (1).

166 Good, "The Verb ΑΝΑΧΩΡΕΩ in Matthew's Gospel," 6.

167 Good, "The Verb ΑΝΑΧΩΡΕΩ in Matthew's Gospel," 10.

of the three-fold pattern are found in Matthew's unique material, with a single exception (Matt 2:12-15; 2:22-23; 4:12-18; 12:15-21; 14:12-14; 15:21-28; 27:5-10). After careful analysis of these passages, Good concludes that "it is not *retreat from* hostility but rather *withdrawal for* the fulfilment of prophecy that demonstrates Matthew's intention in his creation of this pattern."[168]

Matthew's playing down of the role of Herodias and lessening of the Old Testament reminiscence of Jezebel and Esther is noteworthy (cf. 1 Kgs 21, Esth). Herod Antipas was a more prominent figure in Matthew's Gospel from the infancy narrative. Harrington asks, was Matthew familiar with Josephus' *Antiquities* and connects the tradition with Mark's story? As Josephus presented John as another threat to the political stability in Palestine, and was executed by Herod, but he himself is in favor of John (*Ant.* 18:116-119), and thus differs to Mark's presentation of the murdering of John the Baptist (Mark 6:21-28).[169] Thus, Matthew abbreviates Mark and heightens the role of Herod Antipas in the murdering of John the Baptist. The rejection of John and Jesus by Herod was significant in Matthew's Gospel.

Jesus escapes whatever danger he perceives from Herod, but significantly he does not elude the crowds. According to Neil Alexander, Matthew's intention is to tell the reader that Jesus withdraws to the other side of the lake, where Herod Antipas has no authority.[170] However, this kind of speculation may not be useful to understand the text because there is no indication that Jesus is attempting to flee from Herod.[171] Jesus' withdrawing here could well be understood in terms of his grief over the gruesome execution of John the Baptist, probably his cousin brother. Thus, Hagner argues, it is most likely that Jesus withdraws to a solitary place "in order to pray, the death of John perhaps turning his mind to his own approaching passion (cf. v 23)."[172] Matthew, unlike other Gospel writers, hints that Jesus went alone to a deserted place. The phrase ἔρημον τόπον κατ' ἰδίαν "a deserted place by himself" imply that he went without his disciples, and the reappearances of the disciples only in

168 Good, "The Verb ΑΝΑΧΩΡΕΩ in Matthew's Gospel," 12; see also Michael J. Wilkins, *Matthew: The NIV Application Commentary* (Grand Rapids, MI: Zondervan, 2004), 172-173.

169 Harrington, *The Gospel of Matthew*, 217.

170 Neil Alexander, *The New Interpreter's Bible* (Nashville: Abingdon Press, 1995), 323. The traditional site of the feeding, identified by Helena, Constantine's mother, in the fourth century, is Heptagepon, or Tabgha, the seven springs located south of Capernaum, where pilgrims stopped to eat and rest. A beautiful mosaic of the loaves and fish (mid-fifth-century) still identifies the spot.

171 Cf. Hagner, *Matthew 14-28*, 417.

172 Hagner, *Matthew 14-28*, 417.

latter part of the narrative (v. 15) also serve as a pointer that Jesus was alone.[173] Robert H. Gundry also argues that ἐξέρχομαι "coming out" refers to Jesus coming out from his deserted place of privacy.[174]

According to Blomberg, the crowds are presumably Jews from Galilee who have followed him on shore around the lake.[175] As is already mentioned in the earlier chapter, the crowds in Matthew's Gospel are neutral in regard to their position toward Jesus' ministry. However, the ethnic constitution of the crowds in this particular setting and generally in the Gospel needs further investigation.

The word ἔρημος relates to the term for desert in Greek, but one should not imagine a real desert, because the place is near the Lake of Galilee.[176] It is obvious that the place mentioned here is an unpopulated area situated at the east of Galilee.[177] However, the utilization of this word could still be understood as an allusion to Israel's wandering in the wilderness and God's feeding of the Israel with manna.[178] The allusion perhaps provides for the reader a backdrop to understand Jesus' authority, an authority that could be aligned with God's authority in the Old Testament.

While in Mark's Gospel, Jesus' compassion leads to teaching, Matthew expresses it in healing by omitting Mark's metaphor of the sheep and the shepherd. Elsewhere, Matthew also links Jesus' compassion with the healing ministry (9:35-36, 20:34), and did not mention Jesus' teaching again in the summaries of the ministry with the crowds. For Blomberg, the reason may be Matthew's intention to distinguish the crowds from the Jewish leaders as still the objects of Jesus' beneficence, and may also want to distinguish the crowds

---

173 Hagner argues that the disciples, like the crowds must have walked to the spot and articulate the problem posed by the large crowd at the end of the day. Hagner, *Matthew 14-28*, 417.

174 Gundry, *Matthew*, 291.

175 Blomberg, *Matthew*, 232.

176 Harrington, *The Gospel of Matthew*, 219.

177 Blomberg, *Matthew*, 232. However, the exact location is being disputed. Bethsaida as a location is understood as a shift made by Luke. "Most scholars hold that the less populated east bank (toward the north) is the place from which Jesus returns to the other side, to Gennesaret (Matt 14:34), after a nocturnal crossing. Rudolf Schnackenburg, *The Gospel of Matthew*, trans. Robert R. Barr (Grand Rapids, MI: Eerdmans, 2002), 142.

178 Donald Senior, *Matthew*, ANTC (Nashville: Abingdon Press, 1998), 167; Harrington, *The Gospel of Matthew*, 219. For the use of this term and its different forms in Matthew's Gospel, see Matt 3:1, 3; 4:1; 11:7; 23:38; 24:26.

from the disciples.[179] The crowds as being neutral may have been separated from the true followers of Jesus in Matthew's Gospel.[180]

To this relocation, Charlene McAfee Moss argues that "Matthew, associates, at least in part, the *shepherding* response of the compassionate Jesus for 'sheep without shepherd' with his *healing* ministry."[181] This argument stems from the idea that Matthew is aware of the traditions preserved in both Greek and Hebrew readings of Zechariah 10:2, which is consistent with the similar evidence found in exegetical practices at Qumran.[182] Qumran texts where Davidic expectations have been found are influenced by the Old Testament Davidic Shepherd tradition. Apart from Isaiah 11 and Number 24, passages like Ezekiel 34-37, Zechariah 13, and Micah 5 can be identified as traditions with which the interpreters at Qumran engaged.[183]

While the Hebrew version of Zechariah 10:2 contains the term "shepherding," the Greek version has "healing." The healing shepherd-king is also identified as the χριστός κυρίου or χριστοῦ κυρίου "Lord's Messiah or the Lord Messiah" in the *Psalms of Solomon* 17:32 (cf. *Pss. Sol.* 18:7). The vision of a royal shepherd emerges, "the one whose role is to keep sickness and infirmity from the people."[184] Matthew's use of the word ἀσθενείας "sickness" while citing Isaiah 53:4 and the cognate ἀσθενῆσαι that occurs in *Psalms of Solomon* 17:40 assist Moss to identify Matthew's interpretation of Jesus' healing ministry as fulfilment of servant text.[185]

---

179 Blomberg, *Matthew*, 231.

180 Blomberg, *Matthew*, 232; cf. J. A. Comber, "The Verb Therapeuō in Matthew's Gospel," *JBL* 97 (1978): 431-434.

181 Charlene McAfee Moss, *The Zechariah Tradition and the Gospel of Matthew* (Berlin: de Gruyter, 2008), 54. For an argument of the significant of Zech 10:2 that speaks about healing rather than shepherding in LXX in studying Matthew's relocation of Mark's "sheep without a shepherd" with a context of healing, see especially Moss, *The Zechariah Tradition and the Gospel of Matthew*, 49-54.

182 Moss, *The Zechariah Tradition and the Gospel of Matthew*, 54.

183 Young S. Chae, *Jesus as the Eschatological Davidic Shepherd: Studies in the Old Testament, Second Temple Judaism, and in the Gospel of Matthew*, WUNT 216 (Tübingen: Mohr Siebeck, 2006), 151.

184 Pss. Sol. 17:21 "See, O Lord, and raise up for them their king, the son of David at the time which you chose, O God, to rule over Israel your servant." Pss. Sol. 17:32 "...and their king (will be) Lord Messiah." Pss. Sol. 17:40 "...with faith (fullness) and righteousness he will shepherd the Lord's flock and he will not permit illness to be among them in the pasture." Moss, *The Zechariah Tradition and the Gospel of Matthew*, 54; cf. Joseph L. Trafton, "What Would David Do? Messianic Expectation and Surprise in Ps. Sol. 17," in *The Psalms of Solomon: Language, History, Theology*, ed. Eberhard Bons and Patrick Pouchelle (Atlanta: SBL, 2015), 155-174.

185 Moss, *The Zechariah Tradition and the Gospel of Matthew*, 54.

*Damascus Document* such as CD 13:9-10[186] and 4Q521[187] also are interested in a figure like a shepherd who would heal.[188] The fulfilment citation in Matthew 2:6 and a reading of Matthew 8-9 in anticipation of Matthew 9:35-36, may both serve for the confirmation that "the ministry of the Davidic Messiah who will *shepherd* God's people Israel is an important theme in the First Gospel."[189] Therefore, the reason why Matthew changes Mark's metaphor to a context of healing may better be explained as the cause of his christological framework. The framework that encompasses Jesus as the Messiah, the one who possess the authority, not only to heal, but also to control the natural surroundings.

When Jesus got out from his solitary place to meet the crowds, "he had compassion on them and healed their sick." Matthew recounts a few times where Jesus has shown his compassion by healing the sick (14:14, 9:36 and 15:52). In this pericope Matthew omits the reason for Jesus' compassion, which was according to Mark "because they were like sheep without a shepherd" (Mark 6:34). Matthew's vivid statement about Jesus' healing ministry in place of the reason of compassion and Mark's "and he began to teach them many things" (Mark 6:34), according to Daniel J. Harrington, may also imply that the crowds stayed around for Jesus' healing activity than for his teaching.[190] Rudolf Schnackenburg also points out that compassion here implies messianic

---

186 CD 13:9-10 "He shall have pity on them like a father on his sons, and will heal all the "afflicted among them" like a shepherd his flock. He will undo all the chains which bind them, so that there will be neither harassed nor oppressed in his congregation." Translation rendered from Moss, *The Zechariah Tradition and the Gospel of Matthew*, 55.

187 4Q521 "[1][for the heav]ens and the earth will listen to his anointed one, [2][and all th]at is in them will not turn away from the precepts of the holy ones. [3]Strengthen yourselves, you who are seeking the Lord, in his service! Blank [4]Will you not in this encounter the Lord, all those who hope in their heart? [5]For the Lord will consider the pious, and call the righteous by name, [6]and his spirit will hover upon the poor, and he will renew the faithful with his strength. [7]For he will honour the pious upon the throne of an eternal kingdom, [8]freeing prisoners, giving sight to the blind, straightening out the twis[ted] [9]And for[e] ver shall I cling [to those who h]ope, and in his mercy [...] [10]and the fru[it of...] ... not be delayed. [11]And the Lord will perform marvellous acts such as have not existed, just as he sa[id,] [12][for]he will heal the badly wounded and will make the dead live, he will proclaim good news to the poor [13]and [...] ... [...] he will lead the [...] ... and enrich the hungry ones. [14][...] and all ... [...]." Translation rendered from Moss, *The Zechariah Tradition and the Gospel of Matthew*, 55; see also Wayne Baxter, "Healing and the "Son of David": Matthew's Warrant," *NovT 48 (2006): 36-50 (46).*

188 For a tabulation of other biblical texts (Isaiah, Zechariah 10:2, Matthew, one from Q), and also of Pss. Sol. 17 and 4Q521 being compared to highlight messianic expectations, see Moss, *The Zechariah Tradition and the Gospel of Matthew*, 56-57.

189 Moss, *The Zechariah Tradition and the Gospel of Matthew*, 57; cf. Richard Beaton, *Isaiah's Christ in Matthew's Gospel*, NTS 123 (Cambridge: CUP, 2004).

190 Harrington, *The Gospel of Matthew*, 219.

mercy, and healing activity and the distribution of food are also signs of the mercy of God that is seen in Jesus.[191] Therefore, Matthew's inclusion of Mark's word σπλαγχνίζομαι (Luke omits it) is not a simple statement that Jesus is being touched by the crowds, but is an important asset within his christological framework.

The difference in wording thus clearly stems out from the theological concerns of the evangelists. Andrew Purves, in his 1989 book *The Search for Compassion*, argues that Jesus' compassion here is evoked by twofold needs, the need for food, which was met in the feeding miracles, and also the need for spiritual nurturing.[192] He further argues that while Mark focuses the spiritual need and notes that Jesus had much to teach them, for Matthew the immediate need is healing.[193] The healings following the feedinging could be read as an allusion to the Jewish visions of the future time of fulfillment that is often associated with abundant food and healing (e.g., *Jub.* 23:29; 2 Esd. [*4 Ezra*] 7: 123; 8:53; *2 Bar.* 29:7).[194]

The word ἀρρωστος "without strength, weak, sick" is used only here by Matthew, and is commonly translated into English as "sick." It is usually used in reference to a physical state of a person, as also seen in other New Testament writings (Mark 6:5, 13, 16:18, 1 Cor 11:30).[195] The word is a negative form for ῥώννυμι, as a verb it basically means "to be strong, strengthen, have strength" and is also used as "farewell" at the end of a letter (e.g. Acts 15:29).[196] Thus the physical concern heightens in Matthew's feeding story. Jesus' compassion extends to the hungry multitude and fed them to their satisfaction. There is also a deep act of spiritual feeding "with overtones of Jesus' role as divine Wisdom, as Messiah, and as the one who is to feed the church sacramentally."[197]

Matthew's presentation of Jesus' concerns in his Gospel however include both the spiritual needs, and also the physical needs, and the difference in situations suggest differing priorities.[198] Even at this angle, though not explicit as in Mark, it is still clear that Matthew, by using the available traditions as a backdrop also presents Jesus as the compassionate shepherd, precisely as a

191 Schnackenburg, *The Gospel of Matthew*, 142.

192 Andrew Purves, *The Search for Compassion: Spirituality and Ministry* (Louisville: Westminster, 1989), 27.

193 Purves, *The Search for Compassion*, 27.

194 Charles H. Talbert, *Matthew*, PCNT (Grand Rapids, MI: Baker Academic, 2010), 183.

195 The word is translated as "sick" in Mark 16:18, "sick people" in Mark 6:5, "that were sick" in Mark 6:13, "ill" in 1 Cor 11:30.

196 "ῥώννυμι,"*LS&J* 2:1578; cf. "ῥώννυμι,"*VGT*, 566.

197 Ruth B. Edwards, "The Christological Basis of Johannine Footwashing," in *Jesus of Nazareth: Lord and Christ: Essays on the Historical Jesus and New Testament Christology*, ed. Joel B. Green and Max Turner (Grand Rapids, MI: Eerdmans, 1994), 367-383 (367).

198 Purves, *The Search for Compassion*, 27.

healing shepherd-king. What is already noted again comes to crystallization, by deriving from the Old Testament and the later Jewish writings; here Jesus is portrayed as the Davidic Messiah of the final age.[199]

Gundry argues that Matthew's substitution of Mark's "And when the hour had already become late" (Mark 6:35) to an usual phrase "When evening came," (v. 15) is to make the feeding miracle an evening meal, specifically the Lord's Supper for the crowds.[200] This same expression is also used in setting the stage for the Lord's Supper (26:20; Mark 14:17). Thus, the hour has indeed already passed, that is the hour of Jesus' self-sacrifice and therefore the church may eat the Lord's Supper.[201]

The suggestion made by the disciples that the crowd be sent away into surrounding villages to buy their own food is countered by Jesus' direct command: "They need not go away; you give them something to eat" (14:15-16). The "you" in Jesus' reply is emphatic (as is the "we" of 15:33). Here Jesus told them to do the miracle by themselves, after Matthew narrates Jesus' passing on of miracle-working authority to the Twelve (10:1). This passing on of miracle-working ability is also abruptly seen in the next pericope where Peter walks on the water.[202] However, the disciples cannot perform the miracle nor there is no hint that implies what Jesus meant by his emphatic "you." Matthew however makes it clear that after the disciples are endowed with authority, their discipleship becomes more intense.[203] To provide food in the wilderness was perhaps technically not possible apart from miracle, but the Old Testament provide a backdrop where Moses (Exod 16:14-35), Elijah (1 Kgs 17:14) and Elisha (2 Kgs 4:42-44) provide for hungry multitudes.

The disciples' sarcastic response to Jesus' proposal, "Shall we go and buy two hundred denarii worth of bread, and give it to them to eat?" (Mark 6:37) is omitted by Matthew. Again, Jesus' investigation about the amount of the provision in Mark 6:38 "How many loaves have you?" is also missing

199 Cf. Zech 11:5 "and their own shepherds have no pity on them." See also Sir 18:13 "the compassion of the Lord is for every living thing. He rebukes and trains and teaches them, and turns them back, as a shepherd his flock." Compassion, Teaching, and shepherding occur together in Mark's Gospel, but Matthew has healing, which makes it more accurate with the traditions of the expectation of Messiah. Cf. Purves, *The Search for Compassion*, 27.

200 Gundry, *Matthew*, 291.

201 Gundry, *Matthew*, 291; William Loader, *The New Testament with Imagination: A Fresh Approach to Its Writings and Themes* (Grand Rapids, MI: Eerdmans, 2007), 124; Richard A. Jensen, *Preaching Matthew's Gospel: A Narrative Approach* (Lima, OH: CSS, 1998), 128-129.

202 Cf. Blomberg, *Matthew*, 246.

203 James M. Arlandson, "Authoritative Testimony in Matthew's Gospel," *Historical Reliability of the Gospels*, http://bible.org/seriespage/9-authoritative-testimony-matthew-s-gospel.html.

in Matthew's account. Matthew interestingly adds ὁ δὲ εἶπεν, Φέρετέ μοι ὧδε αὐτούς "and he said, 'Bring them here to me,'" the phrase that underlines "the sovereign authority of Jesus."[204]

The disciples in Mark's Gospel fail to understand what Jesus has in mind when the quantity of the provision is asked, and thus they ask about buying bread, but Matthew makes it clear that the disciples are aware of the deficiency of their provision, which is why they count the loaves and fish.[205] The disciples are passively involving in this dramatic act, as the present Φέρετέ is like a motion picture, unlike aorist that is a complete snapshot. Osborne also sees this as a message that conveys the inability to accomplish anything of consequence without Jesus.[206] Thus, Matthew's unique insertion of this phrase "Bring them here to me," is a pointer to understand the sovereignty of Jesus alone in the story. The omission of Mark's disciples' response and Jesus' question about the quantity make Matthew's version vivid and clear, and christological emphasis is readily exposed. However, Matthew's presentation of the disciples weakens the story's allusion to 2 Kings 4:42-44, which is clearly alluded in Mark's Gospel.[207] In the story of Elisha's feeding miracle, his servant questions the quantity of food available to feed one hundred people, which resembles Mark's account of the disciples' action.

Matthew's rendering of the verbs κελεύω and ἀνακλιθῆναι in the scene where Jesus orders the crowd to sit on the grass is another interesting choice. The "grass" suggests that the season is Spring-time and implies that the Passover is near.[208] The word κελεύω "order" which is a strong verb for giving a command and connotes "to state with force and/or authority what others must do."[209] Mark's ἐπέταξεν connotes a softer tone "to arrange, i.e. command" (Mark 6:39). The infinitive ἀνακλιθῆναι "to recline" is also used for "reclining" at banquets and seems deliberate here.[210] Therefore, Matthew conveys that Jesus takes full control of the situation with full authority and the crowd apparently accepted the authority.

---

204 Hagner, *Matthew 14-28*, 415.

205 W. D. Davies and D. C. Allison, *Matthew: A Shorter Commentary based on the Three-Volume International Critical Commentary*, ed. D. C. Allison (London: T&T Clark, 2004), 238.

206 Osborne, *Matthew*, 566.

207 Davies and Allison, *A Critical and Exegetical Commentary*, 2:489.

208 The Passover reminisce the Eucharist, and John explicitly states "the Passover was near" (John 6:4).

209 Johannes P. Louw and Eugene A. Nida, eds. *Greek-English Lexicon of the New Testament: Based on Semantic Domains*, 2nd ed. (New York: UBS, 1988), 425, cited by Osborne, *Matthew*, 566.

210 Osborne, *Matthew*, 566.

For Alan Richardson "The Feeding Miracles imply that the New Age has already arrived; the Messiah has come, and he has given the expected sign of the manna from heaven. Faithful Israel has "sat down" at the Messiah's banquet."[211] Jesus thus miraculously feeds the crowd with little food, and the story is shaped in such a way by Matthew to point backward to the Old Testament texts and point forward to Eucharist, and Eucharist which reminisces a messianic banquet. Moreover, according to Harrington, this forward thrust continues to point "beyond to the kingdom of God pictured in Jewish and Christian petty as a banquet."[212] Jesus' role as a host at a regular Jewish meal is another pointer to the authority embedded in him.

The Jewish custom for the starting of a formal meal is seen in Jesus' breaking of the loaves and blessing of the food to be partaken. This action continued to became the pattern of the Christian communion meal, "the breaking of the bread" or "Eucharist," the main form of worship in the early church and has remained so for today's church.[213] Thus, Joseph Rhymer argues that this may have been one of the reasons why all the evangelists included the miracle story in their respective Gospels.[214] This episode also echoes the spiritual feeding in 26:26-29, and early Christian meals in Acts 27:35, 1 Cor 11:23-24 as well as the stories of Elijah and Elisha (1 Kgs 17:8, 2 Kgs 4:42-44, Deut 8:10).[215]

The use of three successive circumstantial participles κελεύοντας "ordering," λαμβάνειν "take," ἀναβλέψας "looking," all culminated in the final verb of the clause εὐλόγησεν "he gave thanks." This use of participles before the action of Jesus signifies the primary idea of thanking God for the miracle that is about to happen, and thus this sign of foreknowing is another pointer to Jesus' supernatural ability.[216] Thus, "he gave thanks" refers to thanking God for the food.

The sequence of these participles λαμβάνειν "take," εὐλογειν "bless," κλᾶν "break," διδόναι "give" is also similarly used in the account of the Lord's Supper (26:26-27), again suggesting an inevitable association of the two accounts.[217] However, Osborne argues that this same sequence is also found

---

211 Alan Richardson, "The Feeding of the Five Thousand: Mark 6:34-44)," *JBT* 9: 144-149 (148).

212 Harrington, *The Gospel of Matthew*, 221.

213 Rhymer, *The Miracles of Jesus*, 37.

214 Rhymer, *The Miracles of Jesus*, 37.

215 Raymond M. Fowler, *Loaves and Fishes: The Function of the Feeding Stories in the Gospel of Mark*, SBLDS 54 (Chico, CA: Scholars, 1981), 43-148; cf. S. Masuda, "The Good News of the Miracle of the Bread: The Tradition and Its Markan Redaction," *NTS* 28 (1982): 191-219.

216 Osborne, *Matthew*, 566.

217 Cf. Hagner, *Matthew 14-28*, 418.

in the regular meal of Acts 27:35, and it connotes mainly family celebration of the meal, but does not rule out the connection with the Eucharist.[218] The Eucharist which was understood as a foretaste of the meal in the kingdom of God, and the association of both bread (or manna) and fish (or Leviathan) with the messianic feast in Jewish texts (*2 Bar.* 29:3-8, 4 Ezra 6:52) are another significant backgrounds for this feeding story.[219] Some messianic imagery that was later developed in Second Temple period was drawn from the Old Testament literature (e.g., eating Leviathan in *2 Bar.*). But it has to be noted that "there was a broad range of messianic expectations in the period that it is difficult to categorically state "all Jews" believed the messianic period to be like a banquet."[220] As the image of messianic banquet was one of many motifs for the eschaton in the Second Temple tradition, and considering Matthew's inheritance of the tradition in his Gospel, it seems probable that the multitude in Matthew's Gospel understood the feeding miracle as a messianic miracle of the prophet-like Moses.[221]

Matthew also gives importance to the role played by the disciples in distributing the food which Jesus blessed.[222] This may have no connection with the christological significance of the story, but considering how scholars dealt with the difference between Matthew's portrayal of the disciples and the portrayal in his source, it is another important pointer for the difference between Mark's portrayal and Matthew's portrayal of the disciples.[223] It is also significant to see that unlike Mark's version, the disciples' responses to Jesus in both the feeding stories of Matthew's Gospel imply a sense of responsibility. The disciples are responsible to supply food for the crowds (14:15, 15:33) and they know right away the provision at hand (14:17, 15:34), and they are the servers of the meal (14:19, 15:36). Matthew expands the role of the disciples as intermediaries between Jesus and the crowd.[224]

---

218 Osborne, *Matthew*, 567; for a word to word comparison of this story with the Eucharist (Matt 26:20-29) see, Davies and Allison, *Matthew: A Shorter Commentary*, 236.

219 Davies and Allison, *Matthew: A Shorter Commentary*, 236; cf. G. H. Boobyer, "The Eucharistic Interpretation of the Miracles of the Loaves in St. Mark's Gospel," *JTS* 3 (1952): 161-171.

220 Philip J. Long, *Jesus the Bridegroom: The Origin of the Eschatological Feast as a Wedding Banquet in the Synoptic Gospels* (Eugene, OR: Pickwick, 2013), 8.

221 Cf. Davies and Allison, *Matthew: A Shorter Commentary*, 236; see also "The Use of Hebrew Bible Imagery in the New Testament," chapter 2 of Long, *Jesus the Bridegroom*, 10-42, esp. 23-24.

222 Senior, *Matthew*, 167-168.

223 For the summary of different scholarly view on Matthew's portrayal of the disciples in redaction criticism, see Jeannine K. Brown, *The Disciples in Narrative Perspective: The Portrayal and Function of the Matthew Disciples* (Leiden: Brill, 2002), 3-13.

224 Harrington, *The Gospel of Matthew*, 242.

This clause καὶ ἔφαγον πάντες καὶ ἐχορτάσθησαν "They all ate and were satisfied" can be taken as the symbolism of completeness.[225] Osborne rightly argues that the verb χορτάζω which means "eat to the full, be satisfied" fits the idea of the messianic banquet where all the hungry are to be completely satisfied (cf. Mark 5:6, Luke 6:21).[226] The gathering of twelve baskets of leftover also implies the incredibility of the sumptuous meal. This overabundance is also seen in other feeding miracles of the Old Testament and New Testament (1Kgs 17:16, 2 Kgs 4:6-7, 44, 8:8-9, Luke 5:6-7, John 21:6, 11).[227] The term "satisfied" is also used in the fourth beatitude in connection with the hungry that are to be satisfied in the eschatological kingdom. If this idea is link with the satisfaction of the crowds in the story, it may be thought of as foreshadowing the satisfaction of the messianic banquet (cf. Deut 8:10).[228]

The gathering of leftover is done at the command of Jesus in John's Gospel. Matthew and Mark do not contain Jesus' command. Out of Mark's καὶ ἦραν 'κλάσματα δώδεκα κοφίνων πληρώματα' καὶ ἀπὸ τῶν ἰχθύων "and they took up twelve baskets full of broken pieces and of the fish," Matthew mentions only the broken pieces. The number "twelve" is generally interpreted as symbolizing the twelve tribes of Israel.[229]

### 6.4.3. Cosmic Christology in the Passage

France highlights how the Lord's Supper was itself a foretaste of the messianic banquet (26:29), and argues that this dimension is also seen in the feeding story.[230] Blomberg also observes this connection and points out that this large gathering of the common people of Galilee implies the presence of people who were ritually impure.[231] However, the parallel is not developed in Matthew's Gospel, and the substitution of fish for wine may suggest ambiguity for the parallel, but Matthew's employment of the same four verbs in the Lord's Supper narrative (took, blessed, broke, gave - 26:26) makes the parallel convincing.[232]

---

225 Osborne, *Matthew*, 567.

226 Osborne, *Matthew*, 567.

227 Davies and Allison, *Matthew: A Shorter Commentary*, 238.

228 Harrington, *The Gospel of Matthew*, 220; Davies and Allison, *Matthew: A Shorter Commentary*, 238.

229 Harrington, *The Gospel of Matthew*, 220; cf. Fowler, *Loaves and Fishes*; Masuda, "The Good News of the Miracle of the Bread," 191-291.

230 France, *The Gospel of Matthew*, 559.

231 Craig L. Blomberg, *Contagious Holiness: Jesus' Meals with Sinners*, NSBT (Leicester: Apollos, 2005), 105-108.

232 Cf. Douglas R.A. Hare, *Matthew: Interpretation: A Bible Commentary for Teaching and Preaching* (Louisville: John Knox Press, 1993), 166, argues for the ambiguity of the parallel between the feeding story and the Lord's Supper. His main argument is based on the fact that bread and fish constituted the basic ingredients of a peasant's meal in Galilee.

Apart from this, Matthew's banquet is implicitly connected with Herod's bitter banquet, and this can be read in accordance to the difference between the two banquets of the Empire and the Kingdom of God.[233] The aristocracy that looks down on the masses and Jesus' compassion over them is also another clue for colonial interest.[234] Therefore, it is befitting to see this story as having connection with the Lord's Supper as well as the messianic banquet, when located within the overall scheme of Matthew's christological framework. A special eschatological meal was also a central theme at Qumran community. The messianic or heavenly banquets in the Dead Sea Scroll are expressions of the "hope in an imminent heavenly banquet" (1QS 6:4-5; 1QSa 2:11-22).[235]

Gerd Theissen argues that this miracle, as a "gift miracle" story is unusual in its form because there is neither a comment on the reaction of the crowd nor an explicit christological conclusion provided by the evangelist.[236] F. D. Bruner opines that the feeding of the five thousand is in fact the only miracle to appear in all the four Gospels, "perhaps because it shows so comprehensively how Jesus is equal to all human need, whether social or spiritual."[237] Therefore the application of this passage must focus more on Christology rather than the physical implication, and precisely John develops the spiritual import of the miracle by placing Jesus' "Bread of Life" discourse, given in the Capernaum synagogue, shortly after his account of the feeding miracle (John 6:26-59). Keener also argues that the feeding story historically and in the text includes a christological point.[238] Reading the story in the context of other attempted signs-workers in the wilderness in Jesus' day, and the backdrop provided by the idea of Jewish messianic hope, this miracle in the wilderness involves a clear messianic statement.[239]

---

He also points out that Matthew's lack of giving hint like John does, who interprets the event to present Jesus as the bread of life, whose words that are truly nourishing (John 6:35-63). Though he opines that Matthew's feeding story has no anticipation of the Eucharist and the messianic banquet, he still holds that for Matthew it is a messianic meal (not a messianic banquet because the meal does not suite Messiah's victory celebration) since the Messiah is the host who fed his people out of compassion. He is the kind of shepherd-king who cares for his flock.

233 Jensen, *Preaching Matthew's Gospel*, 128.

234 Keener, *A Commentary on the Gospel of Matthew*, 402.

235 Overman, *Church and Community in Crisis*, 218.

236 Gerd Theissen, *The Miracle Stories of the Early Christian Tradition*, trans. Francis McDonagh, ed. John Riches (Edinburgh: T&T Clark, 1983), 104.

237 F. D. Bruner, *The Churchbook* (Dallas: Word, 1990), 530.

238 Keener, *A Commentary on the Gospel of Matthew*, 402-403.

239 Keener, *A Commentary on the Gospel of Matthew*, 402-403; cf. Ben Witherington, *The Christology of Jesus* (Minneapolis: Fortress, 1990), 91 &100; Jos. War 2.261; Ant. 20:169.

### *6.4.4. The Rhetorical Purpose of the Passage*

Jesus' compassion for them is highlighted in this pericope.[240] The story signifies the character of the great host at the messianic banquet that is foreshadowed. Matthew's interest is seen in the christological points embedded in the story. God's caring providence for his people in the present age is clearly depicted by Matthew's unique phrase "*καὶ ἐθεράπευσεν τοὺςἀρρώστους αὐτῶν*" (and cured their sick – 14:14b), and according to William L. Lane, the story "stands in deliberate contrast to the drunken feast of the evil ruler Herod Antipas in Matthew 14:6-11."[241] Thus, it is important to see how Matthew portrays Jesus as possessing the authority to multiply natural elements.

Matthew's portrayal of this miracle story is more interesting when it is compared with the Old Testament feeding miracle stories of Moses, Elijah, and Elisha. As providing food in the wilderness was technically impossible without miracle, the insertion of another unique word *ἔρημος* is significant because the writers of the Gospels use it regularly to identify the wilderness (e.g. Matt 3:1, 3; 4:1; 11:7; Mark 1:3, 4; Luke 1:80; 3:2, 4; 8:29; John 1:23; 3:14). It is clear that Matthew portrays Jesus as being capable of doing what the earlier prophets had achieved.[242] Though the Old Testament narratives did not oppose feeding multitudes by natural means (e.g. 2 Kgs 6:22), and the disciples are also suggesting Jesus to send the crowds to the towns which lay in the vicinity, Matthew's clearly states that Jesus is not willing to send them away but insist on the disciples to provide food. It is also understandable that most of the day's bread would have been consumed by evening, and the "grass" also signifies that the time is spring (near Passover) and the grain stock would be running low by then.[243] By relating this passage with its imperial context, Carter also points out that this feeding is in contrast with the imperial economy, the economy that does not guarantee sufficient food.[244]

Carol B. Wilson's arguments on the shortage of food in this story are also noteworthy.[245] Firstly, a banquet given by Herod before the feeding

240 According to René Latourelle, *The Miracles of Jesus and the Theology of Miracles*, trans. Matthew J. O'Connell (New York: Paulist Press, 1988), 74: Matthew emphasizes the compassion of Jesus but omits Mark's reference to sheep and shepherd, and he also shortens the dialogue between Jesus and the disciples perhaps in order to divide the attention equally between the crowd and the disciples.

241 W. L. Lane, *The Gospel According to Mark*, NICNT (Grand Rapids: Eerdmans, 1974), 227; see also Keener, *A Commentary on the Gospel of Matthew*, 402-403.

242 Keener, *A Commentary on the Gospel of Matthew*, 403.

243 Keener, *A Commentary on the Gospel of Matthew*, 404.

244 Warren Carter, *Matthew and the Margins: A Socio-Political and Religious Reading* (Sheffield, England: SAP, 2000), 327.

245 Carol B. Wilson, *For I was Hungry and You Gave Me Food: Pragmatics of Food Access in the Gospel of Matthew* (Eugene, OR: Pickwick, 2014), 205.

story would have resulted in lack of usual circulation of food (Matt 14:1-12). Secondly, a widespread condition of food shortage is indicated by multitude of hungry people. Thirdly, Matthew's two feeding stories had a scene of Jesus' healing the sick. Wilson thinks of this as an indication that the shortage of food leads to malnutrition and people would be vulnerable to disease. Fourthly, both the narratives take place in the wilderness, an uncultivated land where people "from the lower socio-economic segments of the population went to scavenge when food was scarce."[246]

It was not uncommon in the Old Testament that God used simple object at hand to do great miracles (cf. Judg 6:14-16; 15:15-19). Moses' ordinary shepherd's staff was transformed (Exod 4:1-3) and was also used to part the sea (Exod 14:16). The story of Elisha and the widow is another example, where a jar of oil was miraculously multiplied (2 Kgs 4:1-7). Matthew's narration of Jesus' multiplication of food did not even mention about Jesus' praying, but simply "gives thanks" which is a standard Jewish custom before and normally after meals.[247] Matthew's presentation of Jesus again reflects the cosmic authority over elements of nature, and the absence of Jesus praying for the miracle seems deliberate, as also in other nature miracles. This rhetorical discourse fits perfectly in the working christological framework and cosmological outlook of Matthew.

What Matthew is trying to teach when he mentions the leftovers is not that obvious. There are scholars who think that these numbers (12 baskets in feeding five thousand and 7 baskets in feeding four thousand) are having symbolic significance.[248] Overman argues that the selection of numbers 12 and 7 in Matthew's Gospel "denotes the involvement and hand of God."[249] He further stresses that "When one encounters these numbers within the biblical tradition, including the Gospels, one is aware that God is at work."[250] However, Saldarini sees these numbers as possibly having no symbolic significance.[251]

---

246 Wilson, *For I was Hungry and You Gave Me Food*, 206. For the model description of *uncultivated land*, see 63-75, 101-103.

247 Keener, *A Commentary on the Gospel of Matthew*, 404-405.

248 12 represent the twelve tribes of historic Israel and 7 represent the gentile world. As seen in Luke's Gospel, perhaps 7 or 70 represents the Gentiles (the sending of the 70 in Luke 10:1) and in Acts 6:1 (where seven "hellenists" in contrast to the "Hebrews" were selected to take care of their widows). Overman, *Church and Community in Crisis*, 219; see also Bob Robinson, *Jesus and the Religions: Retrieving a Neglected Example for a Multi-Cultural World* (Eugene, OR: Cascade Books, 2012), 154. Robinson also argues for the Gentile inclusion in Mark's version.

249 Overman, *Church and Community in Crisis*, 219.

250 Overman, *Church and Community in Crisis*, 219.

251 Saldarini, "Matthew," 1036.

Theissen argues that the mentioning of leftovers stresses the abundance of God's miraculous power in Christ.[252] It is also evident from ancient sources that the leftovers of food signify a good host, and Jesus acting as a host or family head is an abundant host.[253] The refusal to squander the leftovers could also imply to teach Matthew's community to trust in God's providence but also to teach them not to neglect what God had already provided.[254]

What is also remarkable in the story is the way Matthew portrays the disciples and their little faith. While the disciples, by seeing the size of what is needed at the moment they could only resort to thinking about the littleness of the human's resources available; but Jesus sees only the greatness of God's resources that will be made available.[255] The eschatological significance is also embedded in the story by a close resemblance with the Lord's Supper, in wording and phrases. Therefore, it may be perhaps fitting to say that Matthew, in his rhetorical discourse shows how to overcome "little faith," that is to see Jesus' cosmic authority over natural elements.

## 6.5. The Walking on the Water (14:22-33)

### *6.5.1. Narrative Framework*

The story of Jesus' walking on the water is another material which is also found in other Gospel writings such as Mark and John. As this passage is inserted right after the feeding of the five thousand in all the four Gospels, Saldarini posits that "the two miracles must have been paired in pre-Gospel traditions."[256] The effect of placing next to the feeding miracle also provides influential emphasis on the identity of Jesus. Matthew's setting out of the question of the identity of Jesus still calls for another answer, which is now unequivocally presented in this story (14:33). This conclusion could also serve well for the previous feeding miracle story.[257]

In this passage Jesus prays alone only in Matthew's Gospel, the phrase for alone is κατ' ιδίαν, which is rare in biblical Greek. There is no certain conclusion from Matthew's use of the phrase.[258] The content or motive of the

252 Theissen, *Miracle Stories of the Early Christian Tradition*, 67.

253 Keener, *A Commentary on the Gospel of Matthew*, 405.

254 Keener, *A Commentary on the Gospel of Matthew*, 405.

255 Keener, *A Commentary on the Gospel of Matthew*, 405.

256 Saldarini, "Matthew," 1033.

257 Hagner, *Matthew 14-28*, 421.

258 For the use of this phrase, see Patrick J. Madden, *Jesus' Walking on the Sea: An Investigation of the Origin of the Narrative Account* (Berlin: de Gruyter, 1997), 105, note 80.

prayer is not known, but the act of prayer before exercising of divine attributes on the sea stresses Jesus' intimacy with God.[259]

"In the ancient Mediterranean world, walking on the water is above all something that a god or God can do, as is stilling a storm at sea."[260] Job 9:8 and Psalm 77:16, 19 are examples where God walks on the waves of the sea, and where Yahweh is both ruler of the waves and able to traverse the sea. In the Old Testament the characterization that God can control waters of the earth and its creative force begins from creation account. God forms and separate the waters to create the seas, the skies, and the land (Gen 1:1-13). God populates the seas with creatures and brings forth all types of fauna to roam the earth and sky.[261] Therefore, Matthew's portrayal of Jesus' divine authority is clear in this miracle.

There are two major differences to be found in Matthew's Gospel and his source Mark's Gospel. Firstly, Matthew's insertion of Peter's walking on the water is not found in Mark's Gospel. Secondly, at the closing of the story, while in Mark's Gospel the disciples lack understanding, but in Matthew's Gospel the disciples prostrate themselves (προσεκύνησαν) and confess Jesus as "Son of God" (θεοῦ υἱος).[262]

In this account, Patrick J. Madden recognizes four remarkable structural similarities to the resurrection appearance in John 21:1-14.[263] Both the narratives take place ἐπι τῆς θαλάσσης (Matt 14:26; John 21:1), but the context requires that the Greek phrase be translated as "upon the sea" in Matthew 14 and "by the sea" in John 21. There is also a lack of recognition in both the accounts. In John 21:4b the disciples did not know the person they saw was Jesus, but in Matthew 14:26 they think they are seeing a ghost. In both the accounts the main character of the Gospels recognizes Jesus, Peter in Matthew 14:28 and the beloved disciple in John 21:7. Peter gets out of the boat in both the accounts; he walks upon the water in Matthew 14:29 and jumps into the water in John 21:7, and presumably swims to the shore (John 21:8).

The Old Testament speaks of the God who out of the void of water brought about creation, and made a path through the Red Sea for the Israelites. God alone is presented as being able to conquer the sea. In antiquity walking on the water is solely a divine ability and is of great interest to people. Even in Greek literature stories about gods and heroes (sons of gods) walking on

259 Saldarini, "Matthew," 1033.

260 Talbert, *Matthew*, 185.

261 Sherri Brown, "Water Imagery and the Power and Presence of God in the Gospel of John," *ThTo* 72 (2015): 289-298 (291-292).

262 Cf. Madden, *Jesus' Walking on the Sea*, 105-106.

263 Madden, *Jesus' Walking on the Sea*, 105.

water was quite common.[264] With these backdrops it is rather clear in what categories the readers of the Gospels must have interpreted Jesus' walking on the water.[265] Thus, Robin A. Parry in his 2014 book *The Biblical Cosmos: A Pilgrim's Guide to the Weird and Wonderful World of the Bible*, argues that "Jesus, like Jehovah, exercises complete control over the chaotic sea and walks upon its waves as on the dry ground."[266] The phrase Θαρσεῖτε, ἐγώ εἰμι (Take courage! I am) makes it more explicit because this expression recalls the phrase with which God identifies God's self in the Old Testament (e.g. Exod 3:14; Isa 41:4; 43:10; 47:8, 10).[267] The ancient readers perhaps understood Jesus' walking on the water in this alluded sense.

### 6.5.2. Analysis of the Passage

*22And immediately Jesus forced his disciples to get into the boat and go on*
*ahead of him to the other side, until he dismissed the crowds. 23After he had*
*dismissed the crowds, he went up to the mountain by himself to pray. When*
*the evening came, he was there alone, 24and the boat was already far from*
*the land, tortured by the waves, for the wind was contrary. 25And in the fourth*
*watch (shortly before dawn) Jesus went out to them, walking upon the sea.*
*26When the disciples saw him walking on the sea, they were troubled and*
*say "It's a ghost," and cried out in fear. 27Immediately Jesus said to them:*
*"Take courage! I am (he). Do not be afraid." 28Peter answering him and said*
*"Lord, if it's you, tell me to come to you on the water." 29And he said "Come."*
*Then Peter got down out of the boat, walked on the water and came toward*
*Jesus. 30But seeing the wind vehement, he was afraid. And when he begins to*
*drown when he saw the wind, he was afraid and cried out, "Lord, save me!"*
*31Immediately Jesus reached out his hand and caught him, and he said" You*
*of little faith, why did you doubt?" 32And when they climbed into the boat, the*
*wind ceased. 33Then those who were in the boat worshiped him, saying, "Truly*
*you are the Son of God."*

Matthew follows Mark in his use of the word ἀναγκάζω "force" to tell how Jesus commanded the disciples to get into the boat. The hurried aftermath of the feeding miracles is made clear in John's account that some of the people were so impressed with the feeding miracle that they tried to make Jesus their

264 In Greek mythologies, Hermes' sandals carry him over the water (Homer, *Od.* 5:54), and Neptune glides over the waters (Virgil, *Aen.* 1:147). It is also noted as a gift that a god can endow to his son. Poseidon gives his son Orion the ability to travel over the sea unharmed (Appollonius of Rhodes, *Argon.* 1:179-184).

265 O. Wesley Allen Jr., *Matthew*, FBPC (Minneapolis: Fortress, 2013), 158; Luz, *Matthew 8-20*, 320.

266 Robin A. Parry, *The Biblical Cosmos: A Pilgrim's Guide to the Weird and Wonderful World of the Bible* (Eugene, OR: Cascade Books, 2014), 44.

267 Allen Jr., *Matthew*, 158.

king (John 6:15). Leon Morris says that Matthew's choice of this word signifies strong action, perhaps to restrain the disciples who may have been sympathetic to the king makers from involving in the situation at hand.[268] The word thus develops a sense of urgency in this context, but shows that Jesus was fully in command.[269] Matthew omits the destination in Mark, which is Bethsaida, situated at the northeast of the Sea of Galilee. Matthew narrates that Jesus and the disciples end up in Gennesaret, situated at the northwest side, below Capernaum (cf. Matt 14:34). The important thing for Matthew is that Jesus forces the disciples to move out of the way until he dismissed the crowds.[270]

Mark, Matthew and John all place the story right after the feeding of the five thousand. The disciples being out on the lake without Jesus being on board, and this temporary separation sets the plot for Jesus' to come from the land and walks on the water. This story is also presented in the same manner as that of other nature miracles, "as a practical response to a difficult situation rather than as a wonder performed for its own sake."[271]

Terence L. Donaldson in his 1985 book *Jesus on the Mountains: A Study in Matthean Theology*, suggests that the terrain in the area around the Sea of Galilee as a location ὄρος is perhaps merely borrowed from Mark.[272] The reason is that, while considering the significance of those passages in the Gospel where a mountain functions as the setting for an event in Jesus' life and ministry, he points out that ὄρος appears five times in sayings material (Matt 5:14; 17:20; 18:12; 21:21; 24:26) are "for the most part taken over by the evangelist from his sources."[273] However, as the phrase κατ' ἰδίαν "privately" used in 14:13 (cf. 17:1) is again deployed in addition with the strengthening phrase μόνος ἦν ἐκεῖ "he was there alone," Twelftree argues that this privacy recalls Moses on Mount Sinai (Matt 14:23; Mark 6:46).[274] He further argues that "Matthew probably intends his readers to notice again the Moses typology explains the insertion of the comment that Jesus "was there alone," for Moses

268 Leon Morris, *The Gospel According to Matthew*, PNTC (Grand Rapids, MI: Eerdmans, 1992), 380-381.

269 Harrington, *The Gospel of Matthew*, 223.

270 The word ἀπο-λύω is used 19 times by Matthew, which is nearly a third of its 65 New Testament occurrences. It is used of releasing a prisoner (27:15) or a debtor (18:27), and of forgiveness (Luke 6:37). It comes to mean "let go, dismiss," and in this sense it is used of divorce in 5:31. Morris, *The Gospel According to Matthew*, 120-121.

271 France, *The Gospel of Matthew*, 566.

272 Terence L. Donaldson, *Jesus on the Mountains: A Study in Matthean Theology* (Sheffield: JSOT, 1985), 12; Hagner, *Matthew 14-18*, 422.

273 Donaldson, *Jesus on the Mountains*, 12.

274 Graham H. Twelftree, *Jesus the Miracle Worker: A Historical and Theological Study* (Downers Grove, IL: IVP, 1999), 130.

is also said to be alone on the mountain (ex 24:2)."[275] This combination of words and phrases could connote two understanding, Moses typology and the motif of Jesus' solitude. It makes it convincing to read Moses typology in the story, especially when considered with the Old Testament narrative of Moses ascending to Mount Sinai and the crossing of the Red Sea.[276] The miracle of Jesus coincidentally took place at the fourth morning watch, which corresponds to the time of God's rescue of his people at the Red Sea.[277] Thus, Matthew's use of this construction "he went up the mountain" in 14:23 and also 15:29 interestingly coincides with Jesus' deeds that would recall Moses' ministry.[278]

However, Hagner and France reject the idea of Moses typology here, and read τὸ ὄρος as representing generally to the hill country near the lake of Galilee.[279] It is difficult to ascertain every instances of Matthew's narrative as symbolism, especially where it hardly connects to ancient traditions. Matthew's uses of ὄρος "mountain, hilly-country" may or may not have an explicit symbolic significance like in Matthew 5:1.[280] To understand it as the hill district as distinct from the lowlands, especially the hills above the Sea of Galilee suffice the scope of the study and are more appropriate in this context. Thus, Matthew's combination of "by himself" and "he was there alone" (14:23) would probably signify not so much of Moses typology but the privacy of Jesus' time before the epiphany.

The sentence, σταδίους πολλοὺς ἀπὸ τῆς γῆς ἀπεῖχεν "the boat was many stadia away from the land" is according to Mark they were "in the middle of the sea." Literally "many stadia," a στάδιον is approximately less than two-tenth of a kilometer. The sea of Galilee is around 30 km in length and a little less than 13 km in width. John says that the boat was "twenty-five or thirty stadia" which is 4.5 km to 5.5 km approximately. These variants however agree to one significant point, that the location of the boat is far away from land. Therefore the distance does not need literal rendering and the emphasis to narrate the

---

275 Twelftree, *Jesus the Miracle Worker*, 130; cf. Andreas J. Köstenberger, L. Scott Kellum and Charles L. Quarles, *The Cradle, The Cross, and The Crown: An Introduction to the New Testament* (Nashville: B&H Publishing Group, 2009), 217.

276 Davies and Allison, *A Critical and Exegetical Commentary*, 2:502; Dale C. Allison, *The New Moses: A Matthean Typology* (Minneapolis: Fortress, 1993), 172-180; cf. Twelftree, *Jesus the Miracle Worker*, 130; Charles Quarles, *Sermon on the Mount: Restoring Christ's Message to the Modern Church*, MSBT (Nashville: B&H, 2011), 22. For alternative suggestion on "Mount Zion" typology, see Donaldson, *Jesus on the Mountains*, 116-118.

277 Twelftree, *Jesus the Miracle Worker*, 130.

278 Quarles, *Sermon on the Mount*, 22.

279 Hagner, *Matthew 14-18*, 422; France, *The Gospel of Matthew*, 156-157. France however did not clearly rule out the use of the phrase as typological parallel with Moses.

280 Harrington, *The Gospel of Matthew*, 224.

wide distance between Jesus and the disciples is clearly conveyed in the three Gospels (cf. Mark 6:47; John 6:19).[281]

Matthew uses βασανίζω "torture" in its participle form to modify the boat, whereas Mark connects it to the disciples, but both texts trace the situation to the "contrary" wind.[282] The term κῦμα (wave) occurs only four times in the New Testament and two times in Matthew's Gospel. Matthew's choice of word may mean that the waves are torturing or harassing not the sailors but the boat.[283] Matthew's use of ἐναντίος "contrary" here signifies that a head wind is against the boat and was tossed by the waves.[284] The duration of their struggle is not clear but Matthew's narration shows that they left right after the meal and had been struggling against natural elements all night, and will be weary. Matthew is painting a scene where even the experienced sailors were struggling and in dire need for help.

Τετάρτῃ δὲ φυλακῇ τῆς νυκτὸς "the fourth watch of the night" is the last watch that occurred between 3:00 AM and 6:00 AM. As there is no such watch in Jewish three watches system, the term here refers to Roman system that divided the time of the night (between 6:00 PM and 6:00 AM) into four watches.[285] A connection with God's intervention against the Egyptians according to Exodus 14:20 ("in the morning watch") is also plausible.[286]

The disciples were terrified and were convinced that they had encountered a φάντασμα "ghost, apparition." An Old Testament example of a ghost is the spirit of Samuel that was raised from the dead by the witch of Endor (cf. 1 Sam 28). Another example of the popular belief that spirits of the night brought disaster to the sea farers is preserved in Talmud: "Rabbah said, Seafarers told me that the wave that sinks a ship appears with a white fringe of fire at its crest, and when stricken with clubs on which is engraven, 'I am that I am, Yah, the Lord of Hosts, Amen, Amen, Selah,' it subsides."[287] Thus Jesus' words to the terrified disciples Θαρσεῖτε, ἐγώ εἰμι· μὴ φοβεῖσθε "Take courage! I am (he). Do not be afraid" is a note to correct their delusive vision and also a call for courage. The phrase "do not be afraid" is a favourite one for Matthew as it appears several times in his Gospel (1:20, 10:26, 28, 31, 17:7, 28:5, 10). Matthew's presentation of Jesus as having special authority

281 Harrington, *The Gospel of Matthew*, 224.

282 Harrington, *The Gospel of Matthew*, 224.

283 According to Morris, the waves are pictured as harassing the sailors. Morris, *The Gospel According to Matthew*, 381.

284 Morris, *The Gospel According to Matthew*, 381.

285 Morris, *The Gospel According to Matthew*, 381-382.

286 Harrington, *The Gospel of Matthew*, 224.

287 B. Bat. 73a; cf. Meg. 3a; 1 En. 60:16; Wis 17:3-4, 15. Lane, *The Gospel of Mark*, 237.

by regularly using this is in terms with the working christological framework of the Gospel.

The expression ἐγώ εἰμι "I am" has a rich background in Isaiah 41:4 and 43:10 where it functions as a divine name (see also Exod 3:14, Deut 32:39). It appears alongside "fear not" in Isaiah 43 several times. The use of such language identifies Jesus as the one who reveals the God of Israel and is uniquely related to that God.[288]

Peter's walking on the water acts as a story within a story, and has no parallel in any other Gospels. Peter's addressing Jesus as Κύριε seems to reflect "an awareness that Jesus shares in the sovereign lordship of Yahweh."[289] The significance of the title is seen in other places in the Gospel and the use in the healing narratives and by the disciples in the stilling of the storm and in this present story. The title here is connected well with the ἐγώ εἰμι of the preceding verse. Peter serves as a spokesperson for the group in decisive points of Matthew's narrative (see 15:15; 16:16; 17:4; 18:21; 19:27; 26:33, 35). Here also he responds to the statement of Jesus. Thus, Peter is portrayed as having perceived the import of Jesus' self-designation ἐγώ εἰμι and he too wants to do what God alone does.[290]

Jesus' command to Peter to walk on the water signifies that Jesus not only has the authority to walk on the sea but also has the ability to share the power and authority with others, which is another motif in Matthew's Gospel (cf. 11:27, 28:18).[291] This observation is crucial because God asks Job "Have you come (LXX: ἦλθες) into the springs of the sea (θάλασσης) or walked in the recesses of the deep?" John Paul Heil understands this question as God's answering to Job who challenged the divine rule over creation, and the implication is thus: if a human being walks on the sea, it is only by divine authority.[292] Davies and Allison therefore argue that this implication points to Jesus as the one who wield divine authority.[293]

The term ἔρχομαι is here employed again by Matthew (14:29) and followed it with προσκυνέω in the later verse (14:33). This combination of words in the LXX is typically a cultic practice of those approaching the tabernacle or temple.[294] The disciples had made a similar plea here as they did

288 Harrington, *The Gospel of Matthew*, 224.

289 Davies and Allison, *A Critical and Exegetical Commentary*, 2:507.

290 Harrington, *The Gospel of Matthew*, 224.

291 Davies and Allison, *A Critical and Exegetical Commentary*, 2:507.

292 John Paul Heil, *Jesus Walking on the Sea*, AnBib 87 (Rome: Biblical Institute, 1981), 61.

293 Davies and Allison, *A Critical and Exegetical Commentary*, 2:507.

294 Johannes Schneider, "ἔρχομαι," *TDNT* 2:666-685; Nicholas G. Piotrowski, *Matthew's New David at the End of Exile: A Socio-Rhetorical Study of Scriptural Quotations*, NovTSup (Leiden: Brill, 2016), 65.

in the stilling of the storm, and the Old Testament background for their cry is found in Psalm 69 (especially vv. 1-2, 14-15) - the cry of those in danger of drowning.[295]

Jesus addresses Peter with the characteristic expression used by Matthew to describe the Twelve, ὀλιγόπιστε. Matthew's presentation of the disciples' faith is neither perfect nor absent, but it is "little" (see Matt 6:30; 8:26; 16:8; 17:20). This initial success of Peter and his subsequent failure provide the model of the "little faith" of the disciples for Matthew.[296] It is also appropriate for Matthew to communicate Jesus' saving power despite inadequate faith.[297] By saving Peter, Jesus calls him to a greater faith, and this saving act is the climax of this story of Peter walking on the water.[298]

The question εἰς τί ἐδίστασας, the same words for doubt διστάζω appears in the climactic scene in 28:16-20 also. Matthew portrays that some of the eleven disciples have "doubted" the presence of the risen Lord. Therefore, instead of having no faith, doubting is how Matthew presents the disciples' position, and also John the Baptist during his imprisonment (cf. Matt 11:2-6).

Matthew's sentence, *καὶ ἀναβάντων αὐτῶν εἰς τὸ πλοῖον ἐκόπασεν ὁ ἄνεμος* helps the story to return to Mark's version. While Mark 6:51 says *καὶ ἀνέβη πρὸς αὐτοὺς εἰς τὸ πλοῖον, καὶ ἐκόπασεν ὁ ἄνεμος*, Matthew's changes the subject to Jesus and Peter and the two co-ordinate clauses were vividly combined to form a single clause.[299] The wind ceased, and at this point Jesus had rejoined the disciples (cf. 14:22) after manifesting something of his true nature. Peter (cf. 14:29) has also returned to the safety of the boat.[300]

The image of the storm being stilled probably echoes Old Testament passages and Second Temple literature (Job 26:11-12; Ps 65:7; 89:9-10; 107:29; Sir 43:23).[301] Though the general admonition found in 4Q185 1:10 "Remember his miracles which he did in Egypt" is in relation to healing and exorcism, there are few "places where the Qumran texts mention signs and wonders in general" (e.g. 1QS 11:23; 4Q504 2:12; 6:1-11; 4Q392). There is also a brief reference to the miracle at the Red Sea set in the context of God's

295 Harrington, *The Gospel of Matthew*, 224.

296 Harrington, *The Gospel of Matthew*, 225.

297 Davies and Allison, *A Critical and Exegetical Commentary*, 2:509.

298 Heil, *Jesus Walking on the Sea*, 64; cf. Davies and Allison, *A Critical and Exegetical Commentary*, 2:507.

299 Cf. Davies and Allison, *A Critical and Exegetical Commentary*, 2:509.

300 Though Davies and Allison argue that Peter was not at the boat during this confession, and they understand the phrase "those in the boat" as excluding Peter. Davies and Allison, *A Critical and Exegetical Commentary*, 2:510; cf. Harrington, *The Gospel of Matthew*, 225.

301 Cf. Jonah 1:15, also compare 4Q381. Harrington, *The Gospel of Matthew*, 225; Davies and Allison, *A Critical and Exegetical Commentary*, 2:509-510.

past intervention; perhaps in a sense of the hope that God will do similar miracle in the great eschatological war that is to come.[302]

As Douglas R. A. Hare argues, the story of Jesus walking on the water in Matthew's Gospel must be interpreted from the Jewish context, but not from the Hellenistic context.[303] Hare also comments on the Greek mythology which contained stories about gods and heroes who displayed the ability to walk on water by virtue of their divine origin and relationship. The Gentile readers might see Jesus as being in the same class with these mythical heroes, and this kind of comparison might have been one of Matthew's intentions in this story.[304]

This approach from the Jewish context yields a very high Christology, that Jesus reveals himself to the disciples as a divine being or God. To support this reading, Jesus' statement to the terrified disciples "Take courage! ἐγώ εἰμι, have no fear," as previously highlighted, reflects the theophanic formula of Exodus 3:14 (I am who I am). These allusions make it clear that for Matthew, this story has christological implications and the portrayal of Jesus as the channel of divine power and authority is in line with his Jewish traditional cosmological worldview.

The same verb προσκυνέω appears also in 2:2, 8, 11, 8:2, 9:18, 15:25, 20:20, 28:9, 17. Matthew's disciples confess that Jesus is the Son of God at the conclusion of the story (cf. Matt 3:17, 16:16, 17:5, 27:54), whereas their heart was hardened and failed to understand according to Mark 6:52. To compare this ending of the story with that of sea rescue narratives in Exodus 14:31, Psalm 107:31-32, and Jonah 1:16 could yield another significant christological motif embedded in the story.[305]

Matthew's omission of Mark's "And they were utterly astounded, for they did not understand about the loaves, but their hearts were hardened" (Mark 6:51c-52) is understood as Matthew's redactional work to present the disciples in a more positive manner.[306] Unlike Mark, Matthew again molds the story in a way to emphasize Christology, and succeeds to do so by inserting christological affirmation. This editing helps the reader to focus more on Jesus than the disciples.[307]

The title "Son of God" in this confession is unmistakably not to be understood in terms of Jesus' wonder-working act, but to be connected with

302 Eric Eve, *The Jewish Context of Jesus' Miracles*, JSNTSup 231 (New York: SAP, 2002), 176.

303 Hare, *Matthew*, 168.

304 Cf. Hare, *Matthew*, 168.

305 Davies and Allison, *A Critical and Exegetical Commentary*, 2:510.

306 Davies and Allison, *A Critical and Exegetical Commentary*, 2:510.

307 Cf. Davies and Allison, *A Critical and Exegetical Commentary*, 2:510.

Jesus' unique status and identity. Instead of the miracle itself, Jesus who performs actions, which the Jewish tradition associates with God alone is a pointer for christological emphasis.[308] Though Matthew already mentioned the identity of Jesus as "the Son of God" in various places (2:15, 3:17, 4:3, 6, 8:29), it is here put on the lips of the disciples for the first time. The centrality of the christological title "Son of God" is seen in its connection to the recurring climaxes in Matthew's Gospel (3:17; 16:13-20; 26-28), and also by its connection with the inclusio that describes the ongoing "presence of God, or Jesus, with the eschatological community" (1:23; 28:20).[309]

In Matthew's Gospel, Jesus is the Son of God in the sense that his origin is in God (1:21), and he perfectly obeys his Father's will (4:1-11; ch. 27), and he also enjoys a unique filial relationship with the Father (11:25-30). The role of Jesus as Son of God is thus to be understood in terms of the presence of God with his eschatological community, and in the person of the Son, God becomes near, so as to dwell among the people (1:23; 28:20).[310] Joel Kennedy states that Jesus as the Son of God in Matthew's Gospel, when closely studied, reveals varied meanings beyond his filial relation to God.[311] Israel was called God's son in Exodus 4:22-23 and Hosea 11:1, and also the king of the earth (2 Sam 7:14; Ps 89:26-27). According to Kennedy, these elements are appropriated by Matthew in his overall Christology. He further argues that Matthew's use of the Son of God, especially in his early chapters "most directly relates to its prior use in the Old Testament in relation to corporate Israel as Son of God and to the king as a representative."[312] Thus, the use of the Son of God title by Matthew is connected to his use of Israel's history and the significant fulfilment theme that he made it prominent in the Gospel.[313]

The unfolding of Matthew's redactional work has also witnessed the disciples growing in knowledge, the growth that will mature in the pre-Easter narrative (16:16). Thus, Davies and Allison argue, "The disciples are beginning to catch up with the readers of the gospel."[314] The readers of the later part of

---

308 Heil, *Jesus Walking on the Sea*, 67; Davies and Allison, *A Critical and Exegetical Commentary*, 2:510.

309 David R. Bauer, *The Structure of Matthew's Gospel: A Study in Literary Design*, BAC (London: Bloomsbury Academics, 2015), 145.

310 Bauer, *The Structure of Matthew's Gospel*, 145.

311 Joel Kennedy, *The Recapitulation of Israel: Use of Israel's History in Matthew 1:1-4:11*, WUNT 257 (Tübingen: Mohr Siebeck, 2008), 6. Luz, *Studies in Matthew*, 93-96, argues that the Son of God title in Matthew's Gospel is both confessional title (vertical dimension) and ethical title (horizontal title).

312 Kennedy, *The Recapitulation of Israel*, 6-7.

313 Jack D. Kingsbury, *Matthew: Structure, Christology, Kingdom* (Philadelphia, PA: Fortress, 1975), 15, 51.

314 Davies and Allison, *A Critical and Exegetical Commentary*, 2:510.

the first century were probably acquainted with a more developed Christology, and that development is followed by the disciples in Matthew's Gospel.

### *6.5.3. Cosmic Christology in the Passage*

Both Matthew and Mark focus on the manifestation of Jesus in their walking on the water narrative. The similarity is seen in their wording and in emphasis to a large extent. Matthew's depiction of Jesus (so also Mark) as the one who does what God does suggests a divine identity for Jesus.[315] The main difference is marked by the portrayal of the disciples in Matthew's Gospel, and the insertion of the episode where Peter walks on the water. The disciples in Matthew's narrative come to the conclusion that Jesus is the Son of God (Matt 14:33), unlike in Mark's Gospel where their hearts remain hardened (Mark 6:52).[316]

However, the sub-theme of discipleship as seen in the stories of the stilling of the storm and the feeding of the five thousand may not be easily discerned in the story without Matthew's addition of Peter's walking on the water. France argues that Jesus' walking on the water is a record of a spectacular instance of his supernatural power and nothing much to do on the lesson in discipleship.[317] It is true that only in Matthew's addition of Peter's experience, rather than in the actual miracle, that an element of thematic interest is present.[318] Therefore this miracle story is a crucial passage for Matthew to communicate the unique identity of Jesus, and is significant to understand Matthew's Christology and also of the Early Church. Matthew informs Jesus' identity with careful and deliberate intertextual quotations and allusions to the Old Testament and Second Temple Literature.

The Old Testament backdrop of the motif of God walking upon the water and the concept of ἐγώ εἰμι, and the disciples' response provide an implicit symbol of "the Creator's control over the unruly forces" of the nature.[319] Carter also argues that Jesus does a "Godlike act" and manifest God's reign over the sea.[320] The portrayal of Jesus as God's son is to recognize him as the agent God has commissioned to reveal God's saving presence and sovereignty.[321] The focus of this miracle story is given on the identity of Jesus, the manifestation of a person who does what God does and speaks as God speaks. Jesus enjoys

315 Harrington, *The Gospel of Matthew*, 225.

316 Harrington, *The Gospel of Matthew*, 225.

317 France, *The Gospel of Matthew*, 566.

318 Cf. France, *The Gospel of Matthew*, 567.

319 France, *The Gospel of Matthew*, 566.

320 Carter, *Matthew and the Margins*, 311-312. Carter lists five "Godlike acts" attributed to Jesus in the story: "walking on water, talking as God, extending his hand, saving from water, calming the storm."

321 Carter, *Matthew and the Margins*, 312.

a special relationship with God, and his possession of sovereignty over the created world makes it clear that the Christology here could be interpreted as cosmic Christology.

France argues that "It is possible to discern several echoes of OT language about God in what is said about Jesus in this pericope as a whole."[322] Rachel Nicholls also sees this miracle story as an allusion to the story of creation and the crossing of the Red Sea, by saying that "the storm recalls the wind, the darkness and the deep which form the scenery" in these events.[323] These events are the "pivotal moments of creation and redemption" in the Old Testament.[324] She further argues that the one who walks on the water and says ἐγώ εἰμι is to be connected with the one "who is to come" (Rev 1:17-18) and whose coming will transform all things (Rev 21:1-16). Therefore, it is significant to see that Matthew's Christology here can be interpreted as cosmic in nature, and envisages all things.

France argues that ἐγώ εἰμι is the most natural form of self-identification, and to trace the divine name in every New Testament use of this common phrase would produce absurd results.[325] He finds it less plausible despite the numinous setting in the story, and changes his suggestion that ἐγώ εἰμι is "an echo of the divine name in Exodus 3:14," a connection between the one who has power over the sea with God who made it.[326] Davies and Allison also regard the "divine name" interpretation as probable.[327] However, Bruner also argues that Jesus' "I am" is not just an everyday self-identification formula, but a divine self-revelation along the lines of Isaiah 43:1-4:

> But now thus says the LORD, he who created you, O Jacob, he who formed you, O Israel: *Do not fear*, for I have redeemed you; I have called you by name, you are mine. When you passed through the waters, I will be with you; and through the rivers, they shall not overwhelm you; ...For I am the LORD your God, the Holy One of Israel, your Savior, ...and I love you (NRSV).[328]

322 France, *The Gospel of Matthew*, 567.

323 Rachel Nicholls, *Walking on the Water: Reading MT. 14:22-33 in the Light of its Wirkungsgeschichte* (Leiden: Brill, 2008), 195.

324 Nicholls, *Walking on the Water*, 195.

325 France, *The Gospel of Matthew*, 569-570.

326 France, *The Gospel of Matthew*, 570.

327 Davies and Allison, *A Critical and Exegetical Commentary*, 2:506.

328 "I am" in combination with the "fear not" has the aura of God's ancient comforting of the people. "Fear not, for I am..." (Gen 15:1; 26:14; 28:13; 46:3, Isa 41:13). Bruner, *The Churchbook*, 75; cf. Luz, *Matthew 8-20*, 408.

Luz, Davies and Allison also agree that the church's later doctrine of the divine nature of Jesus is already seen in this story.[329] Therefore, to see the phrase ἐγώ εἰμι as having connotation with divinity is appropriate, especially considering the emphasis of Jesus' identity and authority in the story. The associations of walking on the water and stilling of the storm in comparison with God's speaking of oneself as ἐγώ εἰμι in the LXX (Isa 41:4; 43:10, 25; 46:4; 51:12) also supported cosmic Christology.[330]

As Carter also points out, the phrase "fear not" usually follows the appearances or words of angels or God as an assurance that God's purposes are good to human beings (cf. Gen 15:1, Isa 42:1-2, 5, 43:2, 3, 11, 15, 25).[331] God's uttering of "I am" to Moses appears before the exodus (Exod 3:14), and during the exile in anticipation to the second exodus and return home (Isa 41:4, 43:10, 47:8, 10). Thus, for Carter, "I am" reveals God's saving presence in circumstances of distress, and this is also evident in Jesus' commission in Matthew 1:21 and 11:25-27.[332]

Matthew's addition of Peter's walking on the water again points to the divinity of Jesus. It is not clear if the story may have been handed down to Matthew as special Peter's tradition or not, the rich background it carries cannot be ignored. The parallelism in regards to a person in danger of drowning and the divine rescue of such a person opens up the emphasis intended in the story.[333] Peter's addressing Jesus as Lord and asking permission (command me) to imitate him in walking on the water also point towards the recognition of Jesus as manifesting and participating in God's rule over all creation.[334]

The appearance of Peter's proposal to Jesus may not be intended to be taken as a model for others, rather perhaps it is Matthew's cautionary remarks for the idea of testing God (cf. Matt 4:5-7).[335] France observes that Matthew's peculiar emphasis on Peter's leading role does not always appear as a model to be followed (cf. Matt 15:15; 16:17-19; 17:24-27; 18:21).[336] When Jesus rescues Peter from drowning, Matthew's language ἐκτείνας τὴν χεῖρα ἐπελάβετο αὐτοῦ could be read in connection with God's extended hand that delivers people from oppressive slavery in Exodus 3:20; 7:5 and from water and other difficulties in Psalm 144:7 (cf. Pss 18:16; 107:28, 30). This adds to the impression that Jesus

329 Luz, *Matthew 8-20*, 408; Davies and Allison, *A Critical and Exegetical Commentary*, 2:512; cf. Bruner, *The Churchbook*, 76.

330 Talbert, *Matthew*, 185-186.

331 Carter, *Matthew and the Margins*, 310.

332 Carter, *Matthew and the Margins*, 310.

333 Harrington, *The Gospel of Matthew*, 226.

334 Carter, *Matthew and the Margins*, 311.

335 France, *The Gospel of Matthew*, 567-568.

336 France, *The Gospel of Matthew*, 568.

acts as God acts in the Old Testament.[337] Moses also stretches out his hand in liberating the people (Exod 4:4; 8:5, 6; 9:22 etc.), and "the phrase "stretch out one's hand" can also signify acts of danger from which humans need saving by God's outstretched hand (Gen 3:22; 22:10-11)."[338] Thus, Carter sees this expression as God's action, and states:

> Jesus again does what God does (cf. walking on the water [14:25-26]; talking as God (14:27]). He continues to manifest God's empire in showing God's sovereignty over the world God created. Extending his hand enables Jesus to accomplish a further action of God. God saves distressed people from water... As Immanuel, so does Jesus.[339]

The "Son of God" phrase which is seen in Jesus' special relationship with the Father in Matthew 11:25-27 and other references made by Jesus (Matt 7:21; 10:32-33; 12:50) may well serve as reminder to spontaneously address Jesus as Son of God.[340] The continuation of this remark in the story from "what kind of a person is this?" in the concluding remark of the stilling of the storm is what makes Davies and Allison to comment "The disciples are beginning to catch up with the reader of the gospel."[341] Hare also states that this remark could be paraphrased as "Now we are convinced that the messianic claim implicit in the feeding miracle was indeed justified."[342] A similar confession is given by the soldiers responsible for crucifying Jesus later in the Gospel (Matt 27:54). Davies and Allison add "What matters is not that Jesus has done the seemingly impossible but that he has performed action which the Old Testament associates with Yahweh alone."[343] Therefore it is significant to accommodate this confession here to identify Jesus, without absurdity fits the overall christological framework of Matthew.

Ben Witherington is contented to see Matthew as a scribe in the Jewish sapiential tradition, and sees this miracle story as resembling that of Wisdom (Sir 24:5-6).[344] He finds Matthew as portraying Jesus as both the wise sage and wisdom itself. James D. G. Dunn criticizes Witherington's commentary

---

337 France, *The Gospel of Matthew*, 571; Gundry, *Matthew*, 300; Carter, *Matthew and the Margins*, 311.

338 Carter, *Matthew and the Margins*, 311.

339 Carter, *Matthew and the Margins*, 311.

340 France, *The Gospel of Matthew*, 571-572.

341 Davies and Allison, *A Critical and Exegetical Commentary*, 2:510.

342 Hare, *Matthew*, 171.

343 Davies and Allison, *A Critical and Exegetical Commentary*, 2:510.

344 Ben Witherington, *Matthew*, SHBC 19 (Macon, GA: Smyth & Helwys, 2006), 1, 20, 245, 338-339, argues that Matthew's Gospel deliberately presents a sapiential portrait of Jesus that is guided by the Solomonic tradition. Cf. E. Anne Clements, *Mothers of the Margin?*

on *Matthew* on the ground that it is more popular than technical, but he acknowledges its unique role of contribution.[345] For Witherington, Matthew understands "his task as interpreting and presenting the life and teachings of Jesus as revelatory wisdom from God," or plainly as the incarnation of God's wisdom.[346] Thus, he suggests that Matthew "so sees his task as interpreting and presenting the life and teaching of Jesus as revelatory wisdom from God."[347] Robert P. Vanda Kappelle in his 2014 book *Wisdom Revealed: The Message of Biblical Wisdom Literature – Then and Now*, also argues that "sapiential thinking and Jewish wisdom literature were important influences" for Matthew's Christology.[348] The present discussion, in addition with these arguments concretizes Matthew's Christology in this miracle story as high Christology.

### *6.5.4. The Rhetorical Purpose of the Passage*

The underestimation of Jesus' cosmic authority over natural elements is again one of the points that could be made out from this passage. Matthew's use of "little faith" is also to be understood in this conceptual framework. Matthew's presentation of the disciples' fear of ghost may serve as the reason why it had not occurred to the disciples that "Jesus could know their plight, walk on water to come to them, or catch up with them in a storm!"[349] However the fear subsides after they recognize Jesus. Matthew's presentation of the story makes it clear that the disciples are improving in the way they perceive Jesus because after knowing the one who came to them, perhaps they also know by now that Jesus would take them through the storm.

From this narrative Peter became more prominent in Matthew's Gospel (10:2; 14:28-31; 15:15; 17:24-27; 18:21).[350] Davies and Allison also suggest

---

*The Significance of the Women in Matthew's Genealogy* (Eugene, OR: Pickwick, 2014), 172.

345 James D. G. Dunn, "How did Matthew go about Composing his Gospel?" in *Jesus, Matthew's Gospel and Early Christianity: Studies in Memory of Graham Stanton*, ed. Daniel M. Gurtner, Joel Willits and Richard A. Burridge (New York: T&T Clark, 2011), 39-58 (35).

346 Witherington, *Matthew*, 7; cf. Daniel M. Gurtner, "The Gospel of Matthew from Stanton to Present" in *Jesus, Matthew's Gospel and Early Christianity: Studies in Memory of Graham N. Stanton*, ed. Daniel M. Gurtner, Joel Willitts and Richard A. Burridge (New York: T&T Clark, 2011), 23-38 (35).

347 Witherington, *Matthew*, 1.

348 Robert P. Vanda Kappelle, *Wisdom Revealed: The Message of Biblical Wisdom Literature – Then and Now* (Eugene, OR: Wipf & Stock, 2014), 198; cf. Ben Witherington, *Letters and Homilies for Jewish Christians: A Socio-Rhetorical Commentary on Hebrews, James and Jude* (Downers Grove, IL: IVP, 2007), 486.

349 Keener, *A Commentary on the Gospel of Matthew*, 407.

350 France, *The Gospel of Matthew*, 253-254.

that this pericope may have foreshadows Peter's later overconfidence at Gethsemane (26:30-35) and denial at Jesus' trial (26:69-75). They also suggest that from this point onward Matthew begins to single out the character of Peter due to his significant relation to the church (16:15-20).[351] Peter's walking on the water was first his own idea (14:28), and was approved by Jesus' response (14:29). Thus Jesus' reproving Peter was not the outcome of Peter stepping out from the boat but it stems out from the doubt that arises even in the presence of Jesus.[352] Keener sees this stepping out from the boat as being an allusion to the priests under Joshua's leadership who led the Israelites to cross the river Jordan (Josh 3:8, 13, 15-17).[353] As Joshua's company trust God, here also Peter is presupposed to be more trusting to Jesus, who had performed so many miracles during their time together. Therefore, Matthew while emphasizing the cosmic Christology did not fail to address the theme of discipleship. Matthew contends to portray that it is always better to look on God's power for sustenance rather than looking to the natural circumstances.

Peter's failure when walking on water is specifically stated by Matthew as the fear of natural circumstances. Rather than trusting on Jesus' cosmic authority, which was already witnessed in the stilling of the storm and feeding miracle, but the initial fear was transferred into a cry for help. Matthew's progressive development of the disciples' faith became clearer in this narrative.[354] The significance however needs to be aligned to the framework of cosmic Christology. To trust the one who possess authority over the cosmos, and even under challenging circumstances to call upon the same. Thus the first confession is suitably inserted by Matthew in this pericope. The messianic implication implicitly witnessed in the story of the feeding miracle is made explicit in this story, especially with the confession added here by Matthew.

## 6.6. Application for Eco-Theology

The belief in relationships among Supreme Being, human beings and nature is a well-known Tribal concept. Human beings and nature are interdependent and maintain close relationship, but the concept gradually changes among the

351 Davies and Allison, *A Critical and Exegetical Commentary*, 2:513-514; cf. Keener, *A Commentary on the Gospel of Matthew*, 407.

352 Keener, *A Commentary on the Gospel of Matthew*, 407.

353 There are opinions that suggested Buddhist parallel for walking on water but the lack of literary correspondences and chronologically questionable arguments, and without mentioning geographical differences make not much sense. Though there are closer Hellenistic parallels and second century Jewish parallels, Joshua's parallel best suited the pericope. Keener, *A Commentary on the Gospel of Matthew*, 407.

354 Keener, *A Commentary on the Gospel of Matthew*, 407.

Mizos after the coming of Christianity and modern development.[355] The giving up of belief in the association among the spirit with natural elements is caused mainly by the condemnation of such acts as superstitious by the early Christian missionaries.[356] The traditional close attachment to natural world ceases and nature becomes mere resources for manipulation and exploitation. However, ecological crisis is still thought of as unserious problem by the majority. This is mainly due to the assumption that poverty and political injustice are seen as the core problem.[357]

The ecological crisis is the outcome mainly of modern industrial and technological growth, and modern lifestyle. The western industrial growth is almost universally accepted as a paradigm of development. This pattern of development evidently resulted in "ruthless exploitation of nature and fellow beings."[358] Samuel Rayan also argues that people's primary objective to maximize profit and competition are the main cause of environmental degradation.[359]

"Eco-Theology seeks to uncover the theological basis for a proper relationship between God, humanity and the cosmos."[360] It is important to read these nature miracles precisely under the framework of Matthew's cosmic Christology so as to rediscover the relationship between the creator, nature and human beings. The reflection of the creation theology is clearly found in the way how Matthew narrates the stories of nature miracles. Especially the Priestly account in Genesis chapter 2, where there is a depiction of creation coming out of chaos. There is also a depiction of the creator God as having the ability "to bring out order and harmony out of turmoil and confusion."[361] The meaning of the story of Jesus' calming the storm provides multi-leveled understanding. The setting that is the darkness of the evening and the chaos at

355 Cf. Yiepetso Wezah and Tereso C. Casino, "Towards a Relevant Theology of Nature: North-East India Tribal Perspective," *TTJ* 14 (2011): 99-115.

356 Wezah and Casino, "Towards a Relevant Theology of Nature," 99-100.

357 Cf. K. C. Abraham, "A Theological Response to the Ecological Crisis," in *Ecotheology: Voices from South and North, ed. David G. Hallman* (Geneva: WCC Publications, 1994), 65-78. (65).

358 K. C. Abraham, *Eco-Justice: A New Paradigm for Church Mission* (Bombay: BUILD, n.d.), 4-5, cited by Wezah and Casino, "Towards a Relevant Theology of Nature," 100.

359 Samuel Rayan, "Ecological Dimension of Our Faith: To Care for the Earth," in *Towards a Theology of Nature* (Madras: Gurukul Lutheran Theological College and Research Institute, 1991), 5, cited by Wezah and Casino, "Towards a Relevant Theology of Nature," 100.

360 Celia Deane-Drummond, *Eco-Theology* (Winona, MN: St. Mary's Press, 2008), xii.

361 Brennan R. Hill, *Christian Faith and the Environment: Making Vital Connections, Ecology and Justice Series* (Eugene, OR: Wipf & Stock, 2006), 82.

the Sea of Galilee, the disciples' panic and Jesus who was sleeping, all depicts the creation from chaos.

The chaotic situation was resolved by the creator and so did Jesus during the storm. The degradation of nature due to the understanding of dominion can be restructured by seeing the relationship between Jesus and natural elements. Therefore, it is important to see the relevancy of nature miracles in developing eco-theology because there are numbers of verses and ideas that could be utilized.

Churches in Mizoram, do considerably well in evangelism and sending out missionaries to different parts of India and also to the world, but the concern for eco-justice is insignificant. As political justice and social justice are linked closely to ecological issue, it is senseless to simply condemn Jhum cultivation. Without providing alternative energy sources, it is impossible to survive especially for the rural marginalized people. Unless the villagers have alternate sources of food and basic needs like fuel, they will continue to destroy whatever natural environment is around them.[362] The churches' teaching on the subject of ecology cannot achieve proper results mainly due to the lack of theological thrust. As greed is identified as the sources of the problem of ecology, more thought has to be given by the church to link theology with ecology. The ascetic or monastic model proposed by K. C. Abraham which is to live in harmony with nature and keeping needs to a minimum is a relevant model to be adopted for the church.[363] The motif of twelve baskets of leftovers warns against waste and responsibility to nature.[364] The wasteful life-style of the rich and the irresponsible use of natural resources are adding more burden to the ecosystem.[365]

Another model called Sacramental/Eucharistic model sees "Life and all its relationships are thought to the worshipful presence of God, where they are constantly being renewed."[366] As all things are received as gifts, they are meant to be shared which is clearly seen in the feeding miracles. Even when the miraculous is set aside the sharing is still to be signified. The Eucharist is seen mainly as a ritual observance of the partaking the flesh and blood of Jesus Christ, but is hardly acknowledge as the imperative of sharing. According to Abraham if this dynamic character of Eucharist is recovered, people could be motivated to be open to God's creation and re-creation.[367] As Psalm 148 affirms the cosmic setting of worship, the feeding miracles also signify the

362 Abraham, "A Theological Response to the Ecological Crisis," 69.

363 Abraham, "A Theological Response to the Ecological Crisis," 73.

364 Hare, *Matthew*, 167.

365 Abraham, "A Theological Response to the Ecological Crisis," 67.

366 Abraham, "A Theological Response to the Ecological Crisis," 72.

367 Abraham, "A Theological Response to the Ecological Crisis," 72.

cosmic nature of Jesus' action. Looking up to heaven and blessing the natural elements and the collection of waste all signifies the cosmic linkage of all creation.

## 6.7. Summary

The approach is to set aside the historicity of these miracle stories and to focus instead on what the narrative meant to Matthew. Within Matthew's Gospel, narrative drives theology, therefore it is important to understand the place of a pericope within the story in order to understand its function. Matthew 14:22-33 is clearly focused on the question of Jesus' identity. Matthew also demonstrates an early belief in Jesus' divinity through his use of allusion, and his "Son of God" language is a christological confession intended to unite Jew and Gentile readers.[368]

While Matthew does not have the more fully developed incarnational Christology that is found in John's Gospel or cosmic Christology found in Pauline corpus, he seems to move further in that direction when compared with Mark and Luke. At Jesus' baptism, Matthew adds the designation "Son of God" to the names already ascribed in chapter 1. It is not agreed however that whether for Matthew this identification in this particular pericope necessarily entails divinity. In this context it could be understood or heard as a reference to kingship. There are arguments that "sonship" in Matthew's Christology is functional rather than ontological.[369] Functional in a sense, Jesus is the son of God because he is obedient. A connection is also to be found in Psalm 2, a royal psalm which is composed for a coronation. Verse 7 says, "You are my son; today I have begotten you."[370]

The identification of three forms of dualism in Matthew's Gospel in a monograph *Apocalyptic Eschatology in the Gospel of Matthew* by David C. Sim seems relevant here.[371] Firstly, an historical dualism where the present age and age to come are sharply distinguished. Secondly, a cosmic dualism that divides "the cosmos or supernatural realm" into two opposing forces. Thirdly, human dualism which divides the righteous and the wicked in human sphere.[372] Nature miracles in Matthew's Gospel come in contact with this proposed second dualism. What John K. Riches thinks about Sim's second dualism is

368 Gurtner, "The Gospel of Matthew from Stanton to Present," 23-38.

369 Anna Case-Winters, *Matthew: A Theological Commentary on the Bible,* Belief (Louisville: WJK, 2015), 33.

370 Cf. Case-Winters, *Matthew*, 33.

371 David C. Sim, *Apocalyptic Eschatology in the Gospel of Matthew* (Cambridge: CUP, 1966), 35-41.

372 Sim, *Apocalyptic Eschatology*, 35; cf. John K. Riches, *Conflicting Mythologies: Identity Formation in the Gospels of Mark and Matthew*, SNTW (Edinburgh: T&T Clark, 2000), 265-266.

significant. He states the difficulty to differentiate precisely the dualism of the human world and the supernatural world. According to Riches, the cause of human wrong-doing could or could not be independent, or a causation of the actions of cosmic forces of evil.[373] He sees that the human dualism and cosmic dualism intertwines especially in the explanation of the parable of the weeds (Matthew 13:36-43).[374] He further argues that Sim's argument that "The righteous are good only in so far as they have aligned themselves with Jesus and his forces in the cosmic struggle" is confusing, especially when viewed under Matthew's understanding of the final judgment.[375]

However, what is important to note here is how Sim understands the role of Jesus and his forces in the cosmic struggle. Matthew's presentation of Jesus in the stories of nature miracles can also be interpreted under this thought. The stilling of the storm and walking on the water may be seen as highlighting the battle between cosmic forces over natural elements. But, the exegesis shows that these natural elements are not presented explicitly as opposing forces to Jesus, but instead the intimate relationship between Jesus and the cosmos is shown. Still, the idea of cosmic Christology is seen repeatedly in these stories of nature miracles. Therefore, it is noteworthy that Matthew moves further than Mark and Luke in the direction of ascribing divinity to Jesus. The stories of nature miracles that are being analyzed serve as pointers for Jesus' divinity, and his cosmic authority. Jesus' incarnation is taken up by John, and Paul also presented a more developed cosmic Christology in his letters.

---

373 Riches, *Conflicting Mythologies*, 267.

374 Riches, *Conflicting Mythologies*, 267.

375 Riches states that what Sim is claiming is not clear. Is it that Matthew views those who do the will of God, but not consciously "aligned with Jesus and his forces in the cosmic struggle, as not good." Riches, *Conflicting Mythologies*, 268.

Chapter 7

# Nature Miracles and Cosmic Christology in Matthew Contextual Implication for Theology of Nature

## 7.1. Introduction

Historians in the discipline of cosmology broadly distinguish three great eras in the history of cosmology: pre-modern, modern and post-modern cosmologies.[1] Pre-modern cosmologies could be understood as lasting up to the seventeenth century, and may be briefly described as being hierarchical, organic, patriarchal, static, fixed and respectful in their relationship towards nature. Modern cosmologies that started from the seventeenth century and lasted up to the middle of the twentieth century could be summed up as being mechanistic, materialistic, reductionist, atomistic and dominating in their relationship with nature. The third era in cosmology is at present in the struggling stage to come to be discussed in any precise manners. However, this post-modern cosmology could not neglect the need for a better relationship with nature.

The cosmology in Matthew's Gospel has been functioning in an ordered unity especially in the narratives of nature miracles. The cosmic context of Christ-event is seen in the languages used by Matthew. Heaven and earth, angels and spirits, earthquakes, wind and storm, above and below, these are just small examples of how Christ-event is presented in a cosmic context.[2] Matthew's frequent use of cosmological language "serves to create and

---

1 Dermot A. Lane, "The Doctrine of the Incarnation: Human and Cosmic Considerations," in *Contemporary Catholic Theology: A Reader*, ed. Michael A. Hayes and Liam Gearon (New York: Continuum, 2000), 209-233 (224).

2 Lane, "The Doctrine of the Incarnation," 227.

establish a theological worldview, one that finds its foundation in Genesis and its consummation in the new Genesis inaugurated by Jesus Christ."[3] Jonathan T. Pennington argues that a variety of cosmological terms that are found in Matthew's Gospel contain strong theological point. And the theme of heaven and earth is central to Matthew's cosmological language.[4] Matthew's understanding of cosmology is closely related to that of Genesis, and shapes his Christology. Thus, for Matthew "the entirety of creation and God's dealings with his creation are consummated in the God-man who took on created flesh, Jesus the Christ."[5]

New Testament Christology is creational but the christological thinking during the modern era of cosmology might be argued as being anthropocentric and ecclesiological. According to Dermot A. Lane, "the missing link in modern Christology has been the absence of a living cosmology."[6] Study on miracle stories in the Gospels and ancient world must focus on miracle stories within their own cultural context or within the cosmological worldview of the tellers of these stories.[7] Instead of reading back the contemporary cosmological worldview into the ancient world, it is thus more appropriate to probe into the miracle stories in order to find out their functions within the ancient world of early Christianity. Therefore, the challenge is to redress the imbalance in New Testament Christology, but not at the expense of anthropological and ecclesiological emphasis.

## 7.2. Miracles and Christology in Matthew's Gospel

The key motif in the healing and nature miracle stories is the focus on Jesus' incomparable power and authority.[8] The healing miracles are important for Matthew's Christology, and the titles "Son of God" and "Servant" portray Jesus as compassionate healer and gentle servant of God. This helps Matthew to be able to define the manner in which Jesus is the exalted Son of God.[9]

The most significant study of miracle stories in Matthew's Gospel was that of Heinz J. Held's article "Matthew as Interpreter of the Miracle Stories."[10]

---

3 Jonathan T. Pennington, "Heaven, Earth, and a New Genesis: Theological Cosmology in Matthew," in *Cosmology and New Testament Theology*, ed. Jonathan T. Pennington and Sean M. McDonough (London: T&T Clark, 2008), 28-44 (28).

4 Pennington, "Heaven, Earth, and a New Genesis," 44.

5 Pennington, "Heaven, Earth, and a New Genesis," 44.

6 Lane, "The Doctrine of the Incarnation," 227.

7 Elaine M. Wainwright, *Towards a Feminist Critical Reading of the Gospel According to Matthew* (Berlin: de Gruyter, 1991), 92.

8 Donald Senior, *The Gospel of Matthew*, IBT (Nashville: Abingdon Press, 1997), 61.

9 Senior, *The Gospel of Matthew*, 61.

10 Heinz J. Held, "Matthew as Interpreter of the Miracle Stories," in *Tradition and Interpretation in Matthew*, ed. G. Bornkamm, G. Barth and H. J. Held; trans. Percy Scott

Held thinks that after surveying Matthew's miracle stories, "it is plain that the message they contain... to Matthew the miracle story is the bearer of a doctrine."[11] He primarily intended to explain the evangelist's intention in retelling the miracle stories by comparing them with the other Synoptic Gospels. Held is right in seeing the collection of miraculous deeds of Jesus as having christological function.[12] Thus, Held holds that Jesus is not only presented as the Messiah of word, but also presented as the Messiah of the deed, especially by the miracle stories.[13]

From a feminist point of view, especially while studying healing miracles, this attention to theological themes obscure the gender reality of the character involved in the stories.[14] This kind of method could best be attributed to the work of Gerd Theissen who deals with the existential function of the early Christian miracle stories.[15] Antoinette Wire further moves this approach forward to come up with a category she calls "demand story" within the healing miracle stories.[16] Such an approach may allow specific attention to the socio-religious marginalization of women which was overcome in the healing miracle stories.[17] However, these are not highlighted to be taken up in this study, but only to highlight the possibility of reading miracle stories within a specific approach that could lead to various understandings. When looking at the nature miracle stories, the approach that seeks to understand the underlying function and embedded themes best suited the study.

Matthew 8-9 does not only have a christological function, but also serves to highlight the themes of faith and discipleship, and similar indication is seen in nature miracle stories. The stilling of the storm has Christology as its main theme, but also highlights other themes or contains other sub-themes, such as faith and discipleship. By the positioning of the miracle stories right after the two sayings of Jesus on the subject of discipleship (Matt 8:19-22), and an addition of Jesus' "Why are you afraid, you of little faith?" (Matt 8:26), Matthew reinterprets traditional materials and enhanced them to develop his

(Philadelphia: Westminster, 1963), 242-245.

11 Held, "Matthew as Interpreter of the Miracle Stories," 210, 219.

12 Held, "Matthew as Interpreter of the Miracle Stories," 246-247.

13 Evert-Jan Vledder, *Conflicts in the Miracle Stories: A Socio-Exegetical Study of Matthew 8 and 9*, JSNTSup 152 (Sheffield: T&T Clark, 1997), 31.

14 Wainwright, *Towards a Feminist Critical Reading of the Gospel According to Matthew*, 93.

15 Gerd Theissen, *The Miracle Stories of the Early Christian Tradition*, trans. Francis McDonagh (Philadelphia: Fortress, 1983).

16 Antoinette Wire, "The Structure of the Gospel Miracle Stories and their Tellers," *Semeia* 11 (1978): 83-118.

17 Wainwright, *Towards a Feminist Critical Reading of the Gospel According to Matthew*, 94.

purpose. Apart from which this miracle story points directly to christological concern, the Christology that has significance connection with Matthew's cosmological framework. The feeding miracle stories though function as messianic banquet; also contain the theme of discipleship. This makes it clear that Matthew's reinterpretation of miracle stories revolves on a broader scope. Though Matthew does not provide explicit christological conclusion, John later develops the function of the story by placing Jesus' "Bread of Life" discourse shortly after the feeding miracle. The messianic allusion and the authority to multiply natural elements could be understood as christological functioning of the feeding miracle stories. Again the story of Jesus' walking on the water is embedded with extra function. Though the theme of faith may seem to be prominent, the christological theme is clearly presented by Matthew. Especially, Peter's confession in the miracle story provided solid basis to argue that Matthew reinterpreted the story to make the christological theme come to the fore front.

Different titles of Jesus helped develop Matthew's Christology, and so did the miracle stories. Birger Gerdhardsson who divides miracle stories into two categories, such as therapeutic miracles and non-therapeutic miracles argues that the therapeutic miracles are worked for the people outside Jesus' group.[18] He further argues that the non-therapeutic miracles are worked for the disciples as a group or individual.[19] However, it is difficult to categorize the feeding miracles under this scheme, but the arching christological theme in all the nature miracle stories is significant. It is also important to note what Gerhardsson has pointed out, that in all these non-therapeutic miracles, the "unknown sides of Jesus' *exousia* are revealed."[20] Though healing miracles are successfully unearthed to develop Matthew's Christology, an attempt of this study on nature miracles could provide more information generally for Matthew's Christology and particularly a basis for cosmic Christology in Matthew's Gospel.

## 7.3. Cosmology and Christology in Matthew's Gospel

As noted before, discussions of Matthew's Christology have often focused the meaning and use of titles in the Gospel. The usefulness cannot be neglected, but it has to be understood that titles represent only a single element in a complex narrative.[21] Luz argues that "the Matthean story of Jesus functions

18 Birger Gerhardsson, *The Mighty Acts of Jesus According to Matthew* (Eugene, OR: Wipf & Stock, 1979), 54.

19 Gerhardsson, *The Mighty Acts of Jesus According to Matthew*, 54.

20 Gerhardsson, *The Mighty Acts of Jesus According to Matthew*, 60.

21 John K. Riches, *Conflicting Mythologies: Identity Formation in the Gospels of Mark and Matthew*, SNTW (Edinburgh: T&T Clark, 2000), 273.

as the predicate and redefines the meaning of the traditional titles."[22] Thus, John K. Riches rightly concludes "that in the end it is the narrative, which determines the meaning of the titles, rather than the titles which give meaning to the narrative."[23]

The title Son of God in Matthew's Gospel is interconnected with his cosmological framework. The title is employed in the major events of Jesus' baptism (Matt 3:17), at Peter's confession at Caesarea Philippi (Matt 16:16), at the Transfiguration (Matt 17:5), at the Trial (Matt 26:63), and Crucifixion (Matt 27:40, 54). When Jesus walks on the water, the disciples cried out in fear and they thought they saw a ghost, and then Jesus replied "Take courage! I am (he). Do not be afraid."

The Old Testament and the Second Temple Judaism provide foundational background for cosmological understanding in Matthew's Gospel. Matthew's description of the sea, the fear and the awestruck of the disciples, and the action of Jesus in the story of the calming of the storm clearly depict the intertextual dependence on these older traditions. Matthew's deliberate use of the word "earthquake" to describe the storm, the word that has eschatological overtones of God's action intensifies the perilous situation, and also exhibits the authority of Jesus. The one who is capable of controlling cosmological elements, and the one who acts as Yahweh did in the Old Testament is a portrayal of Jesus in Matthew's Gospel.

In the story of Jesus' walking on the water, it is possible to discern several echoes of Old Testament language about God which are attributed to Jesus. The allusion to creation story and the crossing of the Red Sea is vividly portrayed. The storm may recall the wind, the darkness and the deep which form the scenery of these Old Testament events. Jesus, by walking on the water and saying ἐγώ εἰμι is hard to be disconnected with the one "who is to come" in Revelation 1:17-18 and the one whose coming will transform all things in Revelation 21:1-16.

Other cosmological language which is not found in nature miracles is one of the favourite word pairs for Matthew. "Heaven and earth" word pair can take a number of forms, such as copulative, thematic, and implied.[24] All these three types of the heaven and earth word pair are found in Matthew's

22 Ulrich Luz, "Eine thetische Skizze der Matthäischen Christologie," in *Anfänge der Christologie* (ed. C. Breytenbach and H. Paulsen; Göttingen: Vanderhoeck & Ruprecht, 1991), 221-235, quoted by Riches, *Conflicting Mythologies*, 273.

23 Riches, *Conflicting Mythologies*, 273, citing Luz, "Eine thetische Skizze der Matthäischen Christologie," 223.

24 Jonathan T. Pennington, *Heaven and Earth in the Gospel of Matthew*, NovTSup 126 (Leiden: Brill, 2007), 194. Copulative pairs are examples where "heaven and earth" appears as one unit, and not separated by prepositions or other words. Thematic pairs use a combination of heaven and earth but with some separation of intervening words or

Gospel. There are three instances where Matthew uses copulative word pairs (5:18; 11:25; and 24:35). In 5:18 and 24:35, Jesus speaks about the passing away of heaven and earth, which could be alluded to the beginning of creation in Genesis 1:1. Jesus addresses the Father as "Lord of heaven and earth" in 11:25 is a reminiscent to the Second Temple literature.[25] The cosmological frameworks of both the Second Temple literature and Matthew's Gospel are conforming to each other quite well, as had been established in the earlier chapter. The other New Testament writings rarely referred to God in this way (cf. Acts 17:24).[26] Matthew, in his concluding narratives presents Jesus as the one who possess full authority in both the spheres of heaven and earth (28:18).

Matthew's framework of cosmology and Christology is observable when the role of mediation is based on authority, because it involves a movement in two directions. Matthew presents Jesus as a mediator whom God had given all authority in heaven and on earth, and thus there is a primary move "from above" to earth, and a secondary movement "from below" to heaven.[27] Regarding the phrase "on earth as it is in heaven" (6:10), Rudolph Schnackenburg argues that "'Heaven and earth' can stand for the whole world (5:18; 11:25; 24:35; 28:18), but it can also counterpoise the divine and human realms (5:34-35; 16:19; 18:18; 23:9)."[28] Therefore, when Jesus is regarded as possessing all authority in heaven and on earth, it is a pointer that cosmology and Christology in Matthew's Gospel play significant parts. Matthew shows his own peculiar christological understanding under his cosmological worldview at the time of his writing. He reveals his christological commitments through the stories of nature miracle inside the framework of his cosmological worldview.

## 7.4. Nature Miracles as basis for Cosmic Christology in Matthew's Gospel

The case of preexistence Christology and cosmic Christology to be found in the Christology of the Synoptic Gospels is plausible, because these kind of christological thoughts are "widespread among various individuals and in various different communities around the Mediterranean well before AD 70."[29]

phrases. Implied pairs occur when heaven is used in conjunction with a word other than earth but one closely associated with it, and thus communicating the same idea.

25 Pennington, *Heaven and Earth*, 194.

26 For detailed survey of implied pairs and thematic pairs, see Pennington, *Heaven and Earth*, 194-196.

27 Kari Syreeni, "Between Heaven and Earth: On the Structure of Matthew's Symbolic Universe," *JSNT* 40 (1990): 3-13 (4).

28 Rudolph Schnackenburg, *The Gospel of Matthew*, trans. Robert R. Barr (Grand Rapids, MI: Eerdmans, 2002), 67, quoted by Pennington, *Heaven and Earth*, 203.

29 Simon J. Gathercole, *The Pre-existent Son: Recovering the Christologies of Matthew, Mark, and Luke* (Grand Rapids: Eerdmans, 2006), 23.

Cosmic Christology in Pauline and Johannine writings is more or less explicit than that of Hebrews and the Synoptic Gospels as well. However, the Synoptic writers, being not strangers to contemporary christological formulation are showing shared thoughts and concepts when they presented their portrayal of Jesus. Therefore, one cannot simply rule out cosmic Christology from these Synoptic Gospels due to their implicit and underdeveloped nature.

To discuss the concept of cosmic Christology, preexistence Christology and Wisdom Christology cannot be sidelined. As early as 48-49 CE, Paul employed wisdom motifs in his Christology, but Gathercole argues that 1 Corinthians 15 and the Philippians hymn were not shaped by it.[30] As the idea of preexistence is seen in various contexts in Pauline writings, the significance is made clear.[31] J. Habermann provides key observation "that Jesus Christ is always the criterion for preexistence in Paul."[32] These kinds of concepts and ideas must have become common thoughts during the time of earliest Christianity, especially due to the widespread influence that Paul had possessed. As Paul did not reflect at length on the preexistence of Christ or the idea of cosmic Christology, it may be a hint that his audiences are familiar with these concepts. This also makes it comprehensible to point at Paul's churches and coworkers as responsible in passing on these ideas and concepts to define Jesus Christ.

Gathercole, therefore speculates that from these co-workers there may well be a Gospel writer.[33] He explained convincingly that wide spectrum of Paul's influence must be found among the Roman, Galatian, Corinthian, Philippian, and Colossian Christians (and among those in Laodicea as well; see Col 4:16). He further elaborates that in addition to Paul himself, his co-workers and co-authors would be well acquainted with this distinctive understanding of Christ. Gathercole challenges the twentieth-century scholarship that was dominated by the view that Mark and Paul were entirely independent. This undermining of the twentieth-century scholarship is clearly seen in recent article of Joel Marcus, who comments "now the tide appears to be shifting, and several scholars have recently contended that Mark should be situated in the Pauline sphere of activity."[34]

---

30 See Gathercole, *The Pre-existent Son*, 31.

31 These various contexts are: atonement, Israel's history, the supremacy of Christ over all things, Christ's role in creation.

32 J. Habermann, *Präexistenz aussagen im Neuen Testament*, Europäische Hochschulschriften (Frankfurt-am-Main: Lang, 1990), 421, cited in Gathercole, *The Pre-existent Son*, 31.

33 Gathercole, *The Pre-existent Son*, 31.

34 J. Marcus, "Mark-Interpreter of Paul," *NTS* 46 (2000): 473-487 (474); also quoted in Gathercole, *The Pre-existent Son*, 42.

As the "we" passages in Acts strongly suggests that the writer of Luke's Gospel was an associate of Paul, perhaps there is a stronger connection between Luke's Gospel and Pauline thoughts. It is also well known and accepted that Matthew relies greatly on Mark's Gospel. With all these in mind, and as Gathercole also concludes, the burden of proof rests heavily on those who would argue for the alternative.[35] The alternative that the Gospel writers are not familiar with Paul's cosmic Christology may not be true. David Oliver Smith in his 2011 book *Matthew, Mark, Luke, and Paul: The Influence of the Epistles on the Synoptic Gospels*, claims that seventy-three (73) passages in Mark's Gospel are derived from Pauline Epistles and Hebrews.[36] He further argues that the vast majority of these passages in Mark's Gospel were adopted by Matthew and Luke.[37]

It is significant to see that nature miracles are the playground for Matthew to relate his theology and his cosmological framework. As it has been said earlier, Matthew follows largely the trajectory of the worldview of the Old Testament and the Second Temple literature. Matthew's cosmology is still fundamentally two-fold, that is heaven and earth, and his theological framework also consists of two oppositional duality.[38] Matthew's cosmology consists of terms like *γῆ* (Earth), *οὐρανος* (Heaven), *κόσμος* (apparently a synonym for earth), *ἅδης* (Hades), *γέεννα* (Gehenna). Hades may be taken as a symbolic reference rather than as a distinct cosmological element because in both the appearances of the term (11:23 and 16:18), they are strongly symbolic.[39] Moreover, the meaning of the reference to Gehenna is unclear, and Matthew's usage mostly points to fire and judgment (5:22, 29, 30; 10:28; 18:9; 23:15; 23:33). The reference to a place that is outer darkness and gnashing of teeth is also found six times (8:12; 13:42, 50; 22:13; 24:51; 25:30). It is still not clear if these references mean the same thing as Gehenna, but this "language of the fire and sentence to hell/Gehenna certainly reflects a Second Temple period development as compared to the OT… and their frequency in Matthew bespeaks their importance."[40] Pennington argues that these images

35 Gathercole, *The Pre-existent Son*, 42.

36 David Oliver Smith, *Matthew, Mark, Luke, and Paul: The Influence of the Epistles on the Synoptic Gospels* (Eugene, OR: Resource Publication, 2011), 1-2.

37 Smith, *Matthew, Mark, Luke, and Paul*, 2. For his analysis and arguments on Mark's use of the epistles, see 36-239.

38 See esp. Chapter Eight, Penington, *Heaven and Earth*, 193-216.

39 The four occurrences of the term in Revelation also are put in apposition with and may simply mean "death" or the angel of death. See Penington, *Heaven and Earth*, 207.

40 Penington, *Heaven and Earth*, 207.

are instruments to speak of a "future judgment and condemnation" and are unlikely to be considered as "a third part of the cosmological structure."[41]

Matthew's portrayal of Jesus is understood in terms of various Christologies, and still cosmic Christology could be added. Matthew in the stilling of the storm explicitly used the word *σῷζω* which was sometimes used to address deities at sea. The term is also understood as pointing to spiritual salvation during the time of the writing of Matthew's Gospel. The double meaning is thus possible. Though spiritual lessons had been drawn out from the story of the stilling of the storm, it must be noted that the christological concern is the main focus. The question, "Who is Jesus Christ?" is answered in a way that shows Jesus' cosmic authority over creation. Matthew's Jesus unlike in Mark's Gospel rebukes the disciples before acting on the tempest, and the delay of the miracle heightens the intensity of the miraculous power of Jesus. The urgency of the miracle may well be subdued by Matthew to communicate his idea of cosmic Christology.

The use of rebuke to natural elements in Matthew's Gospel again is a pointer to anthropomorphizing natural elements. Matthew's cosmology which is related closely to the cosmologies of the Old Testament and Second Temple Judaism that is capable to accommodate this kind of anthropomorphizing. Even if the word "rebuke" is not taken as pointing toward demonic involvement, the immediate calm explicitly depicts Jesus as possessing the Creator's authority. Therefore, the cosmic significance of this miracle story could be observed when careful alignment is made with Matthew's christological framework. Although Matthew does not talk about Jesus' role in creating the universe, miracles such as nature miracles confirm Jesus' cosmic significance. What is vaguely communicated about cosmic Christology is clearly seen in letters such as Colossians and Ephesians.

Matthew may not present Christ as John and Paul did, that is in existential and dynamic terms.[42] Unlike Mark's "teacher" he employs the term "Lord." Mark's question is transformed into a prayer by substituting Mark's term *διδάσκαλε* "teacher" by *κύριε* "Lord." The significance of the use of *προσέρχομαι* in Matthew's Gospel is clearly evident and conclusion could be made that Matthew portrays Jesus in terms of cosmic Christology who deserve such worship and reverence. The argument that Matthew's use of *προσελθεν* "come" and *γονυπετῶν* "kneeling down" to describe the father of the epileptic boy as worshiper is another pointer to Jesus' cosmic relevance. James D. G. Dunn in his article "How did Matthew go about Composing his Gospel?" remarks on the neatness of Matthew's inclusio "And behold, I

41 Penington, *Heaven and Earth*, 207; see also R. T. France, *The Gospel of Matthew*, NICNT (Grand Rapids, MI: Eerdmans, 2007), 156.

42 Cf. Maloney, S.J., *The Cosmic Christ*, 101.

will be with you until the end of the age" (28:20), which is connected with the Emmanuel saying, "God with us" (1:23), and the universal authority (πᾶσα ἐξουσία ἐν οὐρανῷ καὶ ἐπὶ τῆς γῆς) given to the exalted Jesus (28:18) enhances the point of Jesus' cosmic significance.[43]

In Matthew's Gospel Jesus is not simply portrayed as Son of God, son of David, Messiah, Son of Man, or Moses the prophet. Jesus "embodied God's presence and universal authority in a way that no other servant of God had done before him."[44] The goal for Matthew in his writing of the Gospel is seen in Matthew 28:16-20, as it is frequently considered as the key to his theology.[45] The redactional work of Matthew and his stories of nature miracles show that he is sophisticated in his Christology and is interested in Jesus' cosmic significance.

Matthew's presentation of nature miracle stories encompasses the idea of Jesus' divinity and cosmic authority, and these stories propounded cosmic Christology. Dimension of Jesus' authority and majesty is revealed and Jesus' ability in handling any crises, even from natural order is clearly propagated in these nature miracles. What is reserved as God's action is performed by Jesus in Matthew's nature miracle stories, and is a pointer to the concept of cosmic Christology. Jesus possesses the capability to control even the natural phenomena, and acts as Yahweh did in the Old Testament. Cosmic Christology is not incompatible with Matthew's Gospel. The stories of nature miracles provide essential evidence for that cosmic Christology is present in Matthew's Gospel. These nature miracles act as pointers to the progression of faith in the early Christian community. The cosmic significance of these passages points to a Christology that is molded within the cosmic christological conceptual framework of Matthew's Gospel. Though they may not be termed as developed statement of cosmic Christology, but they exhibit the cosmic significance of Christ and the true identity of the human Jesus, who performed miracles attributed to Yahweh's prerogative.

## 7.5. Traditional Religious Cosmology of the Mizos and Theology of Nature

The traditional Mizo religious cosmology is based on the idea of a heavenly being stretched above and the earth below it. Heaven serves as the abode for the high God or Pathian and all other celestial beings, and they frequently visit

---

43 James D. G. Dunn, "How did Matthew go about Composing his Gospel?" in *Jesus, Matthew's Gospel and Early Christianity: Studies in Memory of Graham N. Stanton*, ed. Daniel M. Gurtner, Joel Willits and Richard A. Burridge (New York: T&T Clark, 2011), 39-58 (54-55).

44 Dunn, "How did Matthew go about Composing his Gospel?" 55.

45 U. Schnelle, *The History and Theology of the New Testament Writings* (London: SCM, 1994), 230-231.

the earth habitation and even lived among human beings. Primal worldviews encompass the presence of malignant and non-malignant spirits in the world, so also the traditional Mizo religious worldview. The cosmology is divided into two tiers, an upper tier and lower tier. A high God rules the upper tier or the world beyond the habitat of human beings. There are numerous spirits, good and bad watching and ruling the natural and social worlds. With these spirits of the lower tier the community has frequent interactions. It is now generally agreed that the Mizos believed in one creator and supreme being called Pathian (literally translated as "holy father," holy in the sense of purity), but this Pathian "vaguely figured in the everyday life of the people and occupied no significant place in the religious practices."[46]

However, Lalrinawmi Ralte proposes that there are three supreme beings in Mizo primal religion, namely Khuanu, Pathian and Khuavang.[47] Though Lalsangkima Pachuau argues that this case needs evidential substantiation for its establishment, he describes Khuanu as the one whom the most important sacrifices were offered.[48] C. L. Hminga in his essay "The Traditional Mizo Concept of God," lists five or six names of benevolent spirit-beings.[49] Khuanu is understood as mother of cosmos or cosmic goddess, and also identified as a Pathian's wife.[50] This is why the interest on Mizo traditional understanding of Khuanu seems relevant for this study. Pachuau is of the opinion that Pathian and Khuanu refer to the same being, one the masculine and the other the feminine name.[51] Therefore, to follow Ralte's proposal seems logical, and thus, Khuanu will be taken up as a subject of interest, and an attempt will be made to relate it with cosmic Christology. The traditional Mizo's concept of Khuanu and cosmic Christology in the New Testament could be taken up thus, perhaps to enrich the needed relevant eco-theology for the Mizos.

---

46 Lalsangkima Pachuau, "Mizo "Sakhua" in Transition: Change and Continuity from Primal Religion to Christianity," *International Review* 34 (2006): 41-57 (43).

47 Lalrinawmi Ralte, "Patriarchy and Christianity in the Mizo Church: A Feminist Critique," *Bangalore Theological Forum* 31 (1999): 117-133 (118).

48 Pachuau, "Mizo "Sakhua" in Transition," 43, 55.

49 C. L. Hminga, "The Traditional Mizo Concept of God," in *Toward a Tribal Theology: The Mizo Perspective*, ed. K. Thanzauva (Jorhat: Mizo Theological Conference, 1989), 45-53 (46-51). The benevolent spirit-beings are Pu Vana (literally "grandfather heaven," or heavenly grandfather), Khuanu (mother cosmos or cosmic goddess), vanchung nula (maiden in heaven), Khuavang, and Lasi (mostly connected with the well-being of animals), and a nameless spirit (or unknown spirit) whom one's ancestors worship in the sakhaw worship which, which some think, may not necessarily be seen as god.

50 Cf. Pachuau, "Mizo "Sakhua" in Transition," 43, citing Hminga, "The Traditional Mizo Concept of God," 46-51.

51 Pachuau, "Mizo "Sakhua" in Transition," 43.

The Mizo concept of the interrelationship between God, spirits, human beings, world and nature is not so complicated. The understanding of the cosmos as being isolated from God is not exactly the element of the traditional Mizo worldview. It may be also suitable to see this as the traditional Mizo religious worldview. The conception of the Supreme Being is seen in their worshiping and sacrificing toward the high God. There was a belief that there are celestial beings that are in active contact with human beings. Apart from these there was also a belief that there are numerous kinds of spirit that were generally grouped into two, namely: benevolent and malevolent.[52]

The concept of high God is found in many pre-agricultural societies, and so also among the traditional Mizos "believed in the existence of a benevolent God called Pathian or poetically, Khuanu, who was the creator."[53] The belief in the existence of Pathian and the poetical term Khuanu terms need attention here.[54] These terms will be analyzed briefly in order to understand the traditional conception of the relationship between God and nature. Pathian which probably means Holy Father is a remote being that dwells exclusively in heaven. "Pa" means father and "thian" means pure or holy. Thus, Pathian may also be translated as "Holy Father" and was supposed to be a male person. The belief that Pathian as ultimately good and demand nothing from human beings was prevalent and was offered prayers when the people were placed in extreme difficult situations.[55] According to Lawmsanga the saying "Pathian above is looking down on us" or "our Pathian is good" means that Pathian would ultimately help them.[56] Therefore, though it might not be an active one, but the involvement of the High God within the cosmos is not ruled out in traditional Mizo worldview.

---

52 For more details, see, Saiaithanga, *Mizo Sakhua* [Mizo Religion] (Aizawl: Maranatha Printing Press, 1984; repr., Aizawl: R. Lalmalsawma, 1994); N. E. Parry, *A Monograph of Lushai Customs and Ceremonies* (Shillong: Assam Government Press, 1928; repr., Aizawl: Tribal Research Institute, 1988); H. L. Malsawma, *Sociology of the Mizos* (Guwahati: Spectrum Publications, 2002); Chitta Ranjan Nag, *Mizo Society in Transition* (New Delhi: Vikas Publishing House Pvt. Ltd., 1993); James Dokhuma, *Hmanlai Mizo Kalphung* [Mizo Traditional Ways of Life] (Aizawl: J.D. Press, 1992).

53 C. Lalnunziri Chhangte, "Myth and the Mizo Worldview," *Day Dream Believer*, https://cherriechhangte.wordpress.com/2007/11/28/myth-and-the-mizo-world-view/html.

54 Among several terms that had been used to refer to Pathian, these are the relevant ones: Chunga Mi, Chung Pathian, Khuanu, Pu Vana, Vanhrika, and Khuavang.

55 Sacrifice was made to Pathian only on the days of sechhun and khuangchawi. Pathian was understood as the director of human destiny, and the one who ordained who was to marry whom. Such couples are known as "Pathian samsuih" that means "those whose hairs are joined together by *Pathian*." Lawmsanga, "A Critical Study on Christian Mission with Special Reference to Presbyterian Church of Mizoram," (PhD Diss., University of Birmingham, 2010), 28.

56 Lawmsanga, "A Critical Study on Christian Mission," 28.

Traditional Mizo believed that the cosmos and all nature were created by Pathian.[57] Even though there is no elaborated myth on creation, Pathian was understood as possessing the power to create human beings, cosmos and everything in it. The attitude of the traditional Mizo toward Pathian is not negative, rather they "highly respected Pathian as a good spirit, who never harm nor demand anything from human beings."[58] It is understandable thus that the first translator of the Bible into Mizo language utilized the term Pathian for God, but Ralte states that "Khuanu disappeared from the divine in Christianity."[59] However, though the term Pathian is used in Mizo Bible, Khuanu is still used poetically even in modern Mizo songs and poems, and there seems to be no restrictions culturally or ecclesiastically.

The concept of Pathian especially in its poetical term as Khuanu in traditional Mizo worldview can be utilized in developing Mizo eco-theology.. As the concept of Khuanu encompasses every aspect of cosmic realities, why not use this concept to further the need of relevant eco-theology. Before colonial exploitation the fact that the Mizos respected nature and possessed deep ecological concern is clearly seen when the concept of Khuanu is dealt with. Khuanu's role as creator, provider, and upholder are significant when it is aligned with that of cosmic Christology in the New Testament. The Mizo believed that Khuanu protects the villagers and the animals, and thus the saying arises, "Khuanu in min veng rawh se," which means "May Khuanu protect us." Khuanu relates both Pathian (father God) and this cosmos, and believed to reside in the village, which means Khuanu "is near, active, available, and accessible to human beings."[60]

Wati Longchar states that "The tribal world of culture can be explained only in term of the world of nature."[61] This is also true for the Mizos, and once nature is separated from the society, then the meaning of life cannot be painted on the canvas.[62] The interpretation of the revelation of nature helped them to count seasons and sowed seeds at an appropriate time. Weather, climate,

---

57 Sangkima, *Mizos: Society and Social Change* (Guwahati: Spectrum Publications, 1992), 52.

58 Lawmsanga, "A Critical Study on Christian Mission," 28.

59 Lalrinawmi Ralte, *Crab Theology: A Critique of Patriarchy – Cultural Degradation and Empowerment of Mizo Women* (DMin. Diss., Episcopal Divinity School, Cambridge, 1993), 55.

60 Lalrinawmi Ralte, "The World as the Body of God: Ecofeminist Theological Discourse with Special Reference to Tribal Women in India," *Rethingking Mission*, 2008, https://rethinkingmission.org/wp-content/uploads/2016/07/The-World-as-the-body-of-God-article.pdf.

61 Wati Longchar, *The Traditional Tribal Worldview and Modernity: Focus on North East India* (Jorhat: Limatula LKr., 1995), 24.

62 Longchar, *The Traditional Tribal Worldview and Modernity*, 24.

drought, famine, and prosperity were read from nature, and thus the belief in the revelation of High God in nature was not peculiar.[63] Therefore, it is fitting to relate this worldview with cosmic Christology in Matthew's Gospel, especially to enhance eco-theology among the Mizos.

## 7.6. Summary

Pauline literature may have been used to advocate cosmic Christology in biblical studies, and the consensus had been made in regards to its primacy. James H. Burtness asserts that "the decision forced upon us by Col. 1:15-20 is that what Bultmann calls 'gnostic' – that is, the cosmic dimension of the work of Christ – is actually very close to the heart of the New Testament message."[64]

Cosmic Christology in Matthew's Gospel could be seen in the use of cosmic terms and especially in his utilization of traditions he received from Mark's Gospel. The employment of cosmic languages throughout the Gospel makes it clear that cosmic Christology as we call it now is not an unfamiliar concept to Matthew. Pauline literature which seems to be prior to the Gospels presents a more sophisticated cosmic Christology, and among the Gospel writers, John comes closer to Paul. However, as is already stated, the synoptic Gospels represent a lesser developed cosmic Christology. This includes Matthew's Gospel that portrays the picture of Jesus of Nazareth in cosmic christological pattern.

To really advocate cosmic Christology to the Mizos, it is significant to see that the concept of Khuanu is already available to be disposed of.[65] Ralte, by using Sally McFague's *Models of God* argues that the significance of Khuanu was suppressed and later became invisible and silent. Thus, she made an attempt to rediscover Khuanu in order to utilize the concept for the purpose of developing eco-feminist theology.[66] The element of cosmic creative power is attributed to Khuanu, and thus responsible for the upholding of the universe, but lacks the fierce and destructive elements found in Shakti of Hinduism.[67] The concept of Khuanu could be closely related to the understanding of cosmic Christology in Matthew's Gospel. Matthew's cosmic Christology could be further utilized to develop theology of nature and feminist theology for the Mizos.

---

63 Cf. Yiepetso Wezah and Tereso C. Casiño, "Towards a Relevant Theology of Nature: North-East India Tribal Perspective," *TTJ* 14 (2011): 99-115 (101).

64 James H. Burtness, "All the Fullness," *Dialog* 3 (1964): 257-263 (260).

65 Ralte, "The World as the Body of God," 8.

66 Ralte, "The World as the Body of God," 9-10.

67 Ralte, "The World as the Body of God," 10, citing Vandana Shiva, *Staying Alive: Women, Ecology and Development* (London: Zed Books, 1989), xix.

# General Conclusion

The Christological studies of Matthew's Gospel mostly concentrated on the titles of Jesus and typology. However, miracle stories, especially nature miracles are neglected, and it is important to analyze these miracles to provide contributions to the overall understanding of Matthew's Christology. The understanding of the interrelated connection between God, nature and human being began to cease in this present reality. To connect cosmic Christology with eco-theology is important in order to promote responsibility of the churches in preservation and caring for nature and creation. These questions drive the research and pave way for further discussions: Is it appropriate to interpret nature miracles in Matthew's Gospel as having cosmic Christological significance? Are these miracle stories in Matthew's Gospel to be taken as the projection of Jesus as Lord over nature and the cosmic totality? What did Matthew intend to communicate by these miracle stories?

Though the early Christians' testimony unanimously identifies the apostle Matthew as the author of this Gospel, the nineteenth-century scholarship makes it difficult to identify the real author of the Gospel. The reality of the stages of composition and naming the apostle Matthew as an earlier contributor is significant. Tradition and critical scholarship may not be regarded as opposing each other because the apostle Matthew fits rather well the profile of what modern scholars suggest as the real author of Matthew's Gospel. It is to be noted that little is known in regards to the identity of the apostle Matthew, but among other probable figures he is a suitable candidate for authorship. By placing Matthew's Gospel as early as 60 CE may yield the best sense of the text for the original readers and the Syrian provenance is perhaps the most satisfactory answer to the question of the setting of the Gospel. Matthean community is in the process of creating a distinct community and spreads over a wide geographical area. They were also living in close proximity to a vigorous Jewish community.

The cosmological worldview of the New Testament writers, especially the Gospel writers do not differ much when they are aligned with the Jewish writers. They differ themselves from the Graeco-Roman writings mainly in their understanding of nature, because the latter declined in giving autonomy to nature. God or divine, nature, and miracles were interrelated to each other in these cosmological worldviews of the Old Testament, Second Temple Judaism and New Testament writings. The peculiarity of these traditional worldviews clearly emerges when considered under the same lens with modern science. Therefore, today's consensus inclines more towards situating miracle stories in their own cosmological worldview and theological framework. Modern science is more interested in the actuality and possibility of nature miracles, but the ancient writers give little or no concern for questions of the probability or possibility of these nature miracles. The main reason is the starting point of their working framework.

To locate the Jewish roots of miracle stories in Matthew's Gospel, it is unnecessary to look beyond the cosmological worldview espoused by the Jewish tradition. With this worldview in mind the re-evaluation of Christology proceeds with the identification of how Matthew understands and utilizes the idea of cosmic Christology in his Gospel. Matthew's interest in nature miracles needs reconsideration and reconstruction in order to reinterpret nature miracles as the basis to develop cosmic Christology.

There are various texts and passages in the New Testament that could be accommodated or interpreted under the framework of cosmic Christology. The stages of development may differ, but the presence of cosmic Christology in many passages of the New Testament cannot be ignored. The survey in Chapter Four portrays that though the presentation of Jesus' divinity in Synoptic Gospels may not be easily interpreted as cosmic Christology, but there are hints that suggest Jesus' authority over the creation.

Synoptic Gospels in many instances portray Jesus as God rather than mere human beings. The preexistent nature of Jesus in the Synoptic Gospels is significant to move forward and develop cosmic Christology. It is clear that Johannine writings provide a more developed cosmic Christology than the Synoptic Gospels, expecially because of the use and concept of the term Logos in the prologue of John's Gospel. Christ is also associated with a cosmic role in God's dealing with the cosmos in Pauline corpus. Paul equates Jesus to God, and sees the union between God and Jesus in purpose (Gal 1:1-4). Paul's Christology is framed under the understanding that Christ's coming to the cosmos is for all creation, and not only for humanity.

The Epistle to the Hebrews also claims that the one who upholds all things (Heb1:3) is the exalted Christ, and is also active in a discussion about the dominion of the coming world (Heb 2:5-9). The portrayal of Jesus Christ as the changeless one who founded the cosmos; and though the cosmos deteriorated and decayed, Jesus Christ will roll it up like a cloak and will transform it (Heb 1:10-12) in the "coming world" (Heb 2:5). John's Gospel is explicit but Hebrews is implicit in presenting Logos Christology (e.g. Heb 1:2-4). Furthermore, the preexistent status of Christ is also to be found in several passages (Heb1:5-13; 2:12-13; 5:5-6; 7:17, 21; 10:5-9). Jesus who is the heir of all and both the Creator and sustainer of the universe (Heb 1:1-3) is portrayed through cosmic Christology in Hebrews.

Christologies of the Gospel writings and various literatures from all over the globe are all contextual and is relevant and at the same time irrelevant to a particular socio-cultural context. Christology that arises out of a particular culture and context is not readily adapted or accommodated by another. This does not mean that, any christological interest must be acknowledged, but those that are not in contrast with the Bible must be given a room to develop and prosper. Paul probably synthesizes traditions around him in order to articulate a more complex Christology. This concept influences the thoughts of other New Testament writers, and became prominent in the early church. Cosmic Christology developed partly from Wisdom tradition and involves ecological interests, and also pushes forward the significance of contextual understanding.

For the tribals of Northeast India the idea of incarnation and the relation of Supreme Being with nature are concepts that had been acknowledged from time immemorial. But the inherited Christology is in another perspective an individualistic and otherworldly, and focuses mainly on the death of Christ on the cross, but neglects Jesus' life and ministry. Instead of the emphasis on the salvation of individual soul, and the call to individual for repentance, Christology needs to address the socio-economic, ecological and political problems of contemporary Mizo society. Cosmic Christology with ecological thrust could serve as an exegetical tool to study nature miracles in Matthew's Gospel. The outcome would provide a foundational hermeneutical tool to do contextual Christology.

The exegesis in this study sets aside the question of historicity for nature miracle stories and focuses instead on what Matthew was trying to convey by these narratives. For Matthew, narrative drives theology, it is thus important to understand the place of a pericope within the story in order to comprehend its function. Matthew's Gospel does not contain the more fully developed incarnational Christology that is found in John's Gospel or cosmic Christology found in Pauline writings. But Matthew seems to move a bit further in these directions than other Synoptic writers.

Nature miracles in Matthew's Gospel come in contact with David C. Sim's proposal of second dualism, which is a cosmic dualism. The understanding of the role of Jesus and his forces in the cosmic struggle is significant in this proposed dualism. Jesus in the stories of nature miracles may be accommodated under this thought. The stilling of the storm and walking on the water may be seen as highlighting the battle between cosmic forces over natural elements. However, the exegesis shows that these natural elements are not presented explicitly as opposing forces to Jesus, but instead the intimate relationship between Jesus and the cosmos is to be seen in these nature miracles. Furthermore, the idea of cosmic Christology is seen repeatedly in these stories of nature miracles. Matthew moves further than Mark and Luke in the direction of ascribing divinity to Jesus. The stories of nature miracles that are being analyzed serve as pointers for Jesus' divinity, and his cosmic authority. Jesus' incarnation is taken up by John, and Paul also presented a more developed cosmic Christology in his letters.

Cosmic Christology is advocated in Pauline literature, and the consensus holds to its significance and primacy. The cosmic dimension of the work of Christ is related closely with New Testament theology. The utilization of cosmological terms and traditions from Mark's Gospel help Matthew to communicate cosmic Christology. His employment of cosmological languages throughout the Gospel makes it even clear that cosmic Christology is not an unfamiliar concept for Matthew. Pauline literature which are regarded as prior to the Gospels communicate sophisticated concept of cosmic Christology. Johannine literature also comes close to Pauline writings. However, the Synoptic Gospels represent a lesser or underdeveloped cosmic Christology. But nature miracles in Matthew's Gospel contain rich understanding of Jesus in terms of cosmic christological pattern.

To advocate cosmic Christology for the Mizos, the concept of Khuanu is already available from tradition. The significance of Khuanu was suppressed and later became invisible and silent. Ralte was the first theologian to make an attempt to rediscover the concept of Khuanu in order to utilize it for the purpose of developing eco-feminist theology. The element of cosmic creative power is attributed to Khuanu, and thus responsible for the upholding of the universe. The concept of Khuanu could be closely related to the understanding of cosmic Christology in Matthew's Gospel.

# Bibliography

## Primary Source

Aland, Barbara., *et al.*, eds. *The Greek New Testament.* Edited by 4th rev. ed. Stuttgart: UBS, 1994.

Alexander, Neil. *The New Interpreter's Bible.* Nashville: Abingdon Press, 1995.

Bauer, Walter. *Griechisch-Deutsches Wörterbuch zu den Schriften des Neuen Testaments und der übrigen urchristlichen Literature. A Greek-English Lexicon of the New Testament and Early Christian Literature.* Translated and edited by William F. Arndt and F. Wilbur Gingrich. Chicago: UCP, 1961.

Blass, F., and A. Debrunner. *A Greek Grammar of the New Testament and Other Early Christian Literature.* Translated by Robert W. Funk. Chicago: UCP, 1961.

Elliger, Karl., and William Rudolph., eds. *Biblia Hebraica Stuttgartensia.* Stuttgart: Deutsche Bibelgesellschaft, 1983.

Louw, Johannes P., and Eugene A. Nida, eds. *Greek-English Lexicon of the New Testament: Based on Semantic Domains*. 2nd ed. New York: UBS, 1988.

Metzger, Bruce M. *A Textual Commentary on the Greek New Testament.* 2nd ed. Stuttgart: Deutsche Biblegesellschaft, 2002.

Moulton, Harold K., ed. *The Analytical Greek Lexicon.* Rev. ed. Grand Rapids: Zondervan, 1978.

Moulton, James Hope. *A Grammar of New Testament Greek.* Edinburgh: T&T Clark, 1919.

Mounce, William D. *Basics of Biblical Greek Grammar.* 3rd ed. Grand Rapids: Zondervan, 2009.

Rahlfs, Alfred. *Septuaginta, id est vetum testamentum graece iuxta*. Stuttgart: Württembergische Bibelanstalt, 1935.

Schneemelcher, Wilhelm., ed. *New Testament Apocrypha.* 2 vols. English trans. ed. R. Mc L. Wilson. Philadelphia: Westminster, 1963-1965.

Sparks, Hedley F. D., ed. *The Apochryphal Old Testament*. Oxford: Clarendon, 1984.

*The Holy Bible: New Revised Standard Version.* Grand Rapids: Zondervan, 1989.

## Secondary Sources

### Books

Abraham, K. C. "A Theological Response to the Ecological Crisis." Pages 65-78 in *Ecotheology: Voices from South and North, ed. David G. Hallman.* Geneva: WCC Publications, 1994.

Abraham, K. C. "Christian Ethics: Methodological Issues." In *Doing Christian Ethics: Context and Perspectives*. Edited by Hunter P. Mabry. Bangalore: BTESSC, 1996.

Adams, Dwayne H. *The Sinner in Luke*. TETSMS. Eugene: Pickwick, 2008.

Adams, Edward. "The Cosmology of Hebrews." Pages 122-139 in *The Epistle to the Hebrews and Christian Theology*. Edited by Richard Bauckham et al. Grand Rapids: Eerdmans, 2009.

Aldredge-Clanton, Jann. *In Search of the Christ-Sophia: An Inclusive Christology for Liberating Christians.* Mystic, CN: Twenty-Third Publications, 1995.

Allen Jr., O. Wesley. *Matthew. FBPC. Minneapolis: Fortress, 2013.*

Allison, Dale C. *The New Moses: A Matthean Typology.* Minneapolis: Fortress, 1993.

_______. *The New Moses: A Matthean Typology.* Eugene, OR: Wipf & Stock, 1993.

_______. *The New Moses: A Matthean Typology.* Minneapolis: Fortress, 1993.

_______. *Studies in Matthew: Interpretation Past and Present.* Grand Rapids: Baker, 2012.

Arnal, William E. "The Parable of the Tenants and the Class Consciousness of the Peasantry." Pages 135-157 in *Text and Artifact in the Religions of Mediterranean Antiquity: Essays in Honour of Peter Richardson.* Edited by Stephen G. Wilson and Michael Desjardins. Vol. 9 of *Studies in Christianity and Judaism/Études Sur Le Christianisme et Le Judaïsme.* Waterloo: Wilfrid Laurier University Press, 2000.

_______. *Jesus and the Village Scribes: Galilean Conflicts and the Setting of Q.* Minneapolis: Fortress, 2000.

Arnold, Clinton E. *Ephesians: Power and Magic: The Concept of Power in Ephesians in light of its Historical Setting*. SNTS 63. Cambridge: CUP, 1989.

Assefa, Daniel. "Matthew's Day of Judgment in the Light of 1 Enoch." Pages 199-214 in *Enoch and the Synoptic Gospels: Reminiscences, Allusions, Intertextuality*. Edited by Loren T. Stuckenbruck and Gabriele Boccaccini. Atlanta: SBL, 2016.

Aune, David E. "Magic in Early Christianity." Pages 1507-1557 in *Aufstieg und Niedergang der Römischen Welt*. II. Edited by Hildegard Temporini and Wolfgang Haase. Berlin: de Gruyter, 1980.

_______. *Revelation 6-16*. WBC 52B. Grand Rapids, MI: Zondervan, 1998.

Aus, Roger David. *Feeding the Five Thousand: Studies in the Judaic Background of Mark 6:30-44 par. and John 6:1-15*. SJ. Maryland: University Press of America, 2010.

Bacon, B.W. *Studies in Matthew.* London: Constable, 1930.

Ballentine, Debra Scoggins. *The Conflict Myth and the Biblical Tradition.* New York: OUP, 2015.

Baptist Church of Mizoram. *Zoram Baptist Kohhran Thurin Puanchhuah* (*Baptist Confession*). Serkawn: BCM, 1988.

Barnard, Joy A. *The Mysticism of Hebrews: Exploring the Role of Jewish Apocalyptic Mysticism in the Epistle to the Hebrews*. WUNT 2/331. Tübingen: Mohr Siebeck, 2012.

Barr, David L. *New Testament Story: An Introduction*. 4th ed. Australia: Wadsworth Cengage Learning, 2009.

Bartholomew Craig G., and Ryan P. O'Dowd. *Old Testament Wisdom Literature: A Theological Introduction.* Downers Grove, IL: IVP, 2011.

Bauckham, Richard. *Jesus and the Eyewitnesses: The Gospels as Eyewitness Testimony.* Grand Rapids: Eerdmans, 2006.

_______. *Jesus and the God of Israel: God Crucified and Other Studies on the New Testament's Christology of Divine Identity.* Grand Rapids, MI: Eerdmans, 2008.

_______. *The Theology of the Book of Revelation.* Cambridge: CUP, 1993.

Bauer, David R. *The Structure of Matthew's Gospel: A Study in Literary Design*, JSNTSup. Wiltshire: SAP, 1989.

_______. *The Structure of Matthew's Gospel: A Study in Literary Design.* JSNTSup 31. Sheffield: SAP, 1988.

_______. *The Structure of Matthew's Gospel: A Study in Literary Design.* BAC. London: Bloomsbury Academics, 2015.

Beale, G. K. *Revelation*. NIGTC. Grand Rapids: Eerdmans, 1999.

Beall, Todd S. *Josephus' Description of the Essenes Illustrated by the Dead Sea Scrolls*. SNTSMS 58. Cambridge: CUP, 1988.

Beare, F. W. *The Gospel According to Matthew: Translation, Introduction and Commentary*. San Francisco: Harper & Row, 1982.

Beaton, Richard. *Isaiah's Christ in Matthew's Gospel*. NTS 123. Cambridge: CUP, 2004.

Becker, J. *Paul, Apostle to the Gentiles.* Louisville: Westminster, 1993.

Becker, Michael. "Miracle Traditions in Early Rabbinic Literature: Some Questions on their Pragmatics." Pages 48-69 in *Wonders Never Cease: The Purpose of Narrating Miracle Stories in the New Testament and its Religious Environment. Edited by Michael Labahn and Bert Jan Lietaert Peerbolte. London: T&T Clark, 2006.*

Betz, Otto. "Miracles in the Writings of Flavius Josephus." Pages 212-235 in *Josephus, Judaism, and Christianity.* Edited by Louis H. Feldman and Gohei Hata. Detroit: Wayne State University Press, 1987.

Bevans, Stephen B. *Models of Contextual Theology.* Maryknoll: Orbis, 1992.

Bird, Michael F. *Jesus the Eternal Son: Answering Adoptionist Christology.* Grand Rapids, MI: Eerdmans, 2017.

Black, C. Clifton. III. "Depth of Characterization and Degrees of Faith in Matthew." Pages 604-623 in SBL 1989 Seminar Papers. Atlanta: Scholars Press, 1989.

Blackburn, Barry L. "The Miracles of Jesus." Pages 113-130 in *The Cambridge Companion to Miracles*. CCR. Edited by Graham H. Twelftree. Cambridge: CUP, 2011.

Blackburn, Barry. '*Theios Aner*' *and the Markan Miracle Traditions: A Critique of the Theios Aner Concept as an Interpretive Background of the Miracle Traditions Used by Mark.* WUNT 2.40. Tübingen: Mohr Siebeck, 1991.

Blackburn, Barry. "'Miracle Working THEIOI ANDRES' in Hellenism (and Hellenistic Judaism)." Pages 185-218 in *The Miracles of Jesus*. Vol. 6 of *Gospel Perspective.* Edited by David Wenham and Craig Blomberg. Sheffield: JSOT Press, 1986.

Blomberg, Craig L. *Contagious Holiness: Jesus' Meals with Sinners*. NSBT. Leicester: Apollos, 2005.

_______. *Interpreting the Parables.* Downers Grove, IL: IVP, 1990.

_______. *Matthew.* NAC 22. Nashville: Broadman, 1992.

Bloomquist, L. Gregory. "The Role of Argumentation in the Miracle Stories of Luke-Acts: Toward a Fuller Identification of Miracle Discourse for use in Sociorhetorical Interpretation." Pages 85-124 in *Miracle Discourse in the New Testament*. Edited by Duane J. Watson. Atlanta: SBL, 2012.

Bock, Darrell L. "Dating the Parables of Enoch: A Forschungs bericht." Pages 58-113 in *Parables of Enoch: A Paradigm Shift*. Edited by James H. Charlesworth and Darrell L. Bock. London: Bloomsbury, 2013.

_______. *Luke 1:1-9:50.* BECNT. Grand Rapids: Baker Academic, 1994.

_______. *Proclamation from Prophecy and Pattern: Lucan Old Testament Christology.* JSNTSup 12. Sheffield: JSOT Press, 1987.

Bockmuehl, Markus N. A. *Revelation and Mystery in Ancient Judaism and Pauline Christianity*. WUNT 2. Tübingen: Mohr Siebeck, 1990.

Bohache, Thomas. *Christology from the Margins.* London: SCM, 2008.

Borg, Marcus J. "From Galilean Jew to the Face of God: The Pre-Easter and Post-Easter Jesus." Pages 7-20 in *Jesus at 2000*. Edited by Marcus J. Borg. Oxford: Westview, 1997.

Borgen, Peder. *Bread from Heaven: An Exegetical Study of the Concept of Manna in the Gospel of John and the Writings of Philo.* Leiden: Brill, 1965.

Boring, M. Eugene. *An Introduction to the New Testament: History, Literature, Theology.* Louisville: WJK, 2012.

_______. *The Gospel of Matthew: Introduction, Commentary, and Reflections.* NIB 8. Edited by Leander E. Keck, *et.al.* Nashville: Abingdon Press, 1995.

Bornkamm, G. "The Stilling of the Storm in Matthew 8:23-27." Pages 52-57 in *Tradition and Interpretation in Matthew*. Edited by G. Bornkamm, G. Barth and H. J. Held. Translated by Percy Scott. Philadelphia: Westminster, 1963.

_______. *Jesus of Nazareth.* London: Hodder & Stoughton, 1960.

Bornkamm, G., G. Barth and H. J. Held. *Tradition and Interpretation in Matthew.* Volume 1 *of Wissenschaftliche Monographien zum A.u.N. Testament*. London: SCM, 2014.

Bosch, David J. *Transforming Mission: Paradigm Shifts in Theology of Mission.* New York: Orbis, 1991.

Bouma-Prediger, Steven. *The Greening of Theology: The Ecological Models of Rosemary Radford Reuther, Joseph Sittler, and Jürgen Moltmann.* Atlanta: Scholars Press, 1995.

Bouquet, Alan Coates. *Everyday Life in New Testament Times.* Great Britain: A Carousel Book, 1974.

Bowman Jr., Robert M., and J. Ed Komoszewski, *Putting Jesus in His Place: The Case for the Deity of Christ.* Grand Rapids, MI: Kregel, 2007.

Boxall, Ian. *Discovering Matthew: Content, Interpretation, Reception.* Grand Rapids, MI: Eerdmans, 2014.

Brandon, S. G. F. *The Fall of Jerusalem and the Christian Church: A Study of the Effects of the Jewish Overthrow of A.D. 70 on Christianity.* London: SPCK, 1951.

Bray, Gerald. *Biblical Interpretation: Past and Present.* Downers Grove: IVP, 1996.

Broadhead, Edwin K. *Teaching with Authority: Miracles and Christology in the Gospel of Mark.* JSNTSup. Sheffield: SAP, 1992.

Brown, Jeannine K. "Genesis in Matthew's Gospel." Pages 42-59 in *Genesis in the New Testament.* Edited by Maarten J. J. Menken and Steve Moyise. London: T&T Clark, 2012.

_______. *The Disciples in Narrative Perspective: The Portrayal and Function of the Matthew Disciples.* Leiden: Brill, 2002.

Brown, Peter. *Through the Eye of a Needle: Wealth, the Fall of Rome, and the Making of Christianity in the West, 350-550 AD.* Princeton: PUP, 2013.

Brown, Raymond E. *An Introduction to New Testament Christology.* New York: Paulist Press, 1994.

_______. *An Introduction to the New Testament.* New York: Doubleday, 1997.

_______. *The Birth of the Messiah: A Commentary on the Infancy Narratives in the Gospels of Matthew and Luke.* New York: Doubleday, 1993.

_______. *The Community of the Beloved Disciple.* New York: Paulist, 1979.

_______. *The Death of the Messiah: From Gethsemane to the Grave.* Vol. 1. New York: Doubleday1994.

Bruner, F. D. *The Churchbook. Dallas: Word, 1990.*

Buchanan, George Wesley. *The Gospel of Matthew.* NTS 1. Eugene, OR: Wipf & Stock, 1996.

Bultmann, Rudolf. "New Testament and Mythology: The Mythological Element in the Message of the New Testament and the Problem of Its Re-interpretation." Pages 1-44 in *Kerygma and Myth: A Theological Debate.* Edited by Hans Werner Bartsch. London: SPCK, 1957.

_______. *Jesus Christ and Mythology.* New York: Charles Scribner's Sons, 1958.

_______. *The Gospel of John: A Commentary.* Translated by G. R. Beasley-Murray, R. W. N. Hoare and J. K. Riches. Philadelphia: Westminster Press, 1971.

_______. *The History of the Synoptic Tradition.* Translated by John Marsh. Rev. ed. New York: Harper & Row, 1976.

_______. *The New Testament and Mythology and Other Basic Writings.* Minneapolis: Augsburg, 1984.

_______. *Theology of the New Testament.* Translated by K. Grobel. 2 vols. New York: Charles Scribner's Sons, 1951.

_______. *Theology of the New Testament: Complete in One Volume*. Translated by Kendrick Grobel. New York: Charles Scribner's Son, 1951.

Bummel, E. "The Feeding of the Multitude." Pages 211-240 in *Jesus and the Politics of His Day*. Edited by E. Bummel and C. F. D. Moule. Cambridge: CUP, 1984.

Burger, Christoph. *Jesus als Davids sohn: Eine traditions geschichtliche Untersuchung.* Göttingen: Vandenhoeck & Ruprecht, 1970.

Burridge, Richard A. *Imitating Jesus: An Inclusive Approach to New Testament Ethics.* Rapids, MI: Eerdmans, 2007.

Byrskog, Samuel. *Story as History – History as Story*. WUNT 123. Tübingen: Mohr Siebeck, 2000.

Caird, George B. *New Testament Theology.* Edited by L. D. Hurst. Oxford: Clarendon, 1994.

Callender, Dexter E. "The Primal Man in Ezekiel and the Image of God." Pages 606-625 in *SBL Seminar Papers*, 1998. SBLSP 37. Atlanta: Scholars Press, 1998.

Carson, D. A. "Christological Ambiguities in the Gospel of Matthew." Pages 97-114 in *Christ the Lord: Studies in Christology Presented to Donald Guthrie.* Edited by Harold H. Rowdon. Leicester: IVP, 1982.

_______. "Matthew." Pages 23-670 in *Matthew-Mark.* 2nd ed. EBC 9. Grand Rapids: Zondervan, 2010.

Carson, D. A., Douglas J. Moo and Leon Morris. *An Introduction to the New Testament*. 2nd ed. Grand Rapids, MI: Zondervan, 1992.

Carter, Warren. "Matthew and Empire." Pages 90-119 in *Empire in the New Testament*. NTS. Edited by Stanley E. Porter & Cynthia Long Westfall. Oregon: Pickwick, 2011.

_______. *Matthew and Margins: A Socio-Political and Religious Reading.* Sheffield, England: SAP, 2000.

Case-Winters, Anna. *Matthew: A Theological Commentary on the Bible.* Belief. Louisville: WJK, 2015.

Cassidy, Richard. *John's Gospel in New Perspective: Christology and the Realities of Roman Power.* Maryknoll, NY: Orbis Books, 1992.

Chae, Young S. *Jesus as the Eschatological Davidic Shepherd: Studies in the Old Testament, Second Temple Judaism, and in the Gospel of Matthew.* WUNT 216. Tübingen: Mohr Siebeck, 2006.

Chancey, Mark. *Greco-Roman Culture and the Galilee of Jesus.* Cambridge: CUP, 2005.

Charles, R. H. *A Critical and Exegetical Commentary on the Revelation of St. John.* 2 vols. Edinburgh: T&T Clark, 1920.

Cheon, Samuel. *The Exodus Story in the Wisdom of Solomon: A Study in Biblical Interpretation.* JSPSup 23. Sheffield: SAP, 1997.

Chongloi, Hemkhochon. *Indoi: A Study of Primal Kuki Religious Symbolism in the Hermeneutical Framework of Mircea Eliade.* Delhi: ISPCK, 2008.

Chouinard, Larry. *Matthew.* TCPNC. Joplin, MO: College Press Publishing Co., 1997.

Christensen, Nepper. *Das Matthäus evangelium – ein juden christliches Evangelium?* Aarhus: Universitetsforlaget, 1958.

Clarke, Ernest G. *The Wisdom of Solomon.* CBC. Cambridge: CUP, 1973.

Clarke, Sathianathan. *Dalits and Christianity: Subaltern Religion and Liberation Theology in India.* Delhi: OUP, 1999.

Clements, E. Anne. *Mothers of the Margin? The Significance of the Women in Matthew's Genealogy.* Eugene, OR: Pickwick, 2014.

Clifford, Richard J. *The Wisdom Literature.* IBT. Nashville: Abingdon Press, 1998.

_______. *Wisdom.* NCBC. Edited by Daniel Durken. Collegeville: Liturgical Press, 2012.

Coggins, Richard J. *Sirach.* Sheffield: SAP, 1998.

Colle, Ralph Del. "Miracles in Christianity." Pages 235-253 in *The Cambridge Companion to Miracles.* CCR. Edited by Graham H. Twelftree. Cambridge: CUP, 2011.

Cope, O. Lamar. *Matthew: A Scribe Trained for the Kingdom of Heaven.* Washington: CBAA, 1976.

Corley, Jeremy. "The Book of Sirach." Pages 1188-1254 in *Old Testament.* NCBC. Edited by Daniel Durken. Collegeville: Liturgical Press, 2012.

Cotter, Wendy. *Miracles in Greco-Roman Antiquity: A Sourcebook for the Study of New Testament Miracles Stories.* London: Routledge, 1999.

Cousland, J. R. C. *The Crowds in the Gospel of Matthew.* NovTSup 102. Leiden: Brill, 2002.

Craddock, Fred. *The Pre-Existence of Christ in the New Testament*. Nashville: Abingdon, 1968.

Craig, William Lane. "The Problem of Miracles: A Historical and Philosophical Perspective." Pages 9-40 in *Gospel Perspectives*. Vol. 4. Edited by David Wenham and Craig Blomberg. Sheffield: JSOT Press, 1986.

Crosby, Michael H. *House of Disciples: Church, Economics, & Justice in Matthew.* New York: Orbis Books, 1988.

_______. *Spirituality of Beatitudes: Matthew's Challenges for 1st World Christians.* New York: Orbis Books, 1982.

Crossan, John Dominic., and Jonathan L. Reed. *Excavating Jesus: Beneath the Stones, Behind the Texts: The Key Discoveries for Understanding Jesus in his World.* San Francisco: HarperSanFrancisco, 2001.

Cullmann, Oscar. *The Christology of the New Testament.* London: SCM, 1963.

Culpepper, R. Alan. "The Christology of the Johannine Writings." Pages 66-87 in *Who Do You Say that I Am? Essays on Christology*. Edited by Mark Allan Powell and David R. Bauer. Louisville: Westminster John Knox Press, 1999.

Dalman, Gustaf. *The Words of Jesus*. Translated by D. M. Kay. Edinburgh: T&T Clark, 1902.

Davies, M. *Matthew.* Sheffield, England: JSOT Press, 1993.

Davies, W. D. *Paul and Rabbinic Judaism: Some Rabbinic Elements in Pauline Theology.* 4th ed. Philadelphia: Fortress, 1980.

_______. *The Setting of the Sermon on the Mount.* Cambridge: CUP, 1963.

Davies, W. D., and D. C. Allison. *A Critical and Exegetical Commentary on the Gospel According to Saint Matthew*. 3 vols. Edinburgh: T&T Clark, 1998-1999.

_______. *Matthew 1-7.* ICC. London: T&T Clark, 2004.

_______. *Matthew: A Shorter Commentary based on the Three-Volume International Critical Commentary*. Edited by D. C. Allison. London: T&T Clark, 2004.

_______. *The Gospel According to Matthew.* ICC, 2 vols. Edinburgh: T&T Clark, 1988.

_______. *Introduction and Commentary on Matthew I-VII.* Vol. 1 of *A Critical and Exegetical Commentary of the Gospel According to Saint Matthew.* London: T&T Clark, 1988.

_______. *A Critical and Exegetical Commentary on the Gospel According to Saint Matthew.* ICC, 3 vols. Edinburgh: T&T Clark, 1988.

Deane-Drummond, Celia. *Eco-Theology.* Winona, MN: St. Mary's Press, 2008.

Derrett, J. Duncan M. *Jesus' Audience: The Social and Psychological Environment in Which he Worked.* New York: Seabury, 1974.

DeSilva, David A. *An Introduction to the New Testament: Contexts, Methods and Ministry Formation.* Downers Grove, IL: IVP, 2004.

_______. *Perseverance in Gratitude: A Socio-Rhetorical Commentary on the Epistle "to the Hebrews."* Grand Rapids: Eerdmans, 2000.

Dibelius, Martin. *From Tradition to Gospel*. Translated by Bertram Lee Woolf. New York: Charles Scribner's Sons, 1967.

Dodd, C. H. *According to the Scriptures: The Substructure of New Testament Theology.* London: Nisbet, 1952.

Dokhuma, James. *Hmanlai Mizo Kalphung* [Mizo Traditional Ways of Life]. Aizawl: J. D. Press, 1992.

_______. *Zoram Kohhran Tualṭo Chanchinte* (Histories of the indigenous Churches of Mizoram). Aizawl: D. Buanga, 1975.

Donaldson, Terence L. *Jesus on the Mountains: A Study in Matthean Theology.* Sheffield: JSOT, 1985.

_______. "The Vindicated Son: A Narrative Approach to Matthean Christology." Pages 100-121 in *Contours of Christology in the New Testament*,ed. Richard N. Longenecker. MI: Eerdmans, 2005.

_______. *Jesus on the Mountain: A Study in Matthean Theology.* JSNTSS 8. Sheffield: JSOT Press, 1985.

Douglas, Kelly B., Carter Heyward and Francine Cardman. "Dictionary of Feminist Theologies." Pages 78-85 in *The Strength of Her Witness: Jesus Christ in the Global Voices of Women.* Edited by Elizabeth A. Johnson. Maryknoll, NY: Orbis, 2016.

Drane, John. *Introduction to the New Testament.* Rev. ed. Oxford: Lion Publishing, 1999.

Duane F. Watson. ""Keep Yourselves from Idols": A Socio-Rhetorical Analysis of the Exordium and Peroratio of 1 John." Pages 2981-302 in *Fabrics of Discourse: Essays in Honor of Vernon K. Robbins.* Edited by David B. Gowler, L. Gregory Bloomquist and Duane F. Watson. Harrisburg: Trinity Press International, 2003.

Dube, Musa W. "Savior of the World but not of this World: A Post-Colonial Reading of Spatial Construction in John." Pages 118-135 in *The Postcolonial Bible.* Edited by R.S. Sugirtharajah. Sheffield: SAP, 1998.

Dumbrell, William J. *The Search for Order: Biblical Eschatology in Focus.* Eugene, OR: Wipf & Stock, 2001.

Dunn, James D. G. "Christ, Adam, and Preexistence." Pages 74-83 in *Where Christology Began: Essays on Philippians 2.* Edited by Ralph P. Martin and Brian J. Dodd. Louisville: Westminster John Knox Press, 1998.

_______. "How did Matthew go about Composing his Gospel?" Pages 39-58 in *Jesus, Matthew's Gospel and Early Christianity: Studies in Memory of Graham Stanton.* Edited by Daniel M. Gurtner, Joel Willits and Richard A. Burridge. New York: T&T Clark, 2011.

_______. "Pauline Christology: Shaping the Fundamental Structures." Pages 96-107 in *Christology in Dialogue.* Edited by R. F. Berkey and S. A. Edwards. Cleveland: Pilgrim, 1993.

_______. *Christology in the Making: A New Testament Inquiry into the Origins of the Doctrine of Incarnation.* 2nd ed. Grand Rapids, MI: Eerdmans, 1989.

_______. *Jesus and the Spirit.* London: SCM, 1975.

_______. *The Epistles to the Colossians and to Philemon.* NIGTC. Grand Rapids, MI: Eerdmans, 1996.

_______. *Christology in the Making: A New Testament Inquiry into the Origins of the Doctrine of the Incarnation.* London: SCM, 1980.

_______. *The Theology of Paul the Apostle.* Grand Rapids: Eerdmans, 1998.

Edwards, Denis. *Jesus the Wisdom of God: An Ecological Theology.* New York: Orbis, 1995.

Edwards, Douglas. "The Socio-Economic and Cultural Ethos of Lower Galilee in the First Century: Implications for the Nascent Jesus Movement." Pages 53-73 in *The Galilee in Late Antiquity*. Edited by Lee I. Levine. New York: The Jewish Theological Seminary of America, 1992.

Edwards, James R. *The Gospel According to Mark*. PNTC. Grand Rapids, MI: Eerdmans, 2002.

Edwards, Ruth B. "The Christological Basis of Johannine Footwashing." Pages 367-383 in *Jesus of Nazareth: Lord and Christ: Essays on the Historical Jesus and New Testament Christology. Edited by Joel B. Green and Max Turner. Grand Rapids, MI: Eerdmans, 1994.*

Eichrodt, Walther. *Theology of the Old Testament*. Translated by J. A. Baker. 2 vols. OTL. London: SCM, 1964.

Ellingworth, Paul. *The Epistle to the Hebrews: A Commentary on the Greek Text*. NIGTC. Grand Rapids: Eerdmans, 1993.

Elliot, John H. *A Home for the Homeless: A Sociological Exegesis of 1 Peter. Its Situation and Strategy.* Philadelphia: Fortress, 1981.

Ellis, Earle E. *The Gospel According to Luke.* The Century Bible; Edinburgh: T. Nelson & Sons, 1966.

Eltester, F-W. *Eikon im Neuen Testament.* BZNW 23. Berlin: Alfred Topelmann, 1958.

Esler, Philip F. *The First Christians in their Social Worlds.* New York: Routledge, 1994.

Evans, C. Stephen. *The Historical Christ and the Jesus of Faith: The Incarnational Narrative as History.* Oxford: Clarendon Press, 1996.

Evans, Craig A. *Jesus and His Contemporaries: Comparative Studies. Boston: BAP, 2001.*

Evans, C. F. "The Passion of John," volume 2 of *Explorations in Theology.* London: SCM Press, 1977.

_______. *Jesus and His World: The Archaeological Evidence.* London: SPCK, 2012.

Eve, Eric. *The Healer from Nazareth: Jesus' Miracles in Historical Context.* London: SPCK, 2009.

_______. *The Jewish Context of Jesus' Miracles*. JSNTSup 231. New York: SAP, 2002.

Fauconnier, Gilles., and Mark Turner. *The Way We Think: Conceptual Blending and the Mind's Hidden Complexities.* New York: Basic, 2003.

Fee, Gordon D. *The First Epistle to the Corinthians.* NICNT. Grand Rapids: Eerdmans, 1987.

Filson, Floyd V. *The Gospel According to St. Matthew*. BNTC. London: Adam & Charles Black, 1960.

Fiorenza, Elisabeth Schüssler. *The Book of Revelation: Justice and Judgment*. 2nd ed. Minneapolis: Fortress, 1998.

Fitzmyer, Joseph A. "'Abba and Jesus' Relation to God." Page 28 in *A cause de L'Evangile.* Lectio Divina 123. Paris: Cerf, 1985.

Fletcher-Louis, Crispin H. T. "The Worship of Divine Humanity as God's Image and the Worship of Jesus." Pages 112-128 in *The Jewish Roots of Christological Monotheism: Papers from the St. Andrews Conference on the Historical Origin of the Worship of Jesus*. JSJSup 63. Leiden: Brill, 1999.

Focant, Camille. *The Gospel According to Mark: A Commentary*. Translated by Leslie Robert Keylock. Eugene, OR: Pickwick, 2004.

Fossum, Jarl E. *The Image of the Invisible God: Essays on the Influence of Jewish Mysticism on Early Christology.* NTOA. Freiburg: Universitts verlag Freiburg, 1995.

Fowler, Raymond M. *Loaves and Fishes: The Function of the Feeding Stories in the Gospel of Mark*. SBLDS 54. Chico, CA: Scholars, 1981.

Fox, Matthew. *Meister Eckhart: A Mystic Warrior for our Times.* California: New World Library, 2014.

_______. *The Coming of the Cosmic Christ: The Healing of Mother Earth and the Birth of a Global Renaissance.* Melbourne: Collins Dove, 1988.

France, R. T. *Matthew – Evangelist and Teacher.* Exeter: The Paternoster Press, 1989.

_______. *Matthew*. TNTC. Leicester: IVP, 1985.

_______. *Matthew: Evangelist and Teacher.* Downers Grove: IVP, 1989.

_______. *The Gospel of Matthew*. NICNT. Grand Rapids, MI: Eerdmans, 2007.

Frey, Jörg. "Different Patterns of Dualistic Thought in the Qumran Library: Reflections on their Background and History." Pages 275-335 in *Legal Texts and Legal Issues: Proceedings of the Second Meeting of the International Organization for Qumran Studies Cambridge 1995*. Edited by Moshe Bernstein et al. Leiden: Brill, 1997.

Freyne, Seán. "Reading the Gospels in the Light of the Window of the Evangelists at Chartres Cathedral." Pages 107-120 in *Radical Pluralism and Truth, David Tracy and the Hermeneutics of Religion*. Edited by W. Jeanrond and J. Rike. New York: Crossroad, 1991.

_______. "Urban-Rural Relations in First-Century Galilee: Some Suggestions from the Literary Sources." Pages 75-94 in *The Galilee in Late Antiquity*, ed. Lee I. Levine. New York: The Jewish Theological Seminary of America, 1992.

_______. *Galilee and Gospel: Collected Essays.* WUNT 125. Tübingen: Mohr, 2000.

_______. *Jesus, A Jewish Galilean: A New Reading of the Jesus-Story.* London: T&T Clark, 2004.

_______. *The Twelve: Disciples and Apostles: A Study in the Theology of the First Three Gospels.* London: Sheed & Ward, 1968.

Fuller, Reginald H. *Interpreting the Miracles.* London: SCM, 1963.

_______. *The Foundations of New Testament Christology.* London: Collins, 1965.

Funk, Robert W. *The Acts of Jesus: The Search for the Authentic Deeds of Jesus.* New York: HarperCollins, 1998.

_______., and the Jesus Seminar. *The Acts of Jesus: What Did Jesus Really Do?* New York: HarperCollins, 1998.

_______., and Roy W. Hoover, eds. *The Five Gospels. New York: Macmillan, 1993.*

Gabathuler, H. J. *Jesus Christus Haupt der Kirche-Haupt der Welt*, ATANT. Stuttgart: Zwingli, 1965.

Gager, J. G. "Social Description and Sociological Explanation in the Study of Early Christianity: A Review Essay." Pages 428-440 in *The Bible and Liberation*. Edited by N. K. Gottwald. Maryknoll: Orbis, 1983.

Galipeau, Steven A. *Transforming Body and Soul: Therapeutic Wisdom in the Gospel Healing Stories*. Rev. ed. Carmel, CA: Fisher King Press, 2011.

Garland, D. E. *The Intention of Matthew 23.* NovTSup 52. Leiden: Brill, 1979.

Gathercole, Simon J. *The Pre-existent Son: Recovering the Christologies of Matthew, Mark, and Luke.* Grand Rapids: Eerdmans, 2006.

Geisler, Norman L. *Miracles and the Modern Mind: A Defense of Biblical Miracles. Eugene, OR: Wipf & Stock, 1992.*

*Geivett, R. Douglas., and Gary R. Habermas. Introduction to In Defense of Miracles: A Comprehensive Case for God's Action in History. Downers Grove, IL: IVP, 1997.*

Gerhardsson, Birger. *The Mighty Acts of Jesus According to Matthew.* Eugene, OR: Wipf & Stock, 1979.

Gilbert, M. "Wisdom Literature." Pages 283-324 in *Jewish Writings of the Second Temple Period*. Edited by Michael E. Stone. Philadelphia: Fortress, 1984.

Gnuse, Robert Karl. *Dreams and Dream Reports in the Writings of Josephus: A Traditio-Historical Analysis*. Leiden: Brill, 1996.

Goodacre, Mark. "Redaction Criticism." Pages 38-42 in *Searching for Meaning: An Introduction to Interpreting the New Testament*. Edited by Paula Gooder. Louisville: SPCK, 2008.

Goshen-Gottstein, Alon. "Ben Sira's Praise of the Fathers: A Canon-Conscious Reading." Pages 235-267 in *Ben Sira's God: Proceedings of the International Ben Sira Conference. Durham – Ushaw College 2001*. Edited by Renate Egger-Wenzel. BZAW 321. Berlin: Gruyter, 2002.

Goswami, B. B. "Hill Tribesmen of Northeast India: The Impact of Christianity." Pages 123-129 in *The Tribal World and its Transformation*. Edited by Bhupinder Singh and J. S. Bhandari. New Delhi: Concept, 1978.

Goulder, Michael D. *Midrash and Lection in Matthew*. London: SPCK, 1974.

_______. *Type and History in Acts*. London: SPCK, 1964.

Grabbe, Lester L. *An Introduction to the Second Temple Judaism: History and Religion of the Jews in the Time of Nehemiah, The Maccabees, Hillel and Jesus*. London: T&T Clark, 2010.

Graf, Fritz. *Magic in the Ancient World*. Translated by Franklin Philip. Cambridge: HUP, 1997.

Grant, Robert M. *Miracle and Natural Law in Graeco-Roman and Early Christian Thought*. Eugene, OR: Wipf & Stock, 1952.

Green, Colin J. D. *Christology in Cultural Perspective: Marking Out the Horizons*. Grand Rapids: Eerdmans, 2003.

Griffiths, Jonathan I. *Hebrews and Divine Speech*. LNTS 507. Edited by Mark Goodacre. London: Bloomsbury, 2014.

Groothuis, Douglas. *Jesus in an age of Controversy*. Eugene, OR: Wipf & Stock, 1996.

Grossberg, Daniel. "The Literary Treatment of Nature in Psalms." Pages 69-87 in *Boundaries of the Ancient Near Eastern World: A Tribute to Cyrus H. Gordon*. Edited by Meir Lubetski, Claire Gottlieb and Sharon Keller. JSOTSup 273. Sheffield: SAP, 1998.

Gundry, Robert H. *Matthew: A Commentary on his Handbook for a Mixed Church under Persecution*. 2nd ed. Grand Rapids, MI: Eerdmans, 1994.

_______. *Matthew: A Commentary on His Literary and Theological Art*. Grand Rapids: Eerdmans: 1981.

_______. *The Use of the Old Testament in St. Matthew's Gospel*. SNT 18. Leiden: E.J. Brill, 1967.

Gurtner, Daniel M. "The Gospel of Matthew from Stanton to Present." Pages 23-38 in *Jesus, Matthew's Gospel and Early Christianity: Studies in Memory of Graham N. Stanton*. Edited by Daniel M. Gurtner, Joel Willitts and Richard A. Burridge. New York: T&T Clark, 2011.

Guthrie, Donald G. "The Christology of Revelation." Pages 397-412 in *Jesus of Nazareth: Lord and Christ: Essays on the Historical Jesus and the New Testament Christology*. Edited by J. B. Green and Max Turner. Grand Rapids, MI: Eerdmans, 1994.

_______. *New Testament Introduction: The Gospels and Acts.* Chicago: IVP, 1965.

_______. *New Testament Theology.* England: IVP, 1985.

Gutiérrez, Gustavo. "Statement." Pages 310-311 in *Theology in the Americas*. Edited by Sergio Torres and John Eagleson. Maryknoll: Orbis, 1976.

_______. *A Theology of Liberation: History, Politics, and Salvation. Translated by Sister Caridad Inda and John Eagleson. Maryknoll: Orbis, 1973.*

*Habermas, Gary R. "Did Jesus Perform Miracles." Pages 117-140 in Jesus Under Fire: Modern Scholarship Reinvents the Historical Jesus. Edited by Michael J. Wilkins and J. P. Moreland (Grand Rapids, MI: Zondervan, 1995), 117-140.*

Hagner, Donald A. Matthew 1-13. WBC 33a. Dallas: Word Books, 1993.

_______. *Matthew 14-28*. WBC 33b. Dallas: Word Books, 1995.

_______. *The Jewish Reclamation of Jesus: An Analysis and Critique of Modern Jewish Study of Jesus.* Eugene: Wipf & Stock, 1984.

Hall, Donald E. *Literary and Cultural Theory: From Basic Principles to Advanced Applications.* Boston: Houghton Mifflin, 2001.

Hall, Douglas John. *Imaging God: Dominion as Stewardship.* Grand Rapids: Eerdmans, 1986.

Hanson, Anthony T. *The Prophetic Gospel: A Study of John and the Old Testament*. Scholars Edition in Biblical Studies. London: T&T Clark, 1991.

Hamilton, Catherine Sider. *The Death of Jesus in Matthew: Innocent Blood and the End of Exile*. SNTSMS 167. New York: CUP, 2017.

Hare, Douglas R. A. *The Theme of Jewish Persecution of Christians in the Gospel According to St. Matthew.* Cambridge: CUP, 2005.

_______. *Matthew: Interpretation: A Bible Commentary for Teaching and Preaching.* Louisville: John Knox Press, 1993.

Harrington, Daniel J. *The Gospel of Matthew*. Vol. 1. SPS. Collegeville, MN: The Liturgical Press, 1991.

Harris, Elizabeth. *Prologue and Gospel: The Theology of the Fourth Gospel.* London: T&T Clark, 2004.

Hatina, Thomas R. "From History to Myth and Back Again: The Historicizing Function of Scripture in Matthew 2." Pages 98-118 in *The Gospel of Matthew*. Edited by Thomas R. Hatina. Vol. 2 of *Biblical Interpretation in Early Christian Gospel.* London: T&T Clark, 2008.

Hawthorne, Gerald F. "In the Form of God and Equal with God (Philippians 2:6)." Pages 96-110 in *Where Christology Began: Essays on Philippians 2*. Edited by Ralph P. Martin and Brian J. Dodd. Louisville: Westminster John Knox Press, 1998.

Hayes, Zachary. "Incarnation and Creation in the Theology of St. Bonaventure," Pages 309-329 in *Studies Honoring Ignatius Brady, Friar Minor.* Edited by Romano Stephen Almagno and Conrad Harkins. St. Bonaventure, NY: The Franciscan Institute, 1976.

Hays, R. B. "The Canonical Matrix of the Gospels." Pages 53-75 in *The Cambridge Companion to the Gospels*. Edited by Stephen C. Barton. Cambridge: CUP, 2006.

Headlam, Arthur C. *The Miracles of the New Testament.* London: John Murray, 1914.

Hegermann, H. *Die Vorstellung vom Schopfungsmittler im Hellenistischen Judentum und Urchristentum*. TU 82. Berlin: Akademie, 1961.

Heil, John Paul. *Jesus Walking on the Sea*. An Bib 87. Rome: Biblical Institute, 1981.

Held, Heinz J. "Matthew as Interpreter of the Miracle Stories." Pages 242-245 in *Tradition and Interpretation in Matthew*. Edited by G. Bornkamm, G. Barth and H.J. Held, trans. Percy Scott. Philadelphia: Westminster, 1963.

Helyer, Larry R. *The Witness of Jesus, Paul and John: An Exploration in Biblical Theology.* Downers Grove, IL: IVP, 2008.

Hemer, Collin J. *The Letters to the Seven Churches of Asia in their Local Setting.* JSNTSup 11. Sheffield: JSOT Press, 1986.

Hendrickx, Herman. *The Miracle Stories of the Synoptic Gospels.* London: Geoffrey Chapman, 1987.

Hengel, Martin. *Judaism and Hellenism: Studies in their Encounter in Palestine during the Early Hellenistic Period.* London: SCM, 1974.

Henrichs-Tarasenkova, Nina. *Luke's Christology of Divine Identity.* LNTS. London: T&T Clark, 2016.

Hiddleston, Jane. *Understanding Postcolonialism.* Stocksfield: Acumen, 2009.

Hiebert, Theodore. "Air, the First Sacred Thing: The Conception of חור in the Hebrew Scriptures." Pages 9-20 in *Exploring Ecological Hermeneutics*. Edited by Norman C. Habel and Peter Trudinger. Atlanta: SBL, 2008.

Hill, Brennan R. *Christian Faith and the Environment: Making Vital Connections, Ecology and Justice Series.* Eugene, OR: Wipf & Stock, 2006.

Himmelfarb, Martha. *Between Temple and Torah: Essays on Priests, Scribes, and Visionaries in the Second Temple Period and Beyond.* TSAJ 151. Tübingen: Mohr Siebeck, 2013.

Hminga, C. L. "The Traditional Mizo Concept of God." Pages 45-53 in *Toward a Tribal Theology: The Mizo Perspective*. Edited by K. Thanzauva. Jorhat: Mizo Theological Conference, 1989.

Horsley, Richard A. *Sociology and the Jesus Movement.* New York: Crossroads, 1989.

_______. *Bandits, Prophets, and Messiahs: Popular Movements in the Time of Jesus.* Harrisburg: Trinity Press International, 1999.

_______. *Galilee: History, Politics, People.* Valley Forge: Trinity Press International, 1995.

Hultgren, Arland. *The Parables of Jesus: A Commentary.* Grand Rapids: Eerdmans, 2000.

Hume, David. *An Enquiry Concerning Human Understanding*. 2nd ed. Edited by Eric Steinberg. Indianapolis: Hackett, 1993.

Humphreys, Colin J. *The Miracles of Exodus: A Scientist's Discovery of the Extraordinary Natural Causes of the Biblical Stories.* New York: Harper Collins, 2004.

Hurst, L. D. "The Christology of Hebrews 1 and 2." Pages 151-164 in *The Glory of Christ in the NT: Studies in Christology in Memory of George Bradford Caird*. Edited by L. D. Hurst and N. T. Wright. Oxford: Clarendon, 1987.

Hurtado, Larry W. *How on Earth Did Jesus Become a God? Historical Questions about Earliest Devotion to Jesus.* Grand Rapids, MI: Eerdmans, 2005.

Isaac, E. "1 (Ethiopic Apocalypse of) Enoch: A New Translation and Introduction." Pages 5-89 in *Apocalyptic Literature and Testaments*. Edited by James H. Charlesworth. Vol.1 of *The Old Testament Pseudepigrapha*. Edited by James H. Charlesworth. New York: Doubleday, 1983.

Jackson, David R. *Enochic Judaism: Three Defining Paradigm Exemplars.* LSTS. London: T&T Clark, 2004.

Janecko, Benedict. "Ecology, Nature, Psalms." Pages 96-108 in *The Psalms and Other Studies on the Old Testament*. Edited by Jack C. Knight and Lawrence A. Sinclair. Nashotah: Nashotah House Seminary, 1990.

Jensen, Morten Høerning. *Herod Antipas in Galilee: The Literary and Archaeological Sources on the Reign of Herod Antipas and its Socio-Economic Impact on Galilee*. 2nd ed. Tübingen: Mohr, 2010.

Jensen, Richard A. *Preaching Matthew's Gospel: A Narrative Approach.* Lima, OH: CSS, 1998.

Jeremias, Joachim. "The Lord's Prayer in Modern Research." Pages 80-95 in *New Testament Issues*. Edited by Richard Batey. New York: Harper & Row, 1970.

_______. *Jerusalem in the Time of Jesus: An Investigation into Economic and Social Conditions during the New Testament Period.* Translated by F. H. and C. H. Cave. Philadelphia: Fortress, 1969.

_______. *New Testament Theology: The Proclamation of Jesus.* Translated by John Bowden. New York: Scribner's, 1971.

_______. *The Central Message of the New Testament.* New York: Charles Scribner's Sons, 1965.

_______. *The Eucharistic Words of Jesus*. Translated by Norman Perrin. NTL. London: SCM, 1966.

Johnson, Elizabeth. *She Who is: The Mystery of God in Feminist Theological Discourse.* New York: Crossroad, 1992.

Joy, C. I. David. *Christology Re-Visited: Profiles and Prospects.* Bangalore: Asian Trading Corporation, 2007.

_______. *Hermeneutics: Foundations and New Trends. A Postcolonial Reading of John 4.* Delhi: ISPCK, 2012.

_______. *Mark and its Subaltern: A Hermeneutical Paradigm for a Postcolonial Context.* London: Equinox, 2008.

Kahl, Werner. *New Testament Miracle Stories in their Religious-Historical Setting: A Religionsgeschichtliche Comparison from a Structural Perspective.* FRLANT 163. Göttingen: Vandenhoeck and Ruprecht, 1994.

Kappelle, Robert P. Vanda. *Wisdom Revealed: The Message of Biblical Wisdom Literature – Then and Now.* Eugene, OR: Wipf & Stock, 2014.

Käsemann, Ernst. "A Primitive Christian Baptismal Liturgy." Pages 149-168 in *Essays on New Testament Themes*. SBT 41. Naperville: Allenson, 1964.

Kaye, Bruce N. *The Supernatural in the New Testament.* London: Lutterworth, 1977.

Keating, Daniel. "Thomas Aquinas and the Epistle to the Hebrews: The Excellence of Christ." Pages 84-99 in *Christology, Hermeneutics and Hebrews: Profiles from the History of Interpretation*. LNTS 423. Edited by John C. Laansma and Daniel J. Treier. London: Bloomsbury, 2012.

Kee, Howard Clark. *Medicine, Miracle and Magic in New Testament Times.* Cambridge: CUP, 1986.

Keener, Craig S. "Jesus and Parallel Jewish and Greco-Roman Figures." Pages 85-111 in *Christian Origins and Greco-Roman Culture: Social and Literary Contexts for the New Testament.* Edited by Stanley Porter and

Andrew W. Pitts. Vol. 1 of *Early Christianity in its Hellenistic Context.* Vol. 9 in *Texts and Editions for New Testament Study.* Leiden: Brill, 2013.

_______. *A Commentary on the Gospel of Matthew.* Grand Rapids, MI: Eerdmans, 1999.

_______. *Miracles: The Credibility of the New Testament Accounts.* 2 vols. Grand Rapids: Baker, 2011.

_______. *The Gospel of Matthew: A Socio-Rhetorical Commentary.* Grand Rapids: Eerdmans, 2009.

_______. *The IVP Bible Background Commentary: New Testament.* Downers Grove, IL: IVP, 1993.

Keitzar, Renthy. *In Search of a Relevant Gospel Message.* Guwahati: CLC, 1995.

Kempinski, Aharon., and Michael Avi-Yonah. *Syria-Palestine II: From the Bronze Age to the End of the Classical World [2200 B.C. – 324 A.D.]* Geneva: Nagel, 1979.

Kennedy, Joel. *The Recapitulation of Israel: Use of Israel's History in Matthew 1:1-4:11.* WUNT 257. Tübingen: Mohr Siebeck, 2008.

Kertelge, Karl. "The Epiphany of Jesus in the Gospel." Pages 105-124 in *The Interpretation of Mark.* 2nd ed. SNTI. Edited by William R. Telford. Edinburgh: T&T Clark, 1995.

Khamrang, Khayaipam. "The Tangkhul Naga Tribe (India) between Tradition and Modernity." Pages 35-72 in *Inkulturation zwischen Tradition und Modernitat. Edited by Fritz Frei. Fribourg: Presses Universitaires de Fribourg, 2000.*

Kilpatrick, G. D. *The Origins of the Gospel According to St. Matthew.* Philadelphia: Fortress, 1962.

Kim, Seyoon. *The Origin of Paul's Gospel.* WUNT 2. Edited by Martin Hengel and Otfried Hofius. Tübingen: Mohr, 1984.

Kingsbury, Jack D. *Jesus Christ in Matthew, Mark, and Luke.* Eugene: Fortress, 1981.

_______. *Matthew as Story.* Philadelphia: Fortress, 1986.

_______. *Matthew: Structure, Christology, Kingdom.* Philadelphia, PA: Fortress, 1975.

_______. *The Christology of Mark's Gospel.* Philadelphia: Fortress, 1983.

_______. *The Parables of Jesus in Matthew 13: A Study in Redaction-Criticism.* Richmond: John Knox, 1969.

Kipgen, Mangkhosat. *Christianity and Mizo.* Aizawl: MTC, 1997.

Kirk, J. R. Daniel. *A Man Attested by God: The Human Jesus of the Synoptic Gospels. Grand Rapids, MI: Eerdmans, 2016.*

Klawans, Jonathan. *Purity, Sacrifice, and the Temple: Symbolism and Supersessionism in the Study of Ancient Judaism.* Oxford: OUP, 2006.

Kloppenborg, John S. *The Tenants in the Vineyard: Ideology, Economics, and Agrarian Conflict in Jewish Palestine.* Tübingen: Mohr, 2006.

Koskenniemi, Erkki. "Miracles of the Devil and His Assistants in Early Judaism and Their Influence on the Gospel of Matthew." Pages 84-97 in *Evil and the Devil.* Edited by Ida Fröhlich and Erkki Koskenniemi. LNTS 481. London: T&T Clark, 2013.

Koskenniemi, Erkki. *The Old Testament Miracle-Workers in Early Judaism.* WUNT 206. Tübingen: Mohr Siebeck, 2005.

_______. "Old Testament Figures as Miracle Workers." Pages 77-86 in *Religious and Spiritual Events.* Edited by J. Harrold Ellens. Vol. 1 of *Miracles: God, Science, and Psychology in the Paranormal.* Edited by J. Harrold Ellens. Westport, CT: Greenwood Press, 2008.

Köstenberger, Andreas J. "Baptism in the Gospel." Pages 11-34 in *Believer's Baptism: Sign of the New Covenant in Christ.* NSBT. Nashville: B&H Academics, 2006.

Kristeva, Julia. "Word, Dialogue and Novel." Pages 64-91 in *Desire in Language: A Semiotic Approach to Language and Art.* Edited by Leon S. Roudiez. Translated by T. Gora, et al. New York: CUP, 1980.

Kümmel, W. G. *Introduction to the New Testament.* Nashville: Abingdon, 1957.

Kuruvila, K. P. *The Word Became Flesh: A Christological Paradigm for Doing Theology in India.* Delhi: ISPCK, 2002.

Kysar, Robert. *Voyages with John: Charting the Fourth Gospel.* Waco/Texas: BUP, 2005.

Laato, Antti. *A Star is Rising: The Historical Development of the Old Testament Royal Ideology and the Rise of the Jewish Messianic Expectations.* ISFCJ 5. Atlanta: Scholars Press, 1997.

Lalpekhlua, L. H. *Contextual Christology: A Tribal Perspective.* Delhi: ISPCK, 2007.

Lalsawma. *Revivals the Mizo Way: Forty Years of Revival Movements in Mizoram.* Aizawl: Lalsawma, 1994.

Lane, Dermot A. "The Doctrine of the Incarnation: Human and Cosmic Considerations." Pages 209-233 in *Contemporary Catholic Theology: A Reader.* Edited by Michael A. Hayes and Liam Gearon. New York: Continuum, 2000.

Lane, William L. *The Gospel According to Mark.* NICNT. Grand Rapids: Eerdmans, 1974.

Lategan, Bernard. "Mapping the Hermeneutical process." Pages 65-105 in *Focusing on the Message: New Testament hermeneutics, exegesis and methods*. Edited by Du Toit A. Pretoria: Protea, 2009.

Latourelle, René. *The Miracles of Jesus and the Theology of Miracles.* Translated by Matthew J. O'Connell. New York: Paulist Press, 1988.

Lawrence, Joel. *Bonhoeffer: A Guide for the Perplexed.* New York: T&T Clark, 2010.

Leaney, A. R. C. *A Commentary on the Gospel According to St. Luke.* London: Adam & Charles Black, 1966.

Lee, Aquila H. I. *From Messiah to Preexistent Son: Jesus' Self-Consciousness and Early Christian Exegesis of Messianic Psalms.* Eugene: Wipf & Stock, 2005.

Lee, Bernard J. *The Galilean Jewishness of Jesus: Retrieving the Jewish Origins of Christianity.* Vol. 1 of *Conversation on the Road not Taken.* New York: Paulist Press, 1988.

Lee, Jae Hun. "Günther Bornkamm and Redaction Criticism." Pages 321-340 in *Prevailing Methods before 1980*. Edited by Stanley E. Porter and Sean A. Adams. Vol. 1 of *Pillars in the History of Biblical Interpretation.* Eugene, OR: Pickwick, 2016.

Lefebure, Leo D. *Toward a Contemporary Wisdom Christology: A Study of Karl Rahner and Norman Pittenger.* New York: University Press of America, 1988.

Leske, Adrian M. *The Prophetic Vision and the Real Jesus: Growth of the Prophetic Vision and its Impact on the Mission of Jesus in Matthew's Gospel.* Eugene: Wipf & Stock, 2017.

Lightman, Alan P. *Ancient Light: Our Changing View of the Universe.* Cambridge: HUP, 1991.

Limburg, James. "Quoth the Raven: Psalm 147 and the Environment." Pages 101-112 in *A God So Near: Essays on Old Testament Theology in Honor of Patrick D. Miller. Edited by Brent A. Strawn and Nancy R. Bowen. Winona Lake, IN: Eisenbrauns, 2003.*

Lindars, Barnabas. *New Testament Apologetic: The Doctrinal Significance of the Old Testament Quotations.* London: SCM, 1961.

_______. *John.* Sheffield: JSOT Press, 1990.

_______. *New Testament Apologetic: The Doctrinal Significance of Old Testament Quotations.* London: SCM, 1961.

Lloyd, J. Meirion. *History of the Church in Mizoram.* Aizawl: SPB, 1991.

_______. *On Every High Hill.* Liverpool: CMFMO, 1956.

Loader, William. *The New Testament with Imagination: A Fresh Approach to Its Writings and Themes.* Grand Rapids, MI: Eerdmans, 2007.

Lohse, E. *Colossians and Philemon.* Philadelphia: Fortress, 1971.

Lois, Julio. "Christology in the Theology of Liberation." Pages 168-193 in *Mysterium Liberationis: Fundamental Concepts of Liberation Theology*. Translated by Robert R. Barr. Edited by Ignacio Ellacuria and Jon Sobrino. Maryknoll: Orbis, 1993.

Long, Philip J. *Jesus the Bridegroom: The Origin of the Eschatological Feast as a Wedding Banquet in the Synoptic Gospels. Eugene, OR: Pickwick, 2013.*

Long, T. C. *Matthew.* Louisville: WJK, 1997.

Longchar, Wati A. "Indigenous People's Theologies in Asia: Methods and Perspectives." Pages 147-169 in *Issues in Theological Research: A Methodological Exploration*. Edited by Wati A. Longchar. Bangalore: BTESSC/SATHRI, 2010.

_______. *The Traditional Tribal Worldview and Modernity: Focus on North East India.* Jorhat: Limatula LKr., 1995.

Longenecker, Richard N. "Christological Materials in the Early Christian Communities." Pages 47-78 in *Contours of Christology in the New Testament*. Edited by Richard N. Longenecker. Grand Rapids: Eerdmans, 2005.

Luz, Ulrich. *Matthew 1-7.* Minneapolis: Augsburg, 1989.

_______. *Studies in Matthew*. Translated by Rosemary Selle. Grand Rapids, MI: Eerdmans, 2005.

Macaskill, Grant. *Revealed Wisdom and Inaugurated Eschatology in Ancient Judaism and Early Christianity.* Boston: Brill, 2007.

Macquarrie, John. *Principle of Christian Theology.* London: SCM, 1977.

MacRae, George. "Miracles in the Antiquities of Josephus." Pages 129-147 in *Miracles: Cambridge Studies in their Philosophy and History.* Edited by C. F. D. Moule. London: Mowbray, 1965.

Madden, Patrick J. *Jesus' Walking on the Sea: An Investigation of the Origin of the Narrative Account.* Berlin: de Gruyter, 1997.

Malina, Bruce J., and John J. Pilch. *Social-Science Commentary on the Book of Revelation.* Minneapolis: Fortress, 2000.

Malina, Bruce. "The Social Sciences and Biblical Interpretation." Pages 11-25 in *Bible and Liberation: Political and Social Hermeneutics*. Edited by N. Gottwald. Maryknoll: Orbis, 1983.

Maloney, S. J., George A. *The Cosmic Christ: From Paul to Teilhard.* New York: Sheed & Ward, 1968.

Malsawma, H. L. *Sociology of the Mizos.* Guwahati: Spectrum Publications, 2002.

Manson, T. W. *On Paul and John: Some Selected Theological Themes*. SBT 38. Edited by Matthew Black. London: SCM, 1963.

Marshall, I. Howard. *Luke, Historian and Theologian.* Exeter: Paternoster, 1970.

Martin, Ralph P. *Carmen Christi.* New York: CUP, 1967.

Marttila, Marko. *Foreign Nations in the Wisdom of Ben Sira: A Jewish Sage between Opposition and Assimilation.* DCLS 13. Berlin: de Gruyter, 2012.

Marxsen, Willi. *The Beginnings of Christology, together with the Lord's Supper as a Christological Problem*. Translated by P. Achtemeier and L. Nieting. Philadelphia: Fortress, 1979.

Matera, Frank J. *New Testament Christology.* Louisville: Westminster John Knox Press, 1999.

McDowell, Sean. *The Fate of the Apostles: Examining the Martyrdom Accounts of the Closest Followers of Jesus.* London: Routledge, 2016.

McFague, Sallie. "An Ecological Christology: Does Christianity Have It?" Pages 29-45 in *Christianity and Ecology*. Edited by Dieter Hessel and Rosemary Radford Ruether. Cambridge: HUP, 2000.

_______. *Metaphorical Theology: Models of God in Religious Language.* Philadelphia: Fortress, 1982.

_______. *The Body of God: An Ecological Theology.* London: SCM, 1993.

McKenna, Megan. *Not Counting Women and Children: Neglected Stories from the Bible*. New York: Maryknoll, 1994.

McKenzie, John L. "Aspects of Old Testament Thought." Pages 1285-1287 in *The New Testament and Topical Articles*, JBC 2. Englewood Cliffs: Prentice-Hall, 1968.

Meier, John P. *Matthew.* Collegeville, MN: Liturgical Press, 1980.

Meier, John P. *Rethinking the Historical Jesus: Mentor, Message, and Miracles*. Vol. 2 of *A Marginal Jew: Rethinking the Historical Jesus*. ABRL. New York: Doubleday, 1994.

_______. *The Roots of the Problem and the Person*. Vol. 1 of *A Marginal Jew: Rethinking the Historical Jesus.* ABRL. New York: Doubleday, 1991.

_______. *The Vision of Matthew.* New York: Paulist, 1978.

Metzger, B., and M. D. Coogan, eds. *Oxford Companion to the Bible. New York: OUP, 1993.*

Meynell, Hugo Anthony. *God and the World: The Coherence of Christian Theism*. London: SPCK, 1971.

Michiela, Daniel A. *The Dead Sea Genesis Apocryphon: A New Text and Translation with Introduction and Special Treatment of Columns 13-17.* Leiden: Brill, 2009.

Milavec, Aaron. *Didache: Faith, Hope, and Life of the Earliest Christian Communities, 50-70 C.E.* New York: The Norman Press, 1989.

Mitch, Curtis., and Edward Sri. *The Gospel of Matthew.* CCSS. Grand Rapids, MI: Baker Academics, 2010.

Moberly, R. Walter L. "Miracles in the Hebrew Bible." Pages 57-74 in *The Cambridge Companion to Miracles*. CCR. Edited by Graham H. Twelftree. Cambridge: CUP, 2011.

Moffitt, David M. "Serving in the Tabernacle in Heaven: Sacred Space, Jesus' High-Priestly Sacrifice, and Hebrews' Analogical Theology." Pages 259-279 in *Hebrews in Contexts.* Edited by Gabriella Gelardini and Harold W. Attridge. Leiden: Brill, 2016.

Moltmann, Jürgen. *The Way of Jesus Christ: Christology in Messianic Dimensions*. Translated by Margaret Kohl. Minneapolis: Fortress, 1993.

Morgan, Robert. "Incarnation, Myth, and Theology: Ernst Kasemann's Interpretation of Philippians 2:5-11." Pages 43-73 in *Where Christology Began: Essays on Philippians 2.* Edited by Ralph P. Martin and Brian J. Dodd. Louisville: Westminster John Knox Press, 1998.

Morris, Leon. *Studies in the Fourth Gospel.* Grand Rapids: Eerdmans, 1969.

_______. *The Gospel According to Matthew.* PNTC. Grand Rapids, MI: Eerdmans,1992.

Moss, Charlene McAfee. *The Zechariah Tradition and the Gospel of Matthew.* Berlin: de Gruyter, 2008.

Moule, C. F. D. *The Birth of the New Testament.* New York: Harper and Row, 1962.

_______. *The Origin of Christology.* Cambridge: CUP, 1977.

Mounce, Robert H. *Matthew.* UBCS 16. Grand Rapids, MI: Baker, 2011.

Murphy, Frederick J. *Apocalypticism in the Bible and Its World: A Comprehensive Introduction.* Grand Rapids: Baker, 2012.

Mussner, Franz. *The Miracles of Jesus: An Introduction.* Notre Dame: University of Notre Dame Press, 1968.

Nag, Chitta Ranjan. *Mizo Society in Transition.* New Delhi: Vikas Publishing House Pvt. Ltd., 1993.

Neusner, J. *Formative Judaism: Religious, Historical and Literary Studies.* Chico: Scholars Press, 1982.

Neville, David. *Mark's Gospel Prior or Posterior? A Reappraisal of the Phenomenon of Order*. JSNTSup 222. New York: SAP, 2002.

Nicholls, Rachel. *Walking on the Water: Reading MT. 14:22-33 in the Light of its Wirkungsgeschichte. Leiden: Brill, 2008.*

Nickelsburg, George W. E. *1 Enoch 1: A Commentary of the Book of 1 Enoch*. Edited by Klaus Baltzer. Minneapolis: Fortress, 2001.

Nirmal, Arvind P. "Towards a Dalit Christian Theology." Pages 27-40 in *Frontiers in Asian Christian Theology: Emerging Trends.* Maryknoll: Orbis, 1994.

Nolan, Albert. *Jesus before Christianity.* Maryknoll: Orbis, 1978.

Nolan, Brian M. *The Royal Son of God: The Christology of Matthew 1-2 in the Setting of the Gospel.* Vandenhoeck & Ruprecht, 1979.

Northcott, Michael S. *A Political Theology of Climate Change.* Grand Rapids: Eerdmans, 2013.

Novakovic, Lidija. "Miracles in Second Temple and Early Rabbinic Judaism." Pages 95-112 in *The Cambridge Companion to Miracles*. CCR. Edited by Graham H. Twelftree. Cambridge: CUP, 2011.

Novenson, Matthew V. *Christ Among the Messiahs: Christ Language in Paul and Messiah Language in Ancient Judaism.* Oxford: OUP, 2012.

Nowell-Smith, Patrick. "Miracles–The Philosophical Approach." Pages 392-400 in *Philosophy of Religion: Selected Readings*. Edited by William L. Rowe and William J. Wainwright. New York: Harcourt Brace Jovanovich, 1973.

O'Brien, P. T. *The Epistle to the Philippians*. NIGTC. Grand Rapids, MI: Eerdmans, 1991.

Orchard, Helen C. *Courting Betrayal: Jesus as Victim in the Gospel of John.* JSNTSup 161. Sheffield: SAP, 1998.

O'Day, Gail R. "Miracle Discourse and the Gospel of John." Pages 175-188 in *Miracle Discourse in the New Testament*. Edited by Duane F. Watson. Atlanta: SBL, 2012.

O'Grady, John F. *The Gospel of Matthew: Question by Question*. QQBSC. New York: Paulist, 2007.

Orton, David E. *The Understanding Scribe: Matthew and the Apocalyptic Ideal.* London: T&T Clark, 2004.

Osborne, Grant R. *Matthew*. ECNT. Grand Rapids: Zondervan, 2010.

Osborne, Kenan B. *Sacramental Theology: A General Introduction.* New York: Paulist Press, 1988.

Osburn, Carroll D. *Essay on Women in Earliest Christianity.* 2 vols. Eugene: Wipf & Stock, 1993.

Overman, J. Andrew. *Church and Community in Crisis: The Gospel According to Matthew*. NTC. Pennsylvania: Trinity Press International, 1996.

_______. *Church and Community in Crisis: The Gospel According to Matthew*. NTC. Pennsylvania: Trinity Press International, 1996.

_______. *Matthew's Gospel and Formative Judaism: The Social World of the Matthean Community.* Minneapolis: Fortress, 1990.

Parry, N. E. *A Monograph of Lushai Customs and Ceremonies.* Shillong: Assam Government Press, 1928. Repr., Aizawl: Tribal Research Institute, 1988.

Parry, Robin A. *The Biblical Cosmos: A Pilgrim's Guide to the Weird and Wonderful World of the Bible.* Eugene, OR: Cascade Books, 2014.

Pate, C. Marvin. *The Reverse of the Curse: Paul, Wisdom, and the Law*. WUNT 2. Tübingen: Mohr Siebeck, 2000.

Patterson, Stephen J. *The Gospel of Thomas and Jesus.* Sonomo: Polebridge, 1993.

Patterson, Sue. "Creation and Postmodernity." Pages 84-111 in *The Task of Theology Today: Doctrines and Dogma*. Edited by V. Pfitzner and H. Regan. Adelaide: Australian Theological Forum, 1998.

Paulus, Heinrich. *Exegetisches Handbuch uber die drei ersten Evangelien.* 3 vols. Heidelberg: Winter, 1830-1833.

Pennington, Jonathan T. "Heaven, Earth, and a New Genesis: Theological Cosmology in Matthew." Pages 28-44 in *Cosmology and the New Testament Theology*. Edited by Jonathan T. Pennington and Sean M. McDonough. LNTS. London: T&T Clark, 2008.

_______. *Heaven and Earth in the Gospel of Matthew. NovTSup 126. Leiden: Brill, 2007.*

Pierce, Chad T. *Spirits and the Proclamation of Christ: 1 Peter 3:18-22 in Light of Sin and Punishment Traditions in Early Jewish and Christian Literature*. WUNT 305. Tübingen: Mohr Siebeck, 2011.

Piotrowski, Nicholas G. *Matthew's New David at the End of Exile: A Socio-Rhetorical Study of Scriptural Quotations*. NovTSup. Leiden: Brill, 2016.

Piovanelli, Pierluigi. "A Testimony for the Kings and the Mighty who Possess the Earth: The Thirst for Justice and Peace in the Parables of Enoch." Pages 363-379 in *Enoch and the Messiah Son of Man: Revisiting the Book of Parables*. Edited by G. Boccaccini. Grand Rapids: Eerdmans, 2007.

Pizzuto, Vincent A. *A Cosmic Leap of Faith: An Authorial, Structural, and Theological Investigation of the Cosmic Christology in Col 1:15-20*. BET 41. Paris: Peeters, 2006.

Plummer, Alfred. *An Exegetical Commentary on the Gospel According to St. Matthew.* New York; Stock, 1909.

Pollard, T. E. *Johannine Christology and the Early Church*. SNTSMS 13. Cambridge: CUP, 1970.

Powers, B. Ward. *The Progressive Publication of Matthew: An Explanation of the Writing of the Synoptic Gospels.* Nashville: B&H Publishing Group, 2010.

Propp, William. *Exodus 19-40.* AB 2A. New York: Doubleday, 2006.

Purves, Andrew. *The Search for Compassion: Spirituality and Ministry.* Louisville: Westminster, 1989.

Pushparajan, A. *Ecological World-view for a Just Society.* Delhi: ISPCK, 1992.

Quarles, Charles. *Sermon on the Mount: Restoring Christ's Message to the Modern Church.* MSBT. Nashville: B&H, 2011.

Rasmussen, Larry L. *Earth Community, Earth Ethics.* Geneva: WCC Publications, 1996.

Reed, Jonathan L. *Archaeology and the Galilean Jesus: A Re-examination of the Evidence.* Pennsylvania: Trinity Press International, 2000.

Reid, Duncan. "Enfleshing the Human: An Earth-Revealing, Earth-Healing Christology." Pages 69-84 in *Earth Revealing – Earth Healing: Ecology and Christian Theology.* Edited by Denis Edwards. Minnesota: The Liturgical Press, 2001.

Reinhartz, Adele. "The Colonizer as Colonized: Intertextual Dialogue between the Gospel of John and Canadian Identity." Pages 170-192 in *John and Postcolonialism: Travel, Space and Power.* Edited by Musa W. Dube and Jeffrey L. Staley. London: SAP, 2002.

Reiterer, Friedrich Vincenz. "The Interpretation of the Wisdom Tradition of the Torah within Ben Sira." Pages 209-232 in *Deuterocanonical and Cognate Literature Studies.* Edited by Friedrich V. Reiterer, Beate Ego and Tobias Niklas. Vol. 1 of *The Wisdom of Ben Sira: Studies in Tradition, Redaction, and Theology.* Edited by Angelo Passaro and Giuseppe Bellia. Berlin: de Gruyter, 2008.

Remus, Harold. *Pagan—Christian Conflict Over Miracle in the Second Century.* Patristic Monograph Series 10. Cambridge, MA: The Philadelphia Patristic Foundation, 1983.

Reuther, Rosemary Radford. *Godesses and the Divine Feminine: A Western Religious History.* London: University of California Press, 2006.

Rhymer, Joseph. *The Miracles of Jesus.* Middlegreen, UK: St. Paul Publications, 1991.

Richard, Earl. *Jesus: One and Many. The Christological Concept of New Testament Authors.* Wilmington: Michael Glazier, 1988.

Riches, John K. *Conflicting Mythologies: Identity Formation in the Gospels of Mark and Matthew.* SNTW. Edinburgh: T&T Clark, 2000.

_______. *Matthew.* Sheffield: SAP, 2001.

Richter, Amy E. "Unusual Birth: Enochic Traditions and Matthew's Infancy." Pages 45-72 in *Enoch and the Synoptic Gospels: Reminiscence, Allusions, Intertextuality.* Atlanta: SBL Press, 2016.

_______. *Enoch and the Gospel of Matthew.* PTMS 183. Eugene, OR: Pickwick, 2012.

Riley, Harold. *The First Gospel*. Georgia: Mercer University Press, 1992.

Ringe, Sharon H. *Wisdom's Friends: Community and Christology in the Fourth Gospel.* Louisville: Westminster John Knox Press, 1999.

Robbins, Vernon K. "Argumentative Textures in Socio-Rhetorical Interpretation." Pages 27-65 in *Rhetorical Argumentation in Biblical Texts: Essays from the Lund 2000 Conference*. Edited by Anders Eriksson, Thomas H. Olbricht and Walter Übelacker. Harrisburg: Trinity Press International, 2002.

_______. "Conceptual Blending and Early Christian Imagination." Pages 161-195 in *Explaining Christian Origins and Early Judaism: Contribution from Cognitive and Social Science*. BIS 89. Edited by Petri Luomanen, Ilkka Pyysiäinen, and Risto Uro. Leiden: Brill, 2007.

_______. "Rhetography: A New Way of Seeing the Familiar Text." Pages 81-106 in *Words Well Spoken: George Kennedy's Rhetoric of the New Testamenti*. Studies in Rhetoric and Religion 8. Edited by C. Clifton Black and Duane F. Watson (Waco: Baylor University Press), 2008.

_______. "Sociorhetorical Interpretation of Miracle Discourse in the Synoptic Gospels." Pages 17-84 in *Miracle Discourse in the New Testament*. Edited by Duane J. Watson. Atlanta: SBL, 2012.

Roberts, Alexander. James Donaldson and A. Cleveland Coxe, eds. "Fragments of Papias." Pages 151-155 in *The Apostolic Fathers: Justin Martyr – Irenaeus*. Vol. 1 of *The Ante-Nicene Fathers*. New York: Charles Scribner's Sons, 1903.

Robinson, Bernard P. "Matthew's Nativity Stories: Historical and Theological Quesions for Today's Readers." Pages 110-131 in *New Perspectives on the Nativity.* Edited by Jeremy Corley. London: Continuum, 2009.

Robinson, Bob. *Jesus and the Religions: Retrieving a Neglected Example for a Multi-Cultural World.* Eugene, OR: Cascade Books, 2012.

Rogerson, John W. "The Old Testament View of Nature: Some Preliminary Questions." Pages 67-84 in *Instruction and Interpretation: Studies in Hebrew Language, Palestinian Archaeology and Biblical Exegesis.* Leiden: Brill, 1977.

Ross, John P. "Some Notes on Miracles in the Old Testament." Pages 43-60 in *Miracles: Cambridge Studies in Their Philosophy and History.* Edited by C. F. D. Moule. London: Mowbray, 1965.

Rowley, H. H. *The Relevance of Apocalyptic*. 2nd ed. London: Lutterworth, 1947.

Sagar, Aparajita. "Postcolonial Studies." Pages 562-567 in *Dictionary of Culture and Critical Theory.* Edited by Michael Payne. Oxford: OUP, 1996.

Saiaithanga. *Mizo Sakhua* [Mizo Religion]. Aizawl: Maranatha Printing Press, 1984. Repr., Aizawl: R. Lalmalsawma, 1994.

Saiaithanga. *Thurin Zirna* [*A Study of the Doctrine*]. Rev. ed. Aizawl: SL&PB, 1965.

Saldarini, Anthony J. "Matthew." Pages 1000-1063 in *Eerdmans Commentary on the Bible.* Grand Rapids: Eerdmans, 2003.

Sangkhuma, Z. T. *An Danglamna te* (*Their Distinctives*). Aizawl: Rinzawna, 1991.

Sangkima. *Mizos: Society and Social Change.* Guwahati: Spectrum Publications, 1992.

Schiffman, L. H. *Reclaiming the Dead Sea Scrolls: The History of Judaism, the Background of Christianity, the Lost Library of Qumran.* New York: Doubleday, 1995.

Schleiermacher, Friedrich. *On Religion: Speeches to Its Cultured Despisers.* Translated by John Oman. New York: Harper & Brothers, 1958.

Schnackenburg, Rudolf. *The Gospel of Matthew.* Translated by Robert R. Barr. Grand Rapids, MI: Eerdmans, 2002.

Schnelle, U. *The History and Theology of the New Testament Writings.* London: SCM, 1994.

Scholem, Gershom G. *Major Trends in Jewish Mysticism.* New York: Schocken Books, 1961.

Schreiner, Thomas R. *New Testament Theology: Magnifying God in Christ.* Grand Rapids: Baker, 2008.

Schroer, Silvia. *Wisdom Has Built Her House: Studies on the Figure of Sophia in the Bible*. Translated by Linda M. Maloney and William McDonough. Collegeville: Michael Glazier, 2000.

Schwarz, Hans. *Christology.* Grand Rapids: Eerdmans, 1998.

Schweitzer, Albert. *The Quest of the Historical Jesus: A Critical Study of its Progress from Reimarus to Wrede.* Translated by W. Montgomery. London: A&C Black, 1910.

Scott, James M. "The Division of the Earth in Jubilees 8:11-9:15 and Early Christian Chronography." Pages 295-296 in *Studies in the Book of Jubilees*. Edited by Matthias Albani, Jörg Frey and Armin Lange. Tübingen: Mohr Siebeck, 1997.

Scroggs, Robin. *Christology in Paul and John*. Proclamation Commentaries. Philadelphia: Fortress, 1988.

Seeskin, Kenneth. "Miracles in the Jewish Philosophy." Pages 254-270 in *The Cambridge Companion to Miracles*. CCR. Edited by Graham H. Twelftree. Cambridge: CUP, 2011.

Senior, Donald. *Matthew*. ANTC. Nashville: Abingdon Press, 1998.

_______. *The Gospel of Matthew*. IBT. Nashville: Abingdon Press, 1997.

_______. *The Passion of Jesus in the Gospel of Matthew.* Collegeville, MN: Liturgical Press, 1985.

Shiva, Vandana. *Staying Alive: Women, Ecology and Development.* London: Zed Books, 1989.

Sim, David C. *Apocalyptic Eschatology in the Gospel of Matthew.* Cambridge: CUP, 1996.

Sim, David C. *The Gospel of Mathew and Christian Judaism: The History and Social Setting of the Matthean Community.* SNTW. Edinburgh, T&T Clark, 1998.

Smith, Daniel Lynwood. *Into the World of the New Testament: Greco-Roman and Jewish Texts and Contexts.* London: Bloomsbury, 2015.

Smith, David Oliver. *Matthew, Mark, Luke, and Paul: The Influence of the Epistles on the Synoptic Gospels.* Eugene, OR: Resource Publication, 2011.

Smith, Kevin Gary. *Academic Writing and Theological Research: A Guide for Students.* Johannesburg: SATSP, 2008.

Sobrino, Jon. *Jesus the Liberator: A Historical- Theological Reading of Jesus of Nazareth*. Translated by Paul Burns and Francis McDonagh. New York: Orbis, 1993.

_______. "Christ as Liberator." Pages 237-244 in *Christology: A Global Introduction: An Ecumenical, International, and Contextual Perspective.* Edited by Veli-Matti Kärkkäinen. Grand Rapids: Baker, 2003.

_______. *Christology at the Cross Road.* Maryknoll: Orbis, 1978.

Soares-Prabhu, George M. *The Formula Quotations in the Infancy Narrative of Matthew: An Enquiry into the Tradition History of Mt 1-2*. Analectica Biblica 63. Rome: Biblical Institute, 1976.

Spicq, C. *L'Epitre aux Hebreux.* 2 Vols. Paris: J. Gabalda, 1952.

Spinoza, Benedict de. "Tractatus Theologico-Politicus." Pages 81-97 in *The Chief Works of Benedict de Spinoza*. Translated by R. H. M Elwes. 2 vols. London: George Bell & Son, 1883-1884.

Stadelmann, Luis I. J. *The Hebrew Conception of the World.* AnBib 39. Rome: Pontifical Biblical Institute, 1970.

Stanton, Graham N. *A Gospel for a New People: Studies in Matthew.* Louisville: T&T Clark, 1993.

Stegemann, Wolfgang. "Vagabond Radicalism in Early Christianity? A Historical and Theological Discussion of a Thesis Proposed by Gerd Theissen." Pages 148-168 in *God of the Lowly: Socio-Historical Interpretations of the Bible*. Edited by W. Schottrof and Wolfgang Stegemann. Maryknoll: Orbis, 1984.

Stendahl, Krister. "Quis et Unde? An Analysis of Matt.1-2." Pages 94-105 in *Judentum, Urchristentum, Kirche*. Edited by W. Eltester. Berlin: Topelmann, 1964.

_______. *The School of St. Matthew, and its use of the Old Testament.* Philadelphia: Fortress, 1968.

Strecker, Georg. *Der Weg der Gerechtigkeit: Untersuchung zur Theologie de Matthäus.* FRLANT 82. Göttingen: Vandenhoeck, 1962.

Streeter, B. H. *The Four Gospels: A Study of Origins, Treating of the Manuscript Tradition, Sources, Authorship, & Dates.* London: Macmillan, 1924.

Sugirtharajah, R. S. "Prologue and Perspective." Pages viii-xii in *Asian Faces of Jesus*. FCS. Edited by R. S. Sugirtharajah. Maryknoll: Orbis, 1993.

_______. *Exploring Postcolonial Biblical Criticism: History, Methods, Practice.* Chichester: Wiley-Blackwell, 2012.

Suter, David W. "Enoch in Sheol: Updating the Dating of the Book of Parables." Pages 415-443 in *Enoch and the Messiah Son of Man: Revisiting the Book of Parables*. Edited by G. Boccaccini. Grand Rapids: Eerdmans, 2007.

Sweet, J. P. M. "The Theory of Miracles in the Wisdom of Solomon." Pages 113-126 in *Miracles.* Edited by C. F. D. Moule. London: Mowbrays, 1965.

Swinburne, Richard. *The Concept of Miracle*. NSPR. London: Macmillan, 1970.

Takatemjen. *Studies on Theology and Naga Culture.* Delhi: ISPCK, 1998.

Talbert, Charles H. ed. *Reimarus Fragments.* London: SCM, 1971.

_______. *Matthew.* PCNT. Grand Rapids, MI: Baker Academics, 2010.

Tate, W. Randolph. *Biblical Interpretation: An Integrated Approach.* Grand Rapids: Baker, 1991.

Tatum, W. Barnes. *John the Baptist and Jesus: A Report of the Jesus Seminar.* California: Polebridge, 1993.

Taylor, Vincent. *The Formation of the Gospel Tradition.* London: Macmillan, 1953.

_______. *The Gospel According to St Mark.* 2nd ed. London: Macmillan, 1966.

Teeple, Howard M. *The Mosaic Eschatological Prophet.* Philadelphia: SBL, 1957.

Thanzauva, K. "Issues in Tribal Theology." In Tribal Theology: A Reader. Edited by Shimreingam Shimray. Jorhat: Eastern Theological College, 2003.

Thanzauva, K. "Tribal/Indigenous Interpretation of the Bible: A Keynote Address." Pages 13-25 in Tribal Theology and the Bible: A Search for Contextual Relevance. Edited by Yangkahao Yashum. Jorhat: Eastern Theological College, 2011.

Theissen, Gerd. "Historical Scepticism and the Criteria of Jesus Research: My Attempt to Leap Over Lessing's Ugly Wide Ditch." Pages 549-588 in *How to Study the Historical Jesus*. Edited by Tom Holmén and Stanley E. Porter. Vol. 1 of *Handbook for the Study of the Historical Jesus*. Leiden: Brill, 2011.

_______. "Jesus as an Itinerant Teacher: Reflections from Social History of Jesus' Roles." Pages 98-122 in *Jesus Research: International Perspective*. Edited by J. H. Charlesworth and P. Pokorny. Grand Rapids: Eerdmans, 2009.

_______. *The Miracle Stories of the Early Christian Tradition*. Translated by Francis McDonagh. Edited by John Riches. Edinburgh: T&T Clark, 1983.

_______. *Sociology of Early Palestinian Christianity*. Translated by John Bowden. Phildelphia: Fortress, 1978.

_______. *The First Followers of Jesus: A Sociological Analysis of Earliest Christianity*. Translated by John Bowden. London: SCM, 1978.

_______. *The Gospels in Contexts: Social and Political History in the Synoptic Tradition*. Translated by Linda M. Maloney. Edinburg: T&T Clark, 1992.

Thiselton, Anthony C. *The First Epistle to the Corinthians: A Commentary on the Greek Text*. NIGTC. Grand Rapids: Eerdmans, 2000.

Thompson, James W. *The Beginnings of Christian Philosophy: The Epistles to the Hebrews*. Washington DC: The Catholic Biblical Association of America, 1982.

Trafton, Joseph L. "What Would David Do? Messianic Expectation and Surprise in Ps. Sol. 17." Pages 155-174 in *The Psalms of Solomon: Language, History, Theology*. Edited by Eberhard Bons and Patrick Pouchelle. Atlanta: SBL, 2015.

Travis, Stephen H. "Form Criticism." Pages 153-164 in *New Testament Interpretation: Essays on Principles and Methods*. Edited by I. Howard Marshall. Exeter: Paternoster, 1977.

Tuckett, Christopher M. *Christology and the New Testament: Jesus and His Earliest Followers*. Louisville, KY: Westminster John Knox Press, 2001.

_______. *Q and the History of Early Christianity: Studies in Q*. Edinburgh: T&T Clark, 1996.

Turner, David L. *Matthew*, BECNT. Grand Rapids: Baker, 2008.

Twelftree, Graham H. "Nature Miracles and the Historical Jesus." Pages 1-40 in *The Nature Miracles of Jesus: Problems, Perspectives, and Prospects*. Edited by Graham H. Twelftree, Eugene, OR: Wipf & Stock, 2017.

_______. *Jesus the Exorcist: A Contribution to the Study of the Historical Jesus*. Eugene: Wipf & Stock, 1993.

_______. *Jesus the Miracle Worker: A Historical and Theological Study.* Downers Grove, IL: IVP, 1999-2011.

_______. ed. *The Nature Miracles of Jesus: Problems, Perspectives, and Prospects.* Eugene, OR: Wipf & Stock, 2017.

Urbach, Ephraim E. *The Sages: Their Concepts and Beliefs, trans. Israel Abrahams*. 2 vols. Jerusalem: Magnes, 1975,

van der Loos, Hendrik. *The Miracles of Jesus.* Leiden: Brill, 1965.

van Kooten, George H. *Cosmic Christology in Paul and the Pauline School.* WUNT 2. Tübingen: Mohr Siebeck, 2003.

van Roon, A. *The Authenticity of Ephesians.* Leiden: E. J. Brill, 1974.

van Tilborg, S. *The Jewish Leaders in Matthew.* Leiden: Brill, 1972.

VanderKam, James C. "1 Enoch, Enochic Motifs, and Enoch in Early Christian Literature." Pages 33-101 in *The Jewish Apocalyptic Heritage in Early Christianity*. Edited by James C. VanderKam and William Adler. Assen: Van Gorcum, 1996.

_______. "Enoch Traditions in Jubilees and Other Second-Century Sources." Pages 229-51 in *The Society of Biblical Literature 1978 Seminar Papers.* SBLSP 13-14. Missoula: Scholars Press, 1978.

_______. *From Revelation to Canon: Studies in Hebrew Bible and Second Temple Literature.* Boston: Brill, 2002.

_______. *The Book of Jubilees.* Sheffield: SAP, 2001.

Vanlalchhuanga. *An Zirtirnate* (*Their Teachings*). Aizawl: Goshen, 1984.

Vine, Cedric E. W. *The Audience of Matthew: An Appraisal of the Local Audience Thesis.* LNTS. London: Bloomsbury, 2014.

Viviano, Benedict T. *Matthew and his World: The Gospel of the Open Jewish Christians Studies in Biblical Theology.* Göttingen: Vandenheock & Ruprecht, 2007.

_______. *The Gospel According to Matthew.* NJBC. London: Chapman, 1990.

Vledder, Evert-Jan. *Conflict in the Miracle Stories: A Socio-Exegetical Study of Matthew 8 and 9*. JSNTSup 152. Shefield: SAP, 1997.

Vögtle, Anton. "The Miracles of Jesus against Their Contemporary Background." Pages 96-105 in *Jesus in His Time*. Edited by Hans Jurgen Schultz. Translated by Brian Watchorn. London: SPCK, 1971.

von Rad, Gerhard. *Wisdom in Israel*. Translated by James D. Martin. London: SCM, 1972.

von Thaden, Robert. *Sex, Christ, and Embodied Cognition: Paul's Wisdom for Corinth*. ESEC 16. U.K.: Deo, 2012.

Wainwright, Elaine M. *Towards a Feminist Critical Reading of the Gospel According to Matthew.* Berlin: de Gruyter, 1991.

Walck, Leslie W. "The Son of Man in the Parables of Enoch and the Gospels." Pages 299-337 in *Enoch and the Messiah Son of Man: Revisiting the Book of Parables*. Edited by Gabriele Boccaccini. Grand Rapids, MI: Eerdmans, 2007.

Waltke, Bruce K. *The Book of Proverbs: Chapters 1-15. NICOT. Grand Rapids, MI: Eerdmans, 2004.*

Ward, Keith. *The Big Questions in Science and Religion.* Pennsylvania: Templeton Foundation Press, 2008.

Watson, Duane F. "Miracle Discourse in the Pauline Epistles: The Role of Resurrection and Rhetoric." Pages 189-196 in *Miracle Discourse in the New Testament*. Edited by Duane F. Watson. Atlanta: SBL, 2012.

_______. Introduction to *Miracle Discourse in the New Testament*. Edited by Duane F. Watson. Atlanta: SBL, 2012.

_______. "Introduction." Pages 1-16 in *Miracle Discourse in the New Testament.* Edited by Duane J. Watson. Atlanta: SBL, 2012.

Wells, George A. *Cutting Jesus Down to Size: What Higher Criticism Has Achieved and Where It Leaves Christianity. Illinois: Open Court, 2009.*

Wenham, David. "The Purpose of Luke-Acts: Israel's Story in the Context of the Roman Empire." Pages 79-103 in *Reading Luke: Interpretation, Reflection, Formation*. SHS 6. Edited by C. G. Bartholomew, J. B. Green, and A. C. Thiselton. Grand Rapids: Zondervan, 2005.

Wenham, David., and Steve Walton. *Exploring the New Testament: A Guide to the Gospels and Acts*. Vol. 1 of *Exploring the New Testament*. 2nd ed. Downers Grove, IL: IVP, 2011.

Weren, Wim J. C. *Studies in Matthew's Gospel: Literary Design, Intertextuality, and Social Setting.* Boston: Brill, 2014.

Westcott, Brooke Foss. *Introduction of the Study of the Gospels with Historical and Explanatory Notes.* New York: Macmillan, 1882.

Westermann, Claus. *The Living Psalms.* Edinburg: T&T Clark, 1989.

Westfall, Richard. *Science and Religion in Seventeenth Century England.* New Haven, 1970.

Wilkins, Michael J. *Discipleship in the Ancient World and Matthew's Gospel.* 2nd ed. Eugene: Wipf & Stock, 2015.

_______. *Matthew.* ZIBBC 1. Grand Rapids, MI: Zondervan, 2001.

_______. *Matthew: The NIV Application Commentary.* Grand Rapids, MI: Zondervan, 2004.

Williamson, Ronald. *Philo and the Epistle to the Hebrews.* ALGHJ 4. Leiden: Brill, 1970.

Willits, Joel. "The Twelve Disciples in Matthew." Pages 166-179 in *Jesus, Matthew's Gospel and Early Christianity: Studies in Memory of Graham N. Stanton*. Edited by Daniel M. Gurtner et al. London: T&T Clark, 2011.

_______. "Matthew." Pages 82-100 in *Jesus is Lord, Caesar is Not: Evaluating Empire in New Testament Studies*. Edited by Scot Mc. Knight and Joseph B. Modica. Downers Grove: IVP, 2013.

Wilson, Walter T. *Philo of Alexandria: On Virtues: Introduction, Translation, and Commentary*. PACS 3. Leiden: Brill, 2011.

Windisch, Hans. "John's Narrative Style." Pages 25-64 in *The Gospel of John as Literature: An Analogy of Twentieth Century Perspectives*. Translated by D. Orton. Edited by Mark Stibbe. Leiden: E. J. Brill, 1923.

Windisch, Hans. *Paulus und Christus*. Leipzig: Hinrichs, 1934.

Winston, David. *The Wisdom of Solomon: A New Translation with Introduction and Commentary*. AB 43. Garden City: Doubleday, 1979.

Witherington, Ben. *Letters and Homilies for Jewish Christians: A Socio-Rhetorical Commentary on Hebrews, James and Jude*. Downers Grove, IL: IVP, 2007.

_______. *Matthew*. SHBC 19. Macon, GA: Smyth & Helwys, 2006.

_______. *Revelation,* CBC. Cambridge: CUP, 2003.

_______. *The Christology of Jesus*. Minneapolis: Fortress, 1990.

Witmer, Amanda. *Jesus, the Galilean Exorcist: His Exorcisms in Social and Political Context*. LNTS. New York: T&T Clark, 2012.

Wolfson, Harry Austryn. *Philo*. 2 vols. Cambridge: HUP, 1947-1948.

Wrede, William. *The Messianic Secret*. LTT. Translated by J.C.G. Greig. Cambridge: James Clarke, 1971.

Wright, N. T. *The New Testament and the People of God: Christian Origins and the Question of God*. London: SPCK, 1992.

Yieh, John. *Conversation with Scripture: The Gospel of Matthew*. AABSSS. Harrisburg: Morehouse Publishing, 2012.

Zakovitch, Yair. *The Concept of the Miracle in the Bible*. Tel-Aviv: MOD Books, 1991.

## Journals

Atkinson, Kenneth., and Jodi Magnes."Josephus's Essenes and the Qumran Community." *JBL* 129 (2010): 317-342.

Bacon, Benjamin W. "The Five Books of Matthew Against the Jews." *TEx* 8 (1918): 56-66.

Barnett, Paul W. "The Jewish Sign Prophets – A.D. 40-70: Their Intentions and Origin." *NTS* 27 (1981): 679-697.

Bauer, David R. "The Kingship of Jesus in the Matthean Infancy Narrative: A Literary Analysis." *CBQ* 57 (1995): 306-323.

Baxter, Wayne. "Healing and the "Son of David": Matthew's Warrant." NovT 48 (2006): 36-50.

Boobyer, G. H. "The Eucharistic Interpretation of the Miracles of the Loaves in St. Mark's Gospel." *JTS* 3 (1952): 161-171.

Brown, Raymond E. "Gospel Infancy Narrative Research From 1976 to 1986: Part II (Luke)." *CBQ* 48 (1986): 677-678.

Brown, Schuyler. "The Matthean Community and the Gentile Mission." *NovT* 22 (1980): 1193-221.

Brown, Sherri. "Water Imagery and the Power and Presence of God in the Gospel of John." *ThTo* 72 (2015): 289-298.

Bruce, F. F. "Recent Contributions to the Understanding of Hebrews." *ExpTim* 80 (1969): 260-264.

Burkill, T. A. "The Notion of Miracle with Special Reference to St. Mark's Gospel." *ZBG* 50 (1959): 33-48.

Burtness, James H. "All the Fullness." *Dialog* 3 (1964): 257-263.

Burton, Ernest De Witt. "The Purpose and Plan of the Gospel of Matthew, Part 1." *BibW* 11 (1898): 37-44.

Buse, Ivor. "The Gospel Accounts of the Feeding of the Multitudes." *ExpTim* 74 (1963): 167-170.

Byrne, Brendan. "Christ's Pre-existence in Pauline Soteriology." *TS* 58 (1997): 308-330.

Caird, George B. "Exegetical Method of the Epistle to the Hebrews." *CJT* 5 (1959): 49.

Carter, Warren. "Matthew and the Gentiles: Individual Conversion and/or Systematic Transformation." *JSNT* 26 (2004), 259-282.

Carter, Warren. "The Crowds in Matthew's Gospel." *CBQ* 55 (1993): 54-67.

Charlesworth, J. H. "A Critical Comparison of the Dualism in 1QS III, 13-IV, 26 and the 'Dualism' Contained in the Fourth Gospel." *NTS* 15 (1969): 389-418.

Case, Shirley Jackson. "Jesus and Sepphoris," *JBL* 45 (1926): 14-22.

Chryssides, George. "Miracles and Agents." *RelS* 11 (1975): 319-327.

Church, Philip."Hebrews 1:10-12 and the Renewal of the Cosmos." *TynBul* 67.2 (2016): 269-286.

Clines, D. J. A. "The Image of God in Man." *TynBul* 19 (1968): 53-103.

Comber, J. A. "The Verb Therapeuō in Matthew's Gospel." *JBL* 97 (1978): 431-434.

Cope, O. Lamar. "The Death of John the Baptist in the Gospel of Matthew." *CBQ* 38 (1976): 515-519.

Delio, Ilia. "Christology in the Thought of Zachary Hayes." *FrS* 65 (2007): 107-120.

Deutsch, Celia. "Wisdom in Matthew: Transformation of a Symbol." *NovT* 32 (1990): 13-47.

Diamond, Malcolm L. "Miracles." *RelS* 9 (1973): 307-324.

Donaldson, Terence L. "'For Herod had arrested John' (Matt. 14:3): Making sense of an unresolved flashback." *SR* 28 (1999): 35-48.

Dowling, Maurice. "Proverbs 8:22-31 in the Christology of the Early Fathers." Perichoresis 8 (2010): 47-65.

Draper, J. A. "Wandering Radicalism or Purposeful Activity? Jesus and the Sending of Messengers in Mark 6:6-56." *Neotestamentica* 29.2 (1995): 187-207.

Duling, Dennis C. "The Therapeutic Son of David: An Element in Matthew's Christological Apologetic." *NTS* 24 (1978): 392-410.

Edwards, James R. "The use of Προσερχεσθαι in the Gospel of Matthew." *JBL* 106 (1987): 65-74.

Elliot, J. H. "Social Scientific Criticism of the New Testament and its Social World." *Semeia* 35 (1986): 1-33.

Feiler, Paul Frederick. "The Stilling of the Storm in Matthew: A Response to Günther Bornkamm." *JETS* 26 (1983): 399-406.

Fretheim, Terence E. "Nature's Praise of God in the Psalms." *ExAud* 3 (1987): 16-30.

George, Mathew. "Sources of Tribal Theology." *MisT* 4 (2000): 290-300.

Gibbs, John G. "Pauline Cosmic Christology and Ecological Crisis." *JBL* 90/4 (1971): 466-479.

Glasson, T. F. "'Plurality of Divine Persons' and the Quotations in Hebrews 1.6ff." *NTS* 12 (1966): 270-272.

Gnuse, Robert Karl. "Dream Genre in the Matthean Infancy Narratives." *NovT* 32 (1990): 97-120.

Good, Deirdre. "The Verb ΑΝΑΧΩΡΕΩ in Matthew's Gospel." *NovT* 32 (1990): 1-12.

Gottstein, Alon Goshen. "The Body as Image of God in Rabbinic Literature." *HTR* 87 (1994): 171-195.

Hahn, Robert R. "Judaism and Jewish Christianity in Antioch: Charisma and Conflict in the First Century." *JRH* 14 (1987): 341-360.

Hanson, K. C. "Transformed on the Mountain: Ritual Analysis and the Gospel Matthew." *Semeia* 67 (1994): 147-70.

Harrison, James R. "Modern Scholarship and the 'Nature' Miracles: A Defence of their Historicity and Affirmation of Jesus' Deity." *CH* 3 (2006): 493-510.

Harrison, Peter. "Newtonian Science, Miracles, and the Law of Nature." *JHI* 56 (1995): 531-553.

Hayes, Zachary. "Christ, Word of God and Examplar of Humanity." *Cord* 46.1 (1996): 3-17.

_______. "Christ, Word of God and Exemplar of Humanity: The Roots of Franciscan Christocentrism and its Implications for Today." *Cord* 46.1 (1996): 7-8.

_______. "The Meaning of *Convenientia* in the Metaphysics of St. Bonaventure." *FrS* 34 (1974): 74-100.

Hays, R. B. "The Corrected Jesus." *First Things 43 (1994): 43-48.*

Helyer, Larry R. "Cosmic Christology and Col 1:15-20." *JETS* 37 (1994): 235-246.

Hengel, Martin. "Jesus und die Tora." *ThB* (1978): 152-172.

Hill, David. "Son and Servant: An Essay on Matthean Christology." *JSNT* 6 (1980): 2-16.

_______. "The Figure of Jesus in Matthew's Gospel: A Response to Professor Kingsbury's Literary-Critical Probe." *JSNT* 21 (1984): 37-52.

Holladay, Carl R. "New Testament Christology: Some Considerations of Method." *NovT* 25 (1983): 257-278.

Holland, R. F. "The Miraculous." *APQ* 2 (1965): 43-51.

Jacob, Emmanuel M. "Discipleship and Mission: A Perspective on the Gospel of Matthew." *IRM* 91 (2002): 102-110.

Jeremias, Joachim. "Lord's Prayer in Modern Research." *ExpTim* 71, no. 5 (1960): 141-146.

Jordan, G. J. "The Classification of Miracles." *ExpTim* 46 (1934-1935): 310-316.

Kee, Howard C. "The Transformation of the Synagogue after 70 CE: Its Import for Early Christianity." *NTS* 36 (1990): 1-24.

Keegan, Terence J. "Introductory Formulae for Matthean Discourses." *CBQ* 44 (1982): 415-430.

Kingsbury, Jack D. "The Structure of Matthew's Gospel and His Concept of Salvation History." *CBQ* 35 (1973): 451-474.

Krentz, Edgar. "The Extent of Matthew's Prologue: Toward the Structure of the First Gospel." *JBL* 83 (1964): 409-414.

Lohr, Charles H. "Oral Techniques in the Gospel of Matthew." *CBQ* 23 (1961): 403-435.

Longchar, Wati A. "Reading the Bible from the Perspective of Indigenous People's Experience: A Methodological Consideration." *MITJT* 4 (2003): 41-58.

Longkumar, Bendangla. "Weaving Christology from Tribal Women Perspective: An Ao-Naga Reading." *JTS* 15 (2010): 29-45.

Lovelady, Edgar J. "The Logos Concept: A Critical Monograph on John 1:1." *GJ* (1963): 15-24.

MacRae, George W. "Heavenly Temple and Eschatology in the Letter to the Hebrews." *Semeia* 12 (1978): 179-199.

Malina, Bruce J. "The Literary Structure and Form of Matt. xxviii. 16–20." *NTS* 17 (1970): 87-103.

Manson, T. W. "The Problem of the Epistle to the Hebrews." *BJRL* 32 (1949-1950): 1-17.

Marcus, J. "Mark-Interpreter of Paul." *NTS* 46 (2000): 473-487.

Masuda, S. "The Good News of the Miracle of the Bread: The Tradition and Its Markan Redaction." *NTS* 28 (1982): 191-219.

Matera, Frank J. "The Plot of Matthew's Gospel." *CBQ* 49 (1987): 233-253.

McCarter, P. Kyle Jr. "The Balaam Texts from Deir 'Allā: the First Combination." *BASOR* 239 (1980): 49-60.

McCown, C. C. "Gospel Geography: Fiction, Fact, and Truth." *JBL* 60 (1941): 1-25.

McCullough, J. C. "Some Recent Developments in Research on the Epistle to the Hebrews." *IBS* 2 (1980): 141-165.

McDonough, Sean M. *Christ as Creator: Origins of a New Testament Doctrine. Oxford: OUP, 2009.*

McGinley, Laurence J. "Form-Criticism of the Synoptic Healing Narratives." *TS* 4 (1941): 451-480.

McKenzie, John L. "God and Nature in the Old Testament." *CBQ* 14 (1952): 18-39.

McKinnon, Alastair. "'Miracle' and 'Paradox.'" *APQ* 4 (1967): 308-314.

Michel, O. "Der Abschluss des Matthaus evangeliums." *EvT* 10 (1950-51): 16-26

Migliore, Daniel I. "Christology in Context: The Doctrinal and Contextual Tasks of Christology Today." *Int* 49 (1995): 242-254.

Miller, G. "Intertextuality in Old Testament Research." *CBR 9* (2011): 238-309.

Minear, Paul S. "The Disciples and the Crowds in the Gospel of Matthew," *ATR*Sup 3 (1974): 28-44.

Moule, C. F. D. "Fulfilment Words in the New Testament: Use and Abuse." *NTS* 14 (1967/8): 293-320.

Naveh, Joseph. "The Date of the Deir 'Allā Inscription in Aramaic Script." *IEJ* 17 (1967): 256-58.

Nickelsburg, George W. E. "Enoch, Levi and Peter: Recipients of Revelation in Upper Galilee." *JBL* 100 (1981): 575-600.

Nolland, John. "No Son-of-God Christology in Matthew 1:18-25." *JSNT* 62 (1996): 3-12.

Nwaigbo, Ferdinand. "Cosmic Christology and Eco-theology in Africa." *AFER* 53/2 (2011): 437-461.

Oakley, Todd V. "The Human Rhetorical Potential." *WCom* 16.1 (1999): 93-128

_______. "Conceptual Blending, Narrative Discourse, and Rhetoric." *CogL* 9.4 (1988): 321-360.

Okure, Teresa. "In Him all Things Hold Together: A Missiological Reading of Colossians 1:15-20." *IRM* 360 (2002): 62-72.

Osborne, Grant R. "The Christ of Hebrews and other Religions." *JETS* 46/2 (2003): 249-267.

Pachuau, Lalsangkima. "Mizo "Sakhua" in Transition: Change and Continuity from Primal Religion to Christianity." *IR* 34 (2006): 41-57.

Parsons, Mikeal C. "Son and High Priest: A Study in the Christology of Hebrews." *EvQ* 60 (1988): 195-216.

Pollard, T. E. "Colossians 1:12-20: A Reconsideration." *NTS* 27 (1981): 572-575.

Raja, R. J. "Eco-Spirituality in the Psalms." *VJTR* 53 (1989): 637-650.

Ralte, Lalrinawmi. "Patriarchy and Christianity in the Mizo Church: A Feminist Critique." *BTF* 31 (1999): 117-133.

Redman, Judith C.S. "How Accurate are Eyewitnesses? Bauckham and the Eyewitnesses in the Light of Psychological Research." *JBL* 129 (2010): 177-197.

Rhee, Victor (Sung Yul). "Christology in Hebrews 1:5-14: The Three Stages of Christ's Existence." *JETS* 59 (2016): 717-729.

Rhee, Victor (Sung Yul). "The Role of Chiasm for Understanding Christology in Hebrews 1:1-14." *JBL* 131 (2012): 341-362.

Richardson, Alan. "The Feeding of the Five Thousand: Mark 6:34-44." *Int* 9: 144-149.

Robbins, Vernon K. "The Dialectical Nature of Early Christian Discourse." *Scriptura* 59 (1996): 353-362.

Robinson, J. M. "A Formal Analysis of Colossians 1:15-20." *JBL* 76 (1957): 270-287.

Saucy, Mark R. "Miracles and Jesus' Proclamation of the Kingdom of God." *BSac* 153 (1996): 281-307.

Schuller, Eileen M. "The Psalm of 4Q372 1 within the Context of Second Temple Prayer." *CBQ* 54 (1992): 75-79.

Senior, Donald. "Between Two Worlds: Gentiles and Jewish Christians in Matthew's Gospel." *CBQ* 61 (1999): 14-18.

Smillie, Gene R. "'Even the dogs': Gentiles in the Gospel of Matthew." *JETS* 45 (2002): 73-97.

Smith, Christopher R. "Literary Evidence of a Fivefold Structure in the Gospel of Matthew." *NTS* 43 (1997): 540-551.

Smith, Robert H. "Were the Early Christians Middle-Class? A Sociological Analysis of the New Testament." *CurTM* 7 (1980): 260-276.

Sparks, Kenton L. "Gospel as Conquest: Mosaic Typology in Matthew 28:16-20." *CBQ* 68/4 (2006): 651-663.

Stanton, Graham N. "5 Ezra and Matthean Christianity in the Second Century," JTS 28 (1977): 67-83.

_______. "Revisiting Matthew's Communities." *HTS* 52 (1996): 376-394.

Steenburg, Dave. "The Worship of Adam and Christ as the Image of God." *JSNT* 39 (1990): 95-109.

Styler, G. M. "Stages in Christology in the Synoptic Gospels." *NTS* 10 (1963-64): 398-409

Suter, David W. "Fallen Angel, Fallen Priest: The Problem of Family Purity in 1 Enoch 6-16." *HUCA* 50 (1979): 115-135.

Syreeni, Kari. "Between Heaven and Earth: On the Structure of Matthew's Symbolic Universe." *JSNT* 40 (1990): 3-13.

Thompson, James W. "That which cannot be shaken: Some Metaphysical Assumptions in Heb 12:27." *JBL* 94 (1975): 580-587.

Valantasis, Richard. "The Nuptial Chamber Revisited: The Acts of Thomas and Cultural Intertextuality." *Semeia* 80 (1997): 261-276.

Vashum, Yangkahao. "Jesus Christ as the Ancestor and Elder Brother: Constructing a Relevant Indigenous/Tribal Christology of North East India." JTS 13 (2008): 21-36.

Vermes, Geza. "Hanina ben Dosa: A Controversial Galilean Saint from the First Century of the Christian Era." *JSJud* 23 (1972): 28-50.

Verseput, Donald J. "Jesus' Pilgrimage to Jerusalem and Encounter in the Temple: A Geographical Motif in Matthew's Gospel." *NovT* 36 (1994): 105-121.

Vledder E. J., and A.G. van Aarde. "The Social Location of the Matthean Community." *HTS* 51 (1995): 388-408.

Waddle, Charles W. "Miracles of Healing." *AJP* 20 (1909): 219-268.

Wallace, R. C. "Hume, Flew and the Miraculous." *PQ* 20 (1970): 230-243.

Wedderburn, A. J. M. "Philo's 'Heavenly Man.'" *NovT* 15 (1973): 160-177.

Wezah, Yiepetso., and Tereso C. Casiño. "Towards a Relevant Theology of Nature: North-East India Tribal Perspective." *TTJ* 14 (2011): 99-115.

Wild, R. A. "The encounter between Pharisaic and Christian Judaism: Some Early Gospel Evidence." *NovT* 27 (1985): 105-124.

Williamson, Ronald. "The Incarnation of the Logos in Hebrews." *ExpTim* 95 (1983-1984): 4-8.

Wire, Antoinette. "The Structure of the Gospel Miracle Stories and their Tellers." *Semeia* 11 (1978): 83-118.

Yadin, Yigael. "The Dead Sea Scrolls and the Epistle to the Hebrews." *ScrH* 4 (1958): 133-143.

Zeller, Dieter. "New Testament Christology in its Hellenistic Reception." *NTS* 46 (2000): 312-333.

## Dictionaries

Alexander, T. Desmond., and David W. Baker. *Dictionary of the Old Testament: Pentateuch.* Downers Grove, IL: IVP, 2003.

Arnold, Bill T., and H. G. M. Williamson. *Dictionary of the Old Testament: Historical Books.* Downers Grove, IL: IVP, 2005.

Freedman, David N. *The Anchor Bible Dictionary.* 6 vols. Doubleday: University of Michigan, 1992.

Green, Joel B. Scot McKnight and I. Howard Marshall, eds. *Dictionary of Jesus and the Gospels.* Downers Grove, IL: IVP, 1992.

Hasting, James. *A Dictionary of Christ and the Gospels*. 2 Vols. Honolulu, University Press of the Pacific, 1906.

Kittel, Gerhard. *Theological Dictionary of the New Testament*. 10 Vols. Translated and Edited by Geoffrey Bromiley. Grand Rapids, MI: Eerdmans, 1964-1976.

McKenzie, John L. *Dictionary of the Bible.* New York: Touchstone, 1995.

Martin, Ralph P., and Peter H. Davids. *Dictionary of Later New Testament & Its Development.* Downers Grove, IL: IVP, 1997.

## Unpublished Dissertations

Bird, Adrian. "M.M. Thomas: Theological Signposts for the Emergence of Dalit Theology." Ph.D. diss., University of Edinburgh, 2008.

C., Biju. "Johannine Christology as an Intercultural Christology: A Quest for Hermeneutics in a Subaltern Indian Context." DTh diss., Senate of Serampore College, 2016.

Lawmsanga. "A Critical Study on Christian Mission with Special Reference to Presbyterian Church of Mizoram." Ph.D. diss., University of Birmingham, 2010.

Morphew, Derek Jeffery. "A Critical Examination of the Infancy Narratives in the Gospels according to Matthew and Luke." Ph.D. diss., The University of Cape town, 1980.

Kasher, Rimon. "The Theological Conception of the Miracle in the Bible." PhD diss., Bar-Ilan University, 1981.

Ralte, Lalrinawmi. *Crab Theology: A Critique of Patriarchy – Cultural Degradation and Empowerment of Mizo Women.* DMin. Diss., Episcopal Divinity School, Cambridge, 1993.

## Book Reviews

Bock, Darrell L. Review of *Miracles in Greco-Roman Antiquity: A Sourcebook for the Study of New Testament Miracle Stories*, by Wendy Cotter. *BBR* 10 (2000): 313-314.

Deppe, Dean B. Review of *A Postcolonial Reading of Mark's Story of Jesus*, by Simon Samuel. *CTJ* 44 (2009): 413-414.

Goodacre, Mark. Review of *The Gospel of Mathew and Christian Judaism*, by David C. Sim. *Heythrop Journal* 41 (2000): 334-336.

Seesengood, Robert. Review *Miracles in Greco-Roman Antiquity: A Sourcebook for the Study of New Testament Miracle Stories*, by Wendy Cotter. *Stone-Campbell journal* 4 (2001):140-142.

## Webliography

Arlandson, James M. "Authoritative Testimony in Matthew's Gospel." Historical Reliability of the Gospels. http://bible.org/seriespage/9-authoritative-testimony-matthew-s-gospel.html.

Avioz, Michael. "Splitting the Sea, Manna from Heaven, Defeating Amalek: What Makes Something a Miracle?" *The Torah: A Historical and Contextual Approach,* n.d. http://thetorah.com/what-makes-something-a-miracle.

Callaghan, Peter. "Cosmic Christology and the Reclamation of Christ's Relevance in the 21st Century." *Graduate Annual* 3 (2015): 1-10. http://digitalcommons.las-alle.edu/graduateannual/vol3/iss1/5.

Chhangte, C. Lalnunziri. "Myth and the Mizo Worldview." Day Dream Believer. https://cherriechhangte.wordpress.com/2007/11/28/myth-and-the-mizo-world-view/html.

Florio, Lucio. "Cosmic Christology and Pneumatology: Updating a Traditional Theological Topic to Approach a Dynamic Universe." (paper presented at the program of the Metanexus Institute, Philadelphia, USA, 3-7 June 2006, n.p. https://www.academia.e-du/567401/Cosmic_Christology_and_Pneumatology.

Jeffers, Ann. "The Earth is Full of Your Creatures." The Way. 24-33. http:/www.theway.org.uk/back/s087Jeffers.pdf.

Kelkar, R. R. Bible Meteorology (2010). E-book edition. https://rrkelkar.wordpress.com/books/bible-meteor-ology-by-prof-r-r-kelkar.

McCracken, Andy. Introduction to The Book of Enoch: A Modern English Translation of the Ethiopian Book of Enoch, translation of the Ethiopian text by Michael Knibb. Cedar Hill: Lifeworld International Electronic Library, 2004. http://www.scriptural-truth.com/stuff/BookOfEnoch.pdf.

Montgomery, Eric. "The Image of God as the Resurrected State in Pauline Thought." Bible.org.

https://bible.org/arti-cle/image-god-resurrected-state-pauline-thought.

Ralte, Lalrinawmi. "The World as the Body of God: Ecofeminist Theological Discourse with Special Reference to Tribal Women in India." *Rethinking Mission*, 2008. https://rethinkingmission.org/wpcontent/uplo-ads/2016/07/The-World-as-the-body-of-God-article.pdf.

Roskoski, John. "The Storm-Theophany: A Theology of the Storm." http://www.biblicaltheology.com/Research/RoskoskiJ03.pdf.

Screiner, Patrick. "Matthew's Geographical Overlay: The Return of the Exiled King." Transformed Blog. https://www.western-seminary.edu.